Douglas Murray

Born in 1979, Douglas Murray is currently an
undergraduate at Magdalen College, Oxford
reading English. This is his first book.

SCEPTRE

Bosie

A Biography of Lord Alfred Douglas

Douglas Murray

SCEPTRE

Dedicated with most sincere gratitude
and in affectionate friendship
to
Mary, Viscountess Eccles

First published in Great Britain in 2000 by Hodder and Stoughton
First published in paperback in 2001 by Hodder and Stoughton
A division of Hodder Headline

A Sceptre Paperback

10 9 8 7 6 5 4 3 2 1

ISBN 0 340 76771 5

A CIP catalogue record for this title
is available from the British Library

Typeset by Hewer Text Ltd, Edinburgh
Printed and bound in Great Britain by
Clays Ltd, St Ives plc

Hodder and Stoughton
A division of Hodder Headline
338 Euston Road
London NW1 3BH

Contents

List of Illustrations

Adolescence misled me, youth swept me away, but old age set me right, and taught me by experience that truth I had read long before: that adolescence and pleasure are vain; or rather, it was the Creator of all ages and times who set me right.

Petrarch – letter to posterity

Only yesterday I was being lectured (by a Frenchman) and told that unless I "did something" I would go down to posterity as an appendage of the Wilde affair! It is true that he had never read my poetry.

Lord Alfred Douglas to the French translator
of his poems, 18 January, 1930

Acknowledgements

Over the five years it took to research, write and edit this book I have been fortunate in having the support of a vast number of people. In some cases their input has been directly connected with the text while in others their support has come in practical and emotional ways.

Firstly I should like to thank the dedicatee of this book, Lady Eccles, to whom I owe an enormous debt. As Mary Hyde, she edited the Shaw–Douglas correspondence with great care and brilliance. To me she has been the kindest of hosts as well as one of the most valued correspondents and friends. As the owner of the largest Douglas collection in private hands I am deeply grateful to her for her generosity in letting me see all of her material. She has aided me, and inspired me through the writing of this book. I should also like to record here my gratitude to her late husband, Lord Eccles, a model of kindliness and culture.

I should also like to thank the following:

Sheila Colman at the Estate of Lord Alfred Douglas for permission to quote from his works, both published and unpublished.

The agents who have persevered so tirelessly on my behalf, Belinda Harley and Mary Pachnos. Also Amanda Armstrong at Belinda Harley Associates and Leon Morgan at Davenport Lyons.

Roland Philipps, Roseanne Boyle, Juliet Brightmore, Alexandra Heminsley and Hazel Orme at Hodder & Stoughton. Tina Brown and Jonathan Burnham at Miramax.

There are three people whose knowledge of Douglas and his work has been invaluable. To all of them I owe thanks for their constantly enlivening correspondence, for their generous supplying of material and their general support. They are John Stratford and Julia Wood in this country and, in the Netherlands, Caspar Wintermans.

At both Eton College and Magdalen College, Oxford I have received help from the following individuals as well as the institutions as a whole.

At Eton I am indebted to Angus Graham Campbell, Nick Welsh and Michael Meredith whose excellent teaching inspired me to start writing and, in Michael Meredith's case, as College Librarian, provided me with some of my first sources. At Magdalen the President, Anthony Smith, encouraged me from start to finish and has been an unfailing support and friend. I have gained from the assistance of the archivist, Robin Darwall Smith, the kindness of Barbara Gordon and the great understanding, learning and patience of my tutors, John Fuller and Susan Hitch.

To two other schools I owe a great amount. To Dr Custance, archivist at Winchester College, I wish to express my thanks, as I do to the headmaster, Mr J.P. Sabben Clare whose constant parcels of photos have helped so much in my search to attach names to faces. I also wish to thank Rita Gibbs, archivist at Harrow School for her search which required work way beyond the call of duty to find material on Viscount Drumlanrig.

In this country I should like to thank the staff of the British Library, in particular Sally Brown, Bret Dolman, Christopher Fletcher and Roger Evans, whose friendly and constantly helpful approach made my research at the British Library so enjoyable. Mary Clapinson, Gwydwr Leitch and all the staff at the Bodleian Library, Oxford. The Society of Authors for permission to quote from the letters of George Bernard Shaw. Durham County Record Office, Sussex County Record Office, the National Library of Scotland, Somerset House, the Archive department of Reading University Library, David Gale and the Home Office, the Public Record Office and Don Mead, Peter Vernier and Andrew McDonnell among others at the Oscar Wilde Society.

Hesketh Pearson material granted by permission of A. P. Watt Limited on behalf of Michael Holroyd.

I am grateful to Hugo Vickers for his tips, encouragement, correspondence and friendliness, assets I have enjoyed in equal measure from Ashley Bayston; the late Anthony Powell and Lady Violet Powell as well as the late Sir Rupert Hart-Davis for their correspondence and reminiscences; the Earl and Countess of Sandwich for their hospitality and the chance to use their archive; Tim d'Arch Smith for all his advice and suggestions; Neil Bartlett for his letters on Douglas, Wilde and Drumlanrig; Merlin Holland for his gracious and helpful responses to all my enquiries and for permission to quote from the works of Oscar Wilde; David Falconer for his kindness and work on behalf of the late Michael Holloway; Edward Maggs and others at Maggs Bros Ltd., Berkeley

Square; Geordie Greig for his encouragement and Sir Donald Sinden who was so amusing and informative.

I am grateful to the members of Douglas's family who have volunteered help so graciously including the present Marquess, David Queensberry and Lord Gawain Douglas. My special gratitude goes to Violet Conagham, niece of Lord Alfred himself, who has been kind, helpful and always fascinating.

In America I should like to thank all the staff at the New York public library and in particular those in the Berg collection among whom I must single out Stephen Crook for his welcoming manner to an Englishman abroad. The staff at Princeton University Library for the way in which they helped with every pestering request for obscure items which I could make. All the staff at Four Oaks Farm and in particular Marcia Levinson and Rita Rooney.

The following individuals made my time researching in the States most memorable by their constant acts of kindness: Alfred Bush, Mary Keating, Gordon Roland Adams, Charles Ryskamp, Caroline Seebohm, Rody Shanahan, Mary Anne and all the Trump family and Tom Wright.

Finally a few thanks to those who have supported me during my writing but who have not necessarily had any direct input into the text. To these people who often remain unthanked I would like to express my gratitude.

Firstly for my parents for their unfailing love and support – without whom I could have achieved nothing.

I owe a great deal to Neil and Rosie Colquhoun. For a year they supported me, looked after me and taught me much. I fancy that together we learnt no small amount about human nature at its very best, and at its very worst.

I should also like to record my thanks here to Nita Asut, Dan and Nicola Davey, Dick and Ruth Heslop, Kim Hilder, Gerald and Lorna Maguire, Julie Sheldrick and all those in Scotland who were decent and nice.

Lastly, Sir Anthony and Lady Acland, Ralph Allwood, Bill Bowen, David and Carrie Evans, Tom Fenwick, Benjie Fowler, Sally Groves, John Lewis, Dick Lyon, Ian McAuslan, Richard Mason, Charles and Patsy Mitchell Innes, Simon Over, Joan Palin, Gulliver Ralston, Alastair Sampson, Kevin Smith, Christopher Thompson-Royds, Virginia Valdambrini, Bill and Joan Williams, and everyone else who has shown me kindness during the writing of this book.

Introduction

In the middle of the summer in which I started to write this book I found myself passing through the town of Crawley. I had spent the day in Sussex with one of the few people still alive who had known Lord Alfred Douglas well, and decided to take the detour on my return journey to visit the grave.

My idea of what the site would be like could not have been more wrong. As I pulled off a main road into the small car-park of a red-brick Catholic church I anticipated grand, fountained greenery. Instead there was a yard with no more than a couple of dozen burial plots in it. Douglas's grave was the first I came to. The stone, flat on the ground, read:

> Of your charity
> Pray for the repose of
> the soul of
> Sibyl Queensberry
> Widow of the 8th Marquess of Queensberry
> Died 30 of October 1935
> On whose soul sweet Jesus have mercy
> RIP
> Also her son
> Alfred Bruce Douglas
> Born 22nd October 1870
> Died 20 March 1945
> May they rest in peace

That was it. I had been to Père Lachaise in Paris and seen Oscar Wilde's grave, a winged angel by Epstein, the previous year and found the contrast upsetting: to read the text on Douglas's grave I had to kneel beside the stone and wipe away the grime of years.

This was where the story had ended: the resting place of Oscar Wilde's 'Hyacinthus', a man who had been judged one of Britain's finest poets, a man who, according to John Betjeman, 'gave one a sense of holiday and exaltation whenever one was in his company'.[1] He lay, his mother at his side, forgotten and neglected. I remembered the inscription on Oscar Wilde's rose-bedecked tomb, a quotation from his great *Ballad*, which seemed as suitable for his beloved Bosie as it did for him:

> And alien tears will fill for him
> Pity's long-broken urn,
> For his mourners will be outcast men
> And outcasts always mourn.

In 1995 when I was sixteen and my interest in Wilde and Douglas was growing, Oscar Wilde was finally accorded a memorial in Poet's Corner, Westminster Abbey. In that year, the centenary of the fateful trials, Britain seemed, officially at least, to acknowledge him as her own. Not so Bosie, who – because of the complexity of his own life and actions – has never been championed by any section of society: pagan–Catholic, married–gay, English–Scot, impoverished aristocrat and hearty poet, he remains impossible to pigeon-hole.

I could never be a pure apologist for him, though, and although a book dealing exclusively with the inaccuracies and lies, the smears and cover-ups that have destroyed his reputation would be interesting, it is not this one. My concern is with a poet and a man, not a historical jousting-match.

While I was writing the Home Office agreed, in the autumn of 1997, after more than a year of petitioning, to allow me to see the manuscript of Douglas's prison work. His sole surviving working manuscript, 'In Excelsis' (a riposte to Wilde's prison work, 'De Profundis') had been due to languish, along with other documents relating to him, for a further half-century.

* * * *

It was during his first year at Magdalen College, Oxford, that Lord Alfred Douglas wrote what he later described as his first serious poem. The sentiments expressed in 'Autumn Days' are perhaps no more or less extraordinary than the majority of undergraduate verse, but he was not to leave behind the emotions of his youth. Until the end of his life his passion for the past was so strong that to him the present was often devoid of meaning or purpose. The quality of the poem is, perhaps, not to be found in the technique so much as in its prophetic substance, which rang truer with each year that passed.

> I have been through the woods to-day
> And the leaves were falling,
> Summer had crept away,
> And the birds were not calling.
>
> And the bracken was like yellow gold
> That comes too late,
> When the heart is sad and old,
> And death at the gate.
>
> Ah, mournful Autumn! Sad,
> Slow death that comes at last,
> I am mad for a yesterday, mad!
> I am sick for a year that is past!
>
> Though the sun be like blood in the sky
> He is cold as the lips of hate,
> And he fires the sere leaves as they lie
> On their bed of earth, too late.
>
> They are dead, and the bare trees weep
> Not loud as a mortal weeping,
> But as sorrow that sighs in sleep,
> And as grief that is still in sleeping.

Douglas never belonged to any definable artistic movement – he was allied with many and pitted against most throughout his career – but in the public's consciousness he is most obviously associated with Oscar Wilde and the decadents of the last years of the century into which he was born. Unlike many of his contemporaries Douglas lived on into the twentieth century, railed against it at times, but never identified exclusively with any one period of that history. Some people would have preferred it if Douglas, like Ernest Dowson, had died young, to remain the golden boy – and this might indeed have appealed to him. But his early death would have denied the world an, admittedly select, quantity of poetry, and a fascinating life, both of which throw light not only on his age but ours as well. Always challenging, fighting and perpetually suffering, Douglas still challenges us today, as Wilde's 'Bosie' – immortalised in literature as forcefully as Shakespeare's Mr W.H. – as the zealous convert to Roman Catholicism, fervent litigant, and finally as the dejected and faded beauty of the last sad years.

Douglas's poetry is all that remains of an extraordinary life. He paid dearly for his literary reputation in worldly terms, but writing as an old man, he claimed that he had always been 'if not indifferent to, at least unmoved by, public opinion'.[2] Now many of the quarrels that dogged his turbulent life are faded sensations of a distant age. However, as a poet Douglas had the last word on matters that may now seem obscure. He always knew he was writing for posterity but could hardly have imagined that much of what seemed most important to him would become footnotes in history, while outpourings of emotion in his verse were what his life would eventually be judged on.

A deeply flawed personality, perhaps. A quarrelsome snob or bigot, even. Douglas was a highly complex, but in many ways still lovable figure who, against all odds, has found a place in the history of letters and politics. It was in his youth that his strong personality was formed, and it was at these days he looked back and of which he dreamt in later life. These were the days he saw as his time, a world of innocence and happiness in memory, which in reality had often been very different.

Chapter 1

'The old years that held and fashioned me'

(1870–1889)

The family into which Lord Alfred Douglas was born was one of the noblest houses in Scotland. They had a colourful history and had once possessed great lands, wealth and influence. Towards the end of the eighth century, tradition has it that a chieftain, or king, whose army was losing in battle saw the tide turned in his favour by an unknown warrior. He sent for the man after the battle had been won, and the soldier who conducted him into his presence said, 'Sholto Du-glass. Behold the dark grey man you inquired for.'[1]

A Sir William Douglas died in the Tower of London in 1298 and was succeeded by his son James, Lord of Douglas. But the man who most made a name for the family in its early years was William the 'Black Douglas', nephew of James, who was renowned for having fought in seventy battles. As a friend of Robert the Bruce, it was the Black Douglas who attempted to fulfil that King's dying wish that his heart be taken to the Holy Sepulchre in Jerusalem in a silver casket. It was while engaged on this mission that the Black Douglas met his end. He had travelled with the heart on one of the Crusades but was killed in Spain by the Moors in 1390 before he reached the Holy Land. The Black Douglas's remains were buried, in Melrose Abbey, along with the silver casket containing his friend's heart. It is commemorated in the Douglas coat-of-arms, which bears a heart along with the word 'Forward'. Although his final mission was unsuccessful, the Black Douglas has remained one of the best-known figures in his country's legend. The fierceness and determination that characterised his career emerged in the lives of many of his descendants, along with the gore and sensation.[2]

James I of Scotland conferred the barony of Drumlanrig on the illegitimate son of the 2nd Earl of Douglas, who was killed at the battle of Chevy Chase while fighting the English in 1388, but it was James I of England who, in gratitude for his hospitality in 1617, created the 9th

Baron the Duke of Queensberry, Viscount Drumlanrig and Lord Douglas of Hawick and Tibbers. The second of these titles became the courtesy title by which the eldest son of each Queensberry was known, while the third was often bestowed upon the second son. The complex succession that went on in the family meant that titles often came and went or they were dispersed.

The numbering of the Queensberrys' titles changed after the Second World War, when the 10th Marquess became the 11th. This came about because James, the son of the 2nd Duke of Queensberry, had originally been overlooked: he was reputed to have been 'an idiot from birth'. He became famous as the 'cannibalistic idiot' after an incident in 1707 when he was left alone by his guards in his cell at Holyrood Palace. They planned to watch the riots then taking place in Edinburgh over the Act of Union debate. The 'idiot' escaped and went into the kitchens where he found a cook's boy turning a spit. He seized and killed the boy, then impaled him on the spit and roasted him before the fire. On his father's death, all titles and estates went to his younger brother, who became the 3rd (revised as the 4th) Marquess of Queensberry in 1711. The 'idiot' died at the age of seventeen.

The title Viscount Drumlanrig is reputed by some family members and many others to carry a curse, even for those heirs who do not use it. The 3rd Duke lost his heir while the family, including Drumlanrig's wife, was travelling. Fearing an attack from highwaymen the young man prepared his pistol, but the charge exploded by accident and killed him in the carriage. Another Drumlanrig drowned when he attempted to jump a wide river with his horse and both fell in. Other holders of the title, according to one of their descendants, drank themselves into early graves. The early and often violent deaths that had plagued the family were not only confined to its heirs, though. The 7th Marquess died on 6 August 1858 while out shooting rabbits from the 'accidental explosion of his gun'. However, the national press speculated about the incident: the *Evening Herald* reported that 'in sporting circles a belief is expressed that the death was not accidental; he had recently sustained severe losses', and popular opinion seemed to hold that the Marquess had committed suicide.

However, the family enjoyed some happier, if not entirely reputable, moments in their history. The 3rd Duke and his wife (who had seen their son die in their carriage) were friends and patrons of Jonathan Swift,

Alexander Pope, William Congreve and John Gay among others. Gay's masterpiece *The Beggar's Opera* was written at their house, and they argued with George II over his refusal to grant a licence for its sequel, *Polly*, which, it was claimed, ridiculed Walpole's ministry.[3] The 3rd Duke's cousin, the 4th and last Duke of Queensberry, was the notorious 'Regency Rake' who became known as 'Old Q'. He was one of the most important members of the Hell-Fire Club, the 'Monks of Medmenham'. It was founded by Francis Dashwood, a close friend of George III, met in a restored Cistercian abbey and was filled with Old Etonians. At their meetings the mock-religious order performed acts of devil worship, with Dashwood in the role of Christ, using blasphemy and the black mass as 'sexual stimulants'.[4] However, it seems that what excited Old Q was not so much the perversions, but sex itself: he was sexually active right up to his death at the age of eighty-five when his grave was littered with around seventy letters from various women containing 'open avowals of their adoration or passion'[5] which were gathered together and burnt. He died unmarried and without any recognised issue to succeed him. The dukedom passed to a distant kinsman, the 3rd Duke of Buccleuch. The marquessate, however, passed to the Kelhead line of the house of Douglas, and Sir Charles Douglas, Bt, a descendant of the 1st Earl of Queensberry, became the 5th Marquess of Queensberry.

He never produced a male heir, although he had eight daughters, so on his death the titles went to his brother John, the 6th Marquess. He and his wife Sarah had two children, a boy and a girl. Their son, Archibald William Douglas, succeeded to the title at the age of thirty-six. He had eloped to Gretna Green when he was just twenty-one to marry Caroline Clayton, the one romantic and interesting episode in an otherwise rather dull and unhappy life. He continued to call himself Viscount Drumlanrig, despite the 'curse', and survived his father by only two years. It was he who was found dead with his gun. He was the grandfather of Lord Alfred Douglas.

The 7th Marquess had six children. His first child was a daughter, Gertrude, and the second was his son and heir. John Sholto must have found his father's untimely death especially distressing as he became head of the family at the age of just fourteen. In 1865 his younger brother Francis who was just eighteen was involved in a mountaineering accident on the first climb of the Matterhorn in the Swiss Alps. He had set off with a party of eight, mainly experienced climbers. Progress was easy on the way up and the party beat the Italian team competing against them to be first to the summit. It was during the descent, while trying to negotiate a rocky shoulder on the east face, that disaster struck. The guides had omitted to rope the party firmly together, and the most inexperienced lost his footing and slipped. As he fell he crashed into another climber. Both men tumbled over the cliff, pulling Francis Douglas, who hurtled down four thousand feet of rocky precipices.

There was no way that any of the men could survive such a fall but the subsequent search found only three unrecognisably battered bodies, identifiable only by their clothing. Francis Douglas was never found, even though his elder brother went out to help with the search.[6] Queensberry went ahead of the party and spent a night alone on the mountain searching for his brother's body, coming close to dying from the terrible cold and continual avalanches. Amazed by the force of nature and its ability to take as well as to give life, Queensberry found himself contemplating 'the relation of the body and soul of man',[7] which eventually formed the basis of his atheistic beliefs that while man had the opportunity of eternal life he was not subservient to a god. He expressed his ideas as best he could in a poem many years later,[8] although a more eloquent tribute to the dead mountaineers came in the form of a sonnet about the event by Thomas Hardy. In the wake of Francis's death, Queen Victoria considered banning mountaineering among her subjects.

Queensberry's atheism became more radical as the years passed: asked as one of the Scottish representative peers in the House of Lords to swear the oath of allegiance to God and the Queen, he refused, saying he would not take part in such 'Christian tomfoolery' and that his word should be enough. As a result he was not allowed to take his seat, a decision for which the Prime Minister, Gladstone, apologised.[9] However, as a direct result of this, he was offered the presidency of the British Secular Union and promptly accepted it.

His opinions remained in the public domain and he attracted the limelight again when he tried to stop the third performance of the Poet Laureate's *The Promise of May*. Audiences generally had not reacted well to Tennyson's play and on the first night there had been booing and hissing from a group of atheists objecting to one of the characters, the evil Philip Edgar, an atheist, radical and hedonist, On the night Queensberry took his seat in the front row of the stalls he objected forcefully to the depiction of the atheist and was shouted down. When the scene drew to a close he attempted to explain his feelings to the audience but was promptly ejected from the theatre. Otherwise his life was uneventful, although the Queensberry Rules of boxing took their name from him, and remained the most important development in the sport for many years, and he was a renowned sportsman. However, his greatest ambition, to ride in the Grand National and win, was scuppered when his cousin, who owned what turned out to be the winning horse, deemed Queensberry past his best.[10] Queensberry never forgave him.

The insanity that regularly affected the Queensberry family perhaps most obviously afflicted Queensberry's youngest brother, James (or Jim), who was deeply attached to his twin sister Florrie and heartbroken when she married Sir Alexander Beaumont Churchill Dixie (Sir A.B.C.D. or 'Beau' for short) in 1875. After his attempt to abduct a young girl in 1885, James became increasingly manic. In 1888 he was married to a wealthy woman of his own age with a ten-year-old son and a vast fortune. The union was a disaster from the outset. James was not able to play out the role of Victorian husband and, separated from Florrie, who was in Scotland while he was in London, he drank himself into a deep depression.

* * * *

The woman whom the 8th Marquess of Queensberry took as his wife was quite as determined as the best of the Douglas family members. She was the daughter of Alfred Montgomery, the son of an officer in the East India Company's military service. Born in 1814 and educated at Charterhouse, where he was a contemporary of Thackeray, at the age of sixteen Alfred Montgomery became private secretary to the Marquess of Wellesley, the elder brother of the Duke of Wellington. Wellesley was deeply attached to Alfred's mother, and it was widely rumoured that his choice of private secretary had been influenced by his suspicion that he was the boy's father. Alfred was generally believed to bear a striking similarity in appearance to Wellesley (and if it were true then it would make Lord Alfred Douglas the great-great-nephew of the Iron Duke). He was perhaps best known during his lifetime as a magnificent wit and entertainer. Lisping, stuttering and effete, he was considered a fine conversationalist and companion. It seemed unlikely that he would marry and there are grounds for suspecting that he was homosexual. (His son-in-law, the 8th Marquess, thought he was and it seems had fairly good proof of his suspicion: in later years he implied this strongly, which he would not have done without considerable substantiating evidence.) Certainly the marriage, less than three weeks after Wellesley's death, surprised everyone.

Alfred and his wife, Fanny Wyndham, had little in common. A cousin of the poet Wilfred Scawen Blunt, her family were odd to say the least, with some members being marked by bizarre persecution mania or behavioural habits which kept them from being prominent in society. The couple had two daughters, Sibyl and Edith. Their first child, a boy named Wilfred, died at the age of six.

The marriage of Queensberry and Sibyl Montgomery was also not ideal by any means. Queensberry was attracted to her great beauty: she was delicate and vulnerable-looking, which in many men would stir feelings of protectiveness, though not, as it turned out, in Queensberry. Nevertheless he was totally in love with her and although Alfred Montgomery must have been wary of giving his daughter to the hearty Queensberry, any qualms were laid to rest by the idea that his daughter would become a marchioness, a social advancement that he and his family could not readily turn down.

So, both aged twenty-one, Queensberry and Sibyl married at St George's Church, Hanover Square on Thursday 26 February 1866. The wedding had been planned to take place four days earlier but an uncle of Sibyl's died suddenly and it was postponed. Many of the guests on the impressive list were unable to attend the rearranged service, which was something of a damp squib. It was not a promising start to the marriage.

The bride and groom took a short honeymoon in Essex then headed straight for the family seat of Kinmount in Dumfriesshire. Their arrival there at the end of the Scottish winter cannot have made the bride particularly happy. Kinmount had been built to a neo-classical design in 1812 for the 6th Marquess. With its lakes, woods and rolling borderland landscape, the house looked serene in the finest weather but in the cold and damp of a Scottish winter it was bleak and forbidding.

Queensberry took his role as squire seriously. He became Master of the Dumfriesshire Foxhounds and spent much of his time riding and enjoying country life. Within a year of the marriage the couple's first child was born, which delighted both of them, not least because it was a boy and therefore an heir. In memory of his uncle, they named him Francis.

By the time Sibyl was pregnant again the following year, things had started to go badly wrong between the Queensberrys, as her mother reported to her friend, the Prime Minister Benjamin Disraeli, during a stay at Kinmount. Queensberry, she wrote, was 'very young; only 23. With good abilities and good principles, but suffering from the overwhelming weight of high rank and nothing to do.'[11] Their second son, Percy, was born in 1868, and soon afterwards Queensberry decided to follow his interest in Midlands hunting. In 1869 he moved his stables and his family to Worcestershire where he rented a house called Ham Hill. It was at that house, on 22 October 1870, that their third son was born, Lord Alfred Bruce Douglas.

2

Alfred arrived at a time of particular loneliness in Sibyl's life, and was adored by her over all her children. He became a replacement for her absent husband. Queensberry had just become Master of the Worcestershire Foxhounds and never missed a day in the field, leaving at dawn and returning at dusk. Consequently he spent no time with his wife or children.

Alfred had been named after his Montgomery grandfather and his godfather, Lord Robert Bruce, who had been a friend of Queensberry since they were in the Royal Navy together as young men. The combination of the two names is significant. Alfred had inherited the good looks of the Montgomerys, and particularly resembled his grandfather, but his temperament was a mass of contradictions: he soon showed himself to be a forceful and determined fighter, a wit and a dandy.

After two years at Ham Hill, Queensberry resigned his Mastership and took the family back up to Kinmount, and it was from there that Alfred Douglas's earliest memories dated. They centred, of course, on his brothers and mother. According to Douglas, throughout his childhood he held an 'intense' admiration for his father, which, he wrote, 'was doubtless not at all impaired, but on the contrary greatly increased, by the fact that I hardly ever saw him'.[12] He recorded that Queensberry's children did not see their father for several years at a time, for he was chasing other women as well as the fox and stag. The birth of another son, Sholto, in 1872, and a daughter, Edith, in 1874, did nothing to patch up the relationship between the Marquess and his wife.

However, in his early years at Kinmount life was undoubtedly something like Eden to young Alfred. In those days the family had money, land, influence, power and hordes of servants to care for them and the estate. The impression that all the children retained of their time at Kinmount was one of adventure. Among the rolling woods and lakes lay areas to explore, and a smaller house, owned by the family and hidden among the woods, Glen Stewart, was home to the children's grandmother, the Dowager Marchioness, and later to their aunt Florrie and Beau.

At the age of six Queensberry gave Alfred a pony, which afforded him the opportunity to explore further afield. With Percy, he rode around the estate and up to Glen Stewart. The pair were particularly good friends as well as brothers, and the shared sense of adventure in their youth set the tone of their relationship for the rest of their lives. Together they rode to the village of Ecclefechan where Thomas Carlyle (who was still alive) had been born. There they purchased toy swords with which they carried out reconstructions of their ancestors' feats. On one occasion the game went wrong when Percy almost stabbed out his elder brother Drumlanrig's eye.[13]

It was in these early years that Alfred acquired the nickname by which his family and friends always called him. His mother liked to call him by the West Country diminutive 'Boysie', meaning simply 'little boy', which gradually shortened to 'Bosie'.[14] It was used all his life, and is curiously apt for, in so many ways, he remained at heart a little boy until his death.

*   *   *   *

By the end of the 1870s Queensberry was living in London, apart from his family, but it was not until the next decade that he decided to sell Kinmount. It was a selfish decision that upset the children and his wife. Sibyl, however, would not allow the children to think ill of their father: she wanted them to grow up to love and admire him even if she could not.

While the family were settled in London, Alfred and his eldest brother Francis were sent to Lambrook, a prep school near Windsor. It was not especially eminent, but the children there were all of the aristocracy or royalty – including two of Queen Victoria's grandsons, Prince Victor and

Prince Albert of Schleswig-Holstein. The Queen herself often went to the school from the castle to watch the cricket. Its geographical situation meant that it was a natural feeder for Eton – clearly the path considered at some time for young Alfred.

Francis was only at the school for a term, until he was old enough to go to Harrow, which he did in January 1881. This was against Queensberry's wishes: he wanted his children to go to Scottish schools, even though he had no knowledge of them since he had gone to naval school. Francis did not excel at Harrow. 'He was not a brilliant athlete, nor a distinguished scholar, but one of the larger class of those who make no special mark in work or games, but leave with all their friends pleasant recollections of an honest, strong and upright character, an unfailing cheerfulness, courtesy, and a kindly unassuming demeanour.'[15]

Education at Lambrook must have come as a shock to Alfred after his private lessons at Kinmount. Nevertheless he was happy there. It was therefore with dismay that he faced a sudden change just as he had settled down: after only a year he was forced to leave. What he later termed 'a row' took place. The nature of this is not clear and he says he did not know at the time and did not discover for many years afterwards what had happened.[16] His unwillingness to write or speak about it even fifty or so years later hints that it must have been something serious, perhaps a homosexual scandal, although he certainly was not involved. In fact, it was serious enough for almost every child to leave and the school nearly closed down. Instead Alfred was sent to Wixenford School with his younger brother Sholto. He stayed there for three years.

The few memories he recorded of his time at Wixenford are sketchy. He recalled the headmaster whom he found 'very alarming', and who he thought picked on him, yet he also said that there was almost no punishment, and his days seemed to have passed smoothly enough.[17] He wrote, too, that he was a 'very sensitive' child, and blamed this on his mother, who had made him 'frightfully spoilt'. As a result, he 'suffer[ed] proportionately more at school'.[18] He made one particularly good friend there in Edward Francis Shepherd, an American. Alfred was entranced by Shepherd's accent, which he had never encountered before, and though the other boy was slightly older, the two became close. They parted with sadness when Shepherd left for Eton in 1883.

The separation of Alfred Douglas and Edward Shepherd had not been intended to be permanent, though. Lady Queensberry had put her son down for Eton some time before he was of the age to enter the school, but when Queensberry heard of his wife's plan, he deemed it inappropriate that he had not been consulted and refused to give his consent. He said that he would not have any son of his turned into a 'Belgravian loafer', which Douglas said later, 'was his quaint expression for what he imagined to be the typical and representative results of education at that celebrated school'. Queensberry knew nothing whatsoever about Eton or any other public school, but 'his prejudices once formed were as insurmountable as they were often unreasonable'.[19] Doubtless his decision was based largely on a desire to show his family that he held sway over them even though he saw them so rarely. Inevitably he had his own way and decided that Alfred should go to Winchester, an odd choice since it was further from home than many other appropriate schools (although this might have been the attraction) and because the family had had no previous contact with the school.

Without knowing it, Queensberry was casting the most sensitive and vulnerable of his sons into something of a lion's den. Douglas recalled later that his first two years at Winchester were 'a nightmare'.[20] The school was in the process of being 'cleaned up' when he arrived but still bore a strong resemblance to the Rugby of *Tom Brown's Schooldays*. Bullying was rife, older boys exploiting younger boys, while many cases of torture are recorded. At this point Winchester still had a long way to go before it was dragged into the nineteenth century. Also homosexual activity was rampant.

By then Alfred had exceptional, somewhat feminine good looks. His hair was silky blond, with the faintest hint of curl, his complexion clear and smooth, his lips sensual and his eyes a bright blue. Boys who looked like him were particularly susceptible to attention from their seniors. It is clear that he despised this at first, though after a while he fell into form and it later became a great asset to him.

He only named one boy with whom he had been to bed during his time at Winchester and this was certainly not a sexual encounter. During one summer holiday Alfred went with his housemaster, Trant Bramston and his best schoolfriend, Viscount Encombe (nicknamed 'Jane'), to Zermatt in Switzerland, perhaps so that Douglas might see where his uncle had met his end nearly twenty years earlier. Whatever the justification for the trip, it seems to have been a success. However, when he got home to his mother and siblings, he developed mumps.

Another great friend was one Wellington Stapleton Cotton who was at Wellington College. Alfred and Wellington were keen to spend time together before they returned to their respective schools, but Alfred's mumps prevented a meeting. The friends were not to be separated so easily, though. Through a footman, Alfred pointed out to Wellington that if he got mumps too they would be together and urged him to come to see him despite the prohibition of their mothers. The next morning Wellington climbed through Alfred's bedroom window, got into bed with him and stayed there for half an hour to ensure he caught mumps. The plan failed: Wellington remained healthy, but Encombe went back to Winchester and infected his whole house, who then infected the rest of the school.[21]

Encombe was a most loyal friend to Douglas during his career at school, university and after. He was the heir of the 3rd Earl of Eldon, and the grandson of the famous Lord Chancellor. The two got to know each other well because they were in the same house at school and, although they had a strong relationship, it was not what Douglas would later term 'immoral'. In his *Autobiography* (1929) Douglas set down the three types of relationships that he enjoyed with other boys during his time at Winchester and Oxford.

> . . . I had many fine friendships, perfectly normal, wholesome, and not in the least sentimental. Such was my friendship with Encombe . . . I had other friendships which were sentimental and passionate, but perfectly pure and innocent. Such was my friendship with Wellington Stapleton Cotton. I had others again which were neither pure nor innocent. But if it is to be assumed from this that I was 'abnormal' or 'degenerate' or exceptionally wicked, then it must also be assumed that at least ninety per cent of my contemporaries at Winchester and Oxford were the same.[22]

Friendships like those he shared with Encombe and Stapleton Cotton were rare; the most common were those that were 'neither pure nor innocent', which went largely unrecorded. Forty years later, Douglas was exceptionally brave in admitting to having practised acts that might have consigned him to prison. Few mainstream published books from the period record so candidly an author's admission of homosexual activity. Of course, others wrote accounts of life at public school but only one recorded in detail what could never have been published.

The most famous among Douglas's contemporaries who recorded in detail his sexual activity at school, and afterwards, was Sir Edmund Trelawny Backhouse. His scabrous, unpublished, *Autobiography*, written in Peking in 1943, should be treated with caution: he wrote that his six years at Winchester were 'a carnival of unbridled lust', and claimed to have had sexual relationships with more than thirty boys during his time there,[23] including Alfred Douglas. There is proof that some of his claims were not true, but in 1943, the year before his death, and two years before Douglas's, Backhouse claimed that, 'Bozie (*sic*) would probably not thank me for recalling numerous love episodes at Winchester in which he was usually the ascendant and I the pathic, although positions were sometimes reversed.'[24]

By his third year at Winchester, Alfred was accustomed to this way of life, which probably helped him become at Oxford the most prominent homosexual in the university, among those in the know.[25] Nevertheless, buggery almost certainly did not take place between the Winchester boys and it seems that when they had 'immoral relationships' with other boys they probably went no further than mutual masturbation.

At Winchester, it was more than just the sexual preferences of his contemporaries that rubbed off on Alfred. He arrived at the school with a firm religious faith. Doubts about the existence of God or rebellion against the respect that the Church demanded were simply not considered, and the irreverent behaviour of some older boys in his house shocked him considerably:

> There was a picture of The Last Supper (a reproduction of Da Vinci's picture) hanging over the 'high table' of our House. One of the boys who was a prefect, and certainly the most powerful and influential boy in the House (he was in 'Commoner Six' at football and in the school eleven), used to make a practice of hurling a piece of bread at this picture every time he came in to tea (there being no master then present), his object being to hit the figure of Our Lord.[26]

More painful still, though, was the loss of innocence, which for the rest of his life Douglas tried to regain, striving once again to be in the godly state of childhood:

> I bitterly resent that I was robbed of my virtue and my innocence in my helpless boyhood, by being put into a community which one of its most

distinguished sons compared to hell.[27] If I had escaped untarnished from Winchester and Oxford it would have been a miracle, and I would have been a saint.[28]

Douglas was not a saint, though, so his behaviour and attitude were, as he wrote, 'neither better nor worse than my contemporaries – that is to say, [I became] a finished young blackguard, ripe for any kind of wickedness'.[29]

All this gives the impression that life at school was hell for Douglas, but this is not so. After the *Autobiography* had been published and a biography of him had stated that Douglas loathed his schooldays,[30] he wrote of Winchester in *Without Apology*, 'The plain truth is that, except for about three months before and after my marriage, I have never really been perfectly happy since I left it, and that to this day my most enchanting dream, which comes from time to time even now, is that I am still there.'[31] Part of the reason that he could write this was to do with his circle of close friends: Lord Encombe, whom he always took to tea when his grandfather, Alfred Montgomery, visited him at school;[32] and 'Sunny' Marlborough, or the Marquess of Blandford as he was during his schooldays. (He became the 9th Duke of Marlborough when he was just twenty. He was known as Sunny all his life, though not, as one writer has pointed out, due to any 'sunny disposition',[33] but rather because his father's subsidiary courtesy title was Earl of Sunderland.)

For a variety of reasons, Douglas was popular at school, and certainly not the 'mummy's boy' that some have thought. In fact he excelled in artistic, aesthetic and sporting endeavours. He was affectionately known as either 'Alf' or 'Bosie' by everyone in his house. The nickname had slipped out one day during his first or second year at Winchester. His elder brother Percy had joined the Navy and was about to sail for the Pacific. He sent a telegram to his younger brother which said simply, 'Good-bye, darling Bosie'. It was left for him on a table in Hall while he was out, but before he returned temptation proved too much for another boy. When Douglas got back he was hailed with derisive shouts, ' "Hello, darling Bosie," '[34] and Bosie he remained, through school, university and beyond.

3

As a boy, Douglas was proud of his family, whose fame and prominence impressed many of his contemporaries. At that time his eccentric aunt Florrie was making a name for herself as an explorer. From her first expedition, to Patagonia, she brought home a jaguar, which she kept as a pet and called Affums. Florrie claimed that Affums was 'as friendly as a kitten', though discouraged her nephew from trying to stroke it while it was on its chain in the garden. One day Affums escaped, and found its way to Windsor park where it killed several deer, much to the annoyance of Queen Victoria, who 'made such remonstrances' that when it was recaptured Florrie had to send it to the zoo. She, Beau and her brother Jim would often climb into its cage for a chat.[35]

Home life remained unconventional and it was during his last years at Winchester that Douglas recognised his father for what he was. During school holidays he and his younger sister Edith would spend a couple of weeks with their father in lodgings in Brighton. It was obvious to them that they bored Queensberry: he would suggest they go to the pier and amuse themselves, dishing out sums of money that were 'grossly in excess of what would have been sufficient for the purpose'.[36] Sibyl lived at a house near Bracknell in Berkshire called The Hut, whose name gives no hint of its impressive size, where Queensberry spent no more than a few nights a year. When he did turn up he caused trouble.

On one occasion Sibyl was powerless to prevent her children witnessing his brutality. It was probably this incident that began to turn his children against him. The Hut was near Ascot, and when Alfred was sixteen his mother had arranged for friends to make up a house party during race week. Twenty-four hours before the guests were due Queensberry turned up with a party of his own friends, including his mistress. Sibyl, humiliated, had to put off her guests. From then relations in the family were at breaking point. Queensberry's attempt at a resolution included his suggestion that Sibyl move in with him and his mistress. The following year, 1887, Lady Queensberry petitioned for divorce on the grounds of adultery and cruelty. It was granted without challenge.

If Queensberry ever beat his children it is not recorded, and it seems that his violence towards his wife came in the form of threatening letters, which she received with increasing regularity after the divorce. He found it difficult to communicate with his children. Alfred recorded that from the age of twelve his father talked to him as though he was an adult, repeatedly expressing concern at his brother Jim's drinking – reportedly as many as four bottles of brandy a day on top of the claret, port and champagne he consumed at meals. Conversation initiated by his son, or anyone else, was generally received with a 'stony silence'.[37]

As a boy at Winchester, Douglas always admired and even loved his distant father. He recorded that one of his favourite pastimes was to go to the house library and read through the bound set of old numbers of the *Field* to find references to his father's racing successes in the 1860s and 1870s.[38]

Queensberry's sporting prowess was probably behind his son's greatest achievement at Winchester: he won the school steeplechase of two and a half miles across country in a record time.[39] Queensberry rewarded him with five pounds, a vast amount then for a schoolboy to receive, but then, as Douglas had already realised, Queensberry had 'no idea what was the right amount of money to give a boy'.[40]

It was during the summer of 1887 that Douglas had what was perhaps his most intense emotional relationship during his time at school. It is unlikely that it had a sexual side since he was confident enough of its purity to devote a whole chapter to it in his 1938 book of memoirs *Without Apology*. Eighteen eighty-seven was the year of the Queen's Golden Jubilee, which Douglas described as 'the star-year of my eternity'.[41] Boys of different houses did not generally mix, and older boys certainly had no communication with younger ones of another house, and but for a bout of German measles that confined sufferers to the 'Sick-House', the boys would never have met.

German measles lasted only a few days but the boys were quarantined for three weeks, and it was during the first days of his illness that Douglas set eyes on Maurice Turner, who was two years younger and the son of a housemaster: 'a violent mutual attraction sprang up'. No work was set for patients in the sick-house and only the school matron (the 'kind and delightful' Miss D'Arcy) and the maids were around. They could pass the time in long walks on the school fields, which they had to themselves while everyone else was in lessons, and talking. Maurice was still a child and liked to sing to Douglas the songs he had learnt in the nursery. The boys became inseparable, basking in the sunshine, drinking bottles of ginger beer and telling each other stories.

One morning Douglas realised that he had not seen Maurice since breakfast and surmised that he had returned to normal school life. He was devastated. 'We both thought,' he wrote, 'that he would be there at least another day, which in mid-summer at school is an eternity.' Soon one of the maids arrived to tell him that Maurice was in Miss D'Arcy's room and that he wished to say goodbye. Douglas found his friend sitting disconsolately on the sofa and threw his arms round the younger boy's neck. In front of the matron, they kissed each other and wept openly. She saw nothing reprehensible in this, and, as Douglas put it, he and Maurice knew only too well that, 'owing to the idiotic and rotten conventions of public-school life, he being younger than I, and our not being in the same House, we would hardly ever again be able to see each other except in the distance'. Except on one occasion later that term, when they stole a few whispered words in passing, they never spoke again while they were at school. The only times they met subsequently were when Douglas had left and, as an Old Wykehamist, was able to speak to Maurice when he visited Winchester from Oxford. However, they both knew that their irrevocable parting had come 'on that summer morning in Miss D'Arcy's room'.

Douglas was adamant that his relationship with Maurice Turner should not be misunderstood and made this clear to his readers in a way that he did not when commenting on other youthful relationships. 'Our relationship,' he wrote, '(perhaps I ought to make it clear in this day, when any great friendship between persons of the same sex is generally labelled homosexual as a matter of course) was entirely innocent and idyllic, but it was certainly sentimental to the last degree, which was very far from being the case with most friendships between older and younger boys in my day at Winchester. Immorality there might be, but sentiment no!'[42] In old age he would never have written in such detail of his time with Maurice Turner had their friendship been in any way 'immoral'. It is fascinating, though: not only did it signal the high point in the succession of his encounters with other boys at Winchester, it set a precedent for his future relationships, with both men and women. Thirty-five years later, Douglas expressed his long and deeply felt convictions on the nature of love when he wrote, in his finest and most sustained sonnet sequence, 'In Excelsis',

> For love essentially must needs be chaste,
> And being contracted to unchastity
> (Even in marriage) knows essential loss,
> And falls into a malady of waste,
> Squand'ring the expended spirit's minted fee
> For that which, in the best, is worthless dross.[43]

Eighteen eighty-eight was Alfred Douglas's last year at Winchester, and without doubt his most constructive. During this time he cemented his friendships with people who remained close to him. Foremost among these was George Montagu, Encombe's 'fag', who performed all the usual servile tasks that his position demanded of him. However, he clearly had an easier time of it than most others of his year, for particular attention was paid to him by Encombe's best friend. Four years younger than Douglas, Montagu was to become the 9th Earl of Sandwich,[44] and Douglas described him as 'a fair-haired, blue-eyed pretty boy with engaging manners'.[45] He fell for the boy's charm during his last term, and since their mothers were great friends often stayed at the family's home, which doubtless fired his adoration. Montagu was a boy in whom Douglas could take an almost fatherly interest and he made a bee-line for him whenever he visited Winchester after he had gone up to Oxford.[46]

4

During his penultimate term at Winchester, Douglas, with two friends, founded a school magazine to rival the *Wykehamist*. It was an achievement he remained proud of for the rest of his life. He, Edmund B. Phipps, who was in the same house, and Edmund W. Lidderdale, who was not, produced ten numbers of the *Pentagram*, which was intended to rival and mock the *Wykehamist*. It gave the boys an opportunity to experiment with their own literary ability. Of the five papers Douglas edited during his lifetime, as he admitted, 'The *Pentagram* was the only one that ever showed a profit.'[47] When the last number was published more copies were being sold than there were boys in the school because a number of old boys subscribed to it.

The first issue opens with an explanation of the need for another school magazine: 'The *Wykehamist*, with its active and sleeping editors, is a most respectable journal, whose slowness almost equals its respectability.' They also explained their choice of its title: the shape from which it took its name 'keeps off evil spirits and bad luck generally'. The three editors wrote their often irreverent articles under pseudonyms. Phipps was 'The Pelican', Lidderdale was 'H.H.H.' – Half-way House Hag – and Douglas was 'The Lost Chord'.[48] The three, along with the odd outside contributor, put everything into their magazine from poetry to reports of school matches, but much of their material consists of typical public-schoolboy humour – recounting practical jokes and mishaps that have occurred to friends. There are some more general moments of humour: an article in the sixth issue follows the report of a cricket match against Eton in which Winchester were beaten by ten wickets on the first day and by an innings in the second. Since they could not fault the superiority of Eton on the field they ridiculed the spectators, presumably the Etonian parents. Among five typical examples of such a crowd is, 'II – The Ignorant Party'.

> She: 'Why do they change sides so often? It takes such a long time.'
> He: 'Oh, that's because another bowler is going to bowl at the other end.'
> She: 'But how awfully slow of them! Why don't they bowl from the two ends at once?'[49]

One of Douglas's first prose contributions reveals in embryonic form his anecdotal ability: he describes how on their way back to their house one afternoon the 'Pelican' and 'Lost Chord' decided to chance their luck at a Try Your Strength machine. The 'Lost Chord' had a penny, the 'Pelican' did not, and after a failed attempt to extort the sum from two younger boys and a near descent into violence,

> . . . one of the crowd that was now fast collecting, suggested that they should 'pull, pull together'. No sooner said than done. A moment more, and the Chord had taken up the customary position, with his feet firmly pressed against the supports provided for that purpose, his hands firmly grasping the handles. In an instant the Pelican had seized him round the waist, and on the fall of the coin they got off well together. On entering the 'teens they tired perceptibly, but struggling gamely on, they had just reached 18, when the Lost Chord, whether overcome by the excitement of the moment, or distressed by the unwonted pressure from behind,

suddenly loosed his hold! The sequel is too terrible for publication. There are many who will carry to the grave the memory of the heartrending scene, as the frenzied Fowl, maddened by remorse, bent o'er the prostrate victim of his unfortunate ambition.[50]

Douglas had his revenge on the 'Pelican' (who had accidentally burnt one of his poems) by including in the same issue, when the unfortunate 'bird' was ill, the following short report:

'Yes, I think that's good,' said the Pelican, as he finished reading over one of his own compositions. 'By the way, how do you account for the enormous sale of this week's *Pentagram*?' To him the Chord, 'Well, I expect it had got about the School that you had gone down to Sick House, and so they thought you couldn't have written anything in the number!' and the bird was silent.[51]

The *Pentagram* also gave Douglas the opportunity to publish his verse. Those poems appear to have been his first and were never republished in any of his collections. In his *Autobiography* he recalled, 'I began to write poetry in my first year at Oxford. I had before, in my school days, written verse, chiefly humorous, but none of it was good enough to survive.'[52]

However, the ones he included in the *Pentagram* are of some interest, chiefly because they show Douglas in an endearingly childish vein far removed from the austere work that came out of the traumas that beset him later. It is also of some interest that in these early efforts he is already writing in rigid forms:

Triolets

I

I'm up to books at nine o'clock:
  I haven't done my out of School:
Five past! good heavens, what a shock,
  I'm up to books at nine o'clock.
My 'toys' are shut? Well burst the lock.
Now my straw hat; 'play up' you fool!
I'm up to books at nine o'clock,
  I haven't done my out of School.

II

You writing lines? Yes. So am I,
  For shirking Chapel Sunday last.
Halloa! I hear another sigh:
  You writing lines? Yes. So am I;
That's three of us; and here close by
Another scribbling very fast:
YOU writing lines? Yes. So am I,
  For shirking Chapel Sunday last.[53]

Among the other rhymes and verse in the *Pentagram*, Douglas's stand out as by far the most sophisticated in style. Some are in a more fanciful though less humorous style, but all were dwarfed by one that appeared in the last issue, by Lionel Johnson, a cousin of Douglas.[54] It was a coup for the *Pentagram*'s editors for it was signed 'Ex-Editor of the Wykehamist', which indeed he had been. Although Douglas himself had no lasting admiration for 'A Benediction', describing it in later years as 'a very charming, half-whimsical, half-pathetic poem',[55] Johnson thought highly enough of it to extend its five stanzas to seventy under the title 'Winchester', in which guise it appeared as the last poem in his 1897 collection, *Ireland, with other poems*. The fifth stanza, which closed the *Pentagram*'s final number, went:

Said is my say! so fare you well,
  Lovers and lords of laughter!
(Platitude now.) What Time hereafter
  May bring us, who can tell?
    Then sigh we, alas!
    And fill we the glass,
With *Auld Lang Syne* to the rafter!

The last issue of the *Pentagram* opened with a prose essay, which proved to be uncannily prophetic:

Yes, the play is over; drop the curtain! put out the lights. To-morrow's sun shall look down upon empty houses, cricket fields bare of nets, class-rooms closed, with only the eternal maps on the wall that never disappear, the maps that watch generation after generation come and go, that watch the hairs of their don gradually whiten, the maps that have heard such hundreds of jokes followed by the inevitable burst of applause; the maps that have grown impervious to the jokes, that sit and stare dull and flat, because they know that the applause must die out and float away to the ceiling, that the laugh must cease, and that in the years to come, few, very few hearts, will be as light and brimful of laughter as they are now.[56]

5

Douglas spent his last term at Winchester preparing for his entry to Magdalen College, Oxford in October 1889. After he left, at Christmas in 1888, Gerald Campbell a nephew of Douglas's great-aunt the Honourable Mrs Percy Wyndham, was engaged as his tutor, and the pair passed a few months together in France during which Douglas became fluent in French. He learnt more than that on this trip, though: while staying in an hotel in the South of France he met a woman, whose identity is unknown, with whom he had his first heterosexual affair.

She was apparently the divorced wife of an earl, and Douglas described her as 'a lady of celebrated beauty, at least twelve years older than myself'. She also happened to be a cousin of Campbell. The affair proceeded along what Douglas termed 'classic lines' until one night when his tutor rapped on the bedroom door demanding the return of his 'ravished ewe-lamb'. Douglas appeared in floods of tears in one of the woman's nightgowns to face him. She was apparently blamed by 'whole juries of matrons' who attacked her wickedness in seducing 'an innocent boy'.[57] Douglas was the first to protest that he was far from an innocent boy, but nobody believed him and he was sent back to England in disgrace. However, now that he had experimented fairly successfully with both sexes, he was able to choose which to favour. Although he claimed that if he had stayed with the lady she might have kept him from 'baser promiscuities'[58] this is unlikely: the experience of his Winchester days with this affair qualified him for the position he would take up at Oxford as the leader of 'the cause'.[59]

Chapter 2

'I am the love that dare not speak its name'

(1889–1895)

Douglas went up to Magdalen College, Oxford, in October 1889, just before his nineteenth birthday. For his first year he was given a set of rooms in the eighteenth-century 'New Buildings', where his tiny bedroom overlooked the deer-park. In *Without Apology* Douglas wrote, 'Although I loved it too, I never cared for Oxford quite in the same way as I did for Winchester. Looking back at it now, I realise that my best time there was my first two years, when I was still as much at heart a schoolboy as I was in appearance.'[1] Certainly, in his first years there, Douglas revelled in the liberation he found. His physical appearance, along with his hearty personality and perhaps his title, helped him make friends quickly, and he was noted for his wit and daring from the start. During his first winter at Magdalen, in 1890, the river Thames froze over. Keeping his form up, Douglas was on a run with some friends when the ice was starting to break. They had set a rule that if one of them jumped an obstacle, they all had to. Douglas conceived the idea of jumping from block to block of the ice until they had got to the other side, then to do the same on the way back. In his *Autobiography* he described the inevitable result: 'We all got across safely by something like a miracle. Whereupon I started to cross back again. I jumped on a large floating block of ice, and to my horror it dipped and pitched me right into the swirling, icy water, the block of ice on which I had stepped going clean over my head. When I tried to come up my head bumped against the ice, and meanwhile my companions on the bank were splitting themselves with laughter at my mishap.'[2] Eventually one of the others, 'Tyler' Reid, realised the seriousness of the situation, waded into the river and dragged the stunned Douglas on to the bank.

When Douglas went to Oxford his outlook on life was 'largely sporting and convivial,' although he also confessed to an 'intellectual and artistic side'.[3] He attended the college chapel services every day, even though he had 'lost all belief in religion',[4] and loved to hear the choir, which he believed was the best in the world. His opinion was confirmed when the great violinist Joachim came to a service and, on hearing the choir's rendition of Wesley's 'Exultate Deo', wept at the beauty of the singing. Douglas was an accomplished pianist and made friends with the organist and a number of the 'Academical Clerks', or gentlemen of the choir with whom he spent evenings playing and singing all kinds of music from Wesley to Bach, glees and madrigals. He and his friends were much in demand to perform in 'smoking concerts', which occurred once a week in the Junior Common Room.

He took his rowing seriously, though cross-country running remained his favoured sport, and the one in which he excelled. He won the mile handicap and the two miles (scratch) – indeed, he would have won his Blue but for a crippling knee injury he sustained before a race which he had been tipped to win. He indulged his wicked sense of humour in having cards specially printed with strategically placed blanks to send to his tutors. For instance, when completed

> Lord Alfred Bruce Douglas presents his compliments to . . . and regrets that he will be unable to . . . in consequence of . . .

would read,

> Lord Alfred Bruce Douglas presents his compliments to Professor Smith and regrets that he will be unable to show up his essay on the Evolution of the Moral Idea in consequence of not having prepared one.

The cards won him fame throughout the university and, naturally, amused his friends, though hardly endeared him to the recipients, some of whom were reportedly driven to the 'verge of madness' because 'nothing could be done about them, because they were obviously polite', or so their author claimed.[5] But he found himself in serious trouble – and was gated – for going to the Derby instead of attending lectures and had several other brushes with the Magdalen authorities.

The dean's meeting on 16 January 1890 recorded that the previous December Douglas had failed his end-of-first-term exams, Responsions, and that he was to be gated at 9.00 p.m. for a fortnight. Another meeting, on 26 June 1890, noted that his future residence in the college depended on his being able to satisfy his tutor and the dean in his divinity examination.[6] In January 1891 the tutorial board noted that he would be sent down if he failed to pass the examination in Holy Scripture at the end of the Lent term and that a condition of residence was that he commenced the study of modern literature immediately. In fact, Douglas was reading extensively in areas of literature that interested him. He was also pursuing amorous relationships with both sexes, while setting himself up as the most renowned homosexual in the university where, he later claimed, not only hundreds of undergraduates but also a number of dons were open and practising homosexuals.

2

The 'skits and parodies', as he referred to them in later years,[7] that Douglas had contributed to the *Pentagram* gave him the confidence to write verse in a more serious vein during his first year at Oxford. His first effort, 'Autumn Days', was written at the Hut where his mother was still living. It appeared in the *Oxford* magazine, and among the plaudits he received for it was a note from the president of the college, Herbert Warren, who wrote that he thought the poem 'really passionate and fine', and added, 'I must confess I had no idea that you could do anything so good.'[8] Academically, he was not doing so well and when he was 'ploughed' in mathematics in 'Smalls', his end-of-first-year exams, he was sent down for a term. He spent three weeks studying Euclid, and passed Smalls on his second attempt by having learnt all the propositions in the first book of Euclid by heart.

In the same year, he produced his first sonnet, the area of poetry in which he excelled. In his later work Douglas stuck to the form of the sonnet laid down by the Italian poet Petrarch during the fourteenth century, but in his first attempt he adopted the form Shakespeare had used in his sequence of sonnets. Shakespeare had been his greatest literary love from childhood when his mother had read aloud to him. At Oxford he would stay up late into the night discussing Shakespeare with Lionel Johnson who was an equally great enthusiast and with whom Douglas became far better acquainted.

Shakespeare used the English sonnet form, with the rhyme scheme

ABABCDCDEFEF GG. The Petrarchan sonnet, ABBAABBA CDECDE (or CDCDCD), required four words that rhymed in the octave, or the first stanza, while the Shakespearean sonnet required only two. It was Douglas's theory that the Petrarchan form yielded the finer effect partly because it was harder to master, and he came to believe that 'The more difficult and exacting the form the finer will be the result, provided always that the appearance of ease and naturalness is produced.'[9] His first, somewhat strained, sonnet, 'Amoris Vincula' (The Chains of Love) is a respectable exercise in verse, but contains little of the expertise in technique that would allow him later to explore more moving subject matter.

Only a single sonnet emerged in 1891 and it shows more of the feeling that became his hallmark. 'A Summer Storm' laments the loss of innocent happiness.

> Alas! how frail and weak a little boat
> I have sailed in. I called it happiness,

Here, as in all his sonnets, in the Petrarchan form, for the next four years, the sestets are marred by a faulty rhyme scheme. Later he explained this as due to the influence of Rossetti's sonnets, which, 'are far from being models of perfection as far as form is concerned'.[10] In the 1928 *Complete Poems* he footnoted 'A Summer Storm', 'The worst sonnet I ever wrote!', which was harsh but characteristically truthful.

Along with the poetic output, 1891 brought family tragedy. Queensberry's brother Jim was known as a heavy drinker, and manic depressive. He could not cope with his marriage and his sanity became increasingly questionable. He adored his twin, Florrie, but since her marriage he had been able to spend less time with her, and especially since her move to Scotland. Jim was left without his main support and his decline was rapid. He flew into fits of rage, gibbering and snarling at his wife and her son, then drank himself into a stupor. Matters came to a head in April and Jim's wife turned to Queensberry for advice. He suggested a relaxing fishing holiday alone in Ireland, but, isolated and demented, Jim cracked up completely. On the way back his behaviour was so odd that he was accompanied by an inspector. On his arrival in London he booked into the Euston Station hotel. His wife and Queensberry decided meanwhile that a trip to Scotland should be arranged for him the next morning. They never had the chance to put it to him. In the morning the maid discovered him lying in his room in a pool of blood. The night before he had slit his throat from ear to ear, while standing in front of the mirror.

The suicide of Lord James Douglas brought immense newspaper attention although his death must have been a release for his wife and Queensberry. Nevertheless, the family were devastated, not least by the bizarre events that surrounded his burial. This took place in the family burial-ground in the park at Kinmount. Beau was so upset by his brother-in-law's death that he consumed a vast amount of alcohol, exceeding even his own limits, and his wife banned him from the funeral. To ensure that he would not attend the service she put him to bed, hid his mourning clothes and left without him. Once his wife had left, Beau got up, went to the local inn, borrowed a pair of ill-fitting black trousers from the waiter and left for the funeral thus attired with the addition of a dark overcoat. He arrived just as the coffin was being lowered into the grave. Douglas gave an account of the tragicomic events that followed. Unsurprisingly, 'the appearance, in his strange garb, of poor Uncle Beau at this moment was a fearful shock to Aunt Florrie and all the mourners, and this was accentuated when with loud sobs, and tears running down his cheeks, he threw himself down by the grave and ejaculated: "My God, how I loved that man; we were like a pair of apes!" '[11]

Florrie left a rather more eloquent tribute at the foot of the grave, which read, 'Loved with an undying love by his twin sister Florrie. Here, where he played in childhood's happy days, he now rests.'[12]

The family was dogged by rumours of lunacy and degeneracy, and the series of events that followed provided ample ammunition for gossips and journalists.

3

By 1892 Douglas had moved into a flat in the high street in Oxford with Lord Encombe. There, at number 34, they continued a polite mode of warfare with a Christ Church club, whose rooms were beneath. A battle broke out over the lavatory to which, although it belonged to the club, Douglas and Encombe felt they had right of entry as inhabitants rather than visitors. The correspondence between the aggrieved parties was cordial but when Artie Paget, a friend of Douglas and Encombe, used it club members locked the door from the outside. Paget coolly locked it from the inside and remained in the lavatory for an hour, during which he painstakingly removed all the pieces of the unit and took them with him when he escaped by the window and up a drainpipe. Once the club members had broken into their own lavatory and hired a plumber to restore it they declared themselves willing to admit Douglas and Encombe to membership of that section of the club.

However, by 1892 Douglas was engaged in more than undergraduate high jinks and was writing more verse than ever before. Poetry had become for him a vehicle for expression of a new kind, for at some time in 1891, probably late June, Lionel Johnson took Douglas to visit his friend Oscar Wilde at Wilde's home in Tite Street, Chelsea. By this time Wilde was one of the most famous men in the country. He had been the subject of reams of jokes about his posing and aestheticism for over a decade, and now in his late thirties he had finally lived up to the expectations many people had harboured of his talent. With the publication of *The Picture of Dorian Gray* in 1890 he had begun to be considered as a major writer, which the opening of his first comedy, *Lady Windermere's Fan*, in 1892 was to confirm.

Far from it being love at first sight, Douglas wrote that, 'What really happened at that [first meeting] was just the ordinary exchange of courtesies. Wilde was very agreeable and talked a great deal. I was very much impressed, and before I left, Wilde had asked me to lunch or dinner at his club, and I had accepted his invitation.'[13] On that occasion, a few days later, Wilde presented Douglas with a signed copy of *The Picture of Dorian Gray* – which Douglas had already read, on different estimates, nine or fourteen times running. Later that evening, according to Douglas, Wilde made sexual advances towards him, which he resisted.

When Douglas met Wilde, both had been practising homosexuals for several years. Robert Ross is said to have boasted that he was 'the first boy that Oscar ever had', though whether or not this is true it is impossible to say. What is more certain is that after the birth of his second son, Vyvyan, in 1886, Wilde gave up sexual relations with his wife – financial constraints made it unwise for them to have more children – and was led into homosexuality.

Douglas came further into Wilde's life through a request from Percy

Douglas, who asked Wilde to help out his brother who was in serious difficulties with a blackmailer. The details of the case are vague, but it almost certainly involved a boy in the town of Oxford. Although he claimed later that in these years he still pursued relationships with women, it is much more likely that Douglas was exclusively homosexual. He was an extremely attractive, boyish-looking young man, and his sexual tastes extended no further than to boys of his own age and, more often, to those younger than himself. Wilde was thirty-seven. He had lost what looks he might have had as a young man, and was now large, bloated and coarse-featured; one society hostess referred to him as 'the great white caterpillar'.[14] There was no doubt, of course, that when he met Douglas he was a brilliant and entertaining personality but there was nothing physically to attract the younger man. Nevertheless, Wilde persistently made advances. According to Douglas, they had known each other for six months, during which they had met frequently and Wilde had stayed twice with him in Oxford, before Douglas gave in.

Probably in January 1892, Wilde took Douglas to dinner at the Savoy, then to the theatre and then moved on to supper at the Lyric Club. Douglas was staying with his mother, at her London house in Cadogan Place, though nobody else was there that night except servants. Wilde's family were away, and he was on his own in Tite Street. He and Douglas arrived in the empty house in Chelsea at about two in the morning and, after a couple of hours' chat, Wilde persuaded Douglas to stay the night in the spare bedroom. Years later Douglas wrote, 'I did with him and allowed him to do just what was done among boys at Winchester and Oxford. Sodomy never took place between us, nor was it thought or dreamt of. Wilde treated me as an older boy treats a younger one at school, and he added what was new to me and was not (as far as I know) known or practised among my contemporaries: he "sucked" me.'[15] Douglas's candour in days when such acts could still condemn a man to prison is some proof of the truth of his statement, and his coyness is understandable. However, as he went on, 'Much as I was fascinated by Wilde and much as I really in the long run adored and was "crazy" about him, I never liked this part of the business. It was dead against my sexual instincts which were all for youth and beauty and softness. After a time he tumbled to the fact that I didn't like it at all and only consented to it to oblige him, and he very soon cut it out altogether . . . Except in the case of Wilde I have never in my life had any immoral relations with a man older than myself.' In later years Douglas admitted that just as Wilde had achieved his aim in getting him into bed so, by capturing the attention of this famous figure, 'I got what I wanted.'[16]

When Douglas met Wilde, he was sexually inexperienced although, in his own words, 'no more innocent than any other boys of my age (21)',[17] but his life changed in an important way. In 1890 Wilde had created a scandal, with the serialisation in *Lippincott's* magazine of the unabridged *The Picture of Dorian Gray*. When it was published as a book much of the most overt homosexual subtext was removed, and readers would have been disappointed if they had expected anything racy. Nevertheless, Wilde had dared to do something that few others would have: he put the unspeakable into print – or, at least, suggested it. Under his influence, it was almost inevitable that in time Douglas would adopt an equally unashamed and flagrant attitude.

The character of Dorian Gray was based, if it was based on anyone at all, on John Gray, the minor 1890s poet, who later became the Roman Catholic canon of Edinburgh. As a young man, he had been adopted by Wilde, who dropped him when Douglas came on the scene. At least one letter from Gray to Wilde has survived in which he signed himself 'Dorian', and Wilde often referred to him by this name.[18] Gray was from a working-class background, which he had escaped to some extent in education at cramming schools, but the aristocratic Douglas was a distinct improvement on him in Wilde's eyes.

Wilde's influence over the subjects of his attention is recorded most clearly by André Gide, who later became one of Douglas's most hated enemies for his demonstrably untrue books on him and Wilde. His claim that Douglas once whispered to him that he would 'have' Cyril, Wilde's beloved eldest son, when he was older is just one of the stories which, though unsubstantiated, might ruin a reputation.[19] Although the morality expounded in Wilde's conversation was anathema to Gide, the dizzying effect was persuasive enough to make him question his own moral viewpoint. From Douglas's poetry, it is clear that, before long, Wilde's powerful influence was exerting itself as much in his thoughts and theories as it was in his sex life.

Friendship with Wilde meant that Douglas began to move in a new circle of people. They were cultured, usually witty and sometimes talented. Of them, perhaps the most important was Robert Ross. A Canadian by birth, Ross had become friendly with Wilde in 1886 and their relationship carried on during the young man's time at King's, Cambridge. Whether or not he was 'the first boy Oscar ever had',[20] he was certainly devoted to Wilde, and when he was ousted as Wilde's lover by a series of attractive young men, he grew bitter. When Douglas first got to know him, though, Ross was an amusing and appealing personality. The two quickly became friends, as did More Adey who shared rooms with Ross. The circle included Reginald Turner, the brilliant conversationalist and great friend of Max Beerbohm, and Robert Sherard, a minor poet and great-grandson of William Wordsworth. On the fringes, according to Douglas, was that most extraordinary character Frank Harris. Douglas adored him: he had not only achieved some success as a writer but also in the field as a good shot. Almost without exception these men later wrote about Wilde and Douglas, and all fell out with Douglas.

Perhaps the only member of the Wilde circle who remained Douglas's friend was Ada Leverson. Nicknamed by Wilde 'the Sphinx', she was an adorable and enlightened confidante to him and Douglas, and always remained loyal to Wilde's memory. She was a writer and novelist of some standing, which with her generous nature won her many admirers.

Douglas introduced some of his Oxford friends to Wilde's circle, and one in particular made an impact: Maurice Schwabe had been a friend of Douglas for some years though his introduction to Wilde was unfortunate. Eventually he proved a millstone around Wilde's neck when Wilde tried to deny the allegations made at his trials. It is fairly easy to guess what Douglas's relationship with Schwabe had been, and that Wilde and Douglas were in the habit of swapping their young men.[21]

4

In 1892 Douglas wrote a substantial amount of verse, almost all of it influenced by his now assured homosexuality, including the only poem by him which is still widely known through frequent republication in anthologies. 'Two Loves' takes its title from Shakespeare's sonnet 144:

> Two loves I have of comfort and despair,
> Which like two spirits do suggest me still:
> The better angel is a man right fair,
> The worser spirit a woman colour'd ill.

Republication of 'Two Loves' was banned by its author after the 1896 edition of his poems until 1935 when he gave permission for it to be reprinted so that he could justify his youthful works. In a footnote in the 1935 *Lyrics*, Douglas wrote that he had refused to republish earlier because of the bitterness he felt that the poem had been used against him in the law courts. He explained that it was 'merely the outcome of a classical education and a passion for the sonnets of Shakespeare', and went on, 'Its morality or immorality is in "the eye of the beholder" or, I should say, more properly, the mind of the reader.' The poem is seventy-four lines long, but only the last twelve are famous: they were read out to Wilde in court, and he was asked to explain them. While the poem is simple it has some poetic merit. In the opening section the poet describes a landscape he has seen in a dream, 'a place so strange, so sweet, so fair', and two beautiful young men, one joyous, the other sad, wandering in it. The poem finishes with the narrator asking the sad youth:

> 'Sweet youth,
> Tell me why, sad and sighing, thou dost rove
> These pleasant realms? I pray thee speak me sooth
> What is thy name?' He said, 'My name is Love.'
> Then straight the first did turn himself to me
> And cried, 'He lieth, for his name is Shame,
> But I am Love, and I was wont to be
> Alone in this fair garden, till he came
> Unasked by night; I am true Love, I fill
> The hearts of boy and girl with mutual flame.'
> Then sighing said the other, 'Have thy will,
> I am the Love that dare not speak its name.'

In the 1890s 'shame' was homosexual slang for homosexual love. The first time the word appears to have been used in this way was in André Raffalovitch's poem on Piers Gaveston, 'Tuberose and Meadowsweet', of 1885.

That the last line of 'Two Loves' has remained so famous is some proof of its merit. The idea is not original, but it is originally and beautifully expressed. Douglas himself wrote, 'The poet wishes to strike beautiful notes, not new notes. The medium of poetry remains eternally the same once a language has arrived at its highest point. It is impossible to improve on the language of Shakespeare and the other Elizabethan poets, nor is it necessary to vary their subject-matter. To ask or expect a poet to strike a new note in poetry is exactly like asking or expecting the Nightingale to strike a new note in her perennial song.'[22]

There is no doubt that 'Two Loves' was partly written to impress those who shared the poet's tastes. However, it is more than a hymn to homosexual love. The dedication of the poem to Ada Leverson shows that the poem was intended to be capable of further interpretation, and much is revealed about the poet. From it, and from other poems that were to follow it a few months later, we can see that the poet was still somewhat furtive about his sexuality, perhaps ashamed of it. The boy who represents homosexual passion, or 'shame love' in this Eden is beautiful, yet sad and ill-looking. All the photos of the youthful Douglas show a pose, an image of himself which he cultivated as the wistful and unhappy beauty as assiduously as Wilde posed as a dandy and an exquisite.

Douglas's frame of mind becomes even clearer in his next poem, 'De Profundis' (Out of the Depths). Here he is unequivocal in his celebration of his passions even though he revels in the persecution or unhappiness that they bring. It opens,

> I love a love, but not as other men
> Who tell the world their love for very pride,
> For the cold world loves not my love; and when
> My voice would sing my love I needs must hide,
> Under a cloak of black ambiguous words,

and finishes, without remorse,

> and the fruit
> Of many silent years is like a song
> Sung in a prison by the lips of Fear,
> With a hushed voice and a quick glance behind
> At what is not. Ah! cruel world and drear!
> And yet – I care not, so my love be kind.

The poets of the 1890s, and those before and after them with homosexual inclinations, often had to mask their feelings behind ambiguity or by changing the sex of the beloved. A review in *the Academy* newspaper of Raffalovitch's first book of poems said, 'It is hard to say from internal evidence whether the poems are the work of a man or of a woman.'[23] While many, like Raffalovitch used the method of 'singing with a female voice',[24] Douglas rarely used such tricks in his homosexually erotic verse. In 'De Profundis' he shows his frustration at having to sing with 'lips of Fear'. Yet he gives his poem a personal conclusion – that love, whatever its objects, is true if it is unselfish.

Among the other poems written in this year were several sensual depictions of lovers, fictional or otherwise, again in the fantasy style of 'Two Loves'. These included 'A Winter Sunset' and 'In Summer' which concluded,

> And you came, my love, so stealthily
> That I saw you not
> Till I felt that your arms were hot
> Round my neck, and my lips were wet
> With your lips, I had forgot
> How sweet you were.

'Prince Charming', written at Oxford, once again reveals the poet's taste as still essentially of the schoolboy variety.

Still, it seems, his relationship with Maurice Turner was the ideal. He had, and in some ways retained, what George Bernard Shaw called an 'infantile complex',[25]

Much of Douglas's poetry at this period is simple and ditty-like, a self-gratifying form of expression in which he made little attempt to produce anything of great poetic merit. In 1892 he made his first and only attempt at play-writing, possibly spurred on by Wilde's successes. *When The King Comes He Is Welcome (A Tragedy in One Act)* displays his growing preoccupation with the possibility of a perfect spiritual union between two members of the same sex. The play, by his own later admission, was 'very childish'. Still, he said, it revealed his 'hankering', from an early age, 'after chastity',[26] although he was not practising it at the time.

Eighteen ninety-two produced two further poems from Douglas. One, 'Apologia', drew an unequivocal footnote in the 1935 edition stating that 'The author now repudiates these and similar sentiments in his early poems.' It is one of his best early lyrics, beginning,

> Tell me not of Philosophies,
> Of morals, ethics, laws of life;

The poem is so full of the confidence, indeed arrogance, hope and beauty of youth that it could only have been written by a young man. In contrast the tragedy that was already looming over his life appears all the more destructive.

5

Probably in December 1892, while down from Oxford and staying with his mother in Salisbury for the Christmas vacation, Douglas wrote his sonnet 'In Sarum Close'. He sent it to Wilde in January 1893. It opens

> Tired of passion and the love that brings
> Satiety's unrest, and failing sands
> Of life, I thought to cool my burning hands
> In this calm twilight of gray Gothic things:

and finishes.

> But thou, my love, my flower, my jewel, set
> In a fair setting, help me, or I die,
> To bear Love's burden; for that load to share
> Is sweet and pleasant, but if lonely I
> Must love unloved, 'tis pain; shine we, my fair,
> Two neighbour jewels in Love's coronet.

He described it in the 1935 edition of his sonnets as, 'an example of what I call the "art-for-art's-sake" heresy', and 'It lacks sincerity and is therefore merely an exercise in Verse'. When he wrote this he was out of the artistic and moral grip of Wilde, but at twenty-two he was heavily influenced in every way by the older man which shows clearly in the poem. It delighted Wilde, whose theories had inspired and influenced it, and who must have seen from it that his influence over Douglas was showing not just in his moral, sexual and social life, but, triumphantly for Wilde, in his artistic, creative life. Wilde responded to the poem in one of his most famous letters. Clearly he was not aware that Douglas was already in Salisbury, for his letter, from Lady Mount Temple's house, Babbacombe Cliff in Torquay, where he, his wife Constance and their two sons were staying, reads,

> My Own Boy,
>
> Your sonnet is quite lovely, and it is a marvel that those red rose-leaf lips of yours should have been made no less for music of song than for madness of kisses. Your slim gilt soul walks between passion and poetry. I know Hyacinthus, whom Apollo loved so madly, was you in Greek days.
>
> Why are you alone in London, and when do you go to Salisbury? Do go there to cool your hands in the grey twilight of Gothic things, and come here whenever you like. It is a lovely place – it only lacks you; but go to Salisbury first. Always with undying love, yours,
>
> Oscar.[27]

Wilde must have delighted in the game of acting the disconsolate lover to Douglas, while thrilling to the subterfuge of carrying on a relationship by post, under the noses of his loving wife and children. This was a fine early example of what, in *The Importance of Being Earnest*, is named 'Bunbury'.

In November 1892 Douglas took over the ownership and editorship of the *Spirit Lamp*, an Oxford undergraduate magazine, from Sandys Wilson, an undergraduate at Christ Church. He had written one contribution for the magazine under Wilson's editorship, a witty essay entitled 'An Undergraduate on Oxford Dons', which concludes, 'Let us forgive them, but forget they exist.' Over the Christmas vacation he prepared to relaunch the magazine. His time on the *Pentagram* had given him the experience he needed to run the Oxford publication and in many ways his editorial policy on the *Spirit Lamp* was unchanged. He even persuaded one of his former colleagues, Edmund Phipps, to contribute to it.[28] In all he edited six numbers, the last of which appeared in June 1893.

In the early days there was only one problem with Douglas's editorship of the *Spirit Lamp*: he must have worked on it, for the first full term of his ownership, from outside Oxford, for in the opening months of 1893 he was studying with a private tutor recommended to him by Lionel Johnson. The tutor was Campbell Dodgson, scholar at Winchester and New College, Oxford, Douglas's senior by three years. It was his job to help Douglas cram during the Hilary term which Douglas had been sent down for, having been 'ploughed' in an examination. Campbell Dodgson arrived at Salisbury expecting to enter an environment of study and earnest reformation but, Douglas did not appear until the evening of his tutor's arrival and then only amid 'a flutter of telegrams'.

Next morning he read Plato with enthusiasm for an hour and a half and then, during lunch, announced to his tutor that they would be leaving for Torquay that same afternoon where they would be staying with Mr Oscar Wilde. Dodgson described the journey: 'Our departure was dramatic; Bosie was as usual in a whirl; he had no book, no money, no cigarettes and had omitted to send many telegrams of the first importance. Then, with a minimum of minutes in which to catch our train, we were required to overload a small pony chaise with a vast amount of trunks while I was charged with a fox terrier and a scarlet morocco dispatch-box, a gorgeous and beautiful gift from Oscar. After hurried farewells [to Lady Queensberry], we started on a wild career, Bosie driving. I expected only to drag my shattered limbs to the infirmary, but we arrived whole at the station.'[29]

From Babbacombe Cliff he wrote to Johnson, 'Our life is lazy and luxurious; our moral principles are lax. Bosie is beautiful and fascinating, but quite wicked. He is enchanted with Plato's sketch of democratic man, and no arguments of mine will induce him to believe in any absolute standards of ethics or of anything else. We do no logic, no history, but play with pigeons and children and drive by the sea.'[30] Wilde's mock timetable of 'Babbacombe school', which listed himself as headmaster, Dodgson as second master and Douglas as 'Boys', showed a rough outline for the day. About three hours' work was included, with breaks for sherry, lunch, 'compulsory hide and seek', brandy and sodas ('not to exceed seven for boys') and dinner with 'compulsory champagne', while reading took place in bed for an hour and a half from midnight, with the instruction that, 'Any boy found disobeying this rule will be immediately woken up.'[31]

The set-up at Babbacombe, where Wilde's children were also staying, although Constance had gone to Florence, was only slightly akin to a school. Wilde himself told Dodgson that 'I have succeeded in combining the advantages of a public school with those of a private lunatic asylum, which, as you know, was my aim.'[32] While he was there Douglas certainly got some of his work done, but he and Wilde had a savage quarrel, their first recorded fall-out in two years together. In a fit of rage Douglas stormed out of the household and went to Bristol, leaving Dodgson behind, explaining limply to an astonished Wilde that his young friend had a reputation at Magdalen as not always being responsible for what he said or did.

Once in Bristol, Douglas sent a telegram to Wilde asking his forgiveness, which Wilde instantly granted, and the two joined up together in London where they stayed in adjoining rooms in the Savoy Hotel. As Wilde later acknowledged, it was a fateful visit, for while they were there Douglas had another young man in his room who was seen in his bed by one of the hotel staff. This stay also damaged relations with Wilde's friend Pierre Louÿs who was shocked on entering the rooms to see one double bed with two pillows. He was still with the pair when Constance arrived. She begged Wilde to come home, but he tried to joke that he had been away such a while he could not remember which number his house was. Louÿs observed tears in Constance's eyes as she tried to smile.[33]

Presently Douglas returned to Salisbury and his mother, before his return to Oxford for his final term. Still at the Savoy, Wilde wrote to him.

> Bosie, you must not make scenes with me. They kill me, they wreck the loveliness of life. I cannot see you, so Greek and gracious, distorted by passion. I would sooner be blackmailed by every renter in London than have you bitter, unjust, hating. I must see you soon. You are the divine thing I want, the thing of grace and beauty; but I don't know how to do it.[34]

His infatuation was total, and Wilde saw its destructive side loom when on 21 April as his new play, *A Woman of No Importance*, enjoyed the start of its acclaimed run, the first of a string of blackmailers appeared with the stolen 'Hyacinthus' letter, demanding money for his silence.

Wilde and Douglas were treading a dangerous path. Douglas had befriended a young and unemployed clerk from Oxford called Alfred

Wood, who proved to be less than honest, and when letters from Wilde to Douglas turned up in the hands of blackmailers like Wood with whom they had slept, the two sides of Wilde's homosexual life came together: the romantic love for Douglas and the sexual encounters with rent-boys. Though the former produced Wilde's most dangerous adversary in Lord Queensberry, the latter brought a jury to convict him in court. The sexual relationship between Wilde and Douglas was short-lived, but it was replaced in both by a taste for rent-boys. Maurice Schwabe introduced Wilde to a man called Alfred Taylor, who had already been in trouble with the law and whose rooms in Westminster were to provide the majority of the evidence on which Wilde was convicted. Taylor made a living by introducing wealthy aristocratic men to young working-class lads willing to offer sex for ready money. Transactions of this kind fascinated Wilde, and it is clear from his habit of taking the young men he met through Taylor to dinner that he was interested in their motives as well as their services. The danger of dining these boys under the noses of London society was, as he admitted, 'half the excitement of it'; it was 'feasting with panthers'.

Douglas returned to Oxford for the Trinity term and Wilde made a glorious visit to him in 'Eights Week', during which Douglas arranged a dinner for him on each night of his stay. Of course Wilde won everyone's heart, sportsmen and aesthetes alike. When the periodical the *Ephemeral* attacked his mind and his body, Douglas, who knew the editors, arranged a meeting between the attackers and their victim. Within no time nothing but praise of the venerable playwright was heard from them.[35] Douglas also came under attack in various Oxford papers, including the *Ephemeral*, but found ample room to respond in his own publication, which went from strength to strength. In 1912, almost twenty years after the last issue of the *Spirit Lamp*, the *Morning Post* described it as 'the best of Oxford's many momentary periodicals'.[36] Certainly there can be little doubt today of the quality of the contributions, and Douglas persuaded Wilde to contribute a sonnet and two prose poems, a significant coup: the previous owners of the *Spirit Lamp* had approached him in the spring of 1892 but he had turned them down. Douglas also solicited three pieces, including a poem entitled 'A Friend', from Lionel Johnson; Max Beerbohm, then an undergraduate at Merton College, made his first appearance in print with 'On the Incomparable Beauty of Modern Dress', and an article and poem from the great art historian John

Addington Symonds were published just before his death. Douglas had an astonishing talent for gathering together people to write for his magazine without them expecting payment. Symonds wrote to Douglas to tell him that 'it would give me great pleasure to contribute . . . to your magazine', and since he was enclosing some verses, added, 'Tell me if you would like some prose better when the verse is disposed of – and what sort of stuff you want. I scribble, and would like to scribble for you.'[37]

As editor of the *Spirit Lamp*, Douglas became increasingly confident and published in it material that suited both his tastes and those of its readers. He was cultivating in himself the image of the aesthete, giving in to the cult of Wilde. He admitted in his *Autobiography* that at this time 'it is easy to trace a certain amount of his influence on my style and point of view'.[38] He even gave the *Spirit Lamp* a new subtitle: where it had been 'An Oxford Magazine without News' it became 'An Aesthetic, Literary and Critical Magazine'. After an attack on it in the *Ephemeral*, which referred to it as an 'unholy, decadent academy', and advised, 'Let it gather what withered bays it can find on the grave of Health',[39] he parried,

> Dear sir
> Next to the praise of the cultivated and the admiration of the brilliant, there is nothing so gratifying to the feelings of the editor of a magazine like the *Spirit Lamp* as the abuse of the Philistine and the scorn of the vulgar. Praise and admiration from the brilliant and the cultivated have been freely given to the *Spirit Lamp*, but up to the present, the abuse and scorn of the Philistine have been too infrequent and too sparingly expressed to give me very great cause for pride and self-congratulation . . . I am [therefore] deeply grateful to you.[40]

6

Eighteen ninety-three was an important year for Douglas. His magazine was flourishing and so was his poetry. The issue of 10 March 1893 contained an apology from its editor for the amount of pieces by himself among its pages; he blamed the lack of contributions sent in. His readers' response was to overwhelm him with pieces, which resulted in an astonishing issue on 4 May 1893. It contained a translation into French verse of Wilde's 'Hyacinthus' letter to Douglas, Douglas's own homo-erotic poem 'Sicilian Love Song', and an In Memoriam on the recently deceased former contributor and homosexual John Addington Symonds. Perhaps Douglas's greatest coup was in prompting a contribution from Lord Henry Somerset, an Italian poem 'T'Amo'. Somerset had been in exile for fourteen years and had been the most notorious homosexual before Wilde. Somerset had heeded the advice of his friends and put himself out of reach of the law. He remained infamous in the eyes of the British public, though, and his name in the magazine must have sent shock waves through the university. A note in the editor's 'Answers to Correspondents' section apologised to an A. R. Bayley, who had sent in a story and two poems: 'I like your story very much,' wrote Douglas, 'but I dare not publish it.' He promised to place the verses in the next issue. However, the next number, the last to appear under Douglas's editor-ship, was as lacking in homosexual material as its predecessor was bursting with it and Bayley's poetry was not published. Douglas contributed 'In Summer' which had been written the previous year and did not reveal the beloved's sex. Wilde's prose poem 'The Disciple' is typically decadent, but not conspicuously homosexual. The contribu-tion by J.A. Symonds, 'From the Arabic', featured apparently hetero-sexual lovers, showing Douglas's new-found caution.

Oh when will it be, oh when will it be, oh when,
That she shall be here, and the flute be here and the wine be here?
                    oh then
Her lips shall kiss the lips of the flute, and my lips shall kiss the wine,
And I shall drink music from her sweet lips, and she shall drink
                    madness from mine.

One can only speculate on why the *Spirit Lamp*'s last number was so comparatively tame. Perhaps Douglas had been warned either by the university authorities or by friends that another issue like the May number would land him in serious trouble. Douglas himself had penned its most overt piece: his 'Sicilian Love Song' made no attempt to disguise the sex of the beloved. The last two stanzas contain a particularly heady and overpowering eroticism.

Take wings, relentless light!
Die quick, unlovely sun!
For my love will come with the night
When the dreary day is done.
Come soon! Come soon! sweet night.

His lips are sweet and red;
Where starlight and moonlight mingle
We will make our bridal bed,
Down in the cool dark dingle,
When the long day is dead.

The inclusion of Lord Henry Somerset's poem must have come about through Douglas's friendship with Charles Kains Jackson, who edited the *Artist and Journal of Home Culture* magazine, and who had been consistently friendly towards the *Spirit Lamp*, referring in print to Douglas as 'the Callicles of Magdalen College',[41] and as 'the sweetest harp player'. The *Artist* had a reputation for publishing much 'uranian' material (that is, writing exclusively concerned with the aesthetic appreciation of young male beauty). It was the first magazine to publish Douglas's 'Prince Charming', and Jackson was in constant contact with Somerset.[42] It was not until Douglas himself was forced into exile that he was able to meet up with him.

Just before the last number of the *Spirit Lamp* was published, Douglas wrote another poem in the same mould as 'Sicilian Love Song'. 'Hymn To Physical Beauty' is his clearest and most sustained testimony to homosexual passion. It was published in 1896, in the first book of his poems, by the *Mercure de France*, in Paris, then remained out of print until 1935. Written in three uneven sections, it begins,

Sweet Spirit of the body, archetype
Of lovely mortal shapes, where is thy shrine?

The poet finds in the beauty of the boy an excuse to live and love, but mourns that so few men can appreciate it:

Thou needs must live, seeing he is so fair,
For all his beauty is but part of thee.
Alas! I fear me, in this dreary land,
Thou art distained,

. . .

Spurned in the dust uranian passion lies.

The final stanzas show Douglas's then blatant rebellion against the form of Christianity in which he had been brought up:

> O radiant thing (I will not say divine,
> Thou art more gracious and more beautiful
> Being human merely)
>
> . . .
>
> There be some faithful found who dare to say
> 'We needs must love what is most beautiful.'

The message is simple: we must all admit beauty even if the world denies it.

The most important poetic development of the year were Douglas's sonnets, and he wrote a tribute to his literary hero. However, 'To Shakespeare' is marred by the clumsiness of an inexpert sonnet writer. One editor has suggested that Douglas wrote his sonnet in anger after Robert Ross had jokingly suggested founding an anti-Shakespeare society to 'combat exaggerated bardolatory'.[43]

In August 1894 Douglas visited Shakespeare's grave at Stratford-upon-Avon at the end of a camping holiday with his cousin, the poet Wilfrid Scawen Blunt. Servants went ahead to prepare the camp, so they hardly roughed it, and Blunt recorded that he found Douglas 'a soft traveller'.[44] When they got to the shrine they read Shakespeare's sonnets as 'an appropriate form of prayer'. Douglas records that Wilfrid 'spent an hour kneeling before the tomb of Shakespeare reading to himself some of those marvellous sonnets . . . which are "the high top-gallant of poetry".' He admitted that 'being at that time, I fear, something of a typical under-graduate, I was impudent enough to tell Wilfrid that I thought he was making something of an exhibition of himself, or words to that effect. Wilfrid squashed me appropriately . . . and later I apologised and felt somewhat ashamed of myself.'[45] Blunt ran the Crabbet Poetry Club, which met once a year at his country house and one of whose members was Oscar Wilde. He could barely believe the devotion his cousin showed for Wilde, who had been described by Blunt's twenty-one-year-old daughter Judith as 'a great wobbly blancmange trying to serve underhand',[46] and by Blunt himself as one whose 'skin and hair (dyed) were by now a coarse Milesian brown'.[47]

During their Shakespeare trip Douglas was keen to join Wilde in

Worthing, but Blunt nevertheless had a chance, as he wrote to his cousin Anne, to 'talk to Bosie in the way of precept, in which, as you know, I excel'.[48] By this time Blunt must have seen that something had to be done about his cousin.

7

Douglas left Oxford at the end of the summer term of 1893, having done almost no work and having failed to graduate. His record was abysmal — of the end-of-term exams he passed, four were third class and only one was second (about four-fifths of students achieved first- or second-class marks). Though there was speculation that he was sent down for the blackmailing incident with the local boy this almost certainly did not reach the ears of the college authorities, he was in fact ill for honours, and the university offered him the opportunity to sit a private examination for a degree. He turned the offer down: 'I couldn't possibly stand an examination all by myself,' he responded. 'I really don't care twopence about having a degree.'[49]

This was written from Goring-on-Thames where Douglas was staying with Wilde, and Wilde was delighted: his friend had made the same decision as Swinburne, he said, to remain an undergraduate for the rest of his life. Needless to say, Douglas's parents were not so happy. 'It appears to me that you intend to do nothing,' his father wrote, a few months later. 'I utterly decline, however, to just supply you with sufficient funds to enable you to loaf about.'[50] He had forgotten presumably, in his anger, that he himself had come down from Magdalene College, Cambridge, when he was twenty-two without a degree, which, he said contemptuously later, had never been known 'to be worth twopence to anybody'.[51] Douglas admitted that he had indeed 'made a hash'[52] of his last three terms at Oxford, but this did not help the growing crisis.

Leaving Oxford without a degree should not have affected Douglas's ability to get a decent job — indeed Shelley and the Foreign Secretary of the time, Lord Rosebery, had been in the same position. Douglas, however, did not rush into work, preferring to survive on the allowance his mother made him. He spent the first few months after Oxford in Goring-on-Thames. Wilde's wife and children were with him when

Douglas arrived with his Oxford servants, one of them Walter Grainger. After a while the innocent Constance left, taking the children with her for a seaside holiday, so that the two writers could work. The adoring, demure Constance almost certainly had no idea of the nature of the relationship between her husband and Douglas. She probably viewed their attachment as sentimental but rooted in their common love of the arts, and it is worth mentioning that she and Douglas always got on well. She once confided to him that 'she liked [him] better than any of Oscar's friends'.[53] She was frequently a guest of Lady Queensberry, who also held her in affection.[54]

In Goring during the summer of 1893, Wilde worked on *An Ideal Husband* and proofs of his poem 'The Sphinx', while Douglas attempted a translation of *Salomé* from French, which Wilde had originally written it in. In asking Douglas to translate *Salomé*, Wilde hoped that their names might be able to appear together on the title page of his most infamously decadent work. He had asked Douglas to do the translation because his love blinded him to the young man's faults. Douglas was an undergraduate who spoke and wrote fluently in French, but it was fantasy on Wilde's part to think that he could render into English something that only Wilde could do to his own satisfaction. As it was, the translation was the cause of a major argument. One day, after a weekend when Douglas had had a couple of friends from Oxford to stay, the two had a full-blown quarrel on the croquet lawn outside the house. Wilde said that they must part, they were ruining each other's lives, and Douglas departed for London, leaving, according to Wilde, a vitriolic letter for him.[55] He returned three days later. Both were joyful in their reunion. Some time after that, on 16 August, they went up to London to see the last night of Wilde's *A Woman of No Importance* at the Haymarket, with Robbie Ross, Max Beerbohm and Aubrey Beardsley, who was to illustrate *Salomé*. On this occasion Douglas, Wilde and Ross wore rich clusters of vine leaves in their hair, blatant exhibitionism that embarrassed Beerbohm. The circle had begun to repel as many people as it attracted.

In September Wilde deemed Douglas's translation to be of insufficient merit and asked Aubrey Beardsley to take over. The French edition of the play had been published in the first weeks of 1893, and a limited-edition copy bears an inscription from Wilde to Douglas's friend, Lord Encombe. What is remarkable about the edition is that even though

Douglas had written his own signature opposite, it is claimed he had also written on the dedication page to Piere Louÿs. Someone has scribbled, in imitation of Wilde's own hand, simply 'Bosie from Oscar'.[56] If it was written by Douglas, it represents his wounded feelings at this time, although Peter Ackroyd goes a step further and suggests that it shows that Bosie thought that he had some 'inherent right'[57] to the work.

Douglas's own creative work continued, and at the end of August, while Wilde was in France, he wrote to Kains Jackson, sending him two sonnets to consider for inclusion in the *Artist*. The previous April he had accepted a uranian poem by Douglas, 'Hyacinthus', and the next April published 'Prince Charming', which appeared just before what Douglas called 'a brilliant and daring' article by Jackson on the virtues of 'male comradeship',[58] which forced Jackson to leave the magazine. Little is known of one of the sonnets, which was about Oxford, and the text has not survived. The other, however, has gained a notoriety that its material does not warrant. 'In an Aegean Port' was originally entitled 'A Port in the Aegean', and was not published in England after its appearance in the *Artist* until the 1935 *Sonnets*, for which Douglas changed the last three lines. The last half of the sonnet originally read,

> and I saw thee
> In thy white tunic gowned from neck to knee,
> And knew the honey of thy sugar lips.
>
> Rarer than all the hoarded merchandise
> Heaped on the wharves, more precious than fine pearls,
> Than all the loot and pillage of the deep
> More enviable: oh! food to my starved eyes!
> (That gaze unmoved on wanton charms of girls)
> Fair as the lad on Latmian hills asleep.

In his later amendment, Douglas justified 'sugar lips' by explaining that he had 'been reading translations of Hafiz and other Persian poets' at the time, a source of much inspiration to the uranian poets of the period. However, it might have been better for Douglas if he had just left the sonnet out of the 1935 book, or completely changed the sestet. The last 'corrected' lines read;

> Green pasture for young eyes,
>   Visible dream of tender unripe girls
>   Moon-rapt on Latmian hills, where are thy sheep?

The new lines reek of the worst in forced rhyming, because Douglas was not working with an entire sonnet, but trying to rework existing rhymes to fit a poem he had written forty-two years earlier. The last line, with its irrelevant concern for the sheep, shows the unsuccessful effort of an elderly man to spare his readers the embarrassing morals of his youth.

By this time, many of Douglas's close friends and family were becoming worried about his lack of intention to look for a job. He was arguing frequently with Wilde and their quarrels were at times savagely bitter – caused, at least in part, by Douglas's frustration. Even Wilde, who claimed to cultivate idleness, saw that his younger friend needed something to do. The artist William Rothenstein wrote to a friend that, 'Young Lord Alfred Douglas . . . has been going in for the wildest folly in London, and, I imagine, will shortly have to take a tour round the world, or something of the kind.'[59] Wilde took the somewhat paternal step of writing to Lady Queensberry to advise her to try to persuade her beloved Bosie to do something with his life. In a letter which is both patronising and untrue in parts, Wilde wrote,

Dear Lady Queensberry,

You have on more than one occasion consulted me about Bosie. Let me write to you now about him.

Bosie seems to me to be in a very bad state of health. He is sleepless, nervous, and rather hysterical. He seems to me quite altered.

He is doing nothing in town. He translated my French play last August. Since then he has really done nothing intellectual. He seems to me to have lost, for the moment only I trust, his interest even in literature. He does absolutely nothing, and is quite astray in life, and may, unless you or Drumlanrig do something, come to grief of some kind. His life seems to me aimless, unhappy and absurd.

All this is a great grief and disappointment to me, but he is very young, and terribly young in temperament. Why not try and make arrangements of some kind for him to go abroad for four or five months, to the Cromers in Egypt if that could be managed, where he would have new surroundings, proper friends, and a different atmosphere? I think that if he stays in London he will not come to any good, and may spoil his young life irretrievably, quite irretrievably. Of course it will cost money no doubt, but here is the life of one of your sons – a life that should be brilliant and distinguished and charming – going quite astray, being quite ruined.

I like to think myself his greatest friend – he, at any rate, makes me think so – so I write to you quite frankly to ask you to send him abroad to better surroundings. It would save him, I feel sure. At present his life seems to be tragic and pathetic in its foolish aimlessness.

You will not, I know, let him know *anything about my letter*. I can rely on you, I feel sure. Sincerely yours

Oscar Wilde.[60]

Lady Queensberry followed Wilde's advice, and arranged for her son to stay with her friends Lord and Lady Cromer, the consul-general and his wife, in Cairo.

Douglas had a strong reason of his own for going abroad at this time. As usual, it had to do with a boy. Max Beerbohm explained the problem in a letter to Reginald Turner: Robert Ross had stayed in Bruges with the Reverend Biscale Hale Wortham, who kept a boys' school there and was also the brother-in-law of Ross's tutor at King's, Oscar Browning. Ross had known a pupil there, Philip Danney, since the lad was fourteen. Danney was now sixteen and Ross invited him to 'stay' with him in London. A smitten Ross communicated the boy's presence in London to Douglas, who was still in Goring with Wilde. Douglas's response was to rush to London, seduce the boy and take him back to Goring where, according to Oscar Browning's summary of events, 'On Saturday the boy slept with Douglas, on Sunday he slept with Oscar. On Monday he returned to London and slept with a woman at Douglas' expense.' On Tuesday Danney returned to Bruges – three days late – and when questioned by his headmaster revealed all. His father went to the police, though dropped the idea of prosecution when he realised that although Ross and Douglas would be sentenced to two years each, his own son would spend six months in prison.[61] Wilde's name was kept out of it, but the incident should have served as a warning of the danger that such exploits entailed. Ross hid in Davos, while the visit to Egypt seemed to Douglas like an increasingly useful idea.

The trip was a great success. Although he was distraught that he had received no more than one short letter from Wilde after several weeks away, Douglas kept with him a picture of his friend wherever he went. He was cheered immeasurably by a chance meeting with Encombe at Luxor. Reginald Turner was in Egypt as well, the guest of his wealthy half-brother, who had rented a sumptuous gilded barge, to which Douglas became a frequent visitor.[62]

A few weeks later, when Douglas was staying in a Thomas Cook hotel, he met a man called Robert Hichens. Unknown to Douglas, Hichens had already seen him, though from a distance: Cromer had taken his young guest with him to the races at Gezireh Island, and Hichens had spotted 'a young man, indeed almost a boy, fair, aristocratic, even poetic-looking'.[63] The pair became friends and Hichens revelled in Douglas's increasingly brilliant wit, which the Egypt trip developed – so much so that on his return Max Beerbohm wrote to Turner, 'Is it you who have made him so amusing? Never in the summer did he make me laugh so much, but now he is nearly brilliant.'[64]

They were soon joined by Turner and a new face, E. F. Benson, who had achieved popular success the previous year with his novel *Dodo*, whose heroine was based on the young Margot Tennant, later Mrs Asquith. Hichens was nearing thirty, and had achieved a reputation as a fair journalist. He had had an idea for a novel that would satirise aestheticism and Wilde in particular, and welcomed the chance to follow Benson's example and base it on real-life characters. His meeting with Douglas must have seemed like a godsend, and while he was travelling with Douglas, Turner and Benson up the Nile he got as much material as possible out of Douglas. Then he took his letter of introduction to Wilde back to London and completed his research. The book became one of the decade's greatest successes, but caused much damage to those it sent up. It was titled *The Green Carnation*.

Hichens wrote the book anonymously, though its authorship was soon discovered. At the time of Oscar Wilde's trials Hichens, to his credit, refused to allow a reprint. Thirty-five years later, in his *Autobiography*, Douglas wrote, 'The book did me a lot of harm, and the writing of it (and the appropriation without acknowledgment of a large number of my 'good things' and jokes) constituted a piece of perfidy for which I refrain from reproaching its author because he has publicly expressed his contrition for it.'[65] Hichens finally allowed it to be reprinted in 1949.

Douglas was not impressed by the sights of Egypt, telling his mother that 'Some of the temples and things are quite magnificent in their size and grandeur and massiveness. But all the same I wouldn't give one little bronze Greek head or one broken marble statue for the whole of Egypt put together. The Sphinx however is really beautiful besides being really awesome and splendid.'[66] It inspired him to write a sonnet 'The Sphinx', a distinct improvement on his previous effort in his exercise of the form.

> I gaze across the Nile; flamelike and red
> The sun goes down, and all the western sky
> Is drowned in sombre crimson; wearily
> A great bird flaps along with wings of lead,
> Black on the rose-red river. Over my head
> The sky is hard green bronze, beneath me lie
> The sleeping ships; there is no sound, or sigh
> Of the wind's breath, – a stillness of the dead.

In a letter home to his mother, he wrote that he thought this 'about the best thing I have ever done'.[67] There are fewer of the forced rhymes that dominate some of his earlier attempts.

One aspect of Douglas's poetic expression remained constant during this time and suggests a reason why he never entered his work for the Newdigate Prize at Oxford. He kept 'In Praise of Shame' out of any anthologies of his verse until 1935. Later Douglas had misgivings about it, conjecturing that it had been 'entirely misinterpreted in the law courts by wooden-headed lawyers'.[68]

> Unto my bed last night, methought there came
> Our lady of strange dreams, and from an urn
> She poured live fire, so that mine eyes did burn
> At sight of it. Anon the floating flame
> Took many shapes, and one cried, 'I am Shame
> That walks with Love, I am most wise to turn
> Cold lips and limbs to fire; therefore discern
> And see my loveliness, and praise my name.'

And afterward, in radiant garments dressed,
With sound of flutes and laughing of glad lips,
A pomp of all the passions passed along,
All the night through; till the white phantom ships
Of dawn sailed in. Whereat I said this song,
'Of all sweet passions Shame is loveliest.'

Like 'Two Loves', the poem consists of a comparison between 'Love' and 'Shame Love', but here, Douglas had stopped couching his message with anything approaching subtlety: in the homosexual parlance of the day, the last line was understood to mean, 'homosexuality is the most beautiful love'. However, the elderly Douglas considered that there was more to the poem and it was partly for this reason that he included it in the 1935 *Sonnets*. Of it he wrote, 'I take this opportunity of referring enquirers about its meaning to the last verse of the second chapter of the book of Genesis'. But there can be little doubt that Genesis was not foremost in the mind of the young man who wrote the poem. In 1941, he went further: '["In Praise of Shame"] has not the remotest connection with or reference to homosexuality. Anyone who is not, artistically speaking, ignorant and illiterate . . . could not fail to appreciate this. As to the other poem ["Two Loves"], I do not deny that it contains an allusion to homosexuality, but it is really very harmless and decorous, and if it had been printed for the first time within the last ten years as the work of one of our "modern poets" no one would have turned a hair over it.'[69] That he had no problem in admitting the homosexual content of one poem of the period yet emphatically denied such an interpretation of another suggests that 'In Praise of Shame' might, after all, be an innocent poem. However, in later life he had little affection for 'Two Loves', but held 'In Praise of Shame' in high regard, describing it as 'pretty good'.[70] And, as he pointed out, if it had been written by one of the Auden generation of poets, nobody would have batted an eyelid. For its time, it was an original, bold work. The fact that it has become so infamous is due to the publication in which it appeared (the *Chameleon*) and that it featured in the Wilde trials, in which Wilde was unfairly called to account for it.

8

By the beginning of 1894 Douglas's relationship with his father had soured considerably. Douglas had gone to Paris early in the year to patch up the quarrel with Wilde and the meeting had been a great success. His trip, however, had come to the ears of Lord Currie, in Constantinople, who had recently offered Douglas the job of honorary attaché. Now he withdrew it. He disliked impetuousness, and clearly Douglas was not going to follow the example of his eldest brother, who, at this time, was offered the chance to become a representative peer in the House of Lords. Queensberry saw his third son's rejection by Currie as the consequence of his idleness, while Douglas himself put it down to Currie's 'middle-class fussiness'.[71] The exchange of insulting letters between father and son began in earnest. Queensberry's favourite means of taunting his sons was to suggest that he had not fathered them. The idea was clearly not just to show his own disgust, but to attempt to taint their virtuous mother. It is a testament to his approaching madness that his language and actions became increasingly those of a paranoid.

On 1 April he wrote:

Alfred,

It is extremely painful for me to have to write to you in the strain I must; but please understand that I decline to receive any answers from you in writing in return. After your recent hysterical ones I refuse to be annoyed with such, and I decline to read any more of your letters. If you have anything to say, do come here and say it in person. Firstly, am I to understand that, having left Oxford as you did, with discredit to yourself, the reasons of which were fully explained to me by your tutor, you now intend to loaf and loll about and do nothing? All the time you were wasting at Oxford I was put off with an assurance that you were going to the Bar. It appears to me that you intend to do nothing. I utterly decline, however, to just supply you with sufficient funds to enable you to loaf about. You are preparing a wretched future for yourself, and it would be most cruel and wrong for me to encourage you in this. Secondly, I come to the more painful part of this letter – your intimacy with this man Wilde. It must either cease or I will disown you and stop all money supplies. I am not going to try and analyse this intimacy, and I make no charge; but to my mind to pose as a thing is as bad as to be it. With my own eyes I saw you both in the most loathsome and disgusting relationship as expressed by your manner and expression. Never in my experience have I seen such a sight as that in your horrible features. No wonder people are talking as they are. Also I hear on good authority, but this may be false, that his wife is petitioning to divorce him for sodomy and other crimes. Is this true or do you not know of it? If I thought the actual thing was true, and it became public property, I should be quite justified in shooting him at sight. These Christian English cowards and men, as they call themselves, want waking up.

Your disgusted so-called father,
Queensberry[72]

Clearly at this time Queensberry still had some common sense, for he refrains from libelling Wilde. However, when he burst into Wilde's house to 'have the matter out with him' on 30 June, Wilde recorded that he uttered 'every foul word his foul mind could think of'.[73] Nevertheless, when Wilde asked him, 'Lord Queensberry, do you seriously accuse your son and me of improper conduct?' Queensberry was guarded enough to reply, 'I don't say you are it, but you look it and you pose it, which is just as bad.'[74]

As it happened, Constance was not attempting to divorce her husband. Indeed, it is unlikely that she knew anything about her husband's homosexuality until it all came out in the trials, and Queensberry's accusation probably contains more venom for another reason. In the previous year he had married for a second time. His bride was Ethel Weedon, a seventeen-year-old girl of no social standing, and the union lasted no more than two weeks. Percy, too, had married – a clergyman's daughter – and Queensberry was acquiring increasing distaste for marriage.

His father's letter infuriated Douglas, who took Queensberry at his word on the issue of sending letters. He despatched a telegram designed to send his father's temper spinning out of control: 'What a funny little man you are.'[75]

The telegram says much about Douglas at this time, but, contrary to the claims of one biographer, one cannot 'almost hear Oscar's laughter, mocking and encouraging, in the background'.[76] Wilde would almost certainly have disapproved of his friend's action, and it must have become apparent to Wilde that he was mixed up in a family feud from which he should have remained aloof. As the older, and at this point undoubtedly wiser, of the pair, he might have used his influence to better effect. As it was, Queensberry and his son were more than a match for each other. Douglas later said that his father 'might have guessed that I was quite as obstinate as he was'.[77] Queensberry's madness combined with his son's impulsiveness and Wilde's hatred of others dictating how he should behave became a terrible mixture of emotions which could only lead to disaster.

Queensberry's response to his son was predictable.

> You impertinent young jackanapes. I request that you will not send such messages to me by telegraph. If you send me any more such telegrams, or come with any impertinence, I will give you the thrashing you deserve. Your only excuse is that you must be crazy.[78]

There was nothing unusual in this – father and son constantly accused each other of madness. But what Queensberry had to say next was of greater and more ominous significance.

> If I catch you again with that man I will make a public scandal in a way you little dream of; it is already a suppressed one. I prefer an open one, and at any rate I shall not be blamed for letting such a state of things go on.

Douglas's most interesting response to his father was a poem entitled 'A Ballad of Hate'. It appeared in the *Pall Mall Gazette* and is one of the earliest, most eloquent expressions in the diatribic poetry that Douglas came to master.

> Here's a short life to the man I hate!
> (Never a shroud or a coffin board)
> Wait and watch and watch and wait,
> He shall pay the half and the whole,
> Now or then, or soon or late.
> (Steel or lead or hempen cord,
> And the devil take his soul!)

Nights are black and roads are dark,
(Never a shroud or a coffin board)
But a moon-white face is a goodly mark,
And a trap is a trap for a man or a mole,
And a man is dead when he's stiff and stark.
(Steel or lead or hempen cord,
And the devil take his soul!)

He shall not be shrived or sung.
(Never a shroud or a coffin board.)
The bell of death shall not be rung.
Man to grave and beast to hole,
Earth to earth, and dung to dung!
(Steel or lead or hempen cord,
And the devil take his soul!)

His father's response is unrecorded, but Queensberry wrote a transcription of this poem, and sent it probably to his in-laws – it is indistinctly addressed to a Montgomery – as 'part of his campaign to demonstrate [his son's] iniquity',[79] the following year. Douglas never stated for whom the poem was intended, but in Queensberry's transcription it is headed 'To my Father'. The seven-lined stanzas were clearly too much for Queensberry, and the garbled language and handwriting of the transcription indicate that it is one of the many letters he wrote while in his most unbalanced frame of mind. It contains eccentric spelling, punctuation, syntax and bracketed notes and comments. It begins: 'To my Father (Query am I his "Father")', which implies that Douglas sent a copy to Queensberry. It concludes,

& the devil (again the Christian one I suppose there is no other) take
his soul

(Capital what a fit & such genius is circle of Alfred Douglas. I send you this poem (this that which I wrote last year & which appeared in the Pall Mall. (lucky Pall Mall Title Ballad of Hate. I hated you when I hate you a thousand Times more now and will be seen with you some day. Wishing you my curse & . . . & a speedy death and eternal damnation[80]

The almost incoherent muddle shows how helpless with rage he was at his inability to influence his son.

For Douglas and his father the battle lines were drawn. In the middle was Wilde, though Queensberry did not blame him entirely for his son's idleness and immorality. He was fully aware that Douglas had been involved with other men. From early 1894 to the beginning of the trials on 3 April 1895, father and son waged continual war on each other. As a consequence Douglas had little time to write although he finished two ballads, both of which were admired when they were written.[81] One was 'Perkin Warbeck', for which Douglas took the story from a copy of Holinshed's Chronicles, which was apparently 'supposed to have belonged to Shakespeare and had his reputed autograph on the title page'.[82] It had been lent to him by Jack Benet from his library at Pyt House. The story of a fourteen-year-old boy who is raised to the post of king, despite his lowly social class, because of his beauty fits into a peculiar genre of pastoral idyll. The other ballad was 'Jonquil and Fleur-de-Lys', about two young boys, one a shepherd, the other a prince, who look so similar that they decide to swap roles. Douglas invested this prince-and-pauper tale with rather more homo-erotic overtones, though the feelings are chaste and no 'immoralities' are even hinted at.

XVII

And after that they did devise
For mirth and sport, that each should wear
The other's clothes, and in this guise
Make play each other's parts to bear.

XVIII

Whereon they stripped off all their clothes,
And when they stood up in the sun,
They were alike as one white rose
On one green stalk, to another one.

Oscar Wilde was quoted in an 'interview' that appeared in the *St James's Gazette* on 18 January 1895, as having said that his three comedies to date (*Lady Windermere's Fan*, *A Woman of No Importance* and *An Ideal Husband*) were to each other, 'as a wonderful young poet has beautifully said, "– as one white rose/On one green stalk, to another one." '[83]

9

The slowing-down of his verse production set a trend for Douglas's writing in the coming years. One of his notable successes in 1894, in his own eyes, was his poem for Wilfrid Scawen Blunt's Crabbet Poetry Club. He was the youngest, and the last, to join the club, which had its final annual meeting that year, partly because of the Wilde scandal in 1895, and partly because Blunt's polygamy was discovered. The members (all male) met at Blunt's country house, Crabbet Park, for a weekend, and all had to write a poem on a chosen subject, which that year was 'Civilisation'.[84] It appears that this message did not get to Douglas, who wrote a poem that had nothing to do with it. He fell down in another respect too, and he later wrote that Blunt had 'rather let me down over this, because when he made me a member and said I must write a poem, he gave me no hint as to its nature, and in consequence I wrote a perfectly serious and romantic poem which was in startling contrast to all the rest'.[85] It was a tradition of the club that the poems were of a 'ribald' nature, which Douglas's was not. He said later that he had actually 'faked it up out of another poem which I had already written (not then published) and the only new part was a song at the end "Steal from the meadows, rob the tall green hills" which appeared in all the collected editions of my poetry.'[86] What the first part of the poem was is not known, but the last part appeared in all future collections of his poetry under the title 'A Song'.

> Steal from the meadows, rob the tall green hills,
> Ravish my orchard's blossoms, let me bind
> A crown of orchard flowers and daffodils,
> Because my love is fair and white and kind.

The love of his poem, Douglas said, was a beautiful youth. Certainly it was not Wilde. The poem went down well with the Crabbet members, who found it touching, and Douglas shared the poetry prize with one Geoffrey Webb. He also won the tennis cup, which pleased him enormously. Among others present were George Curzon, Lord Crewe and George Wyndham. Blunt's diary records the high spirits the weekend induced.

We sat in joy at the dinner table till 3 o'clock and then went out to see the sunrise, Cairns playing the bagpipes on the lawn and Mark Napier dancing bare-legged. Then George [Wyndham] and a number more went down into the pond and sang operatic choruses, after which they danced naked on the lawn in full daylight till half past 4.[87]

These were indeed carefree and opulent times on which Douglas would look back with affection in later years.

The year yielded another poem that earned Douglas much praise. 'Impression de Nuit – London' was one of three of his poems that Sir Arthur Quiller-Couch included in his 1912 *Oxford Book of English Verse*. It was clearly influenced by Wordsworth's 'On Westminster Bridge', and the poem is an evocative, if somewhat mannered, description of the capital at night. It was written in the flat of Douglas's friend Charles Gatty, on the top floor of the building that is now the Hyde Park Hotel.

> See what a mass of gems the city wears
> Upon her broad live bosom! row on row
> Rubies and emeralds and sapphires glow.
> See! that huge circle like a necklace, stares
> With thousands of bold eyes to heaven, and dares
> The golden stars to dim the lamps below,
> And in the mirror of the mire I know
> The moon has left her image unawares.

This sonnet still shows the influence of Wilde in its 'jewelled' style, but another from the same year is more in the line of what was to come.

At Winchester and Oxford, Douglas had been friendly with Lucas D'Oyly Carte. However, D'Oyly Carte was unfortunately prone to upsetting Douglas. His letters to his friend are almost entirely made up of apologies for his failings. In one letter, following a passage of humble self-deprecation, he wrote, 'My God how I loathe myself – I really did not mean that letter to be brutal – but I saw it was – I don't mean to be ungrateful, but everything I seem to do has a different effect to what I mean.' He finally admitted, 'Bosie I love you more now than I ever have before. I never did really love you before but I do now.'[88] Eventually, though, Douglas decided that he had had enough. Feeling badly let down he dropped his friend and wrote a sonnet, 'To L', in which his hurt and anger are plain, as he talks of

'Leaving green valleys for the bitter hills'. Invective was characteristic of Douglas's style and manner, both in life and poetry, and he turned on all those friends who let him down in some way, often brutally. He valued loyalty, and nothing enraged him more than a friend who let him down. His public-school attitude to friendship was strengthened by his mother's example: she had always treasured him, protected him and adored him, and in childhood, adulation had come from almost everyone. He took any betrayal by a friend as a direct attack on him, and it was many years before he learnt how to cope with this, and only then because he had to.

At this point the poems still display the forced rhymes and sentiments of the poet who has not yet mastered technique. But there was one exceptional piece of work. At this time Douglas was not at all influenced by the Church, yet during this period of turmoil – many years before he embraced religion – he wrote 'A Prayer', a simple and direct statement of faith.

> Often the western wind has sung to me,
> There have been voices in the streams and meres,
> And pitiful trees have told me, God, of Thee:
> And I heard not. Oh! open Thou mine ears.
>
> The reeds have whispered low as I passed by,
> ''Be strong, O friend, be strong, put off vain fears,
> Vex not thy soul with doubts, God cannot lie'':
> And I heard not. Oh! open Thou mine ears.
>
> There have been many stars to guide my feet,
> Often the delicate moon, hearing my sighs,
> Has rent the clouds and shown a silver street;
> And I saw not. Oh! open Thou mine eyes.
>
> Angels have beckoned me unceasingly,
> And walked with me; and from the sombre skies
> Dear Christ Himself has stretched out hands to me;
> And I saw not. Oh! open Thou mine eyes.

It is a moving account of spiritual struggle. It is probable that, like many of the other poets of the nineties, Douglas felt aesthetically drawn to the Church, but also that he was *trying* to believe. He had no 'intellectual' opposition to religion and later he ascribed his lack of faith to 'moral laziness'. Laziness in believing, or at least in sacrificing parts of himself for it, kept Douglas away from the Church for many years.

10

Meanwhile Queensberry's activities continued to occupy his son's mind. He was stalking Wilde and Douglas, trying to catch them together in restaurants so that he could make a public scene. Although he did not manage this, he caused wave after wave of gossip among those who dined and those who served in the restaurants he attempted to invade. Douglas wrote to him:

> As you return my letters unopened I am obliged to write to you on a postcard. I write to inform you that I treat your threats with absolute indifference. Ever since your exhibition at O.W.'s house, I have made a point of appearing with him at many public restaurants such as The Berkeley, Willis's Rooms, the Cafe Royal, etc., and I shall continue to go to any of these places whenever I choose and with whom I choose. I am of age and my own master. You have disowned me at least a dozen times and have meanly deprived me of money [Lady Queensberry had to support him]. You have therefore no right over me, either legal or moral. If O.W. was to prosecute you in the Central Criminal Court for libel, you would get seven years' penal servitude for your outrageous libels. Much as I detest you, I am anxious to avoid this for the sake of the family; but if you try to assault me, I shall defend myself with a loaded revolver, which I always carry; and if I shoot you or he shoots you, we shall be completely justified, as we shall be acting in self-defence against a violent and dangerous rough, and I think if you were dead not many people would miss you.[89]

Douglas and Wilde were certainly not put off seeing each other by Queensberry's threats and, indeed, when Wilde was staying in Worthing with his family between August and October, writing his next play, Douglas and Percy visited him. Douglas was thus with Wilde for the majority of the time it took him to compose his masterpiece, *The Importance of Being Earnest*. Douglas claimed that much of the repartee in the play was the result of conversations between him and Wilde and it is true that he helped spark in Wilde some of the brilliant exchanges with which the play abounds. Douglas's sense of humour was different from Wilde's but complemented it: Wilde rarely made a joke at someone else's expense, whereas Douglas was liable to be cruel. For example, during a stay in Algiers, Douglas left the hotel to buy something. He was gone for less than an hour but was greeted on his return by a concerned-looking concierge who, relieved, exclaimed, 'Monsieur, you are back! *Votre papa* has been demanding to know where you were, with great noise, for the last hour!' Wilde heard this and was deeply wounded: he believed he looked youthful. Douglas, though, was delighted that the hotel staff thought Wilde 'old enough to be his father'. Afterwards he had only to mention the word *papa* to drive Wilde into a fury.[90]

At this time, though, the arguments between them, which Wilde would record later, became more serious, although the origins were often mundane. While staying in the Grand Hotel at Brighton, Douglas had not looked after Wilde when he was ill even though Wilde had caught his flu from Douglas while nursing *him*. Wilde's demands infuriated Douglas who, after an argument, wrote to him, saying, 'When you are not on your pedestal you are not interesting. The next time you are ill I will go away at once.'[91]

The warfare between Douglas and his father, which escalated in 1894, could not fail to involve the rest of the family. On several occasions Queensberry tried to woo his other sons to his point of view before once again turning to violent language and behaviour. Lady Queensberry obviously supported her Bosie, and the parents wrestled for the affection of their sons. Percy Douglas was on his younger brother's side: he and his wife had experienced Queensberry's wrath all too often. At times Queensberry had tried to explain himself to Percy in almost rational language. Sometime between 1890 and 1894 (he rarely dated his letters properly) he wrote:

> My position with you all is enough to make a man beside himself but of course you cannot help it & it is no fault of yours. I don't think it is any of our faults but the fault of the opinions and laws of these lying hypocritical Christians on the subject of marriage.[92]

He had to blame someone, and when it was not his family it was society. Queensberry's sister Florrie was certain that her brother had a brain disease,[93] and his rage became more intense as he felt himself increasingly lacking control, both emotional and financial, of his sons. As a man of naturally domineering nature, this frustrated him. His eldest son and heir, Francis, Viscount Drumlanrig, was a case in point. Much loved by all the family, he was a particular favourite of his grandfather, Alfred Montgomery, but Queensberry had alienated his son the previous year by hounding Drumlanrig's employer. Queensberry had heard that Lord Rosebery was homosexual, which was true, which led him to believe that Rosebery was having an affair with his son and that Drumlanrig's success was due to this. Queensberry followed the then Foreign Secretary to Hamburg and waited with a dog whip outside Rosebery's hotel, intending to thrash him when he emerged. It was only when the Prince of Wales intervened that he was dissuaded from this course of action. Queensberry's mind was so warped that he supposed Drumlanrig's appointment to the post of lord-in-waiting to the Queen was a direct attack on him. He also had suspicions that Alfred Montgomery was involved in a homosexual intrigue. The stream of abusive letters that followed to Montgomery, Gladstone – then Prime Minister – Rosebery and even the Queen must have been a severe embarrassment to Drumlanrig, who was far from a typical Douglas in temperament, being described as 'an excellent, amiable young man'.[94]

But it was Lady Queensberry who suffered most from her husband's accusations and violence. He still paid her an allowance, in accordance with the conditions of the divorce, but she had to ask lawyers to wrest the money from him. In the summer of 1894 he wrote to Alfred Montgomery: 'Your daughter is the person who is supporting my son [Alfred] to defy me.'[95] In fact Lady Queensberry was always anxious to stop her sons annoying their father, probably because she knew his rage would fall heaviest upon her. As for his son and heir's transition to the House of Lords, Queensberry, still smarting, wrote to Montgomery: 'But your daughter's conduct is outrageous, and I am now fully convinced that the Rosebery–Gladstone–Royal insult that came to me through my other son, that she worked that – I thought it was you.'[96] The belief that his former wife was capable of any such high-powered manipulation shows to what extent the man had lost all sense of reason.

Things worsened for Queensberry with the indignity of the annulment of his second marriage, on the grounds of 'non-consummation' due, apparently, to the genital malformation, impotency and frigidity of the husband.[97] Queensberry contested the judgment, and hired George Lewis to defend him.

The proceedings took place at the worst possible time.

11

Sometime around 11 October 1894, Francis, Viscount Drumlanrig, proposed to the beautiful Alix Ellis. She was the daughter of Major General Arthur Ellis, an equerry to the Prince of Wales. The following week, and as part of his introduction to the family, Drumlanrig was invited for a few days' shooting at Quantock Lodge near Bridgwater in Somerset, the home of the local Conservative MP Edward Stanley, where the Ellises would also be guests. The prospect of this union must have been a joy to all involved: not only were the couple both young and well connected (the marriage would have strengthened the social standing of both families) but it would probably have furthered Drumlanrig's career – even Queensberry would probably not have been dissatisfied, and Drumlanrig had found the happiness and fulfilment to which his good nature should have entitled him.

On Thursday 18 October after lunch, he went off to shoot in a party of five, among whom was Gerald Ellis, his future brother-in-law. Several pheasants were shot early on, but Drumlanrig had no luck. Then he winged a bird, which fell beyond one of the hedges that lay in front of them. The keepers went to search for it but could not find it. Leaving one to continue the search the rest of the party moved on to the next field, but Drumlanrig decided to go and look in the hedge, and informed the party of his decision. Shortly afterwards the others heard a single gunshot. 'I hope he has not shot himself,' one of the young men quipped. 'Oh, no, we won't think that,' the keeper replied.[98] Gerald Ellis went to discover what had happened. He announced that he 'would walk along beside the hedge and see if [he] could find him'.[99]

He found Drumlanrig 'lying on his back parallel with the hedge. The gun was lying across his stomach'.[100] He had died from a single charge of his gun, which had 'entered the mouth, fracturing the lower jaw on the right side, and had passed through the roof of the mouth on the left-hand side'.[101] Death had been instantaneous. Francis, Viscount Drumlanrig, the most promising member of his family, had been twenty-seven. Two days later an inquest at Quantock recorded a verdict of 'accidental death'.

For the family and, of course, Miss Ellis, his death was a devastating blow. The suddenness and horror of it left them deeply scarred.

The received version of events swiftly became that he had committed suicide because he expected public revelation of his alleged affair with Lord Rosebery, but there is no proof that Drumlanrig was having an affair with Rosebery, and the possibility of suicide is even less substantiated. Why would he have chosen the eve of his engagement to kill himself? Perhaps he feared the life change that was coming, but even so suicide was an extreme way out. For a young man so sensitive to those around him, why would he have chosen to take his life in a way so painful to his family, recalling his grandfather's death, and to those with him, who would have to endure the horror of finding his body? It seems unlikely that Drumlanrig would have taken his own life and all the accounts point to an accident. Yet it would have been difficult to shoot himself through the mouth so cleanly by accident. Although he did not believe it at first, towards the end of his life Douglas said that he thought his brother had committed suicide, but the truth will almost certainly never be known.

An immediate consequence of Drumlanrig's death was a reconciliation between the grieving Douglas and Wilde. The separation that had existed since the flu incident ended and the two became closer than ever. Wilde brought his lover flowers for Drumlanrig's grave, and later wrote to him, 'The flowers you took from me to put on your brother's grave were to be a symbol not merely of the beauty of his life, but of the beauty that in all lives lies dormant and may be brought to light.'[102]

Lady Queensberry was devastated by the loss of her son. Wilde recorded how deeply he thought she must have felt the loss 'of the one to whom she clung for comfort and joy in life, and who, as she told me once herself, had from the very day of his birth never caused her to shed a single tear'.[103] He was not far from the mark, although the idea that Lady Queensberry only found joy in her eldest son, or that she had never been disturbed by the turbulent relationship between him and his father is wrong. But Wilde was right when he wrote that Drumlanrig had been 'loved by all who knew him', [104] as the flood of emotion provoked by his death showed. 'He must feel the explosion of love and recognition from all,' wrote his cousin, George Wyndham, 'and at last, in spite of his wonderful humbleness and simplicity guess how much a better man he was than his fellows.' [105]

Over a quarter of a century after her son's death the then Dowager Marchioness of Queensberry described the circumstances surrounding it to her granddaughter. Her account shows that it is unlikely that she read contemporary accounts of her son's death, the pain being too great. It also shows that she held an idealised picture of him into her last years. In her account, Drumlanrig was in Scotland shooting when Miss Ellis emerged, unannounced. In her pleasure at seeing her he ran towards her, and whilst jumping a hedge his gun went off and he was killed in front of her. [106]

The burial took place in the family plot at Kinmount, one of the last such occasions there. Alfred Douglas was the only one of Drumlanrig's brothers who attended: both Percy, now Queensberry's heir, and Sholto were abroad. On the day of the funeral Queensberry was in the midst of his annulment proceedings, and could not be there. The effect on Douglas of having to be one of the sole representatives of the family at the burial of his dear brother was immense. Wilde wrote, 'It is a great blow to Bosie; the first noble sorrow of his boyish life.' [107]

With the death of Drumlanrig, Queensberry realised that Percy and his 'parson's daughter' would lead the family in the next generation. This, perhaps combined with a degree of guilt, spurred him to renew his efforts to assert his influence over the fate of his remaining sons. Only a couple of weeks after the tragedy, Queensberry wrote to his father-in-law, Alfred Montgomery. It was a characteristic epistle showing, perhaps, his own way of grieving.

Sir,

Now that the first flush of this catastrophe and grief has passed, I write to tell you that it is a *judgement* on the whole *lot of you*. Montgomery's, The Snob Queers like Rosebery and certainly Christian hypocrite Gladstone the whole lot *of you* / Set my son up against me indeed and make bad blood between us, may it devil on your own heads that he has gone to his rest and the quarrel not made up between him and myself. It's a gruesome message: If you and his Mother did not set up this business with that cur and Jew fiend *Liar* Rosebery as I always thought –

At any rate she [Lady Queensberry] acquiesced in it, which is just *as bad*. What fools you all look, trying to ride me out of the course and trim *the sails* and the poor Boy comes to this untimely end. I smell a Tragedy behind all this and have already *got Wind* of a more *startling one*. If it was what I am led *to believe*, I of all people could and would have helped him, had to come to me with a confidence, but that was all stopped by you people – we had not met or spoken frankly for more than a year and a half. I am on the right track to find out what happened. *Cherchez la femme*, when these things happen. I have already heard something that quite accounts *for it all*.

Queensberry[108]

Montgomery was shattered by his son-in-law's letter, and never really recovered from the death of his beloved grandson. His health declined and he died shortly after the tragedy's final act began.

For his part, Douglas, overcome with grief, found expression for his feelings only in poetry. He wrote a moving lyric, 'The Image of Death', shortly after the death of his brother, but his finest testimony came in a sonnet he wrote a few months later, in 1895. In 'his last sonnet,' 'Lust And Hypocrisy', Douglas had mastered the form. Now, he had a subject he could write about with true sincerity. It is among his best.

In Memoriam
Francis Archibald Douglas
Viscount Drumlanrig
Killed by the accidental explosion of his gun,
October 18th, 1894

Dear friend, dear brother, I have owed you this
Since many days, the tribute of a song.
Shall I cheat you who never did a wrong
To any man? No, therefore though I miss
All art, all skill, in this short armistice
From my soul's war against the bitter throng
Of present woes, let these poor lines be strong
In love enough to bear a brother's kiss.

Dear saint, true knight, I cannot weep for you,
Nor if I could would I call back the breath
To your dear body; God is very wise,
All that this year had in its womb He knew,
And, loving you, He sent His Son like Death,
To put His hand over your kind gray eyes.

Chapter 3

'The cold world loves not my love'

(1895–1900)

If the Douglas family found the personal apotheosis of its tragedy in the death of its heir it would have to wait another six months for the dénouement.

Relations between Queensberry and his family reached their lowest point in 1895, and the ferocity of the fighting between them was widely commented upon. Queensberry wanted to make his son pay for his disobedience, and revenge his late heir's death on the homosexual he could most easily get at – Oscar Wilde. While his father's behaviour became increasingly and unashamedly manic, Douglas flaunted his relationship with Wilde, creating a scandal to enrage Queensberry. They appeared together in public constantly, which told society that the rumours were true.

Queensberry's outward attacks continued, but, unknown to his family, he had hired private detectives to amass evidence against Wilde and his son, in an attempt to reveal Douglas's activities to his family. He seemed to believe that they only supported his son's fight against him because they were ignorant of his 'associations'.

In a series of letters and telegrams to Percy Douglas and his wife, Minnie, Queensberry showed just how vitriolic he had become: Alfred needed 'the shit kicked out of him', he informed Minnie.[1] As Queensberry attacked Wilde constantly, referring to him as 'a monster' whom he would be justified in shooting in the street,[2] his family must have thought him deranged. Undoubtedly this hardened his determination to reveal the truth. Queensberry had learnt of the exact nature of his son's blackmailing in Oxford and informed Percy of this in an attempt to turn him against his brother. The ploy did not work, which convinced him that another of his sons was, at the very least, a homosexual sympathiser. In his frustration at being ignored by his family Queensberry decided to take his case into the public arena, and began his attempt to goad his son or Wilde into taking out a charge of libel against him. 'This man,' he wrote to Percy of Wilde, 'is a cock sucker.'[3]

For the first half of the year Douglas wrote almost no poetry. The fight was the only thing on the minds of all those involved. As he had said in one of his letters to his father, Douglas had bought a pistol, and carried it with him everywhere. On one occasion it went off accidentally while he was dining at the Berkeley. Queensberry took a horsewhip into the restaurants he visited in his attempt to track down his son with Wilde so that he could give them the thrashing he believed they deserved. Wilde received a sword stick from his friend so that he could protect himself in the event of the Marquess confronting him. In a letter to Robbie Ross in 1897 Wilde claimed that father and son had 'played dice' for his life, and that Douglas had lost[4] but this is an egocentric view of events: he had become involved in a dispute in which the father's aim was simply to 'smash' his son and thus was a subsidiary character. But Queensberry had realised he could destroy his disobedient son and Wilde at a single stroke.

2

Wilde's fame and the respect accorded him as a playwright came to their zenith in the early part of 1895. *An Ideal Husband* was first performed on 3 January and *The Importance of Being Earnest* on 14 February. Douglas was stuck in Biskra, North Africa, where he was attempting to run away with an Arab boy, so did not see the *première* of the great work, but all those critics who had found it difficult to express enthusiasm for Wilde's other plays were there, and praised *The Importance of Being Earnest* effusively. The first night was the pinnacle of the author's success, but in the wings lurked tragedy.

Queensberry had bought a ticket for the opening night, intending to repeat his performance at Tennyson's play of fourteen years before. Fortunately he had bragged to many people of his plans and the ticket was cancelled. When he turned up at the theatre with a bouquet of phallic vegetables he was denied entrance. His next action was more directly confrontational: four days later he went to Wilde's club, the Albemarle in Piccadilly, and left his card, instructing the hotel porter to give it to Wilde. The inscription is unclear, presumably because Queensberry was in one of his uncontrollable rages, but seems to read, 'For Oscar Wilde – Posing as a somdomite [sic]'. In any case, it was a couple of weeks before Wilde received it.

The events that followed are well documented, most notably by H. Montgomery Hyde.[5] Wilde decided to sue Queensberry for libel, and in this was certainly supported by Douglas. Douglas wanted Wilde to approach Sir George Lewis to act for him. He held much material relating to such society cases in his safe, and almost certainly knew that the alleged libel could be justified. However, Lewis was already acting for Queensberry so, perhaps because he wanted an advocate who believed in his innocence, Wilde went to Travers Humphreys and Sir Edward Clarke instead. At the earliest stage Wilde told Douglas that he would not allow him to go into the witness box, because he did not want him to be directly involved in what he knew would be unpleasant proceedings. What was undoubtedly a chivalrous and thoughtful decision did Douglas much harm. As the son of the accused and the link between him and Wilde, it was obvious that his name would come up and his actions would be referred to without his being able to answer certain charges. Most of all, however, he was deprived of the opportunity to show the world what a dreadful man his father was. Later Douglas felt that had he gone into the witness box things might have turned out differently, and perhaps for this reason he sometimes claimed that Clarke had promised to let him appear to save the day.[6] Clarke always denied this,[7] and it is he who should be believed.

Before the trial began, on 3 April, and while Queensberry's team were digging up more of their damning evidence, Wilde and Douglas went off for a week-long holiday in Monte Carlo. It was an unfortunate move to make, and they were asked to leave their hotel after complaints from other guests. Douglas indulged his passion for gambling and clearly both men saw the approaching court case as no serious cause for alarm. While they continued their normal routine, male prostitutes were being gathered to testify in open court to the 'immoral acts' that had taken place between them and Wilde.[8]

* * * *

Queensberry's plea of justification was upheld by the judge and jury after a trial that lasted only two days. Wilde's public account of his withdrawal from the case came in the form of a letter addressed to the *Evening News*:

> It would have been impossible for me to have proved my case without putting Lord Alfred Douglas in the witness-box against his father. Lord Alfred Douglas was extremely anxious to go into the box, but I would not let him do so. Rather than put him in so painful a position I determined rather to retire from the case, and to bear on my own shoulders whatever ignominy and shame might result from my prosecuting Lord Queensberry.[9]

But, as Sir Edward Clarke pointed out, the evidence of Douglas against his father would have been inadmissible anyway. It was not the social or moral conduct in Queensberry's family life that was the subject of the trial but simply whether or not the allegation that Wilde was 'posing as a sodomite' was justified and therefore true. Any evidence about Lord Queensberry's personality would have been disallowed by the judge. Douglas, however, clearly believed that if he had got in even a few hints of his father's disgraceful behaviour towards Lady Queensberry he would be able to lower the court's impression of his father and therefore strengthen the chance of a verdict being given against him. 'What a very bad witness he would make,'[10] wrote Max Beerbohm, speculating on whether or not Douglas would be called to give evidence. Many others thought Douglas too erratic to prove a valuable or reliable witness, though he certainly showed in later years that he was difficult to cross-examine.

What resulted was not support for Queensberry so much as a wave of revulsion against Wilde and the vices of which he was accused. The case against Queensberry failed because when Wilde had decided to prosecute he had no idea of the amount of concrete evidence gathered against him. If he had realised, he would never have taken action. He had evidently thought that any case would be purely about his relationship with Alfred Douglas and the way in which his works might be interpreted: the implications of a very un-British decadence. This was extraordinary folly, and he must have seen that the net was closing around him when he saw the list of witnesses who were being paid by Queensberry to reveal the exact nature of their relationship with Wilde. In the court, when Wilde was questioned about his works he made a mockery of the defence's accusations, overpowering them intellectually, though hardly winning over the jury with his flippancy. However, when the cross-examination came to the subject of rent-boys, Wilde was at a loss. There was no way that he could persuade a jury to believe that his dealings with these members of the lower classes were anything but sexual.

Wilde also found that he did not only have to justify his *own* work. The main literary points scored by Queensberry's team related to a magazine that had been published the previous year. In December 1894 the only number of *the Chameleon* had appeared under the editorship of an undergraduate of Exeter College, Oxford, named John Francis Bloxam. Only one hundred copies were printed but it was perhaps the most overtly homosexual publication to have come out of Oxford in the nineties, and is now the most famous. Its notoriety – which has nothing to do with literary merit – came from the Wilde trials alone. It contained the first publication of Douglas's 'In Praise of Shame' and 'Two Loves' while Wilde himself had contributed a set of some of his finest epigrams, 'Phrases and Philosophies for the Use of the Young'. He recorded his own somewhat distorted recollection of events in *De Profundis*, his letter to Douglas from prison.

> One day you come to me and ask me, as a personal favour to you, to write something for an Oxford undergraduate magazine, about to be started by some friend of yours, whom I had never heard of in all my life, and knew nothing at all about. To please you – what did I not do always to please you? – I sent him a page of paradoxes destined originally for the *Saturday Review*. A few months later I find myself standing in the dock of the Old Bailey on account of the character of the magazine.[11]

Of course Wilde was not tried for the content of *the Chameleon*, and the events surrounding his contribution to the magazine are different from the way he described them. Bloxam had been at Winchester and Oxford with Douglas, and had asked him for a contribution, hoping that he might be able to persuade Wilde to give something. Bloxam himself had published in it a blasphemous short story, 'The Priest and the Acolyte.'[12] In court Wilde claimed that he had requested the removal of his 'Phrases and Philosophies' when he discovered the character of the magazine, but at the time he did not take any such line. He wrote to Ada Leverson about it in a way that showed he had enjoyed its indiscretion.[13]

Wilde was questioned about the Bloxam story and also asked to explain the two poems Douglas had contributed. 'Two Loves' particularly was held up for ridicule and contempt. The ideas and morals revealed in these works by Douglas and Bloxam should not have influenced the decision as to whether or not the libel against Wilde had been written in the public interest and was therefore true, but he was unable to stop what followed. On the second day of the trial, Queensberry's counsel questioned Wilde about Walter Grainger, the young manservant Douglas had brought with him to Goring in the '*Salomé Summer*' of 1893. Asked whether he had ever kissed the man, Wilde replied, 'Oh, dear no. He was a peculiarly plain boy. He was, unfortunately, ugly.'[14] From this it was assumed that Wilde was expressing disappointment at, rather than pity for, the ugliness of the boy. It was a fatal slip. Wilde had held forth for nearly two days, filling the court with laughter by scoring off his opponents and detractors, and suddenly there was silence. The shocked courtroom planted itself firmly behind the QC, who was demanding an explanation for the prosecutor's incriminating answer. The laugh had been lost, the joke was indefensible, and Wilde stood alone in the dock, isolated and despised.[15] It was merely a taste of the revelations to come, and the strength of public feeling that came with them.

It was when the indefensibly sordid nature of the evidence on which Queensberry could draw in his defence became clear that Wilde was advised by his counsel to withdraw from the case and go abroad until the scandal died down. He was not in court for the third and last day to hear his counsel withdraw from the case on his behalf. The jury took only seconds to follow the judge's advice and return a verdict of not guilty on Queensberry. Applause rang through the court, which the judge did not suppress.

When the Queensberry case closed, Wilde had a prolonged consultation with Alfred and Percy Douglas and Robert Ross at the Holborn Viaduct Hotel over what to do next. Alfred Douglas, supported by everyone else who had Wilde's interests at heart, went off to cash a cheque for £200 for Wilde to take abroad, rejoined him at the Cadogan Hotel and tried to convince him to leave the country. Percy Douglas, at Wilde's behest, gave a statement to a reporter, which showed that, at this stage, he, along with many others, saw the matter as being essentially about the Douglas family, and the Marquess of Queensberry in particular. 'You may say from me myself,' Percy assured the reporter, 'that I and every member of our family, excepting my father, disbelieve absolutely and entirely the allegations of the defence. It is in my opinion, simply a part of the persecution which my father has carried on against us ever since I can remember. I think Mr Wilde and his counsel were to blame for not showing, as they could have done, that was the fact.'[16]

But as always, in the Douglas family, things were not so simple and even the claim, 'every member of my family' was open to contention. Queensberry's mother, the Dowager Marchioness of Queensberry, along with his sister, Florrie, and Lord Archibald Douglas issued a statement from Glen Stewart saying that they had not authorised Percy to speak for them and that they repudiated 'any sympathy' with his statement.[17] It was an unfortunate tactical error on Percy's part to think that he could lead the family already, but it demonstrated that the controversies of the Douglases were not to be aired in private.

3

It was clear that after the collapse of his case against Lord Queensberry a criminal prosecution against Wilde was inevitable. Indeed, straight after the court was closed, Queensberry's solicitor had sent all the witness statements as well as shorthand notes of the trial to the public prosecutor, 'in order that there may be no miscarriage of justice'.[18] With the amount of publicity surrounding the case, and to uphold the public's view of justice, the public prosecutor had little choice but to send out a warrant for the arrest of Oscar Wilde on charges of gross indecency.

Having spent the whole day trying to persuade Wilde to escape, the exasperated Douglas dashed off to the House of Commons to consult his cousin George Wyndham MP, to see whether anything could be done and whether or not a warrant had been issued. He learnt that it had, though the public prosecutor and others had deliberately delayed it until the last train for Dover had left London. Few people, except Queensberry's crew, wanted scandal or Wilde's downfall. Many of his friends urged him to leave the country while he had the chance, and if Wilde had gone he might have had the same notoriety and freedom that Lord Henry Somerset had enjoyed. Wilde knew, however, that he could not live the life of an exile, and that if he was fully to realise his potential in life and art, he had to face what lay before him.

Douglas returned from the Commons to find a note from Wilde asking him to get Percy Douglas, George Alexander and Lewis Waller, the managers of the theatres in which his plays were then running, to attend the police court to give bail. He also asked Douglas to come and see him. It was at this point that Wilde discovered who were his real friends. Douglas tried frantically to persuade both managers, who had made a huge profit out of Wilde, to back him now that he was down but both men refused. Constance Wilde's cousin Adrian Hope also refused. Percy Douglas put up the money straight away, though at first bail was refused: public opprobrium was overwhelming and one broadsheet on 20 April carried the following remarks from a friend of Queensberry. 'It is only in a world like London – where people are so cosmopolitan and so indifferent as to allow a parasitic insect like Oscar Wilde to infest society with its nits – that such a grotesque is possible. But at least it is dead and needs no further reference.'[19]

Wilde was committed for trial at the Old Bailey to begin on 28 April. Sir Edward Clarke and Sir Travers Humphreys both asked to represent him without fee.

Rumours circulated constantly that Douglas would be arrested for crimes similar to those of Wilde, and it is proof of Douglas's courage that he stayed in the country throughout. On the evening of Wilde's arrest many men left the country in fear of a tidal wave of prosecutions now that the secret homosexual subcultures of London had been exposed. Among the first to leave were friends and acquaintances of Wilde, many of whom had been mentioned, or associated with him, by the national press. Robbie Ross went immediately to France, but only after he had obtained a promise from his mother that she would help to cover Wilde's legal fees and assist his mother, Lady Wilde, financially. Maurice Schwabe and Reginald Turner left precipitately, and Constance rushed abroad with the children, fearing repercussions on the family. Of Wilde's close circle of friends only Douglas remained, although his mother and the rest of his family pleaded with him to go. George Wyndham MP wrote to his father, the Hon Percy Scawen Wyndham, to say that he had passed on to him the desire expressed by Balfour, Lord Houghton and others that Douglas flee to save his career and reputation: 'Bosie took it very well. He thought I was going to ask him to go at once, and began by saying that nothing on earth would make him leave London until the trial was over. You may be sure that nothing will: he is quite insane on the subject . . . If W(ilde) was released, Bosie would do anything he asked, and no entreaty from you or his mother would weigh with him.'[20]

Wilde was moved from Bow Street police station to Holloway prison and Douglas visited him there every day. Nearly thirty years later Douglas wrote:

> I used to see Oscar every day at Holloway in the ghastly way that 'visits' are arranged in prisons. The visitor goes into a box rather like the box in a pawnshop. There is a whole row of these boxes, each occupied by a visitor, and opposite, facing each visitor, is the prisoner whom he is visiting. The two sides of visitors and prisoners are separated by a corridor about a yard in width, and a warder paces up and down the corridor. The 'visit' lasts, as far as I can remember, a quarter of an hour. The visitor and the prisoner have to shout to make their voices heard above the voices of the other prisoners and visitors. Nothing more revolting and cruel and deliberately malignant could be devised by human ingenuity. Poor Oscar was rather deaf. He could hardly hear what I said in the babel. He looked at me with tears running down his cheeks and I looked at him.[21]

After each visit Wilde wrote to Douglas, and their relationship was strengthened by the persecution.[22] However, just before the start of the trial Wilde's counsel, Sir Edward Clarke, insisted to Douglas that he go abroad: he believed that Douglas's presence would only make his task more difficult. At this Wilde became enormously depressed because the only person he thought or cared about at this time was Douglas. He wrote to the Leversons, 'A slim thing, gold-haired like an angel, stands always at my side. His presence overshadows me. He moves in the gloom like a white flower.'[23] To Robert Sherard, safely in Paris, he wrote, 'Nothing but Alfred Douglas's daily visits quicken me into life.'[24] 'I care less when I think he is thinking of me. I think of nothing else,' he told Ada Leverson.[25] However, Wilde added his voice to Clarke's entreaty. He had at last begun to grasp the enormity of the case in which he was involved and the likely repercussions for his friend as the closest intimate of a man vilified by the loud-voiced populace. It was a tough decision for Douglas to take for he knew that his visits were the only thing keeping up his friend's morale. What perhaps finally convinced him to go were the persuasive yet loyal urgings of his brother Percy.

Percy had told him that he would help in the case even from before the libel action. Now in anticipation of owning a great fortune, as Queens-berry's heir, Percy was borrowing money at a foolish rate. He felt himself responsible for supporting his younger brother financially since he had been cut off by their father, and had given Alfred £250 after Wilde's arrest: Alfred had spent all his own money on the costs of Wilde's case. Percy said that if Alfred went away he would remain in England and help Wilde in any way he could.

Before he left for France, Douglas performed one more act of kindness. Alfred Taylor, who ran the rooms in Westminster in which he introduced respectable clients to out-of-work young men, was being tried with Wilde. Douglas hardly knew him but Taylor, like all the other men who had been associated with Wilde, had been given the oppor-tunity to testify against Wilde in exchange for the prosecution against him being dropped, and had refused. He was different from the lower-class lads who were the main prosecution witnesses: he had been educated at Marlborough and had a strong sense of loyalty to Wilde. Douglas was so impressed by his bravery that he gave £50 to Arthur Newton, Taylor's solicitor, to help with the man's defence.

In their final meeting Wilde kissed the finger Douglas squeezed through the iron grating in the interview room. Both men vowed that they would hold their love for each other, whatever followed – a promise that, in the event, Douglas kept far more conscientiously than Wilde. According to Douglas, Wilde begged his friend 'to let nothing in the world alter my attitude and my conduct towards him'.[26]

Early the next morning, on 24 April, Douglas left the country for France – the same day that a mock auction was held in Wilde's Tite Street house to satisfy his creditors. The proceedings amounted to little more than an organised pillage.

4

In Calais Douglas was able to read the reports of the trial in the newspapers which came over from England daily. Much of the material used in the Queensberry case was restated, although by this time the prosecution had amassed more evidence from chambermaids and other servants relating to Wilde's stays at a number of London hotels, where he 'entertained' young men. The prosecution laid heavy emphasis on Wilde's writings, particularly on his letters to Douglas, which had been 'found' by Alfred Wood. Douglas had given the unemployed clerk several of his old suits, and Wood claimed that he had found the letters in the pockets. Wood was in league with two other blackmailers, Allen and Clibborn, and it is highly improbable that Douglas would have been so careless. A likely explanation is that Wood simply stole the letters from Douglas's rooms at Oxford, where he had worked as a valet.

The fact that the letters were from Wilde to Douglas would have appeared to implicate both men equally and, indeed, towards the end of the following trial the foreman of the jury actually questioned the judge as to why no warrant had been issued for the arrest of Lord Alfred Douglas. The judge said that something more than intimacy would have to be proved if a charge were to be made.[27]

At the trial wore on, Douglas continued to believe he should go into the witness box feeling, as he had in the libel case, that perhaps he could save the day. He telegraphed to Sir Edward Clarke on the third day offering 'certain information' relating to the case. The nature of that information is unclear, but it would seem that it refers to an offer by Douglas to give evidence incriminating to himself that would help to absolve Wilde. Douglas later claimed that the material he had offered related to an incident at the Savoy Hotel, for which Wilde had been charged. Sir Edward Clarke dismissed his offer outright, and Wilde's solicitors informed him that his offer was 'most improper', and asked that he refrain from any further attempt to interfere, which could 'only have the effect of rendering Sir Edward's task still harder than it is already'.[28] But even if Douglas had been answerable to events in Wilde's rooms at the Savoy Hotel, the case against Wilde would not have changed: he was being prosecuted on far more than this single charge. The most damning evidence against him related to the alleged 'corruption' of young men and the goings-on in Taylor's rooms.

The trial of Oscar Wilde at the Old Bailey ended on 1 May with the jury unable to agree on a verdict. This encouraged Wilde's friends and supporters, most of all Douglas, 'I have heard the news, on the whole I think it is a splendid triumph.'[29] His joy was premature. The judge took the unusual step of ordering a retrial, and most of those abroad must have realised now that there were few grounds for optimism. So desperate was the Crown to secure a guilty verdict in this high-profile case that they brought in the Solicitor-General. Important names had come up in the course of the Queensberry trial and in Wilde's subsequent trial, among them that of the then Prime Minister, Lord Rosebery. In a slip of the tongue counsel had mentioned Lord Rosebery's name instead of Lord Queensberry's and the rumours concerning the alleged relationship between Rosebery and Drumlanrig resurfaced. The papers were full of suspicions. 'The evidence given at the Old Bailey seems to affect more reputations than those that have been openly impugned,' noted *The Morning*. The name of one of the men Wilde was accused of having committed acts of 'gross indecency' with (Maurice Schwabe) had to be written down for the judge to see so that the courtroom did not know who it was. He was the nephew of the Solicitor-General's wife, Lady Lockwood. Rumour-mongers in society claimed that there had been a cover up at the highest level. This was something that Alfred Douglas believed. He claimed that the Home Secretary, Asquith, had been told by Rosebery that 'If a second trial was not instituted and a verdict of guilty obtained against Mr Wilde, the Liberal Party would be removed from power.'[30] Douglas claimed, outright, that the Party contained a number of homosexuals, and that the prosecution, conviction and downfall of Wilde took place 'to please a few old men afraid of personal scandal'.[31] Whatever the reasons behind the Crown's determination to get a conviction, Wilde was on trial to show that the crime of which he was accused would be punished, and the law upheld. To an extent, the British legal system was itself on trial: the public wanted blood, and the authorities realised that it had to be pandered to.

Wilde was set bail between the end of the first trial and the beginning of the second at £5,000, which was exceptionally high. Half of the bail had to be supplied by him, and the rest by two sureties. Percy provided £2,000, and the charitable clergyman Stewart Headlam who, although he did not know Wilde well, felt that he was not getting the degree of fair play or Christian charity to which a subject of his country was due, put up the rest. As soon as Wilde was free on bail his friends tried to persuade him to leave the country. Wilde refused to go. He said that he did not want to 'let down his bails', but this was clearly not the only reason: he told Douglas in a letter, 'A dishonoured name, a hunted life are not for me.'[32] Most importantly of all, he was leading himself, knowingly, to the artistic culmination of his career and of his greatest love affair: 'Child of all my imagination, little delicate flower,' he wrote to Douglas, 'I am going to test the power of love, I am going to see if I cannot make the bitter waters sweet by the intensity of the love I bear you.'[33]

*   *   *   *

Wilde's second trial had to end in a conviction. To his disadvantage he was tried in conjunction with, although separately from, Alfred Taylor, whose guilt was far less in question than Wilde's. Fourteen counts were held against Taylor and eight against Wilde. The prosecution insisted that the trial of Taylor be conducted first, and his conviction made Wilde's a foregone conclusion.

On the second day of the trial, when Taylor was found guilty, Queensberry, who had sat in court throughout both trials, rushed to the post office to send one of the last in a long line of telegrams to Percy's wife. Percy had refused to receive any letters from his father, and his solicitor had written to Queensberry to inform him of this. Queensberry's response had been to write all his letters to Minnie, Percy's wife, on the business of his sons and Oscar Wilde. When the solicitor contacted him to tell him that neither letters to his client nor to his client's wife would be received, Queensberry replied to him, 'May I request that you stop this impertinent interference, who the devil are you?'[34] He continued to write to Percy's solicitor and Percy's wife. At times the latter correspondence included such extreme invective and insult that it is barely believable that it was directed to a woman who, furthermore, had nothing to do with the case. Queensberry wrote once with hatred of Percy: 'He certainly has all the appearance to recommend him to the fraternity: white-livered smoothed face, sicked-up looking creature, as if he had come up the wrong way. When he was a child swathed in irons to hold him together it used to make me sick to look at him and think that he could be called my son.'[35] At one point he referred to his son, whose full title was The Douglas of Hawick and Tibbers, as 'The Douglas of Hawick and Shitters'.[36]

When Minnie received the telegram after Taylor's conviction, Percy had had enough of his father's insane hounding. Soon afterwards as he was walking up Piccadilly he spotted his father on the other side of the road. The statements of those who saw or took part in the incident vary wildly, but those of Percy and the friend he was with are the most plausible. Queensberry claimed that, 'He [Percy] came straight at me, almost at a run, and pushed me up against a shop window, at the same time speaking at the top of his voice. I struck him certainly but it was done in self defence.'[37] Percy claimed, 'He must have seen me almost at the same moment as I saw him and during the whole time he was crossing the street he was making grimaces with the apparent idea of attracting my attention. He reached the side of the street on which I was walking some few paces in front of me. I walked up to him and said to him: "Are you going to cease writing these obscene and beastly letters to my wife?" His only reply was to strike me violently under the left eye.'[38] The fight that ensued was watched by a large mob who cheered Queensberry, supposing that Percy was Alfred, and a number of blows were exchanged before the police took father and son to Vine Street police station where they signed to appear at Marlborough Street the following day.

The next morning the business was conducted quickly, partly because Queensberry was in a hurry to get to the Old Bailey where the second trial of Oscar Wilde was to open. Both men were held responsible and bound over to keep the peace for six months, after paying bonds of £500 each. Crowds gathered outside the court to cheer Queensberry to his cab, while Percy was booed and hissed at. The exiled Lord Alfred fumed, 'I would like to know for which of his feats he [Queensberry] was thus greeted. Was it for writing annoying letters to a young lady, or for giving his eldest son a black eye, or simply on account of his general character as shown by his conduct during the past dozen years? I wish somebody would tell me.'[39] Queensberry was guilty, as Douglas later wrote, of 'posing as a moralist'.[40] The British public had been whipped into a frenzy by the popular press as journalists tried to outdo each other in the shock and distaste they could show towards the 'vices' of which Wilde was accused.

Three days after Queensberry and his heir had been bound over, Wilde's trial closed with a predictable verdict of guilty returned by the jury. In sentencing both Wilde and Taylor to two years' hard labour, Mr Justice Wills was administering an unnecessarily harsh punishment for what had only been a crime over the previous ten years since the 'Labouchère Amendment' (1885) had made all homosexual acts, whether committed in public or private, illegal. Yet Wills endorsed the public's bigotry and announced that the case was 'the worst case I have ever tried', and claimed that in his view the sentence, the maximum allowed in law, was 'totally inadequate'.[41] It was adequate enough, however, to destroy Wilde's life, and to deprive him of any chance of ever again seeing his home or his beloved children. In the aftermath of the

'Darling Bosie' – Lord Alfred Douglas at eight
by Hon Henry Richard Graves.

The adoring mother – the Marchioness of Queensberry.

The scene of his father's suicide, Queensberry took his new bride to the family seat of Kinmount immediately after their honeymoon.

Douglas in his early years at Winchester.

Top from left Montagu, Turner, *bottom from left* Blandford and Encombe
– two love interests and two friends.

Douglas (middle) and his co-editors on *The Pentagram*, his first, and most successful, paper.

The end of Winchester (Douglas and friends) 'In the years to come, few, very few hearts, will be as light and brimful of laughter as they are now.'

Ready for the whirligig? The new arrival at Oxford.

Above The condemned
playground – Magdalen.

Right Standing out –
the leader of 'the cause'.

Lord Alfred Douglas by William Rothenstein.

trial the press revelled in the success of the case and their ability to influence it. The *St James's Gazette* led with a call for 'a dash of wholesome bigotry'. The adulterous Queensberry was praised to the rafters and the harlots danced on the pavements.

5

The sufferings of Oscar Wilde in prison were great. His mental and physical breakdown was exactly what many of his enemies had hoped for. Wilde lost any chance of seeing his children again, he lost his name (abroad, Constance and the children had their surname changed to Holland), the ability to write, and at times even his will to live. Wilde had once said that 'If a man could rule over a London dinner table he could rule over the world', [42] but he had realised, during his trials, just how untrue this was. Then, and in prison, he realised that it was only his ability to amuse people which had kept many on his side for so long. When a serious charge was laid against him, Wilde discovered that the British public needed more from a man than amusement to take him into their hearts. Douglas, meanwhile, a member of a noble house, a public-school and Oxford man, had a position by birth that Wilde could never have earned. Douglas had always been treated like a lord, from his days at Winchester and Oxford, right up to the generally respectful remarks made in the press about him, which contrasted starkly with what they wrote of his friend. However, the Wilde trials showed that even social position was not enough to let a man escape unharmed. When the waves of the Wilde scandal broke over his head Douglas found himself treated in a way that was totally alien to him. Previously, Douglas had known people only to be desperate for his company and flattering of his talents. From the time of his exile, he found out what it was to be snubbed, despised, rejected, ostracised and have his talents derided both by people he had known, and those whom he had never met.

Douglas spent his three and a half years of exile in France and Italy, staying with friends who would still have him, or renting apartments. He was never completely without money, but he was rarely well-off. His brother sent funds occasionally as did his mother, but to a young man who had had every luxury lavished on him it was difficult to adapt to his new lifestyle. His father told him that he would give him back his allowance if he renounced Oscar Wilde and agreed never to meet him again, but he could not agree to this.

At this time it must have become evident to Queensberry that he had not only destroyed Wilde, but also his son and, indeed, his family. Whether he had meant to do so from the start is debatable. In one of his letters to Minnie during the trials he wrote that if Percy could see a copy of the *Chameleon* 'it might convince him of the utter folly of his, and of his brother backing this man up, when I am doing all in my power to keep Alfred out of it'. Even more tellingly he continued, 'He goes and throws himself on our swords that mean to hack the other fellow to pieces, and which we can do without touching Alfred.'[43] Sitting in France writing to England, Douglas described himself as 'lying in the lowest hell of misery'.[44] In this situation, though, he found himself able to write poetry for the first time in many months. In the middle of summer he wrote his sonnet 'To Sleep'. It is a heartfelt cry of self-pity, but also a genuine expression of a soul tired of turbulent wranglings against a hostile world.

> Ah, Sleep, to me thou com'st not in the guise
> Of one who brings good gifts to weary men,
> Balm for bruised hearts and fancies alien
> To unkind truths and drying for sad eyes.
> I dread the summons to that fierce assize
> Of all my foes and woes, that waits me when
> Thou mak'st my soul the unwilling denizen
> Of thy dim troubled house where unrest lies.
>
> My soul is sick with dreaming, let it rest.
> False Sleep, thou hast conspired with Wakefulness,
> I will not praise thee, I too long beguiled
> With idle tales. Where is thy soothing breast?
> Thy peace, thy poppies, thy forgetfulness?
> Where is thy lap for me so tired a child?

When Douglas had arrived in France, he had thought he could comfort himself with the idea that it was just the English who had a bourgeois attitude to his artistic and sexual tastes. Within a very little time, though, he had discovered that things were not so different there, and that there was no place on earth where he could find his ideal society of cultured and compassionate fellows to support him. He reverted to poetry for companionship, especially Keats, Shelley, Byron and Shakespeare, and he began to identify himself with the three great romantic poets. His exile, and his conviction that he was being punished for his forward-thinking opinions on society's blinkered attitudes, allied him strongly with Byron and Shelley in particular. Like them, he was of high social and educational ranking, and was being hounded by the ignorant and unworthy. Having been constantly in the company of Wilde for almost four years he was lost without him, missing the gaiety, pleasure and security their friendship had brought him. In response to this he wrote 'Rondeau', a cry of longing.

> This great peace does but magnify
> My great unrest that will not die,
> My deep despair that may not reap
> One poppy, one poor hour of sleep,
> Nor aught but pain to wake and cry
> 'If he were here!'

In the third of his poems on this subject, 'Vae Victis', Douglas compares the cold of England with the warmth of Capri, where he was at the time, yet he concludes the season and weather do not matter:

> For Autumn has found me
> And thrown her arms round me.
> She has breathed on my lips and I wander apart,
> Dead leaves in my heart.

He felt that he, like Wilde, was in prison. 'I think there is no doubt,' wrote Douglas to a friend, 'that if one really loves anyone one feels any sufferings he undergoes infinitely more than if one were undergoing [them] oneself.'[45]

Lionel Johnson tried to help his friend but with little success. He went to visit Douglas and wrote to More Adey asking him to encourage others to do the same. 'It is very important for Bosie's health and peace of mind, that he should be alone as little as possible,' he wrote, adding, 'Most of his Oxford friends seem unable or unwilling, for various reasons, to accompany him.'[46] One of the few exceptions was Lord Encombe who saw him briefly. Douglas could not persuade his greatest Winchester and Oxford friend to come travelling with him, but it was a boost to know that Encombe had not dropped him in the wake of the scandal.[47] Encombe had proved himself a constant friend, remaining supportive of Douglas even though their association might have damaged his own reputation. Douglas also remained in contact with his old friend from *Pentagram* days, Edmund Phipps, who wrote to him of 'To Sleep' as 'particularly effective, and, to me, affecting'. He went on, 'I am afraid you are "learning" a great deal "in suffering", please go on "teaching" it "in song"!'[48] It is a shame that Douglas did not entirely stick to this advice.

Like many other situations in Douglas's life, the hostile reaction he provoked on the continent was largely of his own making. If he had stuck to writing poetry his troubles would have been far less great. However, Douglas felt the same frustration as his father in not being listened to. For both men, inability to influence events was a source of anger and energy. From what many regarded as safety on the Continent, away from the retributive British legal system, Douglas felt he must do all he could to defend his friend. It was with horror that he read the accounts in the British newspapers of Wilde's imprisonment and bankruptcy, and of the requests from the foreman of the jury and members of the public for a warrant to be issued for his own arrest. Yet, again like his father, all he could do was write letters and, in his case, articles. In this way, he dug himself deeper into the crisis. If he had kept quiet many would have forgotten his involvement in the Wilde affair, and many more would not have been given sticks with which to beat him in later years. As it was, Douglas was young and rash. It was impossible for him to ignore the comments in the press after Wilde's sentencing. While a writer in the *Illustrated Police Budget* noted, 'That the sentence was deserved I have not the slightest doubt; but yet I cannot help feeling a kind of sorrow that a man I have admired for his cleverness has, so to speak, gone down to the grave',[49] others were more condescending and immeasurably more vindictive. The *News of the World* claimed that Wilde had got off lightly, but rejoiced that, 'Society is well rid of these ghouls and their hideous practices', finishing, 'It is refreshing to feel that for once, at least, justice has been done.'[50] The *Daily Telegraph* was harsher still:

The man has now suffered the penalties of his career, and may well be allowed to pass from that platform of publicity which he loved into that limbo of disrepute and forgetfulness which is his due. The grave of contemptuous oblivion may rest on his foolish ostentation, his empty paradoxes, his insufferable posturing, his incurable vanity. Nevertheless, when we remember that he enjoyed a certain popularity among some sections of society, and, above all, when we reflect that what was smiled at as insolent braggadocio was the cover for, or at all events ended in, flagrant immorality, it is well, perhaps, that the lesson of his life should not be passed over without some insistence on the terrible warning of his fate. Young men at the Universities, clever sixth form boys at Public schools, silly women who lend an ear to any chatter which is petulant and vivacious, novelists who have sought to imitate the style of paradox and unreality, poets who have lisped the language of nerveless and effeminate libertinage – these are the persons who should ponder with themselves the doctrines and the career of the man who has now to undergo the righteous sentence of the law. We speak sometimes of a school of Decadents and Aesthetes in England, although it may well be doubted whether at any time its prominent members could not have been counted on the fingers of one hand; but, quite apart from any fixed organisation or body such as may or may not exist in Paris, there has lately shown itself in London a contemporary bias of thought, an affected manner of expression and style, and a few loudly vaunted ideas which have had a limited but evil influence on all the better tendencies of art and literature. Of these the prisoner of Saturday constituted himself a representative. He set an example, so far as in him lay, to the weaker and the younger brethren; and, just because he possessed considerable intellectual powers and unbounded assurance, his fugitive success served to dazzle and bewilder those who had neither experience nor knowledge of the principles which he travestied, or of that true temple of art of which he was so unworthy an acolyte. Let us hope that his removal will serve to clear the poisoned air, and make it cleaner for all healthy and unvitiated lungs.[51]

In the knowledge that things could get little worse, and heedless of the consequences for himself, Douglas defended Wilde, and the vices for which he was famed, vigorously. First, he wrote to two journalists, defending homosexuality. His arguments were well put and convincing, but the hostility against anything that showed support for Wilde made sure that Douglas's arguments changed nothing. One letter was ignored while the second drew only a partial response. That was a letter to Henry Labouchère, the MP and editor of *Truth*, who had been responsible for the amendment to the Criminal Law Amendment Act which, in 1885, had made criminal the acts for which Wilde was tried.[52] In his paper, he attacked Douglas, referring to him as 'an exceptional young scoundrel'. In his first letter to Labouchère, Douglas had informed him that he had been naïve to describe the acts of which Oscar Wilde had been convicted as 'not practised by others'. He informed him that, on his 'word of honour', he personally knew of at least fifty men at the top of society who practised such acts, MPs, peers and members of all the smartest clubs. He added, 'At Oxford, where I suppose you would admit one is likely to find the pick of the youth of England, I knew hundreds who had these tastes among the undergraduates, not to mention a slight sprinkling of dons.'[53] Part of the letter was published in *Truth* with a comment from the editor that 'Certainly this exceptional moralist has the courage of his opinions, but these opinions being what they are, it is to be regretted that he is not afforded an opportunity to meditate on them in the seclusion of Pentonville.'[54] This was the common reaction to Douglas's reasoned arguments, and the sentiment was genuine, though Douglas was merely creating more enemies by his outspoken attitude.

The response to his letter did not deter Douglas. In desperation he petitioned Queen Victoria to let Wilde off the rest of his sentence. In that document, though, Douglas put much of his effort into showing what a terrible man his father was: he still felt that this was the only way to discredit the prosecution of Wilde, and attempted to show how brutal one of Her Majesty's peers had been to his family, appealing to the Queen to defend Wilde, reminding her of how Douglas's ancestors had often 'served [her] ancestors on many fields and in many councils'.[55] His work was in vain. The petition was intercepted by the Queen's private secretary who sent it straight to the Home Secretary who sent a formal letter of rejection to Douglas. Its tone is apparent from the Home Office minute that advised: 'Say Petition has been forwarded to S. of S. but he is unable to advise H.M. to comply with its prayer.'[56]

Frustrated by the failure of his letters, Douglas refused to give up his battle. His devotion to his cause was unparalleled in its constancy and purpose. Unlike Wilde's other friends, Douglas worked for him tirelessly, never giving up hope that he might be able to change, if not the sentence, at least other people's attitude to it. He decided to take it into the most public arena of all: the popular press.

6

While passing through Paris on his way to Naples in August 1895, Douglas was asked by the literary magazine *Mercure de France* to write an article on his version of the events of the Wilde case. This was a gift for Douglas, who was stirred up by recent events anyway, for he wrote it as soon as he got to Sorrento. The previous month he had been left by More Adey in a hotel in Le Havre. On his own once more, he decided to do some sailing and hired two young sailors as crew. The local paper discovered this and published an article accusing the young English lord of trying to corrupt the youth of the town. He had to give up the boat and was hounded by the locals. The police were said to be watching him, trying to find the smallest excuse to send him back to England.[57] Douglas had been given a taste of the reception he would attract wherever he went. He wrote to the local paper, 'It is already too evident that the world has the right to insult and injure me because I am Oscar Wilde's friend. That is my crime, not because I was his friend, but because I will be until my death, and even after that if God wills.'[58] It was with the Le Havre incident ringing in his ears that he wrote his defence of Wilde for the *Mercure de France*.

In his article Douglas had several objectives. One was to damn the system that had imprisoned Wilde while another was to justify the love between them and to tell the world that it was not something of which he was ashamed. 'The imprisonment of Oscar Wilde is a shame and an outrage to civilisation,' he declared, adding that, 'Liberty and Justice demand his liberation before the barbarities of the English prison system have killed his body or destroyed his spirit.'[59] He had intended to include some of the letters Wilde had written to him from prison while on trial. He could not contact Wilde to explain why he wanted to use them, because Wilde was allowed to write and receive only one letter every three months, but he thought that Wilde would have no objection to an article intended to restore his reputation at least in France. How wrong he was. When Wilde was informed by Sherard in a visit of the planned publication of his letters he was horrified. He clearly did not understand that Douglas wanted to show what a compassionate and beautiful soul had been locked up in prison. Douglas destroyed the letters in later years, but wrote of them that he believed they would have served to 'rehabilitate Wilde, from a moral point of view'.[60] They apparently showed him far more as an earnest, devoted lover unlike the mannered, high-flown letters that had been read out in court. It was now that Wilde began to turn against his friend.

Meanwhile, Douglas tried to get up a petition signed by French writers who had known, or shown respect for, Wilde in the past. This failed miserably, as did his attempt to raise one in England. The failure of the French petition forced him to understand that the French people were no more or less Philistine and cowardly than their British counterparts. He wrote later that 'in the long run l'hypocrisie Francaise did not appear to differ very much from the English variety'.[61] Such was his anger that he wrote a sonnet 'dedicated to those French men of letters (Messrs. Zola, Coppée, Sardou and others) who refused to compromise their spotless reputations or imperil their literary exclusiveness by signing a merciful petition in favour of Oscar Wilde'.[62]

Douglas was bewildered by Wilde's hostility on the subject of his letters. Sherard wrote to the editor of the *Mercure de France* asking that they refrain from using them, which upset Douglas, who refused to allow the magazine to publish the article without them.

7

For several years Douglas had been encouraged by friends to publish a book of his poetry. Among the publishers he approached was Leonard Smithers, who alongside his reputable publishing firm issued risqué books of erotica. He refused to publish Douglas's poems, though not because he did not admire them: he found Douglas too controversial, famous and provocative a poet, and wanted to protect himself from scandal. However, the *Mercure de France* had a book-publishing wing and made him an offer on his first book of poetry. He accepted it and began preparations for the book, which came out in October 1896. This gave him his first opportunity to write a published article of some length on the Wilde case. In May 1896 the *Mercure de France* asked him for an article consisting of an introduction to his poems with some comments on the trials, which was published by them on 1 June 1896.

When Douglas arrived in Paris in late March 1896 he booked into the Hôtel Brighton, but within a few days was asked by the management to leave. 'I have been sick with rage for a short time,' he wrote to Percy, 'but I am on the whole a philosopher and can manage to put up with anything.'[63] But Douglas had been sick with rage for a long time, and in fact he was quite unable to cope with the hostility shown towards him. His article was clear evidence of this. It was a brave and outspoken defence of Wilde, himself and homosexuality. Unsurprisingly it brought forth a stream of criticism from the public and from journalists. In it he shows his readers that he has a high regard for his own poetry, but he is equally unequivocal in admitting his involvement in the scandal: 'It is curious to reflect that had I had the good fortune to live in Athens at the time of Pericles, the very conduct which at present has led to my disgrace would then have resulted in my glory. Today I am proud that I have been loved by a great poet.' Of his poems he wrote,

> . . . my poems have been represented as a vivid treatment of Greek love. One or two of my poems, it is true, concern Greek love but it is not possible for me to imagine that I should justify myself for dealing with a subject which inspired such poets as Sophocles, Theocritus, Michael Angelo and Marlowe – names selected haphazard. I have very little to say about my book – I will let it speak for itself . . . The volume is exclusively concerned with beauty and I am pleased to think that it is more Greek than any other poetry printed since the death of Keats.

He went on to list great Englishmen who were of the same sexual nature as Wilde, and included Shakespeare. He also declared that 'amid all the heroes of humanity twenty-five per cent at least were sodomites', and continued,

> I give my personal experience when I say that sodomites, and I know a great many, are intellectually superior to other men. Nothing is more ridiculous than the vulgar opinion that as a rule they are physically inferior. In Oxford, for example, they are found principally among the athletes and this is so in nearly all our public schools. In these latter

institutions the practice of Greek love is so general that those 'physically unfit' are reduced to live without love. We may remark that the boys of these schools are drawn from the noblest houses and possess the best blood of England, so that it is safe to predict that a large proportion of our future legislators, lawyers, judges, soldiers and clergy have at least at one time of their lives been sodomites.

His candour was disarming, his language extreme, and the backlash was in kind. In going to press with such opinions Douglas brought on himself the hatred of those members of the establishment who had been the target of his criticism. They would not forget what he had said and the damage he might have done, and the article did a lot of harm in the future to his own cause. But the *Mercure de France* was only a literary magazine, so the scandal of Douglas's remarks was initially felt only in certain, mainly artistic, circles.

Douglas hoped that his article would change attitudes in some way. It was therefore with something akin to astonishment that he received a barrage of criticism, most notably in the press. This prompted him into writing a speedy and unequivocal response. Addressed to four particularly spiteful journalists, Douglas's 'Reply to Certain Journalists' was published in *La Revue Blanche* on 15 June.[64] Among the criticisms he countered was that he had used the Wilde case to advertise himself and his poems. The charge of promoting his poems was thrown since Douglas decided not to release his book, mainly because he had intended to dedicate it to Wilde, who had communicated his disapproval. Without the dedication, Douglas said, he did not want the book published. The accusation of self-promotion to him was ridiculous: why should a man want to tell the public again that he had been involved in the greatest scandal of recent times simply for the sake of it? The idiocy of Douglas's critics in their ignorance of his interpretation of Platonism infuriated and hurt him deeply. He finished the article, a piece of free-flowing invective, answering the second criticism.

Will Mons. Bauer, then, inform me what advantage I am likely to derive from the publication of my article? I should very much like to know what this advantage is and when I shall be able to benefit from it; for just at present that article has brought me nothing but affronts and insults, coarse jests and some startling insight into the crass stupidity and mean lack of generosity of many persons of whom I hoped for better things.

In later years, when the article was used against him in the law courts, he must have realised how serious it had been to register such opinions at the beginning of his career. However, amid great pressure from many quarters, the *Mercure de France* persuaded Douglas to retract his decision not to publish his poems. He came to believe that refusing to publish would be playing into the hands of his detractors, and so the book duly appeared in October of that year.

In many ways this, his first book, was a serious mistake. It was inevitably tangled up with the Wilde case, despite the absence of a dedication. It included the poems that had featured in the court case, and opened with his 'Hymn to Physical Beauty'. The poems were published in English with a French prose translation by Eugène Tardieu, who had translated *The Picture of Dorian Gray* only a year earlier. Undoubtedly the book was a success, but although Douglas's standing as a poet improved as a result, his reputation as a man did not. Because of his connection with Wilde many people read the poems with a sense of morbid curiosity, and Wilde wrote in *De Profundis* that 'The first volume of poems that in the very springtime of his manhood a young man sends forth to the world should be like a blossom or flower of spring, like the white thorn in the meadow at Magdalen, or the cowslips in the Cumnor fields. It should not be burdened by the weight of a terrible, a revolting tragedy, a terrible, a revolting scandal.'[65]

A thousand ordinary copies were printed, along with two exquisite limited and signed editions of fifty and twenty-five copies respectively. The book's frontispiece consisted of a portrait of the author by Walter Spindler. The drawing, which remained a favourite of Douglas, depicted a lily-like, fragile beauty. The presentation copy Douglas gave to Spindler the following September in Naples has survived. It is inscribed by the poet on the title page, 'Walter Spindler from his friend Alfred Bruce Douglas. The portrait of my soul in return for the portrait of my face.'[66] It is clear that Douglas viewed this as an opportunity to reveal himself as a man and a poet: the drawing and the poems supported what he had written in his *La Revue Blanche* article, that he had been loved because he had 'a beautiful soul in a beautiful body'.

There is no doubt that Douglas's *Poems* contained what may now be described as homo-erotic verse, but which is really far better described as Greek. Like all of Douglas's poetry from now on there was nothing explicit in it. What caused consternation was the alarming freedom and openness with which the poet praised the beauty of the male form and its superiority to that of the archetypal embodiment of Romantic perfection, the female form.

Although the book attracted a number of detractors, many others admired Douglas's talent. Not least among his fans was the great symbolist poet, Stephane Mallarmé. He wrote to Douglas some months after publication, and in the year before his own death, to express his opinions.

> Your *Poems*, which can bear that title proudly and simply, reached me in Paris, this winter, late, through complicated circumstances. I have the pleasure of reading them in the original without nevertheless neglecting the translation which renders them miraculously well; but even more in the parallelism of the two languages, I delighted in the first, your own, the original version, which fuses a double instinct which is both French and English. For your verse, depending on your emotion, however much it takes flight and trembles, infinitely, as in your greatest contemporary masters, retains a sureness of touch, unbroken and lucid, which is characteristic of us here.[67]

Mallarmé's joy at being able to read the poems in English was shared by many, and the print-run sold out fairly quickly. Given that the number of English speakers in Paris at this time was recorded by Douglas as 'not one Frenchman in five thousand',[68] this was quite an achievement.

Douglas was pleased with his poems' reception and was happy to be able to consider that he shared with Shelley the honour of having his first book of poetry published on the continent while in exile. Certainly the poems were not 'English', and Mallarmé had been right to notice the French influence. They were not equatable with any English school of poetry. In subject matter, they can be said to link with the 'decadents', but the treatment of their subject is always far from shocking. The generation of poets who had been most identified as 'decadent' lacked sympathy with British life, and the language adopted, specially by Ernest Dowson, took on a French-style lyricism and abstraction of sentiment.

In the lead-up to publication. Douglas had written a large quantity of verse, most notably 'Plainte Eternelle' and 'Rejected', both of which show the influence of the Scottish border ballads he had always loved. Both poems express feelings of inconsolable longing, representative of the emotions Douglas felt at the time, enhanced by his social ostracism and his separation from Wilde.

> Wound me with swords, put arrows in my side.
> (On the white sea the haze of noonday lies.)
> Play with my tears and feed upon my sighs,
> But come, my love, before my heart has died.[69]

However, these poems are seen at times somehow as though he wrote what was expected of him, so the theme sometimes appears forced. It was only in later years when he knew what remorse really was, and how enforced eternal separation really felt, that he wrote about it with profundity. Now, though, Douglas knew that he and Wilde would soon be reunited, and with every letter and poem he wrote in which he mourned their separation their meeting was drawing closer.

8

While Douglas was making his literary reputation in Paris, Wilde was languishing in Reading gaol, and had turned against his friend in the most astonishing way. Douglas had never let slip his promise to Wilde: he waited for two years for Wilde to come back to him; the memory of their last meetings and of Wilde's passionate and devoted letters begging him to hold their love in the period when it would be most at threat had remained with him daily. He had worked ceaselessly, however unsuccessfully, for Wilde's cause, and had endured slights and ridicule for refusing to drop him. In prison Wilde had been unable to stick by his ideals. In a letter written before his conviction Wilde had told Douglas that 'I have had moments when I thought it would be wiser to separate. Ah! moments of weakness and madness.'[70] In prison he was overtaken by a long, sustained moment of weakness and madness. At the time More Adey described the change in Wilde's attitude to Douglas in prison as being no more than 'a passing delirium of gaol moral fever'.[71]

But though the change in attitude might have been 'passing', its consequences were not.

Wilde had felt bitter towards Douglas when he received news of the planned article for the *Mercure de France* and again when he heard of his intention to dedicate *Poems* to him. But it seems that he had turned against him earlier. After Wilde had rejected Douglas's letters in favour of those from his family, Douglas had told Ada Leverson, 'I can't make it out at all . . . Surely Oscar must have sent me some message. I am upset and perplexed by it all. It seems impossible even to find out what is really happening. I am so afraid that some secret influence has been brought to bear on Oscar, or that he has been told some lie about me.'[72] His suspicions were not far off the mark.

In prison Wilde's days had been filled with mind-numbing occupations. The only thing that kept him from losing his mind was the opportunity to reflect on the course of events that had led to the situation he was in. He tried to make some sense of the events that had overtaken him, and for which to a certain extent he had been responsible. He had decided not to leave the country when he had the chance because he intended to play the role of martyr. The idea, initially, of a St Sebastian figure, with arrows piercing him, took on a stronger form in prison. There he equated himself with Christ. The thought of having been brought to downfall by his destiny was comforting in the hell that he now inhabited. But Wilde stretched the comparison with Christ: he needed a Judas to blame, and placed Douglas in this role. However, 'the truth', as Wilde famously pointed out, 'is rarely pure, and never simple'. The state of Wilde's mind in prison was complex, though the facts relating to certain aspects of his time there are clear.

In the last months of his prison sentence, from January to March 1897, Wilde was given the unusual privilege of being allowed to write a substantial document. This was partly because the prison governor wished to encourage him back to writing after the long forced abstention, so that he could start as normal a life as possible once he had left prison.[73] This letter, which took Wilde three months to complete, was a psychological necessity for him. He had to relieve the anger that had built up inside him and had been unexpressed for two years. It was addressed to 'Dear Bosie', signed, 'Your affectionate friend Oscar Wilde', and was originally entitled 'Epistola: In Carcere et Viniculis', (Letter: In Prison and Chains) though it became known as *De Profundis* (From the Depths).[74]

The letter amounts to a sustained attack on his former companion and lover. The prison authorities had wanted to see some improvement in Wilde's conduct since he was such a high-profile case, and in prison he had been encouraged by friends and officials to stay close to his wife. Wilde was distraught at the prospect of not seeing his children again and set out to reconcile himself with Constance. While he was in prison, he had had to limit his letters to the essentials – matters of financial, legal and family importance – and the three-monthly visits were allowed only from people considered reputable. Among those who visited him was Constance, who in February 1896 travelled from Genoa to Reading to tell her husband of the death of his mother.[75] More Adey saw him too, and wrote to Douglas, in a letter both tactful and compassionate, to try to stop him writing any more articles that might potentially damage himself and Wilde: 'Dearest Bosie, you must try to show the love which I know you have for him, by the most difficult of all ways, *waiting*.'[76]

De Profundis contains some of Wilde's finest prose, and sections of it are immensely moving, yet it is also filled with spiteful complaints. Only the fact that he must have been partly out of his mind excuses what must be seen, in places, as the most degrading document ever to come from his pen. The slighting references to Douglas's lowly stature are not only unworthy of Wilde but are also misguided and untrue. He also makes outrageous claims about money, that Douglas volunteered his family to cover the legal fees for Wilde's libel suit against Queensberry then failed to pay up.[77] Percy and Lady Queensberry indeed offered some funding but for Wilde to attack their meanness is curious bearing in mind the generosity both Alfred and Percy Douglas showed him throughout as well as after the trials. Wilde's distorted obsession about money at this time was able to be seen in more than just his gripes against Douglas, he accused many people who had been kind friends to him of ruining his finances including the Leversons, More Adey and Ross.

One of Wilde's most prolonged passages of invective is levelled at Douglas's behaviour in Brighton, where he claims that his friend refused him lemonade when he was ill. Other incidents that had little or no significance at the time are promoted into acts of extraordinary drama. Wilde wished to make an elegant tragedy of his fall but the result in *De Profundis* is a series of pathetically mundane squabbles.

However, this document was without doubt Wilde's most destructive legacy to Douglas. When he left prison he was allowed to take it with him – a rare privilege. As soon as he got to Dieppe, where he met the waiting Robbie Ross and Reginald Turner, he handed it to Ross, and instructed him, after making him his literary executor, to have two copies typed and the original sent to Douglas.[78] In this letter lies the origin of a long, bitter argument that has never been resolved.

Robert Ross always claimed that he had sent Douglas a typescript of *De Profundis*, knowing that Douglas would be likely to destroy it after he had read it. Douglas claimed that he never received it. He said he had received an extended letter from Ross while Wilde was still in prison, with quotes from Wilde, and that after reading a few pages he had torn it up and flung it into the river Marne, which was by his house.[79] If the letter was *De Profundis* then Douglas did not read very far into it, for when part of it was published in book form in 1905 he reviewed it and saw nothing to remind him of the letter he had received.[80] If he had received a typescript of the full letter he would surely have asked if there were other copies of it and where the original was. It seems that the letter Douglas claimed he received and threw in the river was something other than *De Profundis*. On the one occasion that Wilde alluded to it, Douglas thought he was referring to the letter he had actually received from Ross, which contained quotations of what Wilde thought of his former friend, and when Wilde thought that Douglas was referring to it he said, in words to the effect, 'Surely you are not bringing up against me what I wrote in prison when I was starving and half mad.'[81]

Whether or not Ross sent the letter, whether Douglas read it before Wilde's death, one fact is certain: *De Profundis* had a more lasting effect on Douglas than any other of Wilde's works. After its author's death, it was the voice that screamed at Douglas from the grave. Douglas's rage at the letter's lies, his inability to comprehend the attack and to respond to it, built up in him the frustration that destroyed him.

9

When he left prison Wilde agreed that he would never again meet Alfred Douglas. It was one of the conditions Constance Wilde made for her husband if he was to receive an allowance from her. When he heard of it, Douglas went almost mad with grief. Behind the attempt to keep the pair apart was Robert Ross, and Queensberry (who was threatening to shoot both his son and Wilde if they did try to meet). Ross must have seen the opportunity to re-stake his claim to Wilde when Wilde's attitude hardened against Douglas.

Now Douglas was penniless and alone. His one glimmer of hope during the darkest days of his exile had been the release of his friend from prison. Now it had happened, and they could not meet. 'I should die of misery if after all this when Oscar came out there was to be a complete estrangement between us. It is so utterly unjust after all I did and suffered that it seems incredible.'[82] He wrote to Wilde, imploring him to agree to a meeting, knowing that if he could just see him again the old love would return. But Wilde refused, and, though he wrote to him in pleasant terms, would not consent to further the acquaintance.

Douglas was plunged into despair. At times he seemed suicidal, and at one point wrote to Percy to tell him, 'I am sick and tired of this miserable life I lead, always alone, always begging people to come and see me who never come.'[83]

Before long Wilde was feeling similarly frustrated and alone. Like Douglas, he could not finance himself and both were social outcasts. As Wilde sat looking out at the bleak waters of the Channel from the house at Berneval, his mind must have turned towards the only man he could love and who could love him in return. In the previous year, in his *Poems*, Douglas had published some prophetic lines.

> I bent my eyes upon the summer land,
> And all the painted fields were ripe for me,
> And every flower nodded to my hand;
> But Sorrow came and led me back to thee.[84]

And so, although only a few weeks earlier, in mid-June 1897, Wilde had said to Douglas in a letter, 'Don't think I don't love you. Of course I love you more than anyone else. But our lives are irreparably severed, as far as meeting goes',[85] they began to make arrangements to meet. When Ross heard of this he told Wilde's solicitors, who warned Wilde that, if a meeting did take place, Queensberry would come over from London and make a scene. This reduced Wilde to a state of panic so the meeting was called off, but a few weeks later, the plans were revived and the two finally met on 28 August in Rouen. According to Douglas, the day was a great success. 'Poor Oscar cried when I met him at the station. We walked about all day arm in arm, or hand in hand, and were perfectly happy. Next day he went back to Berneval and I returned to Paris, but we had settled that when I went to Naples about six weeks later he was to join me there.'[86] Either at this meeting or at some other point over the next few weeks Douglas gave Wilde, among other presents, a beautiful silver cigarette case which he had had engraved:

> The Phoenix riddle hath more wit
> By us, we two being one are it.
> So to one neutral thing both sexes fit,
> We die and rise the same and prove
> Mysterious by this love.
>
> Bosie.[87]

The quotation from Donne's 'Canonisation' testifies to the enduring power of love after years of suppression and separation. The trials had fanned the fires of the waning friendship that was soon to move into one of its most brief yet happy stages.

A few days after the meeting Wilde wrote Douglas a letter that counts among the most important he ever wrote. It was later cited by Douglas as proof of the ridiculousness of the idea, set down in *De Profundis*, that Wilde 'never wrote anything'[88] when he was with him.

My own Darling Boy,

I got your telegram half an hour ago, and just send you a line to say that I feel my only hope of again doing beautiful work in art is being with you. It was not so in old days, but now it is different, and you can really recreate in me that energy and sense of joyous power on which art depends. Everyone is furious with me for going back to you, but they don't understand us. I feel that it is only with you that I can do anything at all. Do remake my ruined life for me, and then our friendship and love will have a different meaning to the world.

I wish that when we met at Rouen we had not parted at all. There are such wide abysses now of space and land between us. But we love each other. Goodnight, dear. Ever yours.

Oscar[89]

If the relationship wasn't going backwards to the pre-trials days, then it was perhaps going forward into new territory, of care and tranquillity, which had previously been unimaginable.

As arranged, Douglas and Wilde met up in Naples a few weeks later. At the last minute Wilde wrote to Douglas to tell him that he had no money for his fare so Douglas sent him the money. In celebratory mood they forgot financial constraints for two weeks and ran up a large bill in the Hotel Royal where they stayed before finding somewhere more permanent. The bill remained unpaid until several months later when Douglas obtained the money to settle it from his mother.

After the honeymoon things became harder. Neither man had told those close to him what he intended to do. In consequence, correspondence was exchanged with the likes of Ross, who wrote letters Wilde refused to answer for some time, saying that they angered and distressed him too much. 'My going back to Bosie,' he finally informed Ross, 'was psychologically inevitable.'[90] He told those who challenged him that Bosie had offered him love when others had left him struggling. For his part, Douglas told his mother he could not drop Wilde now that he was down, having lived with him when he was at the heights, and insisted that nothing would make him such a 'snob and low filthy hypocrite'.[91] Both men were living on allowances from other people, Douglas from his mother, Wilde from his wife, and the fact that either might be cancelled at any moment gave their reunion an added sense of risk and furtive excitement.

They managed quickly to find a villa to rent by the sea in Posilipo. They hired three or four servants and a cook, and apart from rats infesting the villa (they were sent away by a 'potent witch'),[92] they settled in quickly. In a letter to Ross, Wilde claimed that 'It was necessary that Bosie and I should come together again; I saw no other life for myself. For himself he saw no other: all we want now is to be left alone, but the Neapolitan papers are tedious and wish to interview me, etc. I want peace – that is all. Perhaps I shall find it.'[93] Wilde had his wish, and for the time being both he and Douglas were able to live a life that had seemed lost, and which in many ways suited them better than what had gone before.

The most important ingredient in the success of their stay at Posilipo was that they got on with their own work. It was a great satisfaction to

Wilde that his friend was now a recognised and accomplished poet. Before he had gone to prison, Wilde had liked Douglas's work, but it had been little more than undergraduate verse. Now, in late 1897, Douglas was regarded as among the foremost younger English poets, at least in France. During their time at the villa, Wilde revised and completed what turned out to be his last work, 'The Ballad of Reading Gaol'. He told Ross that all its best stanzas had resulted from his life with Douglas in Naples. The friends intended to collaborate on a libretto for the youthful Dalhousie Young who had given Wilde an advance of £100 to write the work on *Daphnis and Chloe*. Nothing came of the project, though perhaps it was for the best that the friends' literary efforts were kept separate after the lesson learnt from the *Salomé* episode. But it must have made Wilde more aware of his diminishing abilities. By contrast, Douglas's writing was going in a very new direction.

At the villa in Posilipo, Douglas was writing in an atmosphere conducive to thought and inspiration in being free of the anger and persecution that had haunted him in the past. In this atmosphere of calm and love, he wrote some of his finest early poetry, which heralded his arrival as a poet in England.

The City of the Soul was Douglas's first major book to be published in England. Many of the finest poems in it were written at Posilipo, including the sonnet sequence that gave the book its title. There are four, in the Petrarchan form, all showing technical mastery. However, it is not until the end of the sequence that the poet takes up the theme on which he intends to dwell, and reveals a style and order which are, for perhaps the first time, distinctly his own. In the final sonnet of the sequence he combines his technical skill with purity of feeling which, as he said, make up the highest kind of poetry.

> Each new hour's passage is the acolyte
> Of inarticulate song and syllable,
> And every passing moment is a bell,
> To mourn the death of undiscerned delight.
> Where is the sun that made the noon day bright,
> And where the midnight moon? O let us tell,
> In long carved line and painted parable,
> How the white road curves down into the night.

Only to build one crystal barrier
Against this sea which beats upon our days;
To ransom one lost moment with a rhyme
Of passionate protest or austere demur,
To clutch Life's hair, and thrust one naked phrase
Like a lean knife between the ribs of Time.

Although they did not collaborate, the friends influenced each other's work to some extent. Wilde borrowed some aspects of a poem of Douglas's for a stanza in the *Ballad*[94] and though Douglas denied that he 'had assisted Wilde to write his ballad', he certainly advised him, most significantly when he told him to ignore the opinions of Robert Ross on changes to certain sections of the poem.[95] In return Wilde offered advice on his sonnets. Until the 1935 edition of *Sonnets*, the fourth line of the sestet had always previously read: 'Or, if fate cries and grudging gods demur'. Then he 'restored the line to what I originally wrote. Wilde did not like it, and I altered it to please him, but I think my own original version is the better line and makes better sense, though it makes ''passionate'' only two syllables.'[96] Perhaps as the younger and more inexperienced poet he viewed Wilde's opinion then as more important than his original aim. But there can be little doubt that the line he had originally written is superior to Wilde's.

Also written at Posilipo was a set of three sonnets titled, at Wilde's suggestion, 'A Triad of the Moon'. It is not really in the same league as the 'City of the Soul' set, because the ideas behind the sonnets are insubstantial and rather mannered. Lines like 'Ah me, methought, that she should so devise!' do not have the same conciseness, and too many dead words are squeezed in to keep up the form. The poems do not carry the air of ease in composition which is the hallmark of the great sonnets.

Rather more successful was the 'Sonnet on the Sonnet', written at the same time. Douglas was well aware of the great 'sonnet on the sonnet' by Wordsworth, which had been written in defence of the form at a time when it was under fire from critics. One line in particular would have been close to Douglas's heart: 'with this key Shakespeare unlock'd his heart.' Douglas's 'Sonnet on the Sonnet' supports Wordsworth's view of the sonnet's validity.[97] It is his only poetical defence of the form he was to make his own, and a justification for its use.

To see the moment holds a madrigal,
To find some cloistered place, some hermitage
For free devices, some deliberate cage
Wherein to keep wild thoughts like birds in thrall;
To eat sweet honey and to taste black gall,
To fight with form, to wrestle and to rage,
Till at the last upon the conquered page
The shadows of created Beauty fall.

This is the sonnet, this is all delight
Of every flower that blows in every Spring,
And all desire of every desert place;
This is the joy that fills a cloudy night
When, bursting from her misty following,
A perfect moon wins to an empty space.

Both Douglas and Wilde did a substantial amount of literary work at Naples, and their healthy working relationship seems to have pleased them. They had reached the point in their relationship at which they were most content. Although there was almost certainly nothing between them sexually, they loved each other fervently. When Douglas's sonnet 'To Mozart', which was in much the same vein as his earlier sonnet 'To Shakespeare', was refused by a weekly paper called the *Musician*, it was Wilde who was most upset and who wrote to the editor to say so.[98]

The intensity of the devotion the two men felt for each other was only equalled by the level of hatred that the renewal of their friendship caused in others. Reports in the papers of the ménage in Naples came to the attention of the British embassy in Rome. As a result one of the attachés, a friend of Douglas, went to visit them to tell them that their situation was causing embarrassment. Worse, though, was that newspaper reports were seen by Constance, who instantly cut off her husband's allowance. Any feeling of love or pity she still held for him was overwhelmed by her anger that he had gone back to the man she blamed for his downfall. When Wilde's solicitor conveyed this news to him he was deeply upset, and even more so when he learnt that both Robbie Ross and More Adey, who had been such loyal friends throughout his troubles, had supported Constance's action. Moreover Ross had turned against Wilde because of his reunion with Douglas: the man he had always hoped to reclaim as his own had spurned him again for the more talented and beautiful Douglas. Ross was a capable and likeable man but he did not have Douglas's gifts and this led him to desperate measures. He tried to sabotage Wilde's return as an artist – an unforgivable act of treachery and selfishness – by informing Leonard Smithers, who was intending to publish *The Ballad of Reading Gaol*, that Wilde's works had no market value and that he should oppose Wilde being paid extra for serial rights.[99] This action was one of the first of a series aimed at ruining both Wilde and Douglas.

Joining forces with those who wished to separate the lovers was Douglas's mother, the Marchioness of Queensberry. She believed that Wilde had corrupted her son, and, in short, had played Lord Henry Wotton to his Dorian Gray. She corresponded with the man who was to become guardian of the Wilde children, Adrian Hope, and More Adey, to try to arrange a way of breaking up the 'scandalous Naples ménage'.[100] She was finally successful: in December Lady Queensberry told her son that if he did not leave Wilde she would cut off his allowance. It was a fatal blow, for both men had been living on Douglas's money. They had to part for there was no way that either man could make enough money to support them both. Although they could both write, Wilde's name meant that he would not be taken up by any but the most adventurous publisher, while Douglas could earn little from his poetry. It was one of the most difficult decisions Douglas ever had to take.

Douglas and Wilde accepted that they had no option but to separate, and Douglas set out to do as much as he could for his friend. Both men knew that Constance would be likely to restore her husband's allowance once his lover had departed, but Douglas hoped that he might be able to help him more. In a letter to his mother he said that he would leave Wilde on certain conditions: Lady Queensberry should agree to pay Wilde two lump sums amounting to a total of £200, which was more than he received in a year from Constance; she should settle the Naples hotel bill, and pay the rent for the Posilipo villa for another quarter in advance so that Wilde had somewhere to live.[101] It was an incredible demand to make of her even though she had a not insubstantial amount of money at her disposal. Nevertheless, so desperate was she to save her son from the clutches of the man whom she assumed to be the cause of all his problems that she consented wholeheartedly to all the conditions. In another letter to her, Douglas explained his attitude to Wilde and separation.

> Don't think that I have changed my mind about him or that I think him bad or that I have changed my views about morals. I still love and admire him, and I think that he has been infamously treated by ignorant and cruel brutes. I look on him as a martyr to progress. I associate with him in everything. I long to hear of his success and artistic rehabilitation in the post which is his by right at the very summit of English literature, nor do I intend to cease corresponding with him or not to see him from time to time in Paris and elsewhere. I give up nothing and admit no point against him or myself separately or jointly.[102]

Three months later Wilde wrote what Douglas rightly described, years later when he read it, as 'one of the most astonishing products that the history of literature has ever recorded'.[103] In a letter to Robert Ross, Wilde wrote the 'facts' of the Naples period:

> Bosie, for four months, by endless letters, offered me a *"home"*. He offered me love, affection and care, and promised that I should never want for anything. After four months I accepted his offer, but when we met at *Aix* on our way to Naples I found that he had no money, no plans, and had forgotten all his promises. His one idea was that I should raise money for us both. I did so, to the extent of £120. On this Bosie lived, quite happily. When it came to his having, of course, to repay his own *share* he became terrible, unkind, mean and penurious, except where his own pleasures were concerned, and when my allowance ceased, he left . . .
>
>   It is, of course, the most bitter experience of a bitter life; it is a blow quite awful and paralysing, but it had to come, and I know that it is better that I should never see him again. I don't want to. He fills me with horror.[104]

There were no letters 'for four months' from Douglas – the arrangements for the Naples stay were arranged at Rouen in a day. The main income came from Douglas and his allowance, not from Wilde. Wilde did not avoid Douglas in the future – the two remained as close as ever, but their enforced parting meant that they met less frequently.

While Wilde was distorting the facts to try to get some more money for himself from Ross, Douglas remained as loyal as ever. In a letter to his mother after the break-up of the household he told her, 'It is no use wishing that I hadn't ever gone with him to Naples. It was the most lucky thing that ever happened. If I hadn't rejoined him and lived with him for two months, I should never have got over the longing for him. It was spoiling my life and spoiling my art and spoiling everything. Now I am free.'[105]

His obsession with getting back with Wilde had certainly been spoiling his life; whether it had been destroying his art is debatable. However, it is certain that he was anything but free of the friendship.

Soon after Douglas's departure Wilde left the safe haven of the Posilipo villa, with its paid rent, and spent the first £100 of Lady Queensberry's money on a trip to Sicily, where he stayed with the elderly Baron von Gloeden, an infamous homosexual. He also continued to practise and, at least to friends, defend homosexuality. On this he was unrepentant: 'A patriot put in prison for loving his country loves his country,' he wrote to Ross, 'and a poet in prison for loving boys loves boys.'[106] Douglas claimed that, at this period, he was getting away from the crimes with which Wilde was associated, but this is not true: a letter from Wilde to Turner mentions that Douglas was in love with a boy nicknamed 'Florifer', who was only fourteen.[107] Although, as we have seen, Wilde cannot always be believed, his reference to this relationship has been substantiated by others. It is certainly true that, during the last years of his acquaintance with Wilde, Douglas held to the sexual preferences he had acquired at school and university.

There was now only one person to whom Wilde had to defend his sexuality: his wife. After the breakdown of the Naples sanctuary, when he hoped for a restoration of his allowance, he told her that if he had been guilty of anything it was that he had loved too much and that love was better than hate. Constance did not agree with him and remarked to her brother that unnatural love was worse than hate.

10

By this time, Douglas was desperate to return to England. When he parted from Wilde at Naples, he had been away from his home for nearly three years. He was intending to bring out a book of poems in England, but was not sure of the attitude towards him. The public prosecutor replied to an enquiry from Douglas's cousin George Finch that he thought the return of Alfred Douglas was 'very inadvisable'.[108]

During 1898 Douglas and Wilde met frequently and even went on holiday together. Their relationship was more relaxed, but Douglas claimed later that there had been a cooling in Wilde's attitude towards him. In retrospect Douglas blamed his appearance for this: he still looked like a schoolboy, but he was tired. Throughout his life, Wilde had sought beauty, and in his mind, youth was inextricably linked with it. When Douglas began to lose his youth in Wilde's eyes, he began to lose his beauty. In this respect, it is clear that the devotion Douglas felt for Wilde was purer, since Wilde was never physically attractive to him, while physical attraction was clearly important to Wilde.

The problems over Douglas's return to London were resolved by his mother, and he finally arrived in November 1898. His reception was unremarkable. 'I suppose that London takes no notice at all: that is the supreme punishment,' wrote Wilde in a letter to Ross.[109] But although society took little interest in him, the publishing world soon did. Edward Arnold brought out a book of Douglas's nonsense rhymes in the month following his arrival in London. *Tails with a Twist* appeared under the pseudonym 'A Belgian Hare'. In a preface to the 1928 edition of the work Douglas wrote:

> I once wrote a book of pure nonsense; it was called *Tails with a Twist*, and achieved great successes, among them the flattering but (to me) not altogether satisfactory one of being very closely imitated by Mr Hilaire Belloc, in a book which he called *The Bad Child's Book of Beasts*. This book actually appeared before *Tails with a Twist*, but most of the rhymes contained in my book had been written at least two years before Mr Belloc's, and were widely known and quoted at Oxford, where Mr Belloc was my contemporary, and in other places.[110]

Although Douglas's 'pure nonsense' is less brilliantly executed than Belloc's verses, much of it is good, if dated. It was republished as recently as 1979[111] but by then had fallen into the category of children's verse:

> The Eagle is a fearful bird,
> He takes your eye without a word.
>
> And when you're lying in your bed,
> He whets his talons on your head.
>
> And if you move or scream or start,
> He drives his beak into your heart.
>
> To cause pain is his only care:
> How different from the Belgian Hare!

More important to Douglas's reputation was the publication in May 1899 by Grant Richards of *The City of the Soul*. This appeared anonymously because, like *Tails with a Twist*, Douglas's name on the title page of any book would have limited its chances of success. Paranoia was not responsible for the omission of the author's name, but, as we shall see, astute judgement of public opinion. Reviews of the book were almost unanimously good. Lionel Johnson wrote of the author as 'a great unknown', while the *Daily Telegraph* reviewer said:

> *The City of the Soul* is not an essay in the art of writing verse; it is a work of a remarkably high order, and reveals the temperament of a poet who writes because it is in him to do so . . . the verse is throughout chaste, restrained, and as flawless as good poetry may be. But what makes the volume a notable one, and dear to the lovers of all good things, is that it has the one thing needful, and the rarest to meet with – personality . . . The author has achieved great distinction in his sonnets . . . Indeed, all through the book one comes upon lines which are astonishing in their beauty and their distinction.[112]

The contrast between the public's idea of Douglas as a degenerate of the decadent school and his poems' 'chaste' style is striking.

Wilde was among those to whom a presentation copy was sent. Though simply inscribed 'Oscar from Bosie – March 1900',[113] it shows that they were still on intimate terms.

The City of the Soul contains all the major poems Douglas had written up to this point, excluding some that had featured in the *Mercure de France* book, *Poems*, and which he had decided might not only be offensive to English sensibility but not among his best. His earliest poems were included up to his exquisite translations from the French of Baudelaire's 'Le Balcon' and 'Harmonie du Soir', the poems from Posilipo and many he had written during the days of Wilde's imprisonment. There was an 'Ode to Autumn' and, perhaps most movingly, 'Ennui'. In the latter, he approached a subject he had long dwelt on; that the pleasure he had known for so brief a time was now gone.

> The pearls are numbered on youth's rosary,
> I have outlived the days desirable.
> What is there left? And how shall dead men sing
> Unto the loosened strings of Love and Hate,
> Or take strong hands to Beauty's ravishment?
>   Who shall devise this thing,
> To give high utterance to Miscontent,
> Or make Indifference articulate?

The treatment Douglas received when he returned to England is epitomised in one particular incident that goes some way to explaining his frame of mind when writing verses like the above. Among the poems in *The City of the Soul* was 'Autumn Days', and Douglas sent a copy of his book to the president of his old college, Herbert Warren, whose remarks about the poem, made almost a decade earlier, had clearly encouraged him. The book was returned to him with a note explaining that Warren could not accept it. Douglas wrote later, 'It struck me at the time as being rather a brutal and unnecessarily unkind thing to do, and I remember looking up and finding his letter about "Autumn Days", which I had preserved, and reading it again before tearing it up.'[114] It was typical of the sort of thing he had to put up with for the rest of his life as a result of his association with Wilde. Warren was a social climber and an arch-snob, who had been friendly with Wilde when he was at his height of popularity but who had nothing to do with him when he fell from grace. In the same way he had played up to the young lord at his college but rejected him when he realised that acquaintanceship might be a social handicap.

Eighteen ninety-nine also yielded *The Duke of Bewick, a Nonsense Rhyme by The Belgian Hare, Author of 'Tails with a Twist'*.[115] Once again, Douglas hid behind anonymity. He was wise to do so: when *The City of the Soul* ran into its second edition it carried its author's name, at his request, and failed to sell, while the previous print run had sold out quickly. *The Duke of Bewick* is an amusing skit of 266 lines, one of Douglas's lengthiest pieces of light verse. The main character is based not on Queensberry, as the book's illustrator, Tony Ludovici, originally thought,[116] but, as Douglas explained years later to Hugh Walpole, on a minor character in Wilde's *Picture of Dorian Gray*, who, to show his disapproval of Dorian leaves the room in the club, 'in a marked manner', as Dorian enters.[117] This line from the novel amused Douglas, partly, as he explained to his future friend and biographer Rupert Croft-Cooke, because of the deadly earnestness with which Wilde had written it. As Douglas said, '[Wilde's] hatred of being laughed at in even the smallest things was quite morbid.'[118] But perhaps the inspiration came earlier. In 1895 Douglas had told Robert Ross that, 'The Duke of Berwick who was staying here with two women, left the hotel, the day after my arrival and as this is the only decent hotel in the place he is having rather a bad time of it.' He went on impishly to suggest that this prudishness was hypocritical, since, 'He is suspected by some of having sinister designs on a dappled angora lounge goat that browses in a little walled-in garden near the hotel.'[119]

In the wake of the success of *The Ballad of Reading Gaol*, Leonard Smithers had taken on Douglas's new book for publication and commissioned as illustrator the seventeen-year-old Ludovici who said that the author's personality was one that nobody of his age would be likely to forget.

> Lord Alfred Douglas must then have been on the threshold of thirty, and I was instantly struck by his handsome features, charming manner and his still youthful and distinguished appearance. Tall and slim, he was dressed in the elegant négligé style of an artist and as he introduced me to Smithers and motioned me to a chair, he at once made me feel wholly at ease. I was enchanted and faintly bewildered by the simple cordiality of his welcome.[120]

It was a beautifully illustrated and produced book, but a week after publication, Smithers's company collapsed and Douglas's work 'never had a real life as a book at all'.[121]

The failure of such a good book to sell was a bad omen of what was to follow. Nineteen hundred was not only the start of a new era in the calendar, it was the year in which Douglas's world collapsed around him.

11

In the last few years of the 1890s it became clear that the decade would close as definitively as it had begun. The figures who had symbolised its spirit were dying. Among those in the visual arts, Aubrey Beardsley had epitomised the style of the era. The editor of the *Yellow Book*, and a regular contributor to the *Savoy* magazine, died on 16 March 1898, aged only twenty-six. 'He had the fatal speed of those who are to die young,' wrote a friend, 'that absorbtion of a lifetime in an hour, which we find in those who hasten to have done their work before noon, knowing that they will not see the evening.'[122]

Among poets, perhaps none was so representative of his age than Ernest Dowson. His poems prophesied the doom of the era, and '*Vita summa brevis spem nos vetat incohare longam*' perhaps became symbolic of the period. It is a suitable epitaph for all the artists of the age.

> They are not long, the weeping and the laughter,
>> Love and desire and hate:
> I think they have no portion in us after
>> We pass the gate.
>
> They are not long, the days of wine and roses:
>> Out of a misty dream
> Our path emerges for a while, then closes
>> Within a dream.

He died, aged thirty-three, in February 1900. Douglas had to deal with a series of more personal losses too. On 29 January 1900 Wellington Stapleton Cotton died on active service in South Africa. Douglas was desperate with grief, and so determined to do something in memory of his friend that he decided to enlist. First he tried to join a cavalry regiment, but was turned down and advised to try elsewhere. He approached the Cambridge corps, which was entirely made up of gentlemen prepared to pay for their equipment and provide their own horses. Douglas passed all the medical, riding and shooting tests and was accepted, with his cheque of £250. However, a short time later his cheque was returned with a letter informing him that his services were not required. It was a stinging humiliation.

Then on 31 January 1900 the Marquess of Queensberry died. It was no surprise to anyone who knew him: he had clearly been ill for some time. The disorder, which might have sparked off his paranoid attacks, had grown steadily worse. In the aftermath of the Wilde trials, Queensberry's friends deserted him and he started to believe that he was being pursued by 'Oscar Wilders'.[123] Although some writers consider this not impossible,[124] it seems more likely that guilt over his persistent hounding of his own sons and Wilde manifested itself in this way.

There had been a brief reconciliation between father and son the previous year, when they had met and embraced, with Queensberry calling Alfred his 'darling boy' and promising to restore his allowance. All this seemed too good to be true and indeed it was. A week later Douglas received a letter from Queensberry demanding to know the exact nature of his relationship with 'that beast Wilde' before he handed over any money. His son sent back an equally abusive and determined letter, and the two never saw each other again.[125]

When Douglas looked back on his relationship with his father in later years, it was with more charity than he had been able to muster at this point. At first Queensberry had tried desperately to protect his son but had then set to punishing him. In so doing he had squandered a massive amount of the family fortune. Kinmount had been sold in 1893, and with it went almost the last of the Douglases' land in their native country. All that was left for the family was the burial plot. On his deathbed Queensberry saw Sibyl and told her that she was the only woman he had ever loved. However, when Percy arrived Queensberry mustered his last reserves of strength to sit up and spit at him.

Queensberry ended his life with a confusing gesture. On his deathbed he saw his brother, the Very Reverend Canon Lord Archibald Douglas, confessed his sins, renounced his notorious atheistic beliefs, professed his love for and faith in Jesus Christ, and was received into the Catholic Church. Years later Lord Archibald told Douglas that he had given Queensberry conditional absolution, after his brother had said, 'I have prayed with all my heart for the forgiveness of my sins.'[126] In any case, it was an unpredicted ending for an unpredictable man – and, as Alfred Douglas had prophesied years earlier, once Queensberry was dead, not many people missed him.

His death had little effect on the family, and although his children accompanied the ashes to the Kinmount burial ground few tears were shed. The matter of the inheritance was somewhat more engaging, and Douglas realised that his father had not had time to cut him out of the will. Thus, while the bulk of Queensberry's assets went to Percy, Douglas received £8,000 immediately, with another £7,000 to follow. Straight after the funeral Percy and Alfred went to Paris where they met up with Wilde, who observed that the brothers were 'in deep mourning and the highest spirits'.[127]

Wilde's attitude to money had changed during his bankruptcy proceedings and after, and he was no longer able to be extravagant. Therefore he jumped at Ross's suggestion to ask Douglas for a lump sum of £2,000 so that it could be administered as an allowance for him. Ross knew the figure was impossibly high and that Douglas would be bound to refuse, so his and Wilde's relationship would be strained.

However, Alfred and Percy Douglas were already giving Wilde a substantial allowance[128] and this new demand seemed more than greedy. Certainly when Wilde approached Douglas about it he was flatly refused. Douglas was embarrassed and affronted by his friend's request. Between the time of the inheritance and the end of the year Douglas had paid Wilde nearly £400 in cheques and much more in ready money.

Working on spending his inheritance, Douglas bought stables just outside Paris and horses to keep in them. It was the fulfilment of his dream to throw himself into the open-air life he had deserted for most of the decade. Not since his Oxford days had he known such pleasure in sport. The sudden death of Lord Encombe in August must have brought back all the memories of those halcyon days at Winchester and Magdalen. Encombe was not even thirty, and had been married for less than two years. An obituary said of him, 'None held a higher reputation, and none gave brighter promise for the future. He died before he had time to do what might have justified our estimate of his powers.'[129] His passing was of enormous importance to Douglas: not only had he lost his best friend, he had also to realise that life could end at any time in something akin to failure.

It was only a few months later that Douglas had to face an even more disabling grief. Broken by society, ostracised from the very force which had impressed and inspired him in earlier days, Wilde's last years were a tragedy of Shakespearian profundity. His wife had died within a year of his release from prison and with her sudden death had gone any chance of seeing his beloved children again (their guardian, Adrian Hope decided it was not in Cyril and Vyvyan's best interests to be allowed to see their father). He could not write, and realised that he would not complete any more substantial works of art. All he could do was talk and write letters. He, like Dowson, Beardsley and others, had made the nineties and now he, like them, had to fade away and allow in a new era.

Oscar Wilde died on 30 November 1900, in a small Parisian hotel. His death was associated with a fall he had had in prison, which had caused cerebral disturbances that led to encephalitic meningitis. It was a painful and drawn-out end. It was not until 1 December that Douglas found out that his lover, inspiration and dearest friend had died. A letter from Ross a few days earlier had said that Wilde was ill, but that it was 'nothing serious'. Douglas was paralysed with grief when he heard the truth. He had never thought that someone like Wilde could die at the age of just forty-six. [130] He assumed that Wilde's natural *joie de vivre* would carry him through anything.

On his deathbed, like his great adversary just ten months earlier, Wilde was received into the Catholic Church.

The funeral took place on 3 December at the church of St Germain-des-Près and the burial at the cemetery at Bagneux. Douglas paid the funeral expenses and was the chief mourner. He arrived the day before the funeral when the coffin had already been nailed shut so he did not see Wilde's body. His sense of desolation was immense. 'The world seems to be greyer now that he is dead,' he confessed to Percy. 'He was always kind and generous and gentle and forgiving. I was a little afraid you might think I had changed my mind about him in later life. I never did and he was the same to me, always my dearest and best friend, although I found it absolutely impossible to see him as much as formerly in the face of the avalanche of slander and grief of relations etc. both on his side and mine.' [131]

By the end of the decade almost everyone who had given Douglas some reason for living, whether it was because he could quarrel with them (like his father) or because he could love them (like Wilde), had left him. He was the only surviving major figure in the case that had rocked

Victorian England to its core. It took him almost forty years to see the events clearly. In 1938, in *Without Apology*, he was finally able to write the truth about it, while ruminating on the most famous lines from *The Ballad of Reading Gaol*.

It sounds rather conceited, I know, but I have often thought that part of my father's distorted grievance in all this business was caused by jealousy. It never occurred to me at the time, but I believe my father really was fond of me, and I think he sensed somehow that, with the horrible heartlessness of youth I did not appreciate him as he really was, or felt himself to be. I probably showed him (God forgive me) that I thought him rather stupid in comparison with my brilliant friend. I was a spoilt and selfish little beast in those days, I know only too well. Did I perhaps unconsciously wound the feelings of my poor 'Papa'?

The thought which has only recently occurred to me is a terrible one. Did my father really love me all the time, as I certainly loved him before he turned against me, and was he only doing what Oscar says in his great Ballad all men always do, killing the thing he loved? Didn't we all three, Wilde, my father, and I, do it, more or less?[132]

Chapter 4

'Now I have known the uttermost rose of love'

(1900–1907)

Just days after Wilde's death Douglas found the voice he was looking for. When his brother Drumlanrig had died Douglas had discovered that his grief could only be expressed in poetry so after Wilde's death he attempted to write a sonnet. Originally titled 'To Oscar Wilde', it became 'The Dead Poet' and is one of Douglas's most eloquent and moving works, a fine tribute to Wilde.

> I dreamed of him last night, I saw his face
> All radiant and unshadowed of distress,
> And as of old, in music measureless,
> I heard his golden voice and marked him trace
> Under the common thing the hidden grace,
> And conjure wonder out of emptiness,
> Till mean things put on beauty like a dress
> And all the world was an enchanted place.
>
> And then methought outside a fast locked gate
> I mourned the loss of unrecorded words,
> Forgotten tales and mysteries half said,
> Wonders that might have been articulate,
> And voiceless thoughts like murdered singing birds.
> And so I woke and knew that he was dead.

With Wilde gone, Douglas tried to concentrate on his horses. On the race track he could forget the attacks against him and once again be the athletic, popular boy he had been at Winchester and Oxford. He had always dreamed that one day he would be able to run stables and in later years he described this time at Chantilly as the happiest of his life. But although his inheritance from Queensberry was large it was not enough to keep the stables going for long. It never occurred to Douglas to live off the interest from the capital although this, along with his mother's allowance to him, would have given him a handsome £600 a year. Instead he lived well above his means and had a marvellous time. He wrote later that 'My eighteen months, on and off at Chantilly added twenty years of health and vigour to my life.'[1]

In Monte Carlo, where he bought a gelding named Hardi from a casino owner for £250, he made an astonishing amount of money on the roulette tables (over four days with Frank Harris he won £1,600) but it was not a regular enough income to secure either his or his stables' future. He had some notable successes, particularly with Hardi, who won many races for him including the French Derby at Chantilly and a £500 handicap at Maisons-Lafitte. But Douglas saw that things would have to be settled financially. Perhaps his most foolish venture came at the instigation of Frank Harris.

Harris had proved a loyal and generous friend to Wilde, and Douglas had a lot of time for him. He might have seen him as a role model, for Harris bridged the gap between the aesthetes and the hearties, neither stupid and sporty, nor weak and artistic: like Douglas, he had the best of both worlds. Harris was like Douglas in another respect: he was always keen to earn more money to support an extravagant lifestyle, though Harris was willing to get money by any means necessary. It was thus that he duped the trusting Douglas into giving him £2,000. Harris claimed that Douglas was buying into a luxury hotel in France which he said he owned. He lied that the French government had granted permission for him to run roulette and trente-et-quarante there, which were both banned under French law. Douglas believed him and handed over the money. He did not hear anything more for a while and eventually Harris had to admit that the money had been wasted but assured him that it would be returned in due course. It never was, which remained a bone of contention between the two men.[2] Douglas realised that his inheritance was running out, and arrived at a practical solution to his financial predicament: he had to marry, and marry well, preferably a woman with a vast income. He decided, like so many of his generation, that the best option was to search for an American heiress. Moreover, in America the Wilde scandal might not damage his chances as it would in Europe. He wrote later, 'My idea was that I would marry for her money an American girl who had a superabundance of it, and that she would marry me because I had a title and an historic name, and because I knew, and could easily show her, or anyone concerned, that, with plenty of money, there would not be the slightest difficulty in getting back again into the social circle from which I was then partially excluded.'[3]

2

A few months later, a new phase opened up in Douglas's life. It began in an unlikely form with a highly florid letter to him from a young woman named Olive Custance. They had met, in fact, though many years earlier, for in 1887 Olive had been a bridesmaid at the wedding of Douglas's cousin Rachel Montgomery. Douglas wrote back, thanking her for her 'beautiful letter'[4] and they soon entered into an almost daily correspondence.

Olive was descended on her father's side from Francis Bacon and had been born into a wealthy landed family in Norfolk where her father was a magistrate as well as a keen sportsman. From a conventional family, she had grown into an unconventional young woman. She had come to the public's attention as a poet in the mid-1890s. Her book-plate had been designed by Aubrey Beardsley, to whom she sent contributions for the *Yellow Book* when he was its editor. Her first book of poems was published by John Lane in 1900, entitled *Opals*, and won the critics' praise.

Immediately after he had replied to her first letter, Douglas received another communication from her, this time with a bunch of red roses and a copy of her book. He was flattered by her attentions and in his second letter to her he described her poems as 'wonderfully beautiful' and went on, 'I have not seen anything so good for years. I am so glad that they are *really* good.' He concluded with a request: 'I am sending you my photograph. I am afraid it is several years old, but it is the last I had taken and I do not think I have altered much. Will you send me yours?'[5] In his third letter Douglas signed himself her 'loving Prince' in response to Olive calling herself his 'Page'.

By now the pair had met, but only after some difficulty. They had arranged to rendezvous in what is now the Victoria and Albert Museum but they went in through different doors and missed each other. Douglas walked dejectedly back to his rooms off Portland Square thinking the worst. But Olive, governess in tow as chaperone, set off after him. The meeting was a great success and Douglas was stirred by her good looks. Olive was pretty in a boyish way, feminine but not girly. Douglas reported that it was 'love at first sight' for both of them. In his *Autobiography* (1929) he wrote that Olive Custance met every requirement of the ideal person to suit him. She was not only 'well born, beautiful, and outstandingly attractive', she was also, 'intellectual and appreciative of poetry'.[6] And his attraction to her confirmed in him a suspicion he had long harboured, but stated boldly in 1929: 'I believe that almost everyone is more or less bisexual.'[7]

Their next meeting combined Douglas's past and present in a curious way. He and Olive decided that they must meet in secret, without the knowledge of her family, at the Carfax gallery in Ryder Street which was run, among others, by Robert Ross. Ross claimed to be enthusiastic about Olive and helped the couple to steal moments together. Olive had to keep her relationship with Douglas quiet as her parents would not have approved: they were hoping that she would make a good marriage to a respectable and wealthy heir. To this end, in the spring of 1901 Olive was sent to Paris accompanied by a neighbour, Freddie Manners-Sutton, who was not only ten years younger than Douglas but the heir of Viscount Canterbury. The trip backfired. In Paris Olive met the writer Nathalie Barney, who had written to her expressing admiration for her poems. The verse Olive sent her in reply was an almost exact pastiche of Douglas's early homosexual poetry and talked of the love that 'walks with delicate feet afraid/'Twixt maid and maid.'

It was evident that Olive had lesbian leanings, which were nurtured by Nathalie Barney and her friends. During their time in Paris, Manners-Sutton told Olive that he had fallen for her, which she reported to Nathalie who replied, 'Tell him I'm in love with you!' What followed was a muddle of affections and allegiances. Manners-Sutton was unperturbed by Nathalie's statement, but Nathalie wanted Olive to herself and tried to persuade Mrs Custance to allow them to go to Venice together. They did so, deserting Manners-Sutton. Once there, she tried to wheedle Olive's affections away from Douglas, of whom she thought constantly, even suggesting that she herself should marry Douglas and the three of them live in a *ménage à trois*.[8] She wrote a large amount of love poetry to Olive: her 'How Do I Love You' finishes with the lines, 'Of all my cruel loves I love you most,/and since I love you most – ah sweet love me!'

The manuscript of this carries a note to Olive in which Nathalie explained that the poem was 'another proof of the lamentable fact that "all bad poetry springs from true feeling",' and added 'Hope with me for that time when I shall no longer love you – then perhaps I shall be able to sing of you as you deserve.'[9] Olive realised that the threesome wouldn't work and returned to England.

There was no question of Alfred Douglas and Olive Custance marrying: Douglas needed money and the Custance family would not have consented, so the relationship between the two remained intense but fatalistic. In a letter to Douglas during this time Olive asked, 'When shall I get another letter from you . . . and tell me you are pleased with your little Princess?' but reminded herself, 'No! I am not your Princess. She will be very beautiful. But meanwhile love me a little please, kind and beautiful Prince.'[10] Looming before them was Douglas's departure to America, but for a time this looked in jeopardy. Almost completely out of money he went to stay for the summer with Percy on the island of Colonsay, which Percy had rented for the year. The shooting there was particularly good, and Douglas forgot about his troubles in London where, he reported to Olive, 'I was very much harassed . . . by the crude behaviour of money lenders and others.'[11] In September he ventured back to prepare for his departure on the Dominion Line transatlantic ship on the first day of the following month. Olive dreaded his departure as much as he did. His misery at ever having decided to embark on the voyage was acute, but the ticket had been bought and he had to go. Before he left he sent Olive a heart-shaped locket containing a strand of his hair. Olive thanked him straight away:

My own Prince,

The little heart is sweet and I shall wear it even when you have forgotten all about me and married the beautiful rich princess who will give you all those lovely things you ought to have.

I miss you more than I can ever say for I love you beyond everything in the world and I think we shall never be happy together again. Write to me soon and tell me you love your little Page, and that one day you will come back to 'him', my Prince, my Prince.[12]

There is no doubt that their relationship was highly complex. Both had a strongly homosexual nature so the masculine side of Olive attracted Douglas while the feminine side of him attracted her. Before embarking for America Douglas asked her, 'Why can't you dress up as a boy and come with me?'[13] In a later letter he wrote, 'I shan't have anything to do with any horrid princesses or anybody at all, how *could* I after I have known the dear little page?'[14] But at least in falling for a woman who looked like a boy and wanted to act like one, Douglas found himself at last able to have a love affair that was not damned by society. Nevertheless he needed money, and he couldn't get it from Olive.

3

Douglas's ship sailed into Portland, Maine, in mid-October and he had a pleasant time in Boston. He went on to Niagara Falls, then to Buffalo, where his experiences upset him. He wrote to Olive, with whom he was in constant communication, saying, 'Why did I ever come to this country of third-rate snobs and prigs?' He had been 'deeply wounded (stupidly so because I ought to be beyond that now) to find that people here simply don't want to know me, and avoid me'.[15] Olive had also hurt him: she had sent him love letters to her from a female friend. It seems she was trying to make him jealous, and it worked, although she was just as jealous, and quite clearly worried that he would fall in love with someone else when he reached New York. Douglas had gone to America armed with 'heaps of social introductions',[16] including one from Olive to Nathalie Barney, whom Douglas had not yet met. It is clear that Olive started to worry about this meeting once she had organised it – perhaps fearing that Nathalie would try to put her earlier plan into action. Douglas wrote a candid letter to comfort her: 'I have not yet seen Nathalie, but I am sure I shall like her very much, but please don't think for an instant that I shall fall in love with her. You don't seem to realise that you are the only girl I have ever loved or even *looked at* seriously. Do you imagine that because I have found out how sweet and lovely one girl is I shall immediately go and fall in love with others? It is far otherwise I assure you.'[17]

In one of his letters to Olive, Douglas made a most revealing statement about his attraction to her. He wrote, 'You are a darling Baby and you are exactly like a boy and you know perfectly well that I love you better than anyone else, boy or girl. . . . I used to wish you were a boy, now I am glad you are not.'[18] Douglas's misery in America found expression in his letters to her, and drew them closer. In her he had found a confidant as well as a link with home.

Douglas's time in New York was generally pleasant, so he decided to take up the offer of his cousin Percy Wyndham to visit him in Washington. Wyndham was a second secretary at the British embassy. Douglas booked in to a hotel for a couple of days where he found a card for him from the ambassador, Lord Pauncefote. Then he moved into his cousin's rooms and spent two or three weeks with him. Percy Wyndham was a member of the Metropolitan Club in Washington, which claimed to be the most exclusive club in the capital, and proposed Douglas for honorary membership, which was granted. Douglas had frequented the club for about a week when problems arose. Although he was not aware of it at first, one of the club members had raised questions about Douglas's suitability for membership owing to his 'doings in London' and in particular to his friendship with 'objectionable persons'.[19] One evening, unaware of this, Douglas strolled in and ordered a drink. Someone made a highly offensive remark, obviously intended for Douglas's ears, about Oscar Wilde. Douglas finished his drink and walked out. When he arrived at Wyndham's rooms, his cousin told him that he had just received a letter from the club committee asking him to explain why Douglas had been put up for membership in the first place. Wyndham had said that although Douglas had been 'indirectly concerned in the Oscar Wilde scandal' there had been nothing in that which might prevent him taking up membership of the Metropolitan. He had pointed out that Lord Alfred was 'a member of White's Club, one of the most exclusive clubs in London'.[20] Furthermore, he explained, Douglas was 'his cousin and guest, a man of high social position', who was 'on intimate terms with the British Ambassador and Lady Pauncefote'.[21]

But all this could not change the impact on Douglas of the incident, and he did not want to go back there even if they had allowed him to. Things soon got worse: on 23 December the story hit the New York papers, prominently displayed and factually inaccurate. Douglas was embarrassed by this so he decided to give the facts, as well as his side of the story, in a letter to the *New York Herald*, which had first broken the story. It was published on Christmas Eve. He ended, 'Apparently the objection of the Metropolitan Club and the American press in general to me is the frequently stated fact that, having been a friend to Oscar Wilde before his downfall, I continued to be so after his release from prison, and that almost alone among his former friends I attended his funeral. I have never attempted to deny these facts, and I have yet to learn that they constitute a serious indictment against my character, either as a gentleman or a Christian.'[22]

The papers reported that officials at the British embassy were 'indignant at what they regard as the harsh action of the Metropolitan Club',[23] and they had all rallied round to support Douglas. The ambassador, Lord Pauncefote, explained that the members of that particular club were well known never to lose a chance of 'being rude to anyone who was on friendly terms with the British Embassy or himself'.[24] This merely reinforced Douglas's opinions on the country and its inhabitants. He explained in a letter to Olive that 'The women here are charming but the men are with scarcely an exception the most awful cads,' but he added that America 'will be a nice place to live in about 500 years time when the people have got civilised and when they have built up a few traditions of conduct and manners'.[25]

Lady Pauncefote asked Douglas to take her to a concert and then go to dinner at the embassy, which he did, and he remembered the kindness and generosity of the ambassador and his wife for the rest of his life, but this highlighted the lack of civility he had encountered from the natives. Yet despite the support of the embassy, Douglas decided that he could not stay in the city: he felt that he was becoming an embarrassment to Wyndham, who was seeking advancement. He returned to New York.

Douglas was keen to get back to England, but stayed another fortnight in America. The original motive for his journey had not been fulfilled. He wrote to Olive, 'I have met quantities of heiresses but I have treated them only with bare civility! It might have been different if I had met a nice heir. But apparently there are none.'[26] He claimed later that at least three heiresses had been willing to marry him, one of whom had 'quite £20,000 a year',[27] but he came to understand that the idea of his taking any of them as his bride was impossible, and that there was only one reason for this: he was not only deeply in love with Olive, but he wanted to marry her – for love, not £20,000 a year.

There were pleasant moments in New York: the University Club

immediately made him an honorary member, and at the request of
Nathalie Barney, Douglas wrote a translation of Baudelaire's 'La Beauté.'
The translation shows a deep understanding of the French original but
also has the clear fingerprints of Douglas's sonnet style:

> Fair am I, mortals, as a stone-carved dream,
> And all men wound themselves against my breast,
> The poet's last desire, the loveliest.
> Voiceless, eternal as the world I seem.
> In the blue air, strange sphinx, I brood supreme
> With heart of snow whiter than swan's white crest,
> No movement mars the plastic line – I rest
> With lips untaught to laugh or eyes to stream.
>
> Singers who see, in tranced interludes,
> My splendour set with all superb design,
> Consume their days, in toilful ecstasy.
> To these revealed the starry amplitudes
> Of my great eyes which make all things divine
> Are crystal mirrors of eternity.[28]

4

In the last days of 1901, still in New York, Douglas received a letter from a
sixteen-year-old boy, George Sylvester Viereck. He enclosed a sonnet for
which Douglas thanked him. In the first days of 1902 Douglas replied to
another letter from Viereck. It was clear that Viereck was desperate to
meet him and had called at Douglas's rooms three times already without
success. Douglas suggested that they meet for luncheon, which they did. In
the course of a friendly letter he described himself as young and clean-
shaven and, to be sure that Viereck noticed him, he wore a fur coat.[29]
Douglas and Viereck corresponded intermittently for the rest of Douglas's
life, and on his death Viereck wrote a moving sonnet tribute.

Never happy to let an argument settle, Douglas had one more thing to
write before leaving for England. A letter he addressed to the editor of
the *New York Herald* on 11 January was published, at his request, a couple

of days later. In it, he explained that since he was leaving the country early the following week and since he had been asked continually what he thought of the country, he would answer now. He had written a sonnet on America entitled 'The New World', which he included with his letter. He did not ask for any payment, but stipulated that it be prominently printed, which it was, along with a photograph. He wrote that 'as I understand that "sensation" is a *sine qua non* for anything appearing in the American press I wish to create the sensation by dedicating the sonnet to the Metropolitan Club in Washington'. He sent the manuscript of the sonnet to the paper without keeping a copy. It never appeared in any further publication.

> Is this the new world? Nay all this is old;
> The love of self and kindliness denied,
> Malice and Envy and vain boasting pride,
> The hate of beauty and the greed for gold.
> Heads have been emptier still and hearts as cold
> In older worlds than this, and men have lied
> And worms have eaten them, and gods have died
> When this Columbia was a tale untold.
>
> O youngest daughter of Democracy,
> The old sins nestle kindly in thy breast.
> Take these old virtues, too (who runs may read),
> Kindness and Courtesy, and let them be
> Lamps that in all thy lights outshine the rest;
> Then would thy country be New World indeed.

When he came to write his *Autobiography* Douglas remembered the sonnet in which he 'let out at America generally' as 'not very good'.[30]

A day or so before his departure Douglas received another letter from Viereck, who had obviously found unjust the damning comments on his country, to which Douglas replied, 'Of course my sonnet was unjust, *mais que voulez vous?* One can't be just in a sonnet. There is only room in it for one idea and one point of view. I have met many charming people here and seen many interesting and wonderful things in this country and not the least of my pleasures was meeting you.' As he embarked on the voyage home he told the young man that he hoped to see him and hear from him again, and rather poignantly finished, 'You are too clever not to make your mark some time or other. I hope you will have more luck and make a better business of your life than I have done with mine.'[31]

*   *   *   *

'I feel centuries older since I went to America', Douglas told Olive, 'and I think if I had stayed there much longer I should have discovered the secret of eternal middle age.'[32] His return to London brought the news that his mother had given up her house in Cadogan Place, which meant that they both went to stay at Clouds, the house in Wiltshire belonging to Percy Wyndham where Rudyard Kipling was among the luncheon guests. Olive wrote inviting him to a matinée performance of the first revival of *The Importance of Being Earnest* in February. Whether he went is not known, but by early February he had rejoined his brother Percy on Colonsay for the shooting. A hard frost on the mainland, which did not reach the island, 'sent in swarms of woodcock' and Douglas, along with an Argyllshire laird, bagged 147 over five days. There was also a grouse moor, coverts for pheasants, and a vast number of partridges, duck and snipe. Out of the blue a letter arrived from Olive with the news that she was engaged to be married to his old schoolfriend and Encombe's fag George Montagu – at which point, in his own words, 'the blood of a hundred Douglas ancestors surged up, and I said in my heart: "No, you don't!"'[33]

5

George Montagu had remained prominent in Douglas's life ever since Winchester. He had followed Douglas to Magdalen a year after Douglas had left, and Douglas recalled that Montagu had been one of the few who had been 'just as friendly and pleasant'[34] to him after the Oscar Wilde scandal as he had before. For this he had been grateful. However, Montagu's family wanted him to go into politics and with their help he became the Conservative candidate for South Huntingdon. As the electioneering began, he was advised by his family to drop Douglas, whose friendship they considered a liability to anybody wanting to enter the respectable world of politics. To Douglas's surprise, Montagu did so at once, 'without any mitigation or remorse'.

Douglas turned his fury and hurt into a lasting form. In New York he had rediscovered the sonnet as a vehicle for 'the lost art of invective',[35] and considered 'The Traitor' to be among the best he ever wrote.[36] It was included in all subsequent collections of his verse.[37]

> Cast out my soul the broken covenant,
> Forget the pitiable masquerade,
> And that ignoble part ignobly played.
> Let us take shame that such a mummer's rant
> Of noble things, could pierce the adamant
> Of Pride wherewith we ever were arrayed,
> And being with a kiss once more betrayed,
> Let not our tears honour that sycophant.
>
> Let him, on graves of buried loyalty,
> Rise as he may to his desired goal;
> Ay and God speed him here, I grudge him not.
> And when all men shall sing his praise to me
> I'll not gainsay. But I shall know his soul
> Lies in the bosom of Iscariot.

Montagu took his seat in Parliament in the 'Khaki election' of 1900, so all this was behind Douglas when he went to America. It was with dismay that he heard from Olive while he was away that she had met Montagu. Clearly she knew nothing about the split between Douglas and him for she wrote to her 'Prince' that they had got on well. Montagu had found favour with Olive because he had known Douglas well and could do accurate imitations of ' ''Bosie doing'' this, that or the other'.[38] Douglas told her of their falling-out, and in his next letter wrote, 'I hope you have not been seeing too much of the absurd George.'[39] Olive, though, under the impression that it would never be possible for her to marry Douglas, accepted Montagu, his schoolfriend, as a satisfactory second best.

Douglas was livid at the idea of the only woman he had ever loved marrying the man he considered one of the worst traitors imaginable, and decided to marry her himself. He arranged to meet her at Kettner's in London. Over dinner he told her he wanted to marry her and suggested that they elope. She agreed. They met a few days later in Robert Ross's art gallery to work out the finer details of their plan. They decided that things must go on as normally as possible, so Olive would stay that weekend at the Sandwich family's country house so that she could meet Montagu's family. While she was with them Douglas arranged a special licence for their marriage.

Everything went according to plan, though Douglas worried until the last moment that Olive would not turn up. As it was, Olive told her maid of what she intended to do and arrived at the church with her bags packed. Thus, on 4 March 1902, Lord Alfred Douglas and Olive Custance became man and wife at St George's, Hanover Square. Douglas was accompanied by his sister, Lady Edith Fox-Pitt, and the other witness was a friend called Cecil Hayes. Lady Queensberry told her son that she had followed the service in her prayer book at home and that she 'could imagine you two dears standing up together'. She told him that she had 'hoped and prayed for them both'.[40] Well she might – her own marriage to Douglas's father had taken place in the same church.

Another person was present at the wedding. From the back of the church Robert Ross watched as the lover of his greatest friend, the golden Adonis and fated love of Oscar Wilde, married a woman in a Christian ceremony celebrating their love. Douglas had found a love that spoke its name and had a right to do so in the eyes of the law as well as in the eyes of society. As he sat and brooded, Ross took in a scene he would never forget and which he could not forgive.

6

After the ceremony, the newlyweds set off for Paris from Victoria station where they paused only for Olive to send a telegram to let her mother know of the marriage and the address in Paris where they would be staying. A week or so earlier Edward VII had sent a message of congratulation to Mrs Custance on her daughter's engagement. Now the message came through that he was most displeased with the marriage and elopement of Olive with Lord Alfred Douglas. To have married the disgraced and penniless Douglas had been a bad move. Herbert Warren, still president of Magdalen, made it clear where his allegiance lay, and wrote to Montagu: 'You will know how sorry I am to think of how your chivalrous head and your loyal unsuspecting temper must have been tried.'[41]

Colonel Custance went straight to Scotland Yard and demanded to see their records on Lord Alfred Douglas, as Croft-Cooke says, with 'the notion common to his class and period that there were only about a dozen homosexuals in the country and all of them known to the police'.[42] To his surprise the police had nothing on Douglas. Although, in the public's eyes, he was as guilty as Wilde had been, the evidence against him was negligible. Also his marriage had taken place in a perfectly legal manner. On the face of it the Colonel had no reason to object. He must have been furious, but as Douglas was a lord, and since the marriage was a *fait accompli* he clearly viewed it advisable to get on with his daughter and new son-in-law. He and Mrs Custance invited them to spend a fortnight after their honeymoon at the Custance country seat, Weston Old Hall in Norfolk.

Lady Queensberry agreed to pay her son an allowance of £500 a year and wrote to inform the Custances of this fact. She also promised to pay any rents to which they might be liable. Wilfrid Scawen Blunt paid the cost of their eloping to Paris. He was delighted at the union and saw his cousin as having been saved by it. Indeed, the Wyndham family was relieved that Douglas had eloped with a woman, but as Percy Wyndham said to Wilfrid, 'Anything short of murder in the Douglas family is a source of congratulation.'[43]

Colonel Custance was a typical Victorian father with a military background. Ignorant of culture, full of prejudice and used to being in control, he was an imposing figure. Over six feet tall and nearing sixty, he had commanded a battalion in the Boer War. Olive told John Betjeman a story that sums up the kind of man he was. One day she had been walking with him 'down a street in the back of Cromer where some bungalows had been built on Custance land. Her father, who was immensely tall, leaned down and looked in through the windows of a bungalow and said, "Good Lord, do you mean to say people actually live in these things?"'[44]

It must have cost him a lot to allow Lord Alfred Douglas into his house. Their first meeting, oddly, mirrored Queensberry's introduction by his son to Oscar Wilde. Before Queensberry had started his campaign of vitriol he had come across his son dining with Wilde in a restaurant. Queensberry was charmed by him, and likewise, when Colonel Custance met Alfred Douglas he was both impressed and won over.

Colonel Custance's great love in his retirement was field sports, and fishing in particular. Although he no longer rode to hounds he must have enjoyed Douglas's hunting talk, and anecdotes of the shooting in Scotland. His surprise and pleasure were immense and he might even have felt some satisfaction in his daughter's choice. Douglas had never fished, Custance taught him and the two men got on well.

The success of their first visit together to Weston Hall paved the way for many more over the next few years, and when Olive's mother died, a couple of years after her daughter's marriage, Douglas went alone to visit his father-in-law and was a great comfort to him. As Olive later wrote, it was a 'radiant beginning'.[45]

What pleased Colonel Custance most of all was the birth of his grandson, on 17 November 1902. Wilfrid Scawen Blunt gave the child one of his names but refused to be godfather, so Freddie Manners-Sutton stepped in. Christened Raymond Wilfrid Sholto Douglas, he was, as Mary Hyde has written, 'a beautiful infant and became an attractive, affectionate child, healthy but highly strung'.[46] Raymond had been born into an unstable and increasingly fraught environment. Custance and his wife had no son of their own and Colonel Custance interfered in Raymond's upbringing, trying to take over the father's role.

The years of Raymond's baby and childhood were the happiest of Douglas's married life. Not only was he in love with his wife, he was an adoring father, and he was surrounded by his family and friends. His cousin Pamela Wyndham was married to Edward Tennant and they lived together at Wilsford in Wiltshire. On one visit to her she showed Douglas an old farmhouse named Lake Farm, which was up for sale. It was a short walk to the river Avon, with enough trout to keep Douglas occupied for many hours, and seemed perfect. He and Olive moved there two years after Raymond's birth. Able to write poetry at leisure and indulge in as much shooting and fishing as he liked, Douglas was idyllically happy.

7

It would be a mistake to assume that Douglas's marriage led him to some kind of Damascus-style conversion from his previous lifestyle to a settled family one. When he met Olive his homosexual activities were suspended but he did not drop his old friends. Only a few months after his marriage he told his wife in a letter that Maurice Schwabe was staying with him,[47] and he stayed in touch with Reginald Turner, Max Beerbohm and More Adey.

The publication of the first biography of Wilde came in 1902 with Robert Sherard's *The Story of an Unhappy Friendship*. Although there was nothing in it that concerned Douglas he thought the book 'the work of a journalist "a *réclame*" and written for no better object than the desire of the author to put a few shillings in his own pocket'. This was the first of a number of books Sherard wrote on Wilde, all of which tried to whitewash Wilde from any stain of 'sexual sin' and, as Douglas recognised, *The Story of an Unhappy Friendship* showed 'a great deal more about Sherard in it than about Wilde'.[48] In 1902 Walter Ledger wrote to Douglas asking tentatively for information about Wilde's bibliography. Douglas replied, 'You have no reason to apologise to me for writing to me as I regard it as an honour that I should be considered an "authority" on Mr Oscar Wilde's works and that my name should be associated with his.'[49]

In 1905 Robert Ross issued an expurgated edition of *De Profundis*. His introduction to the work hinted that the addressee of the *De Profundis* letter had been himself; indeed, several early writers on Wilde mistakenly claimed this.[50] Douglas reviewed the book in *Motorist and Traveller*, to which he had probably been asked to contribute because he was a well-known driver and car enthusiast. He described it as an 'interesting but rather pathetically ineffective book', and though he conceded that 'the trace of the master hand is still visible, and the book contains much that is profound and subtle on the philosophy of Christ as conceived by this modern evangelist of the gospel of Life and Literature', he concluded that it 'certainly cannot rank within measurable distance of his best work'.[51] Ross was clearly unhappy with Douglas's view and the young novelist Compton Mackenzie recorded in his diary what happened when Douglas interrupted a discussion at Ross's rooms when More Adey and Reginald Turner were also present.

> Douglas came in and stood on the fender fidgeting and scratching himself as usual and kept sliding off it. Then Robbie [Ross] read a letter from G.B. Shaw to point out that *De Profundis* was Wilde's final score off the British public, and that it was a gigantic *blague*, the final pose even in prison.

Douglas said Shaw was probably right and Robbie got angry. Douglas criticised Wilde's life in Paris and Robbie said the one most to blame for that was Douglas himself. Douglas lost his temper, kicked the fender and marched out of the room. He came back for a moment and told Robbie he did not know what he was talking about. Then he slammed the door, and presently downstairs we heard the front door slam.[52]

Croft-Cooke's account of the incident claims that when Douglas tackled Ross on *De Profundis* he

> . . . explained that it was a long letter which Wilde had written in prison to him, Ross, and contained a lot of abuse of Bosie and other people which Ross was cutting out. 'It will make,' he said, 'a very interesting book on Wilde and his character.'
>
> Bosie was furious, particularly when Ross refused to show him the MS. He abused Ross who said: 'If you talk to me like that I'll publish the manuscript as it stands and that will finish you off.'
>
> There were further exchanges in which Ross reminded Bosie of letters of his – presumably to Ross – which he had, and Bosie said he was no better than a blackmailer.[53]

On this occasion in 1905 the quarrel was sorted out, but it alerted Douglas to what Ross was capable of doing. He had sent Ross letters during the nineties that might prove damaging to him now. That Ross had kept these letters was one thing, but to blackmail Douglas with them was quite another. Ross still had the highly compromising letter Douglas had written to him from Biskra in early 1895, in which he reported that he had taken up with a fourteen-year-old lad of incredible beauty who resembled a gazelle (Douglas was twenty-three) with whom he made love once, sometimes twice, every day. Ross knew that one day he might need it.

In 1905 George Montagu married a girl from New York. Douglas had dinner with Edmund Phipps, his old friend from *Pentagram* and *Spirit-Lamp* days, who had met George's bride, Alberta. He told Douglas that he was shocked to find that she was not only ugly but also 'exceedingly common'.[54] Douglas could not help but gloat. George, who had 'treated (Douglas) badly',[55] had come out worst in the end – at least in Douglas's view.

8

Although Wilde and all his circle undoubtedly remained important to Douglas, he took a more philosophical outlook on life and his reputation. Safe in the comforts of family life he became a different man. For a time he ceased to worry about what the world thought of him. In 1905, before moving to Wiltshire, he spent a 'glorious June afternoon' in his garden in Chelsea talking to the Wilde enthusiast Max Meyerfield, who asked him 'the unfortunate question, "Are you not rather afraid of the opinion of posterity?" Douglas's lips curled, he shrugged his shoulders and replied at once: "Posterity! What does posterity mean to me? My son!" '[56]

Posterity, or at least the judgement of oneself in a more general sense, had certainly been on Douglas's mind in 1902 when he wrote one of his finest sonnets, 'Dies Amara Valde'. It owes much in subject matter to the poem that probably sparked it, the thirteenth-century work later incorporated into the mass for the dead, the 'Dies Irae'.

Throughout his youth Douglas nursed a peculiar morbidity, which he lost as he grew older. At sixty-three he recalled an incident after a dinner given for him by Lord Encombe, in celebration of Douglas's twenty-first birthday. He remembered that 'I was so overcome with melancholy at the thought of my "vanished youth" that I retired after dinner to my bedroom and wept.'[57] At thirty-two, when his cousin and friend Lionel Johnson died he was reminded again of his own mortality.

> Ah me, ah me, the day when I am dead,
> And all of me that was immaculate
> Given to darkness, lies in shame or state,
> Surely my soul shall come to that last bed
> And weep for all the whiteness that was red,
> Standing beside the ravished ivory gate
> When the pale dwelling place is desolate
> And all the golden rooms untenanted.
>
> For in the smoke of that last holocaust,
> When to the regions of unsounded air
> That which is deathless still aspires and tends,

Whither my helpless soul shall we be tossed?
To what disaster of malign Despair,
Or terror of unfathomable ends?

Frank Harris, who became, Douglas said, 'the greatest admirer of my poetry', described this as 'the best sonnet ever written in the English language'.[58] Shortly after Raymond's birth, John Lane had brought out Olive's second book of poems, *Rainbows*, but of more interest was her third and last collection which appeared late in 1905. Entitled *The Blue Bird* it contained a dedication 'To My Husband', the end of which contains a fine description of them both.

I have bowed down
Before the light of beauty all my life,
And now, O poet passionate and brave,
O lover with the beautiful sad face,
Like a shy child I bring you all my songs.

Douglas greatly admired all of his wife's poems, but especially those that expressed childishly simple sentiment. Typically her poetry portrayed a little girl's emotions. In a letter to her in 1905 from the Isle of Lewis where he was staying for a week's shooting, Douglas thanked her for a poem she had sent him called 'Angels', which appeared in *The Blue Bird*. He liked its sincerity and told her he thought it 'very beautiful'.[59]

When life is difficult I dream
Of how the angels dance in heaven . . .[60]

He was still writing nonsense verse at this time, and in 1906 Duckworth brought out *The Placid Pug*. The following year saw a reprint of *The Duke of Bewick*, alongside *The Pongo Papers*. *The Placid Pug* was a well-presented book, with humorous illustrations by 'P.P.'. It was a success and Douglas sent copies to all his friends, including Reginald Turner with whom he had dined in Boulogne the previous year.[61] Duckworth brought it out in time for Christmas[62] and sales were fairly good – which was encouraging because, for the first time, a book with his name on the front cover sold:

The Placid Pug
and other rhymes
by
The Belgian Hare
(Lord Alfred Douglas)
Author of 'Tails with a Twist' and 'The Duke of Bewick'

The books also contained verse that had been published in a newspaper: some from *The Pongo Papers* had appeared in Frank Harris's *Vanity Fair*, while those for *The Placid Pug* had appeared in the *English Review*, a weekly paper to which Olive also contributed. The editor of that short-lived organ was a man who would play an unfortunately prominent role in Douglas's life from now on.

9

T. W. H. Crosland had been brought up in the suburbs of Leeds, and was the son of a Nonconformist preacher. Quarrelsome, untidy and an alcoholic, he had a manner that he called blunt but which most termed rude. He could write any kind of prose at speed but, although described by many as a genius, his reputation has survived only through his litigious links with Douglas. One colleague described him as a 'shabby, uncouth, boorish-looking individual with dark, dank locks straying across a pallid forehead'.[63] He had edited the *English Review* with some considerable success: he had got poems out of Olive and Alfred Douglas, as well as from Pamela Tennant, and had done so without paying for them. The Douglases had met him because Olive's *Blue Bird* had been published by the Marlborough Press, which also owned Crosland's paper. It took a little time for Crosland and Douglas to decide that they liked each other: they were polar opposites – the one an aristocratic young poet of 'exceptional beauty',[64] the other a grubby, working-class hack – but something attracted them.

At the end of 1904 Douglas confessed, 'I hardly ever write anything now, only very seldom a sonnet with great effort',[65] and that he felt that what he could produce was not as good 'as what I used to write'.[66] But those of Douglas's completed sonnets from this period that havee survived are certainly up to his best. While staying at La Brague in 1903 he wrote one that first appeared under the title 'Before the Dawn', but later changed to 'Premonition'.[67] It is very much in the same vein as '*Dies Amara Valde*', but perhaps shows even more disillusion and dejection:

> O born to be rejected and denied,
> Scorn of the years and sport of all the days,
> Must the gray future still repeat the past?
> O thrice betrayed and seven times crucified,
> Is there no issue from unhappy ways,
> No peace, no hope, no loving arms at last?

Like 'Dies Amara Valde' the religious imagery is foremost, and in comparing his own sufferings to the sufferings of Christ, Douglas set a precedent for himself that he developed later on. But in this poem, combined with this previously rare religiosity is a reminder of his earlier 'pagan' poems. Love of '*Two Loves*' has become, rather than a physical being, a grand concept along with Truth and, most importantly, Faith. The themes in Douglas's poems were changing from physical to metaphysical preoccupations.

In 1905 Douglas wrote 'To a Silent Poet', which he admitted was about himself, and as his production of verse was declining rapidly, he found himself writing poetry about not being able to write poetry. However it is clear that his muse had not deserted him.

10

Since 1903 he had been engaged with a series of six sonnets he wrote to his wife. He was very much in love with her. 'It is dreadful that you should be so tormented by illness and troubles' he wrote to her, when she had fallen ill in 1906. 'Every wound to you is a sharp knife to my heart. I hate to think that I cannot bear your hurts for you.'[68] They shared a mutual romantic adoration and perhaps saw each other as more than just husband or wife – as something akin to a great event in literature. As Olive wrote to Douglas before his departure to America: 'I read Shakespeare's sonnets and wondered why people should have worried so much who they were written to . . . because, you see, I know it was *you* . . . Shakespeare *must* have met you in another world!'[69]

Douglas's sonnets to Olive were among his most moving, and have attracted critical adulation.

In his 1913 book, *The Genius of Lord Alfred Douglas*, William Sorley Brown noted the first of the six sonnets in particular:

It so happens that the idea contained in this sonnet is similar to that of a certain sonnet of Shakespeare, beginning 'When to the sessions of sweet silent thought'. Some critics have considered this to be a terrible offence, and one individual had the audacity to state in a certain newspaper some time back that the Douglas sonnet was an imitation or 'fakement' of Shakespeare. We recollect having crossed swords with him in this matter, and we endeavoured to show that he was in error. What this reviewer had not considered was the point as to which of the two poets has made the best use of the idea, and, in our opinion, any unprejudiced and competent person who cares to make a comparison between the two sonnets referred to will find that Lord Alfred Douglas gives better expression to the idea than Shakespeare.[70]

To Olive I

When in dim dreams I trace the tangled maze
Of the old years that held and fashioned me,
And to the sad assize of Memory
From the wan roads and misty time-trod ways,
The timid ghosts of dead forgotten days
Gather to hold their piteous colloquy,
Chiefly my soul bemoans the lack of thee
And those lost seasons empty of thy praise.

Yet surely thou wast there when life was sweet,
(We walked knee deep in flowers) and thou wast there,
When in dismay and sorrow and unrest,
With weak bruised hands and wounded bleeding feet,
I fought with beasts and wrestled with despair
And slept (how else?) upon thine unseen breast.

Although it was the first of the 'To Olive' sonnets that caused notice, the last two are perhaps the best. The fifth was probably the one Douglas thought best, as he decided to use it in his *Autobiography*. As he wrote there, whatever his feelings became later for Olive, the poems remain, and 'all the water of the sea will never wash them out'.[71] They are a profound and beautiful testimony to Douglas's love for his wife.

To Olive V

When we were Pleasure's minions, you and I,
When we mocked grief and held disaster cheap,
And shepherded all joys like willing sheep
That love their shepherd; when a passing sigh
Was all the cloud that flecked our April sky,
I floated on an unimagined deep,
I loved you as a tired child loves sleep,
I lived and laughed and loved, and knew not why.

Now have I known the uttermost rose of love;
The years are very long, but love is longer;
I love you so, I have no time to hate
Even those wolves without. The great winds move
All their dark batteries to our fragile gate:
The world is very strong, but love is stronger.

Chapter 5

'When was ought but stones for English Prophets?
(1907–1913)

Few poets can make a living from their poetry and Douglas was well aware of this. He earned almost nothing from his contributions to papers and the books he published never brought in much money.[1] He knew that he had to find work yet he had few qualifications. Perhaps his dealings with newspapers over his poetic contributions led him to consider the world of journalism. Pamela Tennant saw this idea as a way for Douglas out of his rut and asked her husband to buy a paper for him to edit. The *Academy* was being sold for £2,000 and Edward Tennant could easily afford the asking price, but he was a Liberal MP, while Douglas was a 'Diehard' Tory.[2] Tennant was also the brother of Margot Asquith, and therefore the brother-in-law of the next Prime Minister, H. H. Asquith. He clearly had some worries about putting a paper into the hands of his wife's cousin but hoped that Douglas would concentrate the journal on literature.

Douglas's previous experience as an editor was confined to his work on the *Pentagram* and the *Spirit Lamp*. In their own ways, both had been a success, but the *Pentagram* had been designed for Wykehamists and the *Spirit Lamp* for largely homosexual undergraduates. Neither had been reliant on financial success. Douglas was not the ideal choice of editor for the *Academy*, but he was delighted with his new post, and described his appointment to Olive as 'a great victory'.[3]

He was installed in offices in Lincoln's Inn Fields with a secretary and an office boy. The secretary, who was also the sub-editor, was Alice Head, who later became editor of *Country Life*. She admired Douglas and wrote later, 'As all the world knows, he is a great poet, a man of engaging personality. He gave me a taste for good literature and fine poetry and I am everlastingly grateful for his many kindnesses.'[4] Apparently the working environment was congenial and enjoyed by all, including the office boy who always referred to Douglas as 'The

Lord'. Alice Head wrote that under Douglas's editorship the *Academy* reached 'unexampled heights of brilliance',[5] while Douglas modestly described his editorship as being the 'palmy days of that journal'.[6] Certainly, in some aspects, it was a great success. In addition to poems contributed by Olive, Pamela Tennant and himself, he found a large number of talented contributors, including several members of the old Wilde circle, such as Robert Ross, More Adey and Reginald Turner. More importantly, he gave a chance to many of the upcoming generation of writers, who called themselves the 'New Bohemians' and were led by Arthur Machen, though the only member of the group to achieve any lasting fame was Richard Middleton, whom Douglas 'discovered'.

The Academy proved a practice ground for young talent, but Douglas was a strict editor and told his contributors that if they gave him something he judged not of their best he would not print it, for their sake.[7] One talent, some of whose earliest poems were published at Douglas's request, became rather better known in the next decade: Siegfried Sassoon. There were strong similarities between Sassoon and Douglas: both were poets and sportsmen, particularly keen on horses, and both were primarily homosexuals who married in middle age. A contemporary of Sassoon, who also made his name later with his war poetry and who contributed to the *Academy* at Douglas's invitation, was Rupert Brooke, one of the few younger poets Douglas admired – mainly because he could write a successful sonnet. Douglas was always proud that he had spotted Brooke's talent early.

The *Academy* drew praise, but also criticism. T.W.H. Crosland wrote in the *Future*, the magazine he took over after the demise of the *English Review*, 'So far from establishing itself as a literary journal of broad literary dispositions and quality, the *Academy* under Lord Alfred Douglas's editorship, has exhibited a distinct tendency to deteriorate into a feeble organ of the feebler and lesser cults, and at the present moment it is of no more use to the serious principles it might have served than the proverbial headache.'[8] This was typical of the perpetually abusive Crosland, but Douglas admired the harsh northerner's knack with invective. He invited Crosland to join the staff of the *Academy*, first as a contributor then as his sub-editor.

Crosland radically changed the tone of what had been a generally harmless and respectable journal. Under his influence, it became, as Maureen Borland, wrote, 'less a journal of cultural excellence and more an organ of political and religious bigotry'.[9] Alice Head recorded her indignation that, in the intervals between swigging from a brandy bottle Crosland 'alienated most of Lord Alfred's friends and tried to run the business on dubious lines of his own'.[10]

2

Despite Crosland's activities, Douglas continued to oversee the literary side of the journal. Years later he explained his ideas on literary criticism: 'I always told my reviewers that in reviewing a book they were at liberty either to "slate" or praise. "If you slate anyone you must give chapter and verse. You cannot, in any paper that I edit, write 'so-and-so is a bad poet, his lines do not scan and he has no sense of rhythm,' unless you prove what you say by adequate quotation from his own writing." '[11] Thanks to this system the poetry criticism seems to have been uncontentious but feathers were ruffled in other areas of the arts. In May 1908 a review of George Bernard Shaw's latest play, *Getting Married*, was published with the title 'For Shame, Mr Shaw!' The reviewer described it as 'Not a play at all, but a conversation.' He went on to explain that 'Mr Shaw, the vegetarian, teetotaller, non-smoker' did 'not possess a masculine intellect', finishing, provocatively, 'The sooner Mr Shaw learns that he is not in a position to preach the better it will be for him.'[12] Shaw was livid.

'Dear Lord Alfred Douglas, Who on earth have you been handing over your dramatic criticism to?. Your man, who must have been frightfully drunk, has achieved the following startling libel.' Here he quoted the misreports and innuendos in the article and pointed out that they were worth about 'twenty-five hundred pounds apiece' to the manager, producer and others 'libelled'. He generously offered to drop the matter if the substance of the article was withdrawn in the next issue of the *Academy*. On this matter Shaw was certainly in the right; as he pointed out in his letter, 'the writer gives himself away hopelessly at the beginning by saying that he left the house at the end of twenty-five minutes. Later on he describes a scene which he did not wait for, and contrives to get both a libel and a flat mis-statement of fact into his reference.' In suggesting that Douglas arrange for the 'friendliest' way out of the situation, that is the unreserved withdrawal of the article, Shaw asked him to 'let me have a line so that I may try and smooth matters'.[13]

Douglas would have none of it and was fiercely defensive of his reviewer:

> I strongly resent the accusation of being drunk which you bring against the writer of the article. It seems to me that it is characteristic of the feminine quality of your intellect, to which reference was made in the article, to make such an outrageous suggestion. As a matter of fact, I wrote the article myself. If I misheard any particular sentence in the dialogue the error was, on your own showing, a very trifling one, and it is ludicrous to suggest that it is libellous. The part of the play which I heard simply teems with indecencies, and I should be delighted to go into the witness-box in any court and say so.

Douglas finished his letter by informing Shaw that he had no feeling of personal malice towards him, but wrote the review out of duty as a critic. He gave Shaw the address of his solicitors in case Shaw decided to act upon his threat.[14]

Shaw informed Douglas that it was not for himself that he was intervening, but for the managers, producers, actors – and Douglas himself who, he insisted, 'MUST have been drunk – frightfully drunk – or in some equivalent condition' when reviewing his play, adding, 'No normal man behaves like that.' He informed Douglas that he was also insisting that the article be withdrawn to get Douglas 'out of a scrape'.[15]

Douglas replied, with all the aristocratic *hauteur* he could muster:

> Dear Mr Bernard Shaw,
>   Your letter is a piece of childish impertinence, but as it was evidently written in a fit of hysterical bad temper, I shall not count it against you. I am immensely amused by your professed desire to 'get me out of a scrape'. I do not consider that I am in a scrape at all, and I think you will find that I am a person who is very well able to look after himself without any assistance from you.
>   Yours faithfully
>   Alfred Douglas.[16]

In a splendid rejoinder Shaw closed the correspondence, aware that Douglas could drag such a thing out for a considerable time:

Dear Lord Alfred Douglas,

I asked you for a friendly reparation: you have given me a savage revenge. However, perhaps it was the best way out. As you have owned up, we are satisfied; and the public will forgive you for the sake of your blazing boyishness.

There is always the question – Who is to edit the editor? Fortunately in this case there are two Douglases – A.D. the poet and – shall I say? – the hereditary Douglas. Make A.D. the editor. It needs extraordinary conscientiousness, delicacy and Catholicism to criticise unscrupulously, brutally and free-thinkingly, as the *Academy* is trying to do, and, indeed, derives all its interest and value from doing. That hereditary Douglas, when he gets loose from A.D., is capable of wrecking a paper – even of wrecking himself. Most people are – hence the need for editors. Excuse my preaching; I am a born improver of occasions. *Sans rancune*

George Bernard Shaw.[17]

One individual more than capable of 'conscientious, delicate and Catholic criticism' was Ada Leverson, whom Douglas recruited to his list of reviewers. While offering her the opportunity to review Somerset Maugham's new play *Penelope* he told her that, in the *Academy*, 'Nobody is allowed to write "something nice" about a book or a play because the author happens to be a friend, or to attack because he happens to be an enemy. It is necessary to say this because I find that on most if not all other papers, log-rolling and its contrary are taken for granted.'[18]

3

Under Lord Alfred Douglas's rule the circulation of the *Academy* rose every week, but its editor received strong and frequent criticism. In October 1908 he wrote to his wife, 'All this criticism does get on my nerves when I know I am doing the right thing. Nobody likes the *Academy* but on the other hand *they all read it*, and I don't care how angry it makes people as long as they read it. The circulation goes on rising (we are printing extra copies this week) and we have more adverts again. It wouldn't be much use if everybody thought it a dear sweet delightful paper, and the circulation went down and the adverts didn't come in, would it?'[19]

But the criticisms were coming from closer quarters than enraged dramatists and readers. Pamela and Edward Tennant were increasingly agitated at the journal's anti-Liberal tone, and Tennant, who was hoping for a peerage from Asquith (which he finally received, making him Lord Glenconner), made strong representations against Douglas. One of his 'numerous complaints' was directed at an article of Douglas's, which Douglas himself happened to think was 'particularly good'.[20]

Douglas responded with 'Rewards'. In 1896 he had written after Wilde's imprisonment, 'I do not like the British nation. I detest it. As connoisseurs in art they are altogether beneath contempt. They have always stoned the prophets and from time immemorial have sought to immortalise the quacks and indifferent in art. But, after all, their language is mine and I love it. They have a literature which, as regards poetry, is second to none and is equalled only by the ancient Greeks.'[21] He picked up this theme in 'Rewards', which became the sonnet he found most relevant to himself for the rest of his life. In it he had moved away from the 'Greek' ethic he had espoused in 1896 and replaced it with the Christian alternative. Douglas believed that Milton had written a few of the fifty or so great sonnets in the English language[22] and knew them all well. In 'Rewards' he borrowed the rhymes from Milton's great sonnet 'On the late Massacre at Piedmont', which deals with the martyrdom of Catholics and inspired Douglas's use of it.

> From the beginning, when was aught but stones
> For English Prophets? Starved not Chatterton?
> Was Keats bay-crowned, was Shelley smiled upon?
> Marlowe died timely. Well for him, his groans
> On stake or rack else had out-moaned the moans
> Of his own Edward; and that light that shone,
> That voice, that trumpet, that white-throated swan,
> When found he praise, save for 'his honoured bones'?
>
> Honour enough for bones! But for live flesh
> Cold-eyed mistrust, and ever watchful fear,

> Mingled with homage given grudgingly
> From cautious mouths. And all the while a mesh
> To snare the singing-bird, to trap the deer,
> And bind the feet of Immortality.

Tennant cannot have failed to notice the resonances in the poem, which show a turning-point in Douglas's life and work: the homosexual Marlowe, who escaped only in death the persecution Wilde suffered, was not an artist with whom Douglas would willingly associate himself over the next decade, but he was proud to consider himself of the same poetic tradition as Keats and Shelley.

In 'Rewards' he uses the same image of the 'singing-bird' snared, its song stopped, that he had used in 'The Dead Poet' to describe the death of Wilde. Keats had been saved by his poetry from the stones of England and the English, as had Shelley and Wilde, but only after death. Yet if the stones of English prudery and hypocrisy had been flung at Shelley for his views and the way he expressed them, times had changed little in Douglas's eyes. Influenced by Crosland, he formed the idea that their anti-government rantings in the *Academy* matched the stand taken by Shelley a hundred years earlier. However, he was rather more eloquent on artistic matters. In one of the last issues of the *Academy* he wrote, echoing 'Rewards':

> It is a profitless task to speak the peace of beauty into deaf ears, to seek to force her presence upon hearts into whose dark chambers her light has never penetrated, because there is a blindness of the spiritual eye as well as of the physical, a blindness that is from birth, and so incurable. We have piped unto you and ye have not danced, we have mourned unto you and ye have not wept, has been the cry in the hearts of how many singers who have cast their roses and pearls before the feet of swine.

Late in 1909 Douglas published a particularly fierce attack on Asquith, and Tennant wrote to him to tell him that he had gone too far, and that he had decided to sell the paper.

If Douglas was willing to accept this end to his career as an editor, Crosland was not. He persuaded him to fight for it tooth and nail. According to Douglas, Crosland told him to think that 'I was not just the poor dependent on the half-contemptuous whim of the millionaire *nouveau riche* who paid my miserable salary, but the editor of a powerful paper installed into a position from which, if I showed fight, it would be no easy job to oust me.'[23] Crosland persuaded Douglas to let him speak with Tennant. He adopted a 'bullying and aggressive tone'[24] and got what he wanted. Tennant backed down, and agreed to give Douglas the paper along with £500. Since the *Academy* was running at a loss of a couple of thousand pounds a year, the gift was not particularly helpful. Also Crosland's hectoring of Tennant ruined Douglas's previously close relationship with the family.

But the *Academy* remained and the course Douglas took with it was both foolish and damaging.

4

The litigious and libellous career of Lord Alfred Douglas began unspectacularly in 1909, when the undergraduate magazines *The Isis*, at Oxford, and *The Cambridge Magazine*, at Cambridge, almost simultaneously published articles about Wilde, in which the references to Douglas were defamatory. Crosland served a writ on both magazines, at which point both apologised for the libels and offered fifty guineas in damages, along with the dismissal of the editors, to avoid legal proceedings. Both offers were accepted, and Douglas was delighted. The comments had been substantially milder than the insults he had received for years, and the idea that he could be protected from them by the very system that sparked them off gave him great pleasure. He also saw how profitable this legal roulette wheel might prove. He and Crosland headed towards their first major action with all the daring of two naughty schoolboys flaunting a new weapon.

Some of the articles written by Crosland and Douglas in the *Academy* had caused considerable annoyance to various parties, but actual defamation of individuals was a more dangerous game. When the *Academy* fell completely into the hands of Douglas and Crosland, Freddie Manners-Sutton had said to Douglas that if it ever got into financial difficulties he might try to help them find money. Such difficulties arose in the middle of 1909 and Douglas first approached Wilfrid Scawen Blunt, among others, for money. Blunt telegraphed, 'Just leaving for Clouds. You must not count on me in this matter.' Douglas's reply was unworthy of him: 'Did not count on you. I never count on anyone who can't write sonnets'.[25] He entrusted to Crosland the task of asking Manners-Sutton for the help he had offered. Crosland had no idea of the common courtesies involved in taking someone up on a generous offer. He stormed into the situation, demanding £500 from Manners-Sutton, who refused. Crosland, 'doing him a favour', suggested that they settle on a mere £150. This was also refused. Manners-Sutton claimed that Douglas was drawing too high a salary and that he would advance them no money until it was reduced. Crosland reported this to Douglas, who was livid. Although Manners-Sutton stated that he had parted on friendly terms with Crosland, Douglas was given the impression, presumably by Crosland, that Manner-Sutton had behaved with 'gross impudence and brutal insolence'[26] during the meeting. As far as Douglas could see, he had been let down by yet another friend. He wrote to his son's godfather to tell him that he would never again be allowed into his house by either him or his wife. In his *Autobiography* Douglas wrote that his falling out with Manners-Sutton was 'the worst turn Crosland ever did me, and one which let me in for an enormous amount of unpleasantness, grief and regret.[27]

Although the composition of the letter might have vented Douglas's anger and closed the matter in his mind, Crosland could not leave it alone. A few days later, an article was published in the *Academy* that mentioned an unnamed member of a certain noble house who, the article claimed, was 'connected with two publishing firms which carry on two very different classes of business, for while one firm, of which he is the principal shareholder, is engaged in publishing various works and translations of various Christian liturgies, the other has gone in chiefly for dubious stories of a highly spiced character and anything else that will bring grist to the mill without actually compelling the intervention of the police'.[28] At the end of the article was a vague threat that the names of the firms might be revealed in a future issue.

Anybody who knew anything about the publishing world, as many *Academy* readers did, would have known to whom the article referred. Certainly Manners-Sutton had no doubts and his secretary wrote twice to the *Academy* asking that a notice be put into the paper's next issue stating that he was not the individual referred to. Crosland's reply was to the point. 'You say that a paragraph appeared in the *Academy* of June 12 which is a libel upon the Hon. Freddie Manners-Sutton. I am not concerned to give the names of the persons to whom the paragraph in question refers, and if your client chooses to apply what we have said to himself, he is welcome.' He concluded,

> We do not propose to oblige you by stating that Mr Manners-Sutton is not the gentleman referred to. Rather, at our own time and when we have completed our investigations, we shall be disposed to say that he is the gentleman. With regard to the action you threaten, we have only to remark that in our view Mr Manners-Sutton is a person whom it would be difficult for reasonable people to libel. At the same time, if he wishes to make a fool of himself we shall be quite pleased to receive his writ.[29]

Freddie Manners-Sutton did not wish to make a fool of himself but, as Crosland must have known, there was no way that he could let the libel stand. So, Crosland, as promised, was delighted to receive a summons for criminal libel. The action brought a strong response from Douglas, and he informed his wife on 21 July 1909 of what had happened. 'That little beast Freddie has summoned Crosland for libel and the case comes on today . . . There is nothing in it and Freddie has not a leg to stand on. Newton [his own solicitor who had taken the case on for Crosland] says that he thinks he can get the case dismissed right off.' Douglas was confident of this because Crosland was playing a card familiar to him: he had pleaded justification. Manners-Sutton was about to go down the same road as Wilde. Douglas did not see this. He told Olive that Freddie was acting out of spite and malice, and added that Crosland was more than happy with proceedings and was, indeed, rather looking forward to them.[30]

Crosland came up at Bow Street where the magistrate, Sir Albert de Reutzen, suggested that a withdrawal be made and an apology given. Crosland would have none of it, but it was Douglas who spoke out. He shouted to Crosland across the court room, 'Justify, justify up to the hilt,' and turning to Manners-Sutton called out, 'Take him to the Old Bailey!' After that, there was no possibility of a withdrawal so Crosland was committed for trial at the Central Criminal Court. Douglas and Crosland could indeed justify their claims up to the hilt, and knowing this but without thinking to try to save the reputation of a former friend by a settlement, Douglas set himself up to take revenge on a man who had slighted him.

When the case came to court Douglas spent forty minutes in the witness-box and was on the attack from the start. He made speeches to the jury and tackled counsel constantly. About half-way through the cross-examination, counsel appealed to the judge for protection from the witness, which was refused. At the end it was said by some in court that Douglas 'simply ate' the man, who was considered one of the deadliest cross-examiners in the courts. One of the counsel's biggest mistakes was his attempt to drag in Douglas's connection with Wilde, which had nothing to do with the case in hand and was a blatant attempt to sully Douglas's name, which won him sympathy from the jury. It also gave Douglas the opportunity to say something in court that he had longed to say since 1895. When asked if there was 'ever anything to be ashamed of in your relationship with [Wilde]', Douglas stated simply, and without hesitation, 'No, there was not.'[31]

The jury took almost no time to bring in a verdict of not guilty for Crosland, which established that the libels on Manners-Sutton were true and had been published in the public interest. It was humiliating for him, but it also gave Douglas a false impression of the workings of a court. The success of the action and his own shining performance in the box convinced him that the courts were worth reverting to in the future.

Eventually Manners-Sutton and Douglas made up their quarrel when, as arranged by Olive, they met up seven years later. Manners-Sutton died in 1918 and Douglas stayed with him only a couple of weeks before his death. According to Douglas, his friend came to understand that the action taken by him had been ill-advised and that Douglas's support of Crosland, as his friend and employer, had been a matter of principle.

In a nauseating display of gloating pomposity Crosland wrote an article on the outcome of the case, which appeared in the next issue of the *Academy*. He said that Mr Marshall Hall (who had acted for Manners-Sutton) should realise that his bullying cross-examining, 'while no doubt excellent when you are dealing with unintelligent policemen or frightened widows, is apt to get you into serious trouble when persons of average pluck and intelligence happen to come along'. He continued, 'The spectacle of the most relentless cross-examiner at the Bar appealing to the Common Sergeant for protection against a couple of literary persons such as ourselves and Lord Alfred Douglas is one which is long likely to be remembered in the humorous annals of the Old Bailey.'[32]

5

Far more worthwhile than the litigation, though of less public interest, were the activities of the Academy Publishing Company, which published a number of important books. Among these was a reprinted edition of Olive's *Poems*, and, in 1910, Margaret Jourdain's *Outdoor Breviary*. She was a friend of Ivy Compton-Burnett and Douglas considered that she had written 'many good sonnets'.[33] Perhaps the most important publication, though, was Douglas's first book of serious poetry since *The City of the Soul* in 1899. It consisted of nineteen sonnets, which represented all of Douglas's serious poetic achievements for almost a decade. With just twenty-nine pages, *Sonnets* was a flimsy volume, but the poetry contained in it not only showed that Douglas had refined his technique since the nineties but had dropped some of the mannerisms of that period. His use of imagery had matured, largely because he had moved away from the aesthetic attitudes of the previous decade and had adopted a tradition of Christian symbolism, which strikes the reader as more natural to him. 'Premonition' was included, as were 'Dies Amara Valde', 'Rewards', and 'Beauty and the Hunter', which exuded what the poet himself later admitted was 'really Catholic mysticism'.[34] Many of the collection had appeared in the *Academy*, including all six 'To Olive' sonnets. The 'Dedication' to the volume was a new sonnet to Olive, in which Douglas harks back touchingly to his own first completed and not entirely successful sonnet, 'Amoris Vincula'. It shares the gentleness that marks out Oscar Wilde's 'To My Wife, with a copy of my poems'.

> What shall I say, what word, what cry recall,
> What god invoke, what star, what amulet,
> To make a sonnet pay a hopeless debt,
> Or bind a winged heart with a madrigal?
> Weak words are vainer than no words at all,
> The barrier of flesh divides us yet;
> Your spirit, like a bird caught in a net,
> Beats ever an impenetrable wall.
>
> This is my book, and there as in a glass,
> Darkly beheld, the shadow of my mind

> Wavers and flickers like a flame of fire.
> So through your eyes, it may be, it will pass,
> And I shall hold my wild shy bird confined
> In the gold cage of shadowless desire.

Crosland contributed a 'Note' at the end of the book, pontificating that 'the poet of authentic parts should be entirely indifferent to the "reception" which his work may receive at the hands of his contemporaries', and went on, 'Nothing bites so sharply at the heart of the ha'penny reviewer . . . as the appearance of a work of genius. In England at the present moment we have a hundred critics who believe that they know about the sonnet, and we have virtually only two or three critics who really do know. Similarly, we have a hundred poets who have been told by these same critics that they can write sonnets, and we have not more than three poets who really can write them.' What he apparently thought, but fortunately did not say, was that of those two or three critics who 'knew about' the sonnet, he was one and Douglas was another, and that among the three poets who could 'really write' sonnets were himself and Douglas.

A few years after the *Academy* closed, Crosland wrote one of the authoritative texts on the sonnet in his *The English Sonnet*. The opinions he expressed there and in the note to Douglas's 1909 *Sonnets* resemble Douglas's views put forward in his journalism and in his prefaces to his own and others' books. However, dogmatic adherence to traditional form and expression on which Douglas and Crosland insisted was not only didactic, it was limiting to their criticism. If the Petrarchan form was the only form of the sonnet worth writing then, of course, other poets were falling short. Certainly Crosland and Douglas knew what they were talking about – no other critic of the day had the same knowledge of the sonnet, its history and practice – but their criticism became somewhat simplistic. However, they profoundly admired each other's poetry, and Crosland concluded his 'Note' to Douglas's *Sonnets*,

> There is . . . a common impression abroad that English literature is very
> rich in proper sonnets. In point of fact it is not so rich as the vulgar
> imagine. Leaving out Shakespeare, who is a sonneteer to himself, Milton
> gave us a few good sonnets; Keats has given us a similar few: and the same
> holds true of Wordsworth, of Matthew Arnold, of Rossetti, and of

Swinburne. To this general few — probably not more than a hundred all told — a good number of the sonnets in this present book must be added. Several of them are as fine as the best, and, comparisons apart, several of them will stand on their pure merits so long as poetry is esteemed and so long as the English language is understood. And if anybody should think that the present writer oversteps the mark in thus assaying, what he has a perfect right and qualification to assay, let such a person go back and read again — and compare.

His words were bold but not outrageous, but they must have considerably bloated Douglas's ego. Such extravagant praise would be difficult to live up to.

The sale of *Sonnets* went well: the first edition of 500 copies sold out in a few weeks and the second edition almost as fast.[35] This probably helped make up John Lane's mind to issue *The City of the Soul*, for which Douglas wrote a preface.[36] In it he set down many of his ideas on aesthetics and poetry, advocated traditionalism in literature, and admitted that he had considered revising some of the blemishes he could now see in his early work. Having defined poetry as that which cannot be said in prose and stating that to write poetry for any other reason is 'to sin against the high muses', he added, 'A rigid application of this touchstone to the mass of contemporary poetry would have the result of wiping out at least ninety per cent of it from the necessity of consideration, which would be a very good thing indeed.' If applied to all of his poetry, he said, some of the verses in the latter part of the volume, that is, predominantly, the earliest ones, 'would not survive it'. 'These poems are the poems of extreme and comparative youth,' he informed his readers, 'and the interest they possess would, I believe, be impaired by revisions which a mature technical knowledge and a great alteration in point of view would dictate.' He had, of course, acquired a more mature technical knowledge since the first editions of the book, but of more interest is the 'great alteration' in the point of view of the poet, and why it had come about.

In November 1911 Douglas informed his wife that the *Mercure de France* were requesting permission to reissue the poems they had published in 1896, but that he would not allow it.[37] He was ashamed of their technical immaturity and of the content of some. He hoped that poems like 'Hymn to Physical Beauty' and 'Two Loves' would be forgotten. As he looked back at these works he must have seen how foolish he had been to set out at such an early age his ideas, loves and preoccupations. Extolling the virtues of homosexual rather than heterosexual passion had seemed a brave thing for an Oxford undergraduate of the 1890s to do, but it was a dangerous legacy for a twentieth-century husband and father.

6

Perhaps Douglas's attempt to break as cleanly as possible from his past provided part of the incentive for his increasingly intense religious belief. He had begun to adopt High Anglicanism from around the time he took over the *Academy*, and as the years passed his conviction grew. The article that had made Tennant drop the paper in 1908 had been about the suppression by Asquith of certain aspects of a Catholic procession around Westminister Cathedral. So Douglas's opinions had been entrenched for some time before, in May 1911, he faced up to what he had in the past described as 'tomfoolery'[38] and became a Catholic.

It is no surprise that Douglas made this turn-around during the first decade of the century: Rome provided a draw that was primarily aesthetic and secondarily spiritual. Wilde's preoccupation with Rome while an undergraduate at Oxford had been dominated by the former rather than the latter, but Douglas's conversion, as he was entering middle age, left him open for the rest of his life to the worry of lapsing into his old ways, and to the then suspicious attitude in Britain to Catholicism. But none of this seemed to worry him. He stated at the time, and never changed his mind, that becoming a Roman Catholic was quite the best thing he had ever done.[39]

Douglas's conversion highlighted the foolhardiness of a court action in which he had been involved the previous year. Spurred on by the success of the Manners-Sutton case, he responded, in attacking mode, to an article that appeared in the *Daily News* claiming that the *Academy* had passed into Roman hands: 'Your remarks regarding *Academy* in yesterday's *Daily News* are a combination of malicious falsehood, spiteful innuendo,' he telegraphed the writer, 'Presume this is a method of retaliating for unfavourable review in *The Academy*. I call upon you to withdraw and apologise or send me the name of your solicitors.'[40] The article's author, the Nonconformist Dr Horton, did not withdraw so in June 1910 a libel action began. It was a senseless piece of litigation for although Douglas had not yet converted, his views on Protestantism, as aired in court, showed that he was a Catholic in all but name. At the same time, his contributors, in particular Arthur Machen, were predominantly High Anglican. Douglas's objection was raised partly on the fact that none of the *Academy* staff or writers was a Catholic, but this did not change the impression that the paper gave as 'an organ of Catholic propaganda'.[41]

One significant aspect of the case was that the legal team employed by the *Daily News* was headed by Sir Edward Carson – the cross-examiner who had brought down Wilde's case against Queensberry. Mixed emotions welled in Douglas as he finally faced the man who, fifteen years earlier, he had been desperate to confront to save Wilde and reveal how flawed Queensberry was.

The jury took fifty minutes to decide that they could not agree on a verdict and when the judge, Mr Justice Darling, asked them to try again it took them just fifteen to agree in favour of the defendants, the *Daily News*, though with a rider that Horton should have checked his facts more carefully before writing the article. It was not an unjust outcome, but the effects were unfortunate. Because he had to meet the costs of the action Douglas had no option but to sell his only asset, the *Academy*. George Wyndham negotiated a deal by which Lord Howard de Walden and Lord Fitzwilliam bought the paper but they immediately sacked Douglas as editor.[42] The case should perhaps have taught him that the courts were not always the best place in which to settle a dispute, but it did not.

During these sometimes turbulent years the Douglas family life was rather unstable, with either Douglas or Olive away for much of the time, but Douglas was an affectionate father and found much amusement in his son. He was delighted to be able to report to Olive in October 1911 that he had just returned with Raymond from a production of *Romeo and Juliet*, which had thrilled their son. Apparently, while Raymond had admired Juliet he also expressed the opinion to his sympathetic father that Romeo was 'a very handsome man'.[43] After the sale of the *Academy*, Douglas had more time to dedicate to his son and sport. He continued to go up to Scotland to shoot and took with him the cocker spaniel named Winston, who had recently joined the household. The Douglases seemed basically happy with their marriage, and if either felt closeted in their lifestyle, there were plenty of opportunities for them to go off alone. What threw the spanner into the works was Douglas's decision to convert.

In 1908, Olive's mother had died and Colonel Custance was left alone and isolated at Weston Hall. He had ample opportunity to brood on past slights and review his life, and reserved a particularly irrational bitterness for Roman Catholicism. Custance had only one sibling, a sister, and much to his chagrin she had married a Catholic and converted. Custance believed that his sister had been taken from him. With Catholics, *en masse*, as an enemy, there was no way that he would ever accept Douglas's decision. Most worrying to Custance were the implications of this for his daughter and grandchild. Although Douglas had thought Olive would follow him into the Church she did not do so immediately, and the battle was fought instead over Raymond's soul.

Custance was horrified at the idea of Raymond converting but Douglas was so committed to his faith that a few months later Raymond was instructed and received into the church. There were, of course, practical changes that Raymond's reception into the Catholic Church entailed. Foremost among these was the choice of a public school: Douglas selected Ampleforth, the most prominent school in Britain for Catholic boys. This enraged Custance, but, for a time, there was little he could do about it. He sat back to consider his next move.

Custance was not the only person to have a run-in with Douglas over his conversion. Shortly after he had been received Douglas wrote to Wilfrid Scawen Blunt and apologised for the abusive letters he had written over the *Academy* episode. But Blunt was not to be moved. He told his cousin, 'Your trespass against me was a small matter and easy to forgive, but your sins against others of your friends [presumably Manners-Sutton] in the last two or three years have been less forgivable, and you must not expect me to condone them or give you any further countenance.'[44] It was a harsh but fair appraisal of the situation, which a rather more humble convert would have found easier to swallow. Douglas stormed back at him with a letter that showed how little in him had changed. 'Of what value has your countenance ever been to any man? To be known as your friend or associate has always been something in the nature of a social handicap.'[45] Blunt noted receipt of this letter in his diary and that it was what he 'expected and indeed intended, for I had rather have him as an enemy than a friend',[46] and mused 'Whatever he may have done by becoming a Catholic, it has not brought him to the point of repenting his sins', all of which was substantially justifiable. On the sale of the *Academy*, engineered through George Wyndham and others, he recorded, 'They agreed that it would have been wiser to let him go bankrupt. But they consider him quite harmless to effect anything except annoyance.'[47] It soon became obvious to them all that Douglas could do far more than create 'annoyance'.

7

The question of why Douglas behaved as he did during the next few years is difficult to answer. Why did he alienate almost all of his family and former friends? To begin with, it was a family trait. Lady Queensberry told Wilde that she felt Alfred to have been the only one of her children to have inherited 'the fatal Douglas temperament'. Many thought that during the last years of his life Queensberry suffered an acute form of persecution mania, as had his brother, long before his suicide. However, Lord Alfred Douglas had wit, charm, beauty and intelligence, which his father's generation generally lacked. Perhaps the suspicious and paranoid side of his father's nature would not have appeared in the optimistic, trusting and care-free young man, to take him into a quarrelsome and litigious middle age, without the Oscar Wilde affair.

From the time of the trials people slighted, vilified, slandered and abused Douglas. It had happened so often that Douglas started to see insult where none was intended from the first few months after the collapse of the case against his father in 1895. By the end of the first decade of the twentieth century he had decided that rather than allow this to happen without retaliation he would go on the attack. He had said in the Manners-Sutton case that he had nothing to be ashamed of in his relationship with Wilde but he would soon change his mind. He was renowned as having been homosexual, which he appeared to have suppressed in himself, but he was now a Roman Catholic: his sexual extravagance in his early life was not only an offence against the law, punishable with imprisonment, but also a sin against God, punishable with damnation. The only way for him to survive was to turn completely. He would lie about his relationship with Wilde and deny any improprieties, which he had had to do at the time, and he would break away from his friends of the Wilde period. He had to make sure that nobody in his new life had been involved with or could remind him of the Wilde débâcle. Of those who remained there was one who had risen to the fore as the primary advocate of Wilde: Robert Ross.

According to Ross, he had suggested to Douglas between 1900 and 1901 that, with the money he had inherited from his father's death, he should buy the copyright in all of Wilde's works, thus making a fine investment for himself and putting the estate in the black. At the time, Douglas turned it down but he came to realise that he had forgone a good money spinner. It was his bitterness at not having taken Ross up on his offer that, according to Ross, was the real cause of their falling out. But there was more to it than that. Part of Douglas's growing irritation with Ross centred around the fact that Ross was doing so well with the Wilde estate and had resurrected Wilde's name as an artist long before many people thought it possible. From his point of view, Ross had finally claimed back Wilde for himself, albeit posthumously. In a way it was his revenge for the back-seat role that the advent of Douglas had forced him into with Wilde. Both men still cared passionately for Wilde and his memory, but while Ross gained prestige and respect for his association with Wilde and his work for him, Douglas received nothing but abuse. The situation initially erupted in 1905 with the publication of the edited version of *De Profundis*, but that was only a trial run for the most damaging period in the lives of both men.

In 1908 the *Collected Works of Oscar Wilde* were published in a limited-edition fourteen-volume set and also in a cheap edition. For copyright reasons Ross ensured that everything that Wilde had written, however obscure or trivial, including his work as a reviewer, was included. The cheap edition was a great success and along with the financial benefit to the Wilde estate came an increase in the public's estimation of his genius. Distaste for Wilde's 'vices' might have obscured interest in his works for a time, but, with memories of the trials fading, appreciation of the works was easier to come by. The formal public reacceptance of Wilde came in December 1908, within a decade of his death. The event was a dinner at the Ritz, with about a hundred and sixty guests, in honour of Robert Ross and in recognition of his work for the estate of Oscar Wilde. Reginald Turner was among those on the organising committee for the dinner. Douglas told him that he did not want to attend. It was a mistake, because it meant that a sense of exclusion developed in Douglas's mind, and he saw those who attended, such as Frank Harris, Christopher Millard (soon to become Wilde's bibliographer) and More Adey, as members of a group to which he did not belong.

He had missed the point: the dinner was not to honour Wilde, but to honour Ross's work on Wilde's behalf. Many people were there whose connection with Wilde was tenuous or non-existent, but they were friends of Ross. They included members of both Houses of Parliament, aristocrats, artists and others who simply added to the glittering list of names present, and the evening was a great success. Alice Head, Douglas's former secretary, had received an invitation. She knew almost nothing of Wilde, or of Douglas's involvement with him, and recalled being 'inexpressibly puzzled to find that most of the speakers seemed so choked with emotion that they could hardly utter their words. On all sides I noticed people apparently ready to dissolve into tears and sobs.'[48] The charged atmosphere, at least in part, must have come from the presence of Wilde's sons, known since the trials as Cyril and Vyvyan Holland, the former seated beside William Rothenstein, the latter by Somerset Maugham.[49] Had Douglas gone to the dinner he would have been able to restore his friendship with Cyril and Vyvyan, and to share in the open pride in Wilde's achievements. But although he had only himself to blame for his exclusion, he still felt left out.

Of course, at the time of the Ritz dinner, Douglas was still editing the *Academy*, and in the background of a looming feud with Ross lurked Crosland. Crosland despised homosexuality, he despised Wilde, and he despised everything he thought Wilde had stood for. When he saw that Douglas was in contact with most of the Wilde group, he used him to get at them and, in particular, Ross.

Crosland was undeniably a gifted man, but he was always embittered by the success of others, particularly financial, which he himself could never achieve and which he saw that Wilde had had. The re-evaluation of the reputation of a man whom Crosland loathed not only as a human being but also as a writer drove him to distraction. He persuaded Douglas that they were fighting for decency in letters, and encouraged him to view Wilde as a figure with whom he should not want to associate and as an immoral writer. He made Douglas feel like a crusader and fighter in the tradition of his greatest ancestors. In one sonnet written after he and

Douglas had successfully defended a libel action against them he included a sestet addressed to Douglas:

> Chiefly to you this victory, by God's grace,
> Most "disagreeable Witness" with the thrust
> That withers liars in their obscene place –
> The honour in which kings have put their trust,
> The name that was a name at Chevy Chase,
> Shine on, serene above the smirch and dust.

On the *Academy* Crosland had led Douglas into a campaign against Ross. Crosland told Douglas that, from various things he had heard, he had decided that Ross was an unsuitable character to be contributing to the *Academy*. A review Douglas had asked Ross to write was printed, but only after Crosland had changed its contents entirely. Ross was understandably put out and decided not to write for the paper again, as Crosland had hoped. The relationship between Ross and Douglas was further strained.

A few weeks after the Ritz dinner Olive, who was desperate to make peace between her husband and Ross, wrote asking him to lunch. He sent back a refusal, explaining that he had a prior engagement. Olive tried again, imploring Ross to come, 'You must know I always love to see you,' and added simply, 'Because I am afraid you and Bosie are not friends just now, I am sorry.'[50] Ross explained to her why he did not want to come. He knew, he explained, that he and her husband would be bound to argue. 'I am with the opposite side on every controversial matter discussed by the *Academy*, which moreover attacks all the people who are my personal friends and most of the books and authors I happen to admire,' he told her. He complained that Douglas was the only one among all of his and Wilde's former friends who had sent no congratulatory words on the dinner at the Ritz. With admirable kindliness he concluded, 'I have no hostile feelings whatever because I know Bosie too well and have known him too long. But I decided some time ago to deny myself the privileges coincidental to friendship with him.'[51]

Douglas wrote back to him after he had seen Ross's letter to Olive:

As to your absurd dinner to meet the Duchess of Sutherland and other people who have nothing whatever to do with Oscar or literature, I certainly did not feel inclined to go to a function to meet Frank Harris, Robert Sherard and about 20 other people with whom Oscar was not on speaking terms when he died. As to your determination to forgo my friendship, as you have raised the point, I may say that the boot is very much on the other leg. I gave up going to your house because I disapproved of your views, your morals and most of your friends. My own views have changed and I do not care to meet those who are engaged in active propaganda of every kind of wickedness from anarchy to sodomy.[52]

This statement was actionable in itself, but Ross was advised against proceeding by his solicitor, Sir George Lewis. Douglas finished with a paragraph that would soon be proved sadly misguided in respect of More Adey: 'I agree with you that it is better that we should keep apart. I don't consider that you have ever been a real friend of mine, in the sense that More and others have been my friends. And I may tell you frankly that I don't think your character has improved with age.'

Ross was so incensed by what he felt to be a campaign against him by Crosland and Douglas that he agreed to give evidence against Crosland in the Manners-Sutton case, which Douglas saw as an attempt by Ross to damage him. From then on he realised that Ross was against him and he was against Ross. Both men began to try to keep themselves aloof of anything that might give the other ammunition to use against him, and to influence mutual friends to take one side or the other. Douglas, believing that More Adey was more on his side than on Ross's, told him that Ross was being watched by detectives, which would put off friends from visiting him. He also said that Ross had been involved in a number of liaisons with servants and named the establishments where they worked.

8

Ross was friendly with the director of the British Museum, Sir Frederick Kenyon, and late in 1909 offered to deposit the manuscript of Wilde's prison letter to Douglas in the museum. All parties realised that there would have to be a lengthy seal on the manuscript and that it could not be seen in the lifetime of the generation involved. After reading the whole

MS, and consulting Randal Davidson, then Archbishop of Canterbury, Kenyon informed Ross that he felt the British Museum to be 'the best place for a work which cannot be made public for a considerable time, but which may be of great interest to future generations'.[53] The trustees agreed with the director, and on 13 November accepted the gift with the condition that it be locked up for fifty years.

On one matter the British Museum do not appear to have acted with particular foresight. Alfred Douglas was the addressee of the letter and was also the person from whose gaze the benefactor most wanted the MS to be kept. They acknowledged that 'Although in the form of a letter addressed to Lord Alfred Douglas, there is nothing to show that it was ever sent to him.'[54] Ross had assured them that, on the day after his release, Wilde had handed him the MS 'with a request that I should keep the manuscript for possible publication after his death, and cause two typewritten copies to be made; one of which was to be sent to him and the other to Alfred Douglas'.[55] The museum authorities presumably took it on trust that Ross had carried out Wilde's instructions, that Douglas had been sent a copy of the letter by Ross and that he was aware of its contents. To their minds the manuscript could slumber in the vaults of the museum for fifty years – little did they realise that it would be out in less than four.

Although Ross no longer had the original of *De Profundis*, he still had copies to show to anyone should Douglas try to deny anything Wilde claimed in it, and with his conversion and new stand on homosexuality – Ross's in particular – it did not seem unlikely that he would. Without Douglas's knowledge Ross had possession of a work that might ruin him entirely, the original of which was out of his reach. If Douglas had been aware of the contents of *De Profundis* then it is inconceivable that he would have embarked on his campaign against Ross.

As it was, Douglas was sinking deeper into financial crisis while Ross was climbing high in his profession as an art specialist, usually with the help of people whom Douglas detested, such as Edmund Gosse. However, it was not until 1912 that the pressure started to build. In May of that year Ross was elected to the National Art Collections Fund's executive committee, a position of both responsibility and respectability. In August he applied for a new post as valuer of pictures and drawings for the board of the Inland Revenue set up, according to Douglas, especially for him by Asquith, the Prime Minister.

Also, Douglas's relationship with his father-in-law had continued to deteriorate in the wake of his conversion. It struck rock bottom over Olive's 'entailment'. In the absence of a male heir, it was to Olive that the family estates at Weston Longeville had been left, while the Colonel had a life interest. In early 1911 he suggested to Olive that she should break the entail and agree to a resettlement in which she would surrender her rights in return for an annual income of £600 during his lifetime, and at his death a life interest with the remainder to Raymond.[56] It was clear to a suspicious mind like Douglas's that there must be a catch in the agreement, and he was right. Olive, understandably, trusted her father and, against the advice of her husband, signed the agreement without a written promise from Colonel Custance to provide her with the £600: he had insisted that his word was good enough.

Once the documents were signed Colonel Custance wrote to his daughter to say that unless Raymond was handed over to him he would not pay her an allowance, and that all other payments to her, such as her son's school fees, would be stopped. He was particularly vehement on the point that the boy's father must not take him away on his own. Douglas, however, removed Raymond from his prep school in Sleaford, Lincolnshire, and took him to the house of the Dowager Marchioness of Queensberry. He was angry with his wife for not listening to him when he had warned her of what would happen. They quarrelled bitterly, and it was some months before they were reconciled. Douglas did not blame her for what had happened, though. He wrote to her, 'I do understand that what you have done has been forced on you by your father and that villain Lewis and I forgive you.'[57] George Lewis, of Lewis and Lewis, was the son of the George Lewis who had been a friend of Wilde and who had extricated Douglas from the blackmailing incident at Oxford. He was not only Colonel Custance's solicitor: he was also instructed by Robert Ross. Douglas realised that Lewis must be privy to certain information from his father's days and decided that it was no coincidence that he was acting for the two men who were his chief enemies: Lewis must be out to get him. Douglas concluded that he would stand up and fight, which meant he had to attack first.

From 1911 to 1912 Douglas bombarded his father-in-law with letters until Custance told him that any more would be thrown unopened on the fire. Douglas reverted to his father's device of sending postcards and telegrams. In this way he told Custance that he believed him to have acted dishonestly and fraudulently and informed him that he was taking legal advice as the matter would have to be fought in court. In a postcard the next day Douglas wrote that there was 'no doubt whatever that [Custance] was a despicable scoundrel and a thoroughly dishonest and dishonourable man'.[58] When he threatened to inform the Colonel's clubs, bank, family, friends and all the tenants on his estate, Custance had no choice but to go to George Lewis and cause a summons to be issued for the arrest of his son-in-law on a charge of criminal libel. This was served on 26 February 1913.

9

In 1912 the dispute between Douglas and Ross had become fully public and something of a scandal. In March of that year a book had appeared by the young Arthur Ransome – who had not yet made his name as the author of *Swallows and Amazons* – entitled *Oscar Wilde: A Critical Study*. It was the first work on Wilde by a man who had not known his subject personally and who treated him as a serious artist. The book had been commissioned by the publisher Martin Secker, who suggested that Ransome should meet Robert Ross as an authority on Wilde. The meeting was arranged, and many more took place during which Ross gave Ransome generous amounts of information and help. In a subsequent legal statement Ross claimed that he had shown Ransome no letters or documents relating to Douglas. However, it is evident from the finished book that Ross had shown Ransome a copy of *De Profundis* and the letter he had received from Wilde written after the break-up of the Naples ménage, which claimed that Douglas had left him penniless.

The book was a success. The Times Book Club put it on its list and many leading reviewers and critics praised it highly. Douglas had not been consulted on it, so read it when the general public did so. It was dedicated to Ross for all the help and encouragement he had given its author. It was an unfortunate gesture: it meant that Douglas read the book as a Ross-inspired work. Ross had not been consulted about the dedication, and he had refused to read the final proofs, fearing that he might disapprove of some of the content and that this would change the perspective of a book that brought a fresh voice to the Wilde story.[59]

Unfortunately Ransome had made a number of statements that should not have been included (such as the implication that Douglas's friendship was unworthy of Wilde and that he had deserted him), and which Ross might have excised.

Ross had insisted that Douglas's name should not appear in the book, and this was respected, but Douglas was implicated in it, and anyone who knew anything about the case could have identified the references to him. When referring to *De Profundis*, Ransome said that it 'was not addressed to Mr Ross but to a man to whom Wilde felt that he owed some, at least, of the circumstances of his public disgrace',[60] which could only have referred to Douglas, who wrote immediately to Ross: 'I now write to ask you whether it is true that the MS of *De Profundis* consists of a letter addressed to me, and if so why you have concealed the fact from me all these years. I should also like to know why you published the letter as a book without my knowledge or consent.' He clearly felt strongly that any letter to him was his property and not to be tampered with by anyone else. He stated unequivocally, 'Hitherto I have always been under the impression that *De Profundis* was a letter written by Wilde to *you* but containing abusive or scandalous references to me which you had suppressed. Of course if this latter version of the affair is correct there is no more to be said. But if Ransome's version is correct, matters assume a very different and very serious aspect.'[61]

Indeed Ross had allowed Douglas and the public to believe that *De Profundis* had been written to himself but now, fifteen years after its composition, Douglas was made aware of its exact nature. It was explained to him by George Lewis in reply to the letter Douglas had sent to his client Ross:

The manuscript of *De Profundis* consists of a document in the form of a letter addressed to you, the original of which was entrusted by Mr Oscar Wilde to Mr Ross *with directions that he should not part with it but that he should send you a copy of the letter*, which he did in the year 1897; so that you are already aware of this fact which has never been concealed from you. The manuscript was published after Mr Oscar Wilde's death *in accordance with his directions to Mr Ross* and the reason why it was published without your name was out of consideration for you. This was also why Mr Ross decided that many passages in the manuscript should be omitted from the form in which it was published, and this your letter shows was within your knowledge.[62]

George Lewis's letter was packed with inaccuracies: as we have seen, Wilde had told Ross in a letter to send the original to Douglas, keep one copy and send the other to Wilde. Douglas's letter to Ross shows that he had not known that *De Profundis* was addressed to him.

After receiving Lewis's letter, Douglas telephoned him and requested a meeting. He explained to Ross afterwards why he had done this.

> I merely wished to put on record that I had been shamefully deceived by you over the *De Profundis* matter. As you must be perfectly well aware, I have never, until I saw it stated in Ransome's book, had the slightest inkling that the MS of *De Profundis* was a letter addressed to me by Wilde or that there was any connection between the letter you sent me in 1897 (which I destroyed after reading the first half dozen lines) and the book. Had I been aware of this I should have used every endeavour to prevent the publication of the book [in 1905] by appealing to the sense of decency and honour which at that time I did not doubt you possessed. Failing that I should have applied for an injunction.
>
> Wilde, after his release from prison, only referred to the letter sent by you to me at Nogent-sur-Marne in 1897 and on that occasion implored me to forgive him for having written it.

The Nogent-sur-Marne letter was the one from Ross in which he quoted Wilde, and Douglas admitted in his *Autobiography* that 'It is quite possible that this letter of Ross' contained extracts from Wilde's *De Profundis* letter to me.'[63]

Douglas continued:

> You now ask me to believe that Wilde was so base and so vile as to have left you in the possession of the original letter (of which I burnt the copy) and to have agreed with you that it was to be published in whole or in part after his death, and this at a time when he was on terms of the most affectionate friendship with me and was receiving large sums of money from me. Whether it is true or not that Wilde was a party to your action (and I prefer to believe that it is not true and that in spite of his degradation he was not quite as bad as that) there can be no question as to

your part in the matter. You admit it and positively glory in it and you have made a lot of money by it.[64]

Douglas was devastated. He disliked Ross for the way he had tried to monopolise Wilde's memory, for his homosexual activities, which he had heard included the corruption of young boys, and also for the blackmail of himself. He felt persecuted because a dead man, his lover and the most defining character of his life, was supporting the accusations of Ross from beyond the grave.

Crosland urged him to act straight away. Accordingly Douglas issued writs for libel against Ransome, the author of the libels, Martin Secker, their publisher, and The Times Book Club, their distributor. The action brought an immediate withdrawal and apology from Secker, but the other two parties accepted the writs. Douglas himself had no doubts about who the case was really against. 'You filthy bugger and black-mailer,' he wrote to Ross, 'my libel action against Ransome henceforth becomes an action against you and it will be so conducted.'[65] Ross also saw that it was him Douglas was really hoping to punish, and accordingly offered to pay Ransome's legal costs, which the author, who had a family to support, could not easily raise. Ross suggested to Ransome that he instruct George Lewis as his counsel, and Lewis suggested that a plea of justification be entered.

During the period that elapsed before the case was heard Douglas was given access to two documents that had been cited to justify the libels that had appeared in Ransome's book. The first was the complete text of *De Profundis*; the second was the letter Wilde had written to Ross during March 1898 claiming that Douglas had deserted him and left him penniless, which, Douglas called 'one of the most astonishing products that the history of literature has ever recorded'.[66] He could see no reason why Wilde had lied about the arrangements at Naples or why he had so vilified him straight after Douglas had secured his future and they had parted amicably. It did not occur to him that Wilde had been manip-ulating Ross into giving him money. Far worse, though, and of more lasting hurt to Douglas, was the letter he had been meant to read fifteen years earlier, and which he now read as his friend, lover and greatest companion's final words to him. He had no way of replying to Wilde now, and he felt anger, bitterness and hatred as he contemplated the treachery of the man to whom he had given his youth. In *De Profundis*

Wilde had written of hate and Douglas's capacity for it, and it is one of
the saddest ironies of the whole case that Wilde's letter unleashed in
Douglas the greatest tide of hatred he had ever felt. Wilde wrote:

> Hate blinds people. You were not aware of that. Love can read the
> writing on the remotest star, but Hate so blinded you that you could see
> no further than the narrow, walled-in, and already lust-withered garden
> of your common desires. Your terrible lack of imagination, the one really
> fatal defect of your character, was entirely the result of the Hate that lived
> in you. Subtly, silently, and in secret, Hate gnawed at your nature, as the
> lichen bites at the root of some sallow plant, till you grew to see nothing
> but the most meagre interests and the most petty aims. That faculty in
> you which Love would have fostered, Hate poisoned and paralysed.[67]

Wilde was wrong: the hatred Douglas had felt for his father was
equalled by the love he felt for Wilde. Now Wilde's words sounded
prophetic, and Douglas's love for him turned to hate, which he vented on
Ross as the recipient and withholder of *De Profundis*. It caused Douglas to
behave in a manner almost identical to that which his father had
employed with Wilde and, like his father, he expressed his views with
all the bigotry and force possible. 'Don't imagine that the production of
this MS will make the slightest difference to my line of conduct,' Douglas
warned Ross. 'I am going straight ahead with my action and my only
hope is that you will go into the witness box and give me a chance of
having you cross-examined.'[68] He set about sending Ross letters of such a
libellous and offensive nature that Ross had to claim they were untrue. It
was a replay of the Wilde–Queensberry case, and Douglas even told
Ross, 'It is my intention to give you a very severe thrashing with a horsewhip. I am bound to come across you one day or another when occasion
serves and you shall be whipped within an inch of your dirty life.'[69]

Perhaps the most dramatic event occurred at a party on 29 November
at the London home of the Tennants, by now Lord and Lady Glenconner.
Among the guests were the Prime Minister, his wife, Margot Asquith,
and, of course, Ross. He had had serious misgivings about attending a
function at the house of his enemy's cousin, but having consulted George
Lewis, who assured Ross that Douglas would not be there, Ross accepted
the invitation. But Douglas had indeed been invited, and when he saw
Ross was determined to make a scene. He made a noisy entrance, strode

across the room to Ross and, in a manner reminiscent of his father, declared, 'You have got to clear out of this: you are nothing but a bugger and a blackmailer.'[70] He was clearly pleased,[71] not only with his alliteration but with the fact that he felt both claims could be substantiated. Ross was a homosexual and he had also blackmailed Douglas with the threat of using various letters, including *De Profundis*, against him. One account of the incident says that Ross's friends pushed him away from Douglas into an adjoining room but Douglas pursued him, still shouting. Ross escaped behind a broad table but Douglas lunged at him as Ross ran into the next room, leaving Douglas 'shouting with rage at being baulked of his prey'. Hilaire Belloc's sister recorded that 'certain of the words which Lord Alfred had shouted were quite unknown to me'.[72] Ross hurriedly took his leave and a livid Margot Asquith took him back to Downing Street to recover from the shock of such a public humiliation.

The trouble did not stop with Ross's exit from the party. Ross himself wrote to Glenconner the next day and apologised for the incident, explaining that he was doing so 'not merely because of the unpleasantness to myself but for being the occasion of discord under your hospitable roof'. He added, 'Had I known that Alfred Douglas was likely to be there I would not have availed myself of Lady Glenconner's kind invitation. I do not propose to trouble you with the origin or causes of Douglas's alleged grievance against me; but if you wished for any immediate explanation Sir George Lewis would, I am sure, place all the information you want before you.'[73] He said that he did not want to burden them 'with the details of the sordid and revolting persecution which I have endured for the last four years. That will no doubt be made public when the pending litigation is heard.'[74]

While Ross was trying to excuse the behaviour of the night before, Douglas opened the second round: he wrote Ross one of his most offensive and threatening letters.

Robert Ross

I could not make a scene last night at my cousin's house or I would have kicked you out. You may be quite sure that you will *never* be asked to the house again. I shall take care that your true character is made known to everyone I know. It is fortunate in one way that you had the impudence to come to Lady Glenconner's house last night, because my anger was so obvious that a complete explanation was inevitable. This explanation I gave to all and sundry. You will not find many respectable houses open to you in future. There is a bad time coming for you and all your gang.

Alfred Douglas.[75]

10

At this time, Douglas discovered which friends were willing to stand up for him and help, and how many would desert him now that he was in serious trouble. In the last days of 1912 he received a letter from William Sorley Brown, editor of the *Border Standard*, who became his loyal supporter not just in his court actions and crusade against vice in literature and life, but also of his poetry. He wrote to Douglas to congratulate him on the first issue of a new, but short-lived, paper called the *Antidote*, which Douglas and Crosland had just brought out.

At this point Sorley Brown published a pamphlet, which he lengthened into a book, entitled *The Genius of Lord Alfred Douglas – An Appreciation*. It was, as the title suggests, a glowing tribute to Douglas as a poet, but as a work of literary criticism it was poor: its style was almost identical to that of Douglas and Crosland, and it was even dedicated to 'T.W.H. Crosland – In admiration of his brilliant work as critic, satirist, and poet during the days when "The Academy" was so ably edited by his friend Lord Alfred Bruce Douglas'. In a note at the beginning Brown wrote, 'The name of Lord Alfred Douglas is usually linked with that of Oscar Wilde. As to the poetic genius of the latter the public knows all that it wants to know: of the genius of the former the public yet knows too little, but there can be no doubt that Lord Alfred Douglas is a truer and greater poet than Wilde.'[76] In Douglas criticism, and even when the writer is trying to show that Douglas has a reputation apart from Wilde, his name is constantly linked to, and his work compared with, Wilde, thus negating the notion that he can be read as a poet in his own right.

Of course, when *The Genius of Lord Alfred Douglas* was published there had been only two volumes of Douglas's serious poetry, but Sorley Brown's praise was extravagant: 'In "The City of the Soul" there is something akin to the sigh which rises from the earth at the coming of a summer dawn. And both that work and the volume of "Sonnets" reveal a rich sense of music and a vision of beauty that assuredly give this poet a place among the "fixed and radiant stars" in the firmament of the immortals.'[77] He quoted a number of Douglas's sonnets and lyrics but what is absent is more noteworthy than what is present. None of the poems from the *Mercure de France* and the *Spirit Lamp* period, which are open to homosexual interpretation, are mentioned, and perhaps for this reason he felt able to write that Douglas

> is the finest poet that Magdalen has produced. Mr Robert Ross, Oscar Wilde's literary executor, considers that Wilde is 'the only real poet on the books of that institution'. Of course a man who has behaved to Lord Alfred Douglas in the way that Mr Ross has behaved is capable of saying and doing anything, and the above statement, which is made in a volume of Wilde's 'Selected Poems' is a perfect insult to all lovers of poetry. Lord Alfred Douglas is a far greater poet than Oscar Wilde, and one has only to read the poems of both to realise this.[78]

Some time before the Ransome trial, Crosland read the full version of *De Profundis*. Now he had a reason to express his open hatred of Wilde, claiming that the letter showed Wilde's baseness: first that he could write in such a way at all and then had concealed it from Douglas so that his reputation might be destroyed after Wilde was dead: 'I shall be told to remember that Wilde was a man of genius, and that he is dead. In view of what is happening under our noses, I refuse to forget that he is fearfully alive, that his genius belonged essentially to the stews, and that he spent his last literary strength on the deliberate production of a work which is disgraceful to humanity.'[79] Crosland prefaced his rhetoric with his new poem, which took its title from the Biblical line 'Whomsoever is without sin amongst you let him cast the first stone'. 'The First Stone' is a despicable attack on Wilde, the unpleasantness of which has rarely been equalled. Its conclusion refers to the grave in Paris with the great Epstein monument over it to which Wilde's body had been transferred a few years earlier.

> The dubious dust
> Hidden in Père la Chaise
> Beneath the Epstein stone
> Is not thy monument,
> Not for thy memory:

> But on a Rock called Shame
> Sunken in letters of lead
> Which may not be effaced
> Till the slow clocks of Time
> Shall strike the ages out,
> Men read:-

> Oscar Fingal
> O'Flahertie Wills Wilde

> WHOSE SOUL WAS ALL A SIN,
> WHOSE HEART WAS ALL A LUST,
> WHOSE BRAIN WAS ALL A LIE.[80]

Then Douglas considered it a 'terrible and astonishingly brilliant indictment of Wilde', and that 'If Oscar Wilde has been wronged, all I can say is that he owes it to his evil genius, Robert Ross.'[81] He did not entirely lose his critical judgement though, for he realised that 'though a stinging piece of invective', it was 'of course not poetry'.[82]

By this point Douglas had earned himself a reputation for vindictiveness on all fronts. He still missed no opportunity to criticise Asquith: in one of his letters to the newspapers, when the debate over the attempt to flood the upper chamber with newly created peers to carry through the Parliament Bill was raging, Douglas hit out straight to the top.

As long as the King wished to be a King and not a puppet we were all prepared to fight to the last for him and if necessary die in the last ditch for him, but as his majesty has now definitely decided to take up the position of a sort of glorified Lord Mayor or 'President of the Republic' it seems to me that there is nothing left to fight for. What does it matter now whether 500 or 5000 new peers are made or not? The peers are supposed to derive their position from the King as the Fountain of Honour, but his present Majesty has disposed of all this old fashioned notion by definitely acquiescing in the monstrous theory that the particular politician who happens to be Prime Minister at any given moment can make as many peers as he chooses. I am not a peer myself but as the younger son of a peer of ancient creation I am glad to think that there was a time when Kings did not run away before the first shot was fired. Of course you won't print this letter – you have neither the pluck nor the sense – but I wish you would contrive that it should somehow reach the eyes of the King; it would do his majesty good to know what is thought of his attitude by thousands of his subjects.[83]

And as if insulting the King and Prime Minister were not enough, he did the same to many members of his own class, including those who might have been useful to him. In 1910, when the Duke of Richmond refused him entrance to the private stand at Goodwood, he could not possibly have imagined for how long Douglas would harbour resentment. In the midst of his battles with Ross and Colonel Custance, he told Richmond, in a letter written on 5 August 1912, that he was planning to write a book entitled 'Inglorious Goodwood' dealing with the decline of the 'sport of Kings' into the mire of 'commercialism' for which, primarily, Douglas blamed him: 'I propose to dedicate this work to your Grace and I should be glad to have your Grace's permission to do so. As I do not possess the Privilege enjoyed by your Grace of being descended from the bastard son of a French whore I am not in a position to offer your Grace actual "cash down" for your Grace's good offices in the matter.'[84] The incident still rankled with him twenty years on. In his *Autobiography*, he wrote 'Of course as long as the Duke of Richmond has a Private Stand he is at liberty to refuse admission to persons of better birth than himself, while admitting any kind of *nouveau riche* or dubious profiteer.'[85]

11

By early 1913 Douglas was having to defend himself on all sides and even he did not have the energy for this. A free pamphlet was published in London by someone signing himself E.G.O. who was clearly a member of Ross's circle, entitled *The Writing on the Ground*. The title echoed the biblical theme adopted by Crosland in 'The First Stone', with the suggestion that in here were listed the sins of those who had dared to throw stones when they were not without sin themselves. The number of people who read it were probably few, but it was a direct attack on Douglas. Certainly Douglas was justified in feeling persecuted when he read it: it contained some information and stories of Douglas's doings privy then only to members of the Wilde circle and also a poem by Aleister Crowley, reprinted from his book *The Winged Beetle* of 1910. It was entitled 'A Slim Gilt Soul' and contained many allusions to Wilde, his writing and Douglas's relationship with him, also implying that Douglas had turned his amorous attentions from young boys to young girls.

> Sure no one like yourself can be
> Past-Master in virginity.
>
> . . .
>
> You would be welcome on the stage
> To amuse and to instruct the age
> – A shining light in opera-bouffe;
> Giton, and Judas, and Tartufe!

The Winged Beetle was privately printed and probably had not reached Douglas at that time. With *The Writing on the Ground*, though, it came to his attention. 'More crass and abominable libels were never put into type,' he wrote.[86] He wanted to take legal action over Crowley's insinuations but for once he did not. As his nephew later wrote, 'In this he was well advised. Aleister Crowley was a rich man and an experienced litigant, with a power of invective that left nothing to be desired.'[87] Douglas himself could equal Crowley in invective, but by this stage his finances were in a very rocky state which might explain why he never took Crowley to court.[88]

The main point made by the author of *The Writing on the Ground* was that Douglas was hypocritical in protesting against physical and literary decadence in others, which was supported by quotations from various homosexual passages of 'Hymn to Physical Beauty', 'Prince Charming' and 'Two Loves'. In the last paragraph the writer suggests that the book be brought to the attention of Lord Alfred Douglas in the hope that he might 'crush the perpetrator' of such decadent works. The pamphlet is only interesting in that it puts down on record the views that many people held and still do hold about Douglas's actions during these years, and the author made clear his opinion of Douglas: 'This crawling creature (would we could hope him to be mere victim of Religious mania!) is, by vilifying his dead friend, seeking to right himself with Heaven. – "Oh, fears of Hell and hopes of Paradise!" ' This was the stand taken by the Ross camp, of whom none could understand how Douglas had the gall to criticise in others what he had practised himself – but the point is not what Douglas *had* practised but rather what he was practising *then*. There is no doubt that since he had fallen in love with Olive, married and rejected his homosexual friends, Douglas had believed himself heterosexual. The 'persecutions' he felt that he suffered mainly at the hands of Ross were, he saw, directly attributable to homosexuality. As a Catholic he would not condone sinning in any way, but as a young man, a young 'pagan' he had had no moral qualms because he had had no belief. As he explained, what he could not forgive, in Ross (also a Catholic) in particular, was the idea of someone knowing that they were sinning yet going on doing so. 'There is nothing in the world so bad,' he wrote, 'as a bad Catholic.'[89] Just as Douglas had settled down to a relatively normal family existence, with his new-found faith and circle of friends, the past rose up, largely by his own doing, and brought his world crashing down around him.

On 14 January 1913 Lord Alfred Douglas was made bankrupt on a money-lender's petition. For years he had had to borrow, always, like his elder brother, expecting to come into vast capital. The money he earned from his writing and editing was enough to support his family but not for all the litigation, and for some time bankruptcy had seemed inevitable. His membership of White's was terminated immediately. This did not bode well for what was to follow.

An article in the *Star* newspaper referred to the libel case against Douglas coming from his father-in-law and described it as 'the long postponed trial of Lord Alfred Douglas'.[90] This caused him to write to the paper, explaining that the case was not 'long postponed' but rather had to be held back so that he had time to put in his plea of justification, which was particularly necessary since he had 'three other actions pending'.[91] In a letter to the Home Secretary, Reginald MacKenna, on the day of the *Star* article, Douglas wrote, 'I now appeal to you to exercise your authority to prevent me from being made the victim of an act of injustice on the part of the Recorder of London who is actuated,' Douglas claimed, by 'personal spite against me'. He pointed out that 'I am entitled to Common Justice and will put up with no less.'[92] MacKenna replied, explaining that he had no authority to interfere in the matter. Predictably Douglas was so infuriated by the polite but unhelpful reply to his request that he dispatched another letter to MacKenna:

> It is eminently characteristic of a member of the present discredited and shuffling administration to cause such a reply to be sent to a letter involving a matter of grave public interest. It is not true that the Home Secretary 'has no authority to interfere'. The proper course for you, Sir, to take, would be to consult the Attorney General and to convey through him to the Recorder of London the opinion that it is highly improper that he should try my case under the circumstances and considering that he is (1) a personal friend and neighbour of the Prosecutor Colonel Custance and (2) actuated by spite and malice against me the Defendant. You cannot pertinently plead that you are ignorant of these facts because such ignorance arises from your own refusal to listen to their recital which I have offered to make to you. By running away from your responsibility you are making yourself together with the Recorder of London and the notorious solicitor Sir George Lewis a party to a plain and obvious conspiracy to defeat the ends of Justice. I warn you that the conspiracy will fail and that you will all three be the sufferers in the long run. I am keeping a copy of this letter and shall make its contents public at the proper time and in the proper place. I have the honour to be, Sir, your obedient servant, Alfred Bruce Douglas.

This time the letter, considered by officials at the Home Office to be, alternately, 'amusing' and 'preposterous', generated no response.[93]

An adjournment was granted, but on 8 April the Recorder of London described Douglas as being 'oblivious of the motto' of his class, 'Noblesse oblige', described his letter-writing as 'scurrilous' and his conduct as 'disgraceful'. In a letter to the editor of *The Times*, to whom, along with every other paper, Douglas offered the entire correspondence relating to the matter, he stated, 'These accusations I utterly deny and I challenge the Recorder to repeat them outside the Court when he is not protected by his privilege as a Judge and I will proceed against him for libel.'[94] When his letters explaining his actions were not published he imagined it was due to a 'boycott' and that various people were out to stop him having his say. Douglas wrote again to the Home Secretary telling him exactly what he intended to do:

Now I give you all fair warning that the whole of these facts will come out. As soon as the case of Rex v Douglas is disposed of, I shall write a pamphlet setting forth all the facts and embodying the letters that I have written to the Recorder, to you, and to other persons; and I shall demand that the Recorder be removed from the Bench. The lives and characters of His Majesty's subjects are not safe when such people are allowed to occupy the position of judges. If I had not been a man of exceptional determination and utterly devoid of fear in a righteous cause, I should by this time have been tried, convicted, and sentenced by the Recorder, without being given a chance of putting in my plea of justification. I have pledged my word to my counsel and my solicitor that I will not write any further letters to the Recorder till after my case is disposed of, but I am under no pledge to refrain from writing to you, and I hereby formally demand an official enquiry into the matter.[95]

Of course, Douglas did not get his official enquiry, and his counsel and solicitor requested him to refrain from any more letter-writing. They had enough to deal with as it was.

On 18 April 1913 Douglas's case against Arthur Ransome and The Times Book Club came up before Mr Justice Darling. The Book Club was claiming that they had not been aware of any libellous comments in the book. Essentially Douglas objected to three statements: that *De Profundis* had not been written to Ross but 'to a man to whom Wilde felt he owed some, at least, of the circumstances of his public disgrace';[96] that Wilde had wished to live a life of natural simplicity after his release and that this had been 'flung aside' due to the 'iterated entreaty of a man whose friendship had already cost him more than it was worth';[97] that, relating to the Naples period, Wilde's 'friend, as soon as there was no money, left him'.[98] Cecil Hayes represented Douglas, while F.E. Smith (later a Lord Chancellor) represented The Times Book Club. From the start it was obvious that Douglas's counsel was outweighed by the experience of those representing the defendants. The jury would have to decide whether or not Douglas had been the cause of Wilde's downfall and whether or not he had deserted Wilde at Naples when all the money had gone. In 1895 Douglas had wanted to go into the witness box to show the world how evil his father was, and later to defend the love he had shared with Wilde. After Wilde's death he had hoped to justify their relationship. Above all, he had wanted the opportunity to say what he

'[The disciple] stands behind one's throne, and at the moment of one's triumph whispers in one's ear that, after all, one is immortal'. Wilde at the time of the writing of *Dorian Gray*.

Left 'When we mocked grief and held disaster cheap' – Wilde and Bosie at Oxford – 1893.

Below 'No Wonder people are talking as they are' – *A dream of decadence on the Cherwell* – a contemporary's view.

Bosie and companion – on one occasion he said that this was his brother Drumlanrig with him and on another that it was one of the boys implicated in the Wilde trials, Maurice Schwabe.

For Oscar from Bosie Feb 2 1894

'Your slim gilt soul walks between passion and poetry'.

'History preserves in amber his beauty'. (Richard Ellmann)

The Marquess of Queensberry in 1896 – 'Posing as a moralist'.

The picture of Alfred Douglas.

After prison. Bosie reunited at Naples with Oscar who told a friend – 'I want peace – that is all. Perhaps I shall find it'.

'A martyr to progress'.

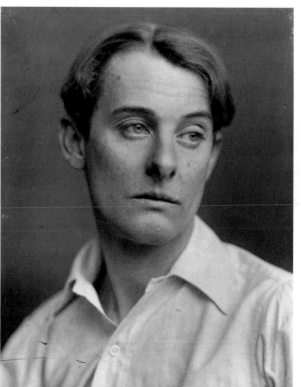

Above 'They are not long, the days of wine and roses' – Oscar Wilde on his deathbed.

Left 'I gazed at (Bosie) across the gulf that separates the 19th from the 20th century ... while he passed a petulant hand through his rebellious golden curls'. (Max Beerbohm)

had to say and be listened to. But, with the discovery of the contents of *De Profundis* and the picture emerging in his mind of a conspiracy hatched by Wilde and Ross to ruin him, his memories of Wilde would have to be distorted.

From the moment Douglas entered the witness box things went badly for him. The court saw the bank book that showed he had given Wilde a substantial amount of money, but he was not able to say how Wilde had spent it. Then the trial was taken out of the hands of either Douglas or his counsel. Within minutes of the opening of Douglas's cross-examination, it became clear that Ransome's team were planning to damage his reputation before the jury so that they would lose any sympathy they might have felt for him. F. E. Smith and his colleagues realised that substantial gain could be made from tarring Douglas with the same brush as Wilde and documents and letters were produced to suggest that Douglas was himself a sodomite and the corrupter of Wilde.

For the first time Douglas saw what it must have been like for Wilde to stand in the dock in 1895 and, indeed, for a time it looked as though this case would be a replay of that one. The letters from Wilde to Douglas, which Carson had produced in 1895, were read out again here, and so shocked was Mr Justice Darling by the details that he asked the members of the press to make their reports of the trial 'as disguised as possible' saying that 'it would do incalculable harm to public morals if they [the details] were published'.[99] Then Douglas was faced with a barrage of questions on the article he had written in 1896 for *La Revue Blanche*. It must have been obvious to him now that he had little hope of swinging judge or jury to his side. The 1896 article was accompanied by the letter Douglas had written, just after Wilde's prosecution, to Henry Labouchère, claiming that the vices of which Wilde had been convicted were practised by countless other people. Obviously this implied that Douglas was not only familiar with the practices but that he indulged in them himself. The translator of the *La Revue Blanche* article was brought out by Ransome's team to testify that it was indeed by Douglas. Foremost among those who could barely believe this was Douglas: the opinions expressed in the article, the open defiance and breaking of sexual and social conventions that permeated it must now have seemed alien to him. He repudiated it and the letter – but, nevertheless, he had written it, and for that he was held accountable.

The counsel leading for The Times Book Club then showed Douglas the manuscript of *De Profundis*. It was a significant moment: the first physical contact between the original of the letter and the intended recipient who had never received it. It had been specially taken out of the vaults of the British Museum for the occasion. The junior defence counsel was asked to read from it. Before he could begin, Douglas's counsel proposed that the whole of the letter should be read, not just extracts. He claimed that only through a complete reading could the court see that Wilde's moods were passing, and that if his opinions could swing so clearly in prison his attitude before and afterwards might also have changed significantly. The judge agreed and Ransome's junior counsel began.

It was perhaps the most destructive and wounding moment not just of the case but of Douglas's life so far, when he heard what he took to be Wilde's final verdict on him read out. During the reading he asked if he could leave the witness box. The judge refused him. When the reading was resumed on the second day of the trial it took Mr Justice Darling twenty minutes to realise that Douglas was not there. It took a quarter of an hour, during which the reading continued, to locate him. The judge rebuked him strongly for missing the reading of the letter, which was intended to be for his benefit as he was to be questioned on it. In fact Douglas had spent the morning in another court, trying to persuade the Recorder of London to postpone the public examination into his bankruptcy; his request was granted, and the case was left to be heard in June.

Douglas sat and listened to Wilde's attack on him. It damned his 'gross lack of imagination', his mind, his lusts, his poetry, his attempts to communicate with Wilde in prison, and revealed Wilde's rage at the attempts Douglas had made to help his friend, his articles and his desire to dedicate *Poems* to him. In court he had already been damned for the articles he had written in defence of Wilde, now Wilde was damning him for writing them. He heard Wilde refer to his friendship as unworthy of him, and dissect minor incidents that had taken place twenty years before so that the court saw them as evidence that Douglas had indeed been his ruin. Wilde even complained that Douglas had had an adverse influence on his work.

I arrived at St James's Place every morning at 11:30, in order to have the opportunity of thinking and writing without the interruptions inseparable from my own household, quiet and peaceful as that household was. But the attempt was vain. At twelve o'clock you drove up, and stayed smoking cigarettes and chattering till 1:30, when I had to take you out to luncheon at the Café Royal or the Berkeley. Luncheon with its liqueurs lasted usually till 3:30. For an hour you retired to White's. At tea-time you appeared again, and stayed till it was time to dress for dinner. You dined with me either at the Savoy or at Tite Street. We did not separate as a rule till after midnight, as supper at Willis's had to wind up the entrancing day. That was my life for those three months, every single day, except during the four days when you went abroad. I then, of course, had to go over to Calais to fetch you back. For one of my nature and temperament it was a position at once grotesque and tragic.[100]

Douglas might have disproved this by producing certain of Wilde's other letters, such as that written from Dieppe, when he said, 'I feel that my only hope of again doing beautiful work in art is being with you' and 'I feel that it is only with you that I can do anything at all',[101] but their otherwise passionate content would have worked against rather than for Douglas.

By this point it was obvious that nothing could save him. Eventually the jury intervened and said that they had heard enough. This was fortunate for Douglas, though it deprived the courtroom of hearing the most charitable, beautiful and moving section of the letter:

How far I am away from the true temper of soul, this letter in its changing, uncertain moods, its scorn and bitterness, its aspirations and its failure to realise those aspirations, shows you quite clearly. But do not forget in what a terrible school I am sitting at my task. And incomplete, imperfect, as I am, yet from me you may have still much to gain. You came to me to learn the Pleasure of Life and the Pleasure of Art. Perhaps I am chosen to teach you something much more wonderful, the meaning of Sorrow, and its beauty. Your affectionate friend

Oscar Wilde.[102]

But in court in 1913 Douglas was learning only the horror of increasing humiliation and defeat. Like a caged animal, he lashed out occasionally, which made things worse. After being constantly interrupted while trying to answer questions put to him by Campbell, representative of Arthur Ransome, Douglas snapped, 'You must allow me to finish my answer if you wish to get the truth,' ominously adding, 'but perhaps you don't wish it.'

This drew a swift response from the judge. 'Don't be impertinent to the learned counsel,' said Darling.

'I accept your lordship's rebuke,' Douglas answered.

'You will not only accept my rebuke, but you will act upon it,' came the stern reply.

Douglas had alienated everyone of importance in the courtroom, and when, over the next few days, the defence witnesses were called it might have seemed that little more damage could be done. But one made an impression, not on the court so much as on Douglas. It was More Adey, who had been persuaded into giving evidence by Ross. As we have seen, in one of his earliest letters of vitriol to Ross, Douglas had written, 'I don't consider that you have ever been a real friend of mine, in the sense that More and others have been my friends'. [103] It hit Douglas hard to see his old friend ranged against him – but worse followed. Among other things, Adey told the court that the £200 Douglas had given to Wilde was part of a 'debt of honour', rather than a gift, making up some of the expenses that the Queensberry family had promised to pay before the trial. This devastated Douglas who had discussed the matter many times with Adey, who had been an intermediary for the money, and he let him know, in no uncertain terms, what he thought of him. On 23 April he wrote,

Dear More,

I see that yesterday you were recalled by the Judge to give evidence, you, too, playing the Judas Iscariot to me, your old friend. You deliberately misled the jury.

You know perfectly well, for I have discussed the matter with you a dozen times, and you discussed it with my solicitor, that the £200 was sent to Wilde in November, 1897, within a week of my leaving him at Naples, and you also knew perfectly well that this £200 formed no part of any debt of honour.

I wish you joy of what you have done, knowing as you do that I have for years led a clean, straight life, and have struggled hard to be a good Christian and a good Catholic, and knowing that Ross, who put up Ransome to write the book, is a filthy beast and to this day a habitual sodomite and corrupter of young boys.

Our friendship is at an end. I shall never speak to you again. It is no business of mine to seek revenge on you or on Ross, but the reckoning will surely come sooner or later.

Alfred Douglas[104]

Here Douglas showed that he had no doubt Ross was behind the whole thing, but Ross was never called to the witness box. When Hayes asked why he had not been summoned, the judge told him that he could call him if he wished, though Hayes could not cross-examine Ross as his witness as he would be bound by Ross's answers. Ransome was never called as it was decided that there was nothing he himself could have proved. It was others who had given him evidence and it was they who should give witness to the court. Douglas, of course, felt that Ross had not been given the grilling he deserved and for this reason felt that he had not had 'satisfaction'. Hayes also complained that the defendant's counsel had missed the main points at issue and had 'thrown mud in the eyes of the jury, so that they should not see the clear issue. The defence,' he claimed, 'had thrown nothing but brimstone and thunderbolts.'

The judge summed up against Douglas, which, considering Douglas's behaviour, was unsurprising. He told the jury that they should not regard *De Profundis* as wholly true, though that was not to say it was wholly untrue.

It took one hour and fifty minutes for the jury to reach a verdict. They returned their decision that the words complained of were indeed a libel, but that they were true, that therefore Ransome had been justified in publishing them and that The Times Book Club had been justified in circulating them. Both the defendants were to be awarded costs.

Douglas was financially and emotionally ruined. He swore straight away that he would revenge himself on Ross. His request to appeal was turned down when it became obvious that he would be unable to secure the costs. The day after the close of the case, Darling called Cecil Hayes and F. E. Smith to see him. Douglas had sent Darling a copy of his letter to More Adey and the judge told both counsels that they were to pass on to him any other such communications. The letter he said, was, undoubtedly libellous and if either Ross or Adey wanted to take action they could. They declined, but this meant that the final confrontation would be postponed rather than avoided.

Just days after the end of the Ransome trial Douglas was in court again, this time to answer the charge of libelling his father-in-law. The action had been complicated by another action, which Custance, with Lewis's help, had been preparing: an attempt to take Raymond away from his father. On the charge of libel Douglas was advised not to put in a plea of justification by his solicitor, who obviously thought it would be better if Douglas just accepted what was coming to him and, indeed, he did. He admitted that, after losing the Ransome case 'my nerve went . . . and I was demoralised'.[105] Accordingly, Douglas withdrew all accusations and tendered an unequivocal apology to Colonel Custance. He was bound over, on his own recognisances, to the sum of £500 at the Recorder's suggestion.

12

After the trials Douglas went to stay with the brother-in-law of his sister, Lady Edith Fox-Pitt, and took Raymond with him. When he returned to the home he had had since *Academy* days in Hampstead, he found the house nearly empty. Olive had left him and taken her furniture with her. All he had left, apart from his mother, was his son. But now moves were afoot to deprive him of Raymond. Lewis was trying to get total custody of Raymond for Colonel Custance.

It was Douglas's lowest moment. The new life he had made in the wake of the Wilde scandal had been torn apart. He wanted revenge on all those who had aided his downfall. But for the time being, as he sat alone in the empty house, he dwelt on his bitterness, burned all the photographs of his wife, along with everything else that reminded him of her, and wrote two of his most tragic sonnets. One was to Olive, and the other a more general lament. 'Behold, Your House Is Left Unto You Desolate', is a devastating follow-up to the beautiful 'To Olive' sonnets.

> Alas, for Love and Truth and Faith, stone dead,
> Borne down by Hate to death unnatural,
> Stifled and poisoned! From the empty hall
> To the dismantled chamber where the bed
> Once held its breathing warmth, the soundless tread
> Of sad ghosts goes by night. Timid and small
> One creeps and glides; I saw her shadow fall
> Behind me on the floor uncarpeted.

> Poor wistful semblance of too weak remorse
> Why have we met in your forsaken room,
> Where the pale moon looks in on emptiness
> And holds a lamp to ruin? Fragile force,
> You come too late, my cold heart is a tomb
> Where love lies strangled in his wedding dress.[106]

By the end of the sonnet his feelings for Olive are no longer expressed as 'Love', an exalted, divine phenomenon, but 'love', a parody of true affection: Olive had deserted him when he needed her most. 'Stones For Bread' is about all the others who betrayed him:

> We clothed with white and shining loveliness
> The soul of the belovèd. And anon
> We saw it gleam, red hate, behind her eyes.
> The imagined loyalty of friends was less
> Than the least benefit we fed it on.
> Daily our hope is born and daily dies.

Douglas had brought much upon himself. He had been vindictive and cruel in his search for retribution, and with the zeal of the newly converted he had used religion as an excuse to condemn others, but he had struggled for years to suppress in him what he now condemned in Ross. Now though, he had opened up his past. Alice Head had recorded that, although they were close when she had worked with Douglas in the *Academy* days, she had not known the exact nature of the scandal surrounding him, explaining, 'They didn't tell women anything in those days.'[107] Now, thanks to his efforts to vindicate his past, nobody who read the papers could have been ignorant of the facts.

In his *Autobiography* he admitted, which he could not in 1913, that his own conversion and righteousness 'does not give me the right to condemn others. I see that now, though at one time I thought it did. There was a time, when I went after Robert Ross, when I succeeded, I fear, in "kidding myself" into believing that I was carrying on a sort of purity crusade.'[108] He continued to kid himself for some time. In the wake of the trials he had one objective in mind: to 'go for' the man he thought had masterminded his downfall, Robert Ross, and indeed he went for him with all the ferocity, persistence and insanity of Queensberry against Wilde. Now Wilde, as the co-conspirator with Ross in keeping *De Profundis* as a weapon against Douglas, which was how Douglas saw it, was also an enemy. As his father's system had worked with Wilde, Douglas decided to use it against Ross.

As Douglas had heard in court, during the reading of *De Profundis*, Wilde had seen the similarity between father and son. Now Douglas would prove him right. Douglas's mother had tried hard to prevent her children from becoming like their father and had tried to set an example of moral behaviour to them. Douglas, however, was proving the truth of one of Wilde's most flippant epigrams: that 'All women become like their mothers. That is their tragedy. No man does. That is his.'[109]

Chapter 6

'I bayed the pack alone'

(1913–1923)

When Douglas watched Wilde's case against Queensberry collapse, then read of Wilde's prosecution, he had felt able to express some of his anger in print. Now having seen the muck raked over in the Ransome case, John Long, an enterprising though controversial publisher, approached Douglas and offered him a substantial £500 advance for a book on Wilde, if it could be finished by July 1913, before all the interest caused by the Ransome trial had died away. The deadline was impossibly close for Douglas, although he needed the money badly and wanted an opportunity to refute the ideas about him sparked by the press.

Crosland, however, could knock up a readable book in a matter of weeks and saw that this was not only a glowing financial opportunity for him but a chance to exercise his pet hatred and, he hoped, destroy Wilde's reputation for ever. He said to Douglas, 'You will never write this book as it ought to be written. Even now, after all that has happened, and after you have got the complete proof of what an unspeakable swine Wilde was, you are still too "soft" about him to put it right across him as you ought to do,' and concluded, 'You had much better let me write the book altogether, you of course giving me the facts and revising it after I have put them into shape.'[1] Douglas agreed, not fully realising that Crosland would use him as a mouthpiece for his own prejudices.

Oscar Wilde and Myself has remained a favourite source among Wilde apologists, who have naturally found much in it to dig out and show revulsion at. Certainly there is no defending the book, and Douglas was naïve in the way he handled its creation. He admitted that Crosland pushed him to include more and more invective against Wilde and Ross and worked the book into a list of falsified excuses for himself. 'At the time I wrote or endorsed that book,' he admitted, years later, 'I had really persuaded myself that it represented a true picture of me. In truth it merely presented a picture of what at that time I wished to be supposed to be.'[2] Douglas wished to be supposed a heterosexual and an ardent, unblemished Catholic, so he could not admit to any love affair with Wilde. In any case Crosland would have been too horrified at the thought that Douglas had been a homosexual to have remained his friend, and Douglas needed Crosland, who, he said, was 'the only real friend I have ever had'.[3] Therefore, within the opening pages of the book Douglas states that the reason why he had never written about his relationship with Wilde before was because 'I have always known that there was nothing in our friendship of which I need be ashamed', and 'I looked to time and the facts to set me right.'[4] The tone of the text is, in the main, a cross between deeply wounded and vicious.

> The revelation of his [Wilde's] perfidy and vileness which came to me when, about a year ago, I first got knowledge of the existence of the unpublished portion of 'De Profundis', the shock of horror, indignation and disgust which the reading of that abominable document produced in my mind, and the ever-recurring reflection that during the last few years of his life and after his release from prison, when he was professing the greatest friendship and affection for me and living – for a time in part, and ultimately altogether – on my bounty, he was all the time the secret author of a foul and lying attack on me and on my family which he had arranged to make public after my death, combine to make the task of reconstructing a semblance of my old feeling for him almost a hopeless one.[5]

Douglas originally intended that *Oscar Wilde and Myself* would contain a complete reproduction of the whole text, including the so-called 'suppressed' portions, of *De Profundis*. He would add his own comments on all the allegations Wilde had made as marginal notes. In this way he would have the last word on the matter, which nobody alive could then dispute. But Douglas had not taken Ross into account. When Ross heard what he was intending to do, he took out an injunction to delay publication of the book. But although, as copyright holder, Ross could prevent the re-publication in Britain without his consent of any Wilde work, the same did not hold true in the USA where copyright was not protected. Therefore Ross, with the assistance of his secretary Millard, arranged for the production of the required twenty-five copies of *De Profundis* to secure copyright in the States. The intention of Douglas's book was further distorted by the publishers' purging of many of the more libellous passages regarding Ross, although the attacks on him that were allowed to stand are substantial enough. Problems arose over the book at every turn and delay after delay meant that it missed the gossip-market it might have found had it come out earlier.

2

Douglas's crusade on vice ironically came at the same time as his own record of virtue was tarnished. Shortly after Olive left him, a woman appeared providentially during the Custance libel case and offered him money. He was moved that a stranger should want to help him so, although he turned down her offer, he began to see her regularly and she filled the void in his life created by Olive's departure. Her name was Doris Edwards[6] and she helped Douglas through a trying period but also lured him into 'immorality'.

For some weeks he took her everywhere with him in innocent friendship, explaining to her that as a Catholic he could not have an affair with her. In the end, though, he succumbed to temptation and slept with her.[7] However, Douglas might have been pushed into this relationship: both he and Doris knew they were being followed by detectives hired by George Lewis and Colonel Custance. The intention presumably was to collect enough evidence against Douglas for Olive to be able to divorce him easily without any stain on her reputation. Douglas knew that his relationship with Doris would make his wife jealous and, indeed, when she heard of it through her father it did. She immediately telephoned him. After nearly four months of separation he recorded that the sound of her voice made him realise how much he loved her and that he wanted to repair the breach in their relationship.

The reconciliation did not last long, and took place during the public examination of Douglas's bankruptcy. During this period Douglas wrote to his wife about his affair with Doris. The tone of the letter is reminiscent of those he sent to her from America. He told her he still loved her but that

You have done a dreadful thing to me, and perhaps the most dreadful of all, in fact certainly the worst thing of all, is that you drove me out of the state of grace and holiness into mortal sin. I was good and in spite of all the suffering and persecution I was going through I was happy. I went every morning at 6 or 7 o'clock to communion and used to feel lifted right up to Heaven and I had no hate for anyone in my heart. I used to pray every day for your father and for Ransome and Ross and even George Lewis, and I really meant it.

Then when that Chancery case came on and you appeared against me, I turned bitter, for the first time, but even then I did not let go of the sacraments, and although I had met and known Doris for some time I utterly refused to do wrong with her.

He went on to say that, after the Chancery case,

I went to France and she came over to me and we spent a week together, but we were living in separate hotels and perfectly innocent and happy. It was simply on my part the ache of the void of love of a woman. I had got used to you 'loving' me and making a fuss of me, in the intervals of hating and abusing me, and I could not refuse love when it came to me. Now I have fallen into living in sin and I am utterly miserable. It is like going back into a hot blazing desert after being in a cool shady wood.

Then he made an extraordinarily frank admission:

You know I am not like other men and that it is possible for me to have a Platonic friendship with a pretty woman.

Then as regards you and me, there is nothing to do but wait and see what happens. Things may come right in the end somehow or other. I do still love you. I thought I had got over it, and for a short time I really did hate you. But I do understand now what you have done has been forced on you by your father and that villain Lewis and I forgive you.

He signed himself 'Your loving Boy',[8] but the test of his love came when she left him for the second time. Once again she returned to her father, whom Douglas considered as much his enemy as Ross. For her part Olive was caught between her husband, whom she loved, her father, whom she loved, and her son, who was, like her, the object of the quarrel. Clearly each party tried to vilify the other to her and she did not have the energy to make a decision between them. Olive made her biggest mistake when she agreed to give evidence against her husband, which Douglas found difficult to forgive.

But the real victim of the war between Douglas and Custance was the now thirteen-year-old Raymond. The courts had ordered that the boy's time should be shared between his father and his grandfather, which Douglas found impossible to accept and continually challenged. Constant arguments arose over it and Douglas informed his father-in-law that the whole Queensberry family considered the arrangement 'quite impossible'.[9]

In a series of letters to Olive after her second desertion he informed her that, although he had not lost all love for her, he could not help despising her for the way she had behaved towards him. He also felt aggrieved at some of the things he was hearing second-hand about what Olive was saying.

I am getting a little bit tired of your continual libellous and slandering assertions that I have been 'cruel' to you. You know perfectly well that it is a damnable lie to say so. So far from being cruel to you I have been extraordinarily good and long-suffering and patient with you. Having treated me in a most abominable way you try to put yourself right by slandering me and telling lies about me. It is a mean and despicable dodge and it is worthy of you, but it will do you no good in the long run.

Everyone who knows us and knows what I have had to endure from you and your horrible family knows that I have always been kind and loving and generous to you. What you call being 'cruel' is my refusing to let you make a public exhibition of yourself with Jack Stirling, Filson Young (you wanted to go and stay in an hotel with him in the west of Ireland and I was 'cruel' enough to prevent you) and other men.

So far from my ever having been cruel to you the boot is entirely on the other leg. You have been brutally cruel and heartless in your treatment of me and you have admitted it over and over again, and what is more all the world knows that it is a deliberate and wicked lie to say that I have ever been cruel to you.[10]

Douglas emphasised that he had suffered despite being a good father. The constant attempts to take Raymond from him made him more angry than anything else, particularly when Olive claimed that what she was doing was for Raymond's sake. As Douglas knew only too well, it was Olive's father who was making the decisions for her and it was he who wanted Raymond. Douglas claimed that Olive had not only been a bad mother but had also been a frequently absent one. A letter from his wife during the period when it was her turn to have the child drew a particularly vicious response from Douglas: 'I am glad that you have at last discovered that Raymond is a "clever and interesting child". That is at any rate a welcome change from your usual way of abusing him and saying how much you hate him and wish he had never been born.'[11]

Certainly Olive's attitude towards Raymond was ambivalent. She was attached to him but clearly found him a burden and motherhood difficult. She seemed incapable of taking on the adult role motherhood demanded and found it easier to be swayed by her father or husband than to make decisions herself. Perhaps she liked the fact that her father still controlled her life, both emotionally and financially, although she was in her forties. Ten years after she left her husband Olive admitted to a friend, 'I have always remained a child at heart.'[12]

3

Olive's departure was provoked, at least in part, by the constant pressure her husband was under as he juggled his quarrels and court cases. In the autumn of 1913 he acquired a few more enemies. The first was Frank Harris. It had been Harris who, shortly after Queensberry's death, had swindled Douglas out of a substantial part of his inheritance. Douglas did not bear him any grudge for this, but during this year, possibly the worst in his life, he actually came to blows with Harris. It was one of the few recorded physical fights of Douglas's life, though probably just one in a long list of Harris's. He had been a liar from birth but he was also a bully.

Whether or not Harris had a grudge against an individual he was capable of publishing the most outrageous lies about them. He had recently been to prison for contempt of court after printing some malicious lies about an enemy while a case involving him was in progress.[13] At the time of the fight with Douglas, he was busy writing his biography of Wilde, which, judging by the defamatory statements it contained about Douglas, was quite possibly the source of the violence. Afterwards, Douglas wrote to him:

> You are entitled to all the honour and glory you can extract from the fact that as you weigh about 3 stone more than I do and as I made no attempt whatever to hit you first you succeeded in grabbing me by the collar and forcing your thumb into my wind-pipe, thereby reducing me to impotence. All this I cheerfully concede to you. But would it not be more to the point if you could pretend even to yourself that you have behaved otherwise than as a blackguard?

Douglas listed Harris's offences towards him, then went on, 'If you can deny all these things, then you must be even more clever at deceiving yourself than you are at deceiving other people. If you cannot (and you know in your own heart that you cannot) deny them, then your own conscience must be your own punishment.' Douglas said he thought that Harris would probably not live much longer (which, unfortunately for Douglas, did not prove true) and told him, in the words of the sonnet Harris had admired so fervently, that he left him now, 'To what disaster of malign Despair,/Or terror of unfathomable ends?'[14]

Douglas's quarrel with Harris ended a friendship that had endured on and off since the nineties.

Another argument was instigated at this time by someone who did not even know Douglas. This was Christopher Millard, secretary to Ross. He had got into 'trouble' as a schoolmaster, then gone into journalism before publishing *Oscar Wilde Three Times Tried* (1912), a first and brilliant account of the Wilde trials, as well as the impeccable *Bibliography of Oscar Wilde* (1914) both of which appeared under his pseudonym, Stuart Mason.[15] Millard, a graduate of Keble College, Oxford, was undoubtedly a brilliant young man but, as Rupert Croft-Cooke, who knew him in his later years, wrote, although 'the work he did for Ross in editing the accounts of Wilde's trials and drawing up his enormous Bibliography was valuable . . . his indiscretions helped to ruin Ross when litigation began'.[16] Millard's name had inevitably come up in the cases Douglas had fought that had reference to Ross and, although much rumour circulated about Douglas's activities regarding his persecution of Ross, it appears that for a time Douglas indeed hired detectives to watch him. Millard's name came up in conjunction with the homosexual activities of

Ross's coterie. Certainly he was an indiscreet, overt homosexual who was bound to be frightened when Douglas's hounding of Ross became well known. Thus Millard wrote to Douglas without having had any previous contact with him. The content of his letter is clear from Douglas's reply, of 11 November 1913, written from his house in Church Row, Hampstead. It is one of the most interesting expressions of Douglas's viewpoint during the whole period.

Sir,

I am in receipt of your letter. You are under a strange delusion if you imagine that it is any part of the duty of a Catholic to endorse the evil doings of other Catholics. If you were not a Catholic and did not know perfectly well the wickedness of the life you are leading and the corruption you are spreading among the young, there might be some excuse for you. As it is there is none. There is nothing in the world so bad as a bad Catholic. God forbid that I should judge other people and if it were merely a question of yielding to temptation I could sympathise with you. But with you and your ex-employer Ross it is a question of deliberate propaganda and exaltation of vice in its worst form. As you have chosen to write to me you cannot complain if you get your answer, but I can assure you that, apart from general principles, I have not and never have had the slightest feeling against you personally. I know you only by sight and I have no 'satisfaction' at all in thinking that anything I have done has had the effect of 'ruining' you 'irretrievably' as you say it has. For my part I think that anything that has the effect of cutting you off from a man like Ross, who is probably the foulest and most filthy beast drawing the breath of life, can only be an ultimate gain to you; and if there were anything I could do to help you to get out of the quagmire of corruption in which you are floundering I should be most pleased to do it.

Yours very truly,

Alfred Douglas.[17]

Clearly Millard did not take Douglas up on his kind offer of help for in March 1914, when Douglas had a 'Letter To My Father-In-Law' put into pamphlet form Millard got a prominent mention. By then Douglas was trying to make Ross realise that the time had come when, unless he wanted his name to be irreparably ruined, he had to stand up in a libel action and deny the allegations made by Douglas and Crosland, which they could substantiate. In the circulated 'Letter To My Father-In-Law', Douglas informed Custance that

> You went to [George Lewis] because you knew that he was the solicitor of the notorious Sodomite, Robert Ross, of Georgian House 10 Bury Street St James, literary executor of Oscar Wilde, and because you knew that Lewis was acting for Ross and a *protégé* of his [Ransome] in proceedings which I had taken against that *protégé*. With your eyes open you thus allied yourself with what everybody now admits to be one of the foulest gangs of ruffians in modern history. I refer to George Lewis, Ross the Sodomite, Christopher Millard, otherwise Stuart Mason, who as you are well aware has served a sentence for an indecent assault on a boy, and their aiders and abettors.

He hammered home the message to his readers in the closing lines:

> We are told by St Paul to suffer fools gladly. I am free to admit that speaking for myself I have not suffered you over gladly, but on one thing you may plume yourself, namely that the literary executor of Oscar Wilde (Robert Ross), his ex-convict 'secretary' Christopher Millard alias Stuart Mason, George Lewis the solicitor, and the horde of filthy personages who have made the West End of London a sort of third City of the Plain will go down to their graves heaping blessings on the noble name of Custance.[18]

Nineteen fourteen brought a strange mix in fortunes for Douglas. Twice more he applied to Mr Justice Eve in the Chancery Court requesting full custody of Raymond. On both occasions Colonel Custance and Olive successfully opposed him. The result was that Douglas could have his son for only two-fifths of the year. All the parties wanted what was best for Raymond but in the end the tug-of-war – over everything from which school he was to attend to who was going to get him fitted for a new pair of trousers – took its toll. Raymond became confused by the competition for him. Although the Custance libel case of 1913 had ended with Douglas giving a full apology for and withdrawal of his claims he forfeited the recognisances under which he had been bound over when, in late 1913 and early 1914, he continued to make the same allegations, passing around letters about Custance's attempts to break up his marriage, and his attempts to gain Raymond for himself by whatever means. There was only one possible outcome from such a reckless course of action.

A court order was sent to Douglas telling him to attend the Old Bailey on 6 March for judgement to be passed on his case. He knew that imprisonment was likely as he had already broken the conditions of the earlier settlement. He wrote to the Recorder of London, informing him that since he believed it inconceivable that he would receive a fair trial at the hands of the Central Criminal Court he would not attend. He had started his career in litigation believing that the courts were a sound means of proving his innocence, but the continual rejection of his appeals for custody of Raymond, along with the fiasco of the Ransome trial, had made him lose any trust in fair play as a ruling principle in the English legal system. Most worrying of all, though, was that Douglas saw that a trap had been laid for him by Lewis with Custance and Ross. He saw that once he was in prison for libelling Custance, Lewis would apply for a warrant for his arrest for criminally libelling Robert Ross, and he would be unable to collect the evidence he needed to justify his libels. Therefore he would be 'done for ever'.[19] Consequently, for the second time in his life, this time to protect himself, rather than a friend, from the law, Alfred Douglas escaped across the Channel to the sanctuary of France.

Once Douglas was safely abroad, Ross might have thought it unlikely that he would cause any more trouble, but Crosland took the persecution of Ross a stage further. Early in the year he had sent a series of letters to Ross goading him into suing him for libel. Crosland was more willing than Douglas to attack Wilde, and through him Ross, so it was as one 'perpetuating the cult of Oscar Wilde' that Crosland attacked him. The statements he made were grossly offensive and he knew it. He told Ross that 'From the public point of view it is the highly respectable Ross labouring generously for the much maligned and greatly suffering Wilde and bringing him into his own. From my point of view, and in the case of the facts, it is one dirty Sodomite bestowing lavish whitewash upon another.'[20] He taunted Ross that 'If these letters do not contain the truth about you there can be little question that you would have taken a certain and obvious legal remedy.'[21] The 'legal remedy' to which Ross had now to resort, was no such thing.

4

Crosland was arrested as he was returning home late on Sunday 12 April. He told the police he was surprised that they wasted their time arresting him when they should have arrested Ross long ago. It was exactly the attitude Queensberry had expressed when he had been arrested almost twenty years earlier. Crosland was charged at Marylebone with having conspired with Lord Alfred Douglas to 'unlawfully, falsely, and corruptly to charge Robert Baldwin Ross with having committed certain acts with one Charles Garrat'. This was not the only charge against Crosland and Douglas: unknown to Douglas, Ross had also issued, on the advice of Sir George Lewis, an extra writ against Douglas accusing him of criminal libel.

Every weekend Crosland crossed to Boulogne, his fares paid by Douglas's mother, to consult Douglas over the action they should take. Douglas and Crosland had gathered considerable evidence against Ross although it was not all reliable. Charles Garrat, the boy whom Crosland had tried to persuade to testify to having committed indecent acts with Ross, claimed during the case never to have seen Ross. Years later when Millard was an old man, he told Rupert Croft-Cooke that although he had bedded Garrat, there had been no sexual relations between Ross and the boy.[22]

As always in a case involving Crosland there were dramatic scenes. At one point he got so heated that his own counsel asked him to calm down, to which he replied, 'I have been ten years trying to bring this thing about and I am here now, very happy and comfortable.' He frequently rebuked the prosecuting counsel with lines like, 'Keep a civil tongue in your head,' and at one point, asked by F. E. Smith, who was acting for Ross, whether it was true that he had taken it upon himself to 'regulate the private life of Mr Ross', he replied, 'Oh, no. I don't object to Ross making a pig of himself; what I mind is his making a sty of the world.'[23] It was a particularly over-the-top claim, even for Crosland, but it was a desperate attempt to bring the court over to his side.

Ross did not shine in the witness box. He had some serious claims to deny, and his attempts to do so were not convincing. Crosland's manner in the witness box won favour with those in the courtroom who wanted to show open disgust at anything to do with the crimes being discussed, and while Crosland had scored points with his brusque and determined answers Ross seemed merely to be sniping. The time Ross spent in the witness box brought back unhappy memories. His own solicitor put in *Dorian Gray* and read Wilde's infamous statement that 'There is no such thing as a moral or an immoral book. Books are well written, or badly written. That is all.' Ross was asked if there was such a thing as an immoral book to which he replied, 'Yes, I know heaps of them. Lord Alfred Douglas' *Poems*, for instance.'[24] Such a 'clever' answer did not win the court's favour although, ironically, they would probably have supported it if they had read the 1896 *Mercure de France* edition. Millard's appearance in defence of Ross was a serious error of judgement for he had been found guilty of the crimes of which Ross stood accused and which he claimed constituted a libel. Questioned about Wilde, Ross informed the court that he had tried to persuade his old friend to give up his relations with 'gutter perverts'.

It was in his summing-up that the judge indicated that anyone who had been a friend of Wilde's might reasonably be suspected of similar tendencies, unless they were vigorously and often denied. It was quite clear whom he backed, and the jury reinforced his opinion when they returned a verdict of 'not guilty' for Crosland amid loud applause from the back of the court. It was another unpleasant replay of 1895.

The acquittal encouraged Crosland at home and Douglas abroad. Ross was losing the fight, and they saw that it was just a matter of time before they had him cornered. For his part Ross was convinced that his former friend was clinically insane. In January 1914 Vyvyan Holland, the younger son of Oscar Wilde, married. Ross was terrified that Douglas would 'come and make a scene'. Holland was gracious enough to acknowledge in his memoirs, many years later, though, that Ross 'need not have worried as Douglas, eccentric though he may have been, was too well bred to make a fuss at my wedding'.[25] The incident showed that Ross himself was acquiring the same persecution mania as his enemy.

But Ross had cause to worry, for Douglas was determined to bring him down. Later in the year *Oscar Wilde and Myself* was finally published. The delay had largely been due to Ross's having forbidden use in it of Wilde copyright material. He and Robert Sherard, among others who were featured in the book, could still have sued for libel but did not and Ross wrote simply, 'I can only hope that the press will not discuss it too much.'[26]

Oscar Wilde and Myself vented the burning hatred of both Crosland and Douglas for Ross and Wilde, kindled by *De Profundis*. The book contains a chapter that challenges Ross to allow Douglas to publish *De Profundis*, 'word for word and line for line, without omitting or curtailing anything, and over it I will publish my reply, and the public at large shall be left to judge between Oscar Wilde and Lord Alfred Douglas'.[27] Crosland/ Douglas even claimed that on inspection of the released manuscript after Douglas's death, 'Wilde will be disgraced and confounded on his own evidence.'[28] The problems of the book as it stood were obvious to Douglas: 'It is very difficult to reply to an attack which one is unable to quote, and I can only say that I have met the difficulty as best I could.'[29] Having said this he declared the work to be 'my own present to Mr Ross and to the weeping worshippers of Wilde', continuing that it 'can be opened and read by him who runs while we have still a little breath'.[30]

Their growing hatred of anyone whose private life differed from their own was their other reason for writing *Oscar Wilde and Myself*. For Crosland this is understandable: he was a bigot and posed as a moralist even though he was neither perfect nor aspiring to be. The case of Douglas is rather more complex: there is no doubting he believed that Wilde and Ross had set out to ruin him. On the other hand he had been an unashamed and open homosexual, who had been as reckless in print as he had in his behaviour. His conversion to heterosexuality came at roughly the same period in his life as had Wilde's to homosexuality. For Douglas homosexuality was simply something in which he and most of his friends had engaged at school and university, and in some cases carried on into early adulthood. There is no doubt that from the time of his marriage onwards Douglas engaged in no homosexual activity. Perhaps at times he felt an attraction to a girlishly pretty boy but it is clear that, for him, the switch from one form of behaviour to another had not been a problem. As a Catholic, he saw homosexuality as a sin, and that giving in to that sin was wrong. Douglas had been well informed that Ross was corrupting young boys which disturbed him to the extent that he felt Ross's crimes should be made known in the public interest.

If *Oscar Wilde and Myself* were simply the expression of Douglas's hatred, a discussion of Wilde as a swine would have sufficed with the odd flash of aristocratic arrogance – 'Wilde's father was certainly a knight; but heaven alone knows who his grandfather was'[31]. But Crosland made sure that the book attempted to destroy Wilde as a literary figure as well.

Thus his every work was damned, except *The Ballad of Reading Gaol*. Crosland was allowed to make as much as he wanted of the split infinitives in the prose works and dismiss the 'minor verse', but when it came to the *Ballad* Douglas would not allow it to be touched.[32] Perhaps aside from the technical brilliance of the poem, which he admired, Douglas found in the Christian theme of that poem an inkling of the forgiveness he should have felt for Wilde. Wilde had been forty-four when he wrote the *Ballad*, the same age that Douglas was when he gave his name to the despicable book against his former friend.

5

Reaction to *Oscar Wilde and Myself* was almost uniformly horror – 'Hypocrisy can go no further, nor falsehood be more impudent. It is a monstrous travesty of the truth, which filled me with disgust,'[33] André Gide wrote in his *Journal*. Reviews appeared on the day of publication in *The Times* and the *Daily Telegraph*, but the book achieved little success except among those who followed the career of Lord Alfred Douglas. It gained him many enemies, particularly those who supported Ross's efforts to bring the works of Oscar Wilde to the fore. When, some time before publication, George Sylvester Viereck (who had befriended Douglas in America) wrote to him asking whether he could quote some of the book in a paper, Douglas replied, 'I rather doubt whether my book will commend itself to you as it is a strong attack on Wilde, not only on his character but on his work which I have dealt with critically in a way which has not been applied to it before.'[34] A member of the public was so concerned about the content of the book that he wrote to the Home Office asking why the Home Secretary did not suppress it, explaining, 'It is nothing more or less than blackmail of the living and calumniation of the dead.'[35] Max Meyerfield summed up the impression of many when he wrote that Douglas had done Wilde the favour of 'turning one of his paradoxical sayings into a commonplace truth: "It is always Judas who writes a man's biography." '[36]

With the outbreak of war against Germany, Douglas decided to join the army. He wrote to Lord Kitchener to ask if he could help but was turned down: he was, after all, a man with a past who was living in

France with three warrants out for his arrest, and he was also forty-four. For a while he half-heartedly contemplated entry into the French Foreign Legion, but decided, wisely, to return to England. He crossed the Channel with an overwhelming sense of doom, saying the rosary over and over again. As soon as he walked down the landing stairs of the ship at Folkestone a plain-clothes detective arrested him. He thought he was being arrested over the Custance business, but it turned out that a warrant had been issued over the criminal libel of Ross, of which Douglas had not been aware. For five days he was kept in Brixton prison and then at Wormwood Scrubs, where on arrival he was given stale bread and cocoa and allowed to bath before being sent to his cell. Years later he recalled the experience.

> I was put on the second and top floor of the sinister and forbidding-looking iron and steel house, smelling strongly of gas, with its rows and rows of numbered cells, to which I was destined. I was in the third or hard-labour division, and I must therefore, I imagine, have been in the same building where Oscar Wilde had been confined. I thought of him as I 'went to bed' (a plank bed and no mattress), and said to myself: 'Poor Oscar, however did he manage to stand this for two years?' That was the first time I had had a comparatively soft thought about him since I read the 'unpublished part' of 'De Profundis'.[37]

Because of various complications that arose, so Douglas claimed, from the deliberate efforts of George Lewis, he spent more time in prison than was strictly necessary, and the longer he was there the more he panicked. Having refused to eat as he thought he was to be released at any moment, he was starving and close to breakdown. He wrote that, in the morning,

> The door was again opened, and my untasted breakfast was removed by a prisoner, who eagerly took possession of my bread and stuffed it into his shirt. I sat for a time in a dazed condition, hearing the noise of walking and tramping outside. Then a fierce looking 'officer' looked in and shouted angrily at me: 'What are you doing here? Why haven't you made your bed? What do you think you are doing? You ought to be in the shed!' I looked at him with wide eyes and then burst into tears. I buried my face in my hands and sobbed.

The officer took pity on the new prisoner, who, he thought, judging by the nearly perfectly preserved good looks, was still a boy, and showed him how to do all the jobs he needed to do in prison. 'He then conducted me down two flights of iron stairs and out of the dreadful hall into the open air, and so to the shed, a large building, where about a hundred prisoners were working at sewing sacks and picking oakum. I was given some oakum to pick. Either before or after that, I forget which, I had an hour's "exercise," walking round and round a yard, with a hundred and fifty or so other prisoners.'[38] It was a lesson in humility, which he could, perhaps, have done with earlier.

After a night in Wormwood Scrubs, Douglas was granted bail, which was guaranteed in part by his cousin Sholto. The fighting spirit of his ancestors was now boiling up in Douglas's veins and he was ready for a fight. He went out and found a solicitor ready to go every round, but once Douglas had told him of claims he would make to plead justification he was told, 'Unless you can get a lot of real evidence, apart from your own, you will not have a chance.'[39]

So Douglas set out to get it. He travelled the country, from one end to the other, following every lead, searching for people who would testify against Ross. Every time he came to a dead end, he prayed to St Antony of Padua, the patron saint of lost things for whom he had a special affection, and tried again.

When the case against Douglas of criminally libelling Robert Ross came up in the Central Criminal Court in November, he had amassed fourteen witnesses to testify that Ross was a sodomite. For his part Ross was worn out by the battles he had already fought and, like Wilde in 1895, he was at a disadvantage: the courts did not like to support any behaviour that might be construed as homosexual in a climate hostile to it. With the war going on, fears of 'the English vice' being publicised arose not only because it might have a damaging effect on the impression given of the country abroad but also because it was feared that morale at home might be weakened by reports of such perversion. As a consequence, press reports were suppressed as far as possible. For Douglas the trial was one of his most glorious moments.

When Douglas searched for evidence to prove that Ross was 'a corrupter of young boys right down to the present day',[40] he went back to the early nineties and found men willing to recall their experiences at Ross's hands twenty years earlier. He also produced those who would testify to Ross's more recent activities, but some of these testimonies were tainted or insubstantial. The trial inevitably wandered away from the subject in hand, and included as much about literature and its damaging effects as it had in 1895 when prosecuting counsel had won sympathy with the jury by the reading of passages from 'immoral' works of art. Just as in 1895, many of the works mentioned were not those of the defendant or the prosecutor. H. G. Wells took the stand to testify to the moral integrity of his friend Ross, and Comyns Carr, acting for Douglas, made capital from allegations about the 'improper' works of Wells. He questioned Wells on a review of his book *Ann Veronica*, which had appeared in the *Academy* under Douglas's editorship. The review had damned Wells's book, claiming that it glorified the cohabitation of unmarried couples. 'Have you not,' persisted Carr, 'constantly written advocating the view that the ordinary ideas of marriage are nonsensical?'

'I have done nothing of the sort,' was Wells's reply.

But association with all kinds of immorality or immoral writings helped to nail the case against Ross. Just as Douglas had been ruined in the Ransome case by the jury's being fed information that had nothing to do with the case but which discredited his moral character, here the technique was turned on Ross. Edmund Gosse, Ross's great friend, gave evidence for his character and Cyril Holland said that Ross had been a second father to him, adding that Ross had never made personal gain of so much as a penny from the estate of Oscar Wilde – a claim Douglas always rejected. But these witnesses were not enough to take away the stain that had fallen on Ross's character. A boy by the name of Smith testified that he had been associated with Ross and that he had 'painted and powdered his face'. Such a statement on its own was enough to bring to the surface all the most conventional English bigotries, as was another that Ross had been at a New Year party at which twenty or thirty men had danced together. Another man pointed to Ross and declared, 'That is the man,' when referring to an individual who had corrupted his brother. The witnesses for Ross were respectable figures, but they could not deny the charges against him, while the collection of people assembled by Douglas could point to specific incidents. It was this that impressed the jury.

On the charge of blackmail made by Douglas against Ross, Douglas told the court that moral blackmail existed where a man kept letters written by friends until they could be produced twenty years later in court. The judge agreed with this, and his summing-up was strongly against Ross. 'I waited and waited,' he said, 'but I waited in vain for any moral expression of horror at the practice of sodomitical vices.' Ross's fate was sealed as Mr Justice Coleridge informed the court that 'I don't recollect that there is a copy or extract which has been produced indicating that he disapproves or that he views this kind of vice with disgust . . . I would say that is the attitude of the man and his mind towards this kind of perversion of sex.' In 1914 that was enough for Ross to lose his case and for society to turn against him.

The outcome was that the jury could not agree on the verdict and the case was adjourned. Douglas claimed that 'the foreman of the jury and 8 other jurymen waited for me outside the court when it was over to tell me that they were all in my favour except this one [juryman] who said *on the first day of the trial* that he would never bring in a verdict against Ross. The foreman told me that they would have stopped the case after Ross's cross-examination if it had not been for this one man.'[41] Douglas and his solicitor saw Lewis go up to the stubborn juryman after the case, touch him on the shoulder and walk out of the court with him. In a letter to one friend Douglas reported that the juryman had reported to the judge that the jury was divided (and the *double-entendre* was intended) into two 'camps',[42] and he always believed that the rogue juryman had been planted there by Lewis.

When the fresh hearing came up in December, Ross entered a plea of *nolle prosequi*, which meant effectively that Douglas's plea of justification would remain on the files and that Ross had admitted his guilt. Ross was forced to pay Douglas's costs and all out-of-pocket expenses, which amounted to about £600. Douglas therefore felt able to tell Olive, 'The triumph over Ross and Lewis is complete.'[43] Certainly for a time it seemed that Douglas had won, but a few weeks later Ross received £700 and a testimonial signed by three hundred people, stating their high opinion of Ross as a man of letters. It was endorsed by the Asquiths, Lady Ottoline Morrell and George Bernard Shaw representing a generation of writers, and by Robert Sherard, Ada Leverson and More Adey, representing the Wilde circle. For Douglas, it proved how stupid the English were. When he heard that Ross intended to use the money to create a scholarship fund for young boys he nearly went out of his mind. He wrote a satire that ran into four editions, selling thousands of copies, and remained in print as a pamphlet for some years called *The Rossiad*.

Referring to the signatories of the Ross testimonial he wrote in the person of Gosse talking to Ross:

> Three hundred names! you understand
> That's the big fish I mean to land.
> 'Letters and Art' to fill the ranks,
> A few Professors, and some cranks,
> A Bishop, (Anglican, I fear,
> I can't work miracles, my dear,)
> A brace of snobbish journalists,
> (Garvin for one,) some 'optimists,'
> Nine or ten 'cultivated' Peers,
> Some gushing ladies, poor old dears,
> Victims to vapours and anaemia,
> And then the riff-raff of Bohemia
> To swell the list and fill it out,
> The Press will do the rest no doubt.
> You'll see, they'll take it 'lying down,'
> There's not an editor in town
> Who'll dare to raise a single whine
> When Asquith bids him toe the line.

It concluded with a cry to the country, playing on the basest wartime fear of an enemy within.

> Two foes thou hast, one there one here,
> One far, one ultimately near,
> Two filthy fogs blot out thy light:
> The German, and the Sodomite.

The poem was sometimes funny, sometimes nauseating, but it was snapped up when it appeared in the shops, and caused a minor scandal when a number of retailers refused to stock it. Some people were shocked by Douglas's behaviour but he had no qualms: Ross had tried to ruin him so he had defended himself using Ross's own weapons.[44]

6

The war years were wasted years in every sense for Douglas. Young poets whom Douglas had first published, such as Siegfried Sassoon and Rupert Brooke, fought on the fields of Flanders for a nation that, in Douglas's estimation, was not worth the price paid for it in human lives. He hated pacifism because he associated it with cowardice, but he saw that British complacency had meant that a generation of young men had been sacrificed for a country riddled with moral decay. His attitude was epitomised in a poem he wrote at this time, entitled 'All's Well With England'. In it he aired his grievances against Ross, Margot Asquith and her husband ('Old Squiffy') but also railed against the hypocrisy that could allow moral opposites to co-exist.

> Out there in Flanders all the trampled ground
> Is red with English blood, our children pass
> Through fire to Moloch. Who will count the cost?
> Since here at home sits merry Margot, crowned
> With Lesbian fillets, while with front of brass,
> 'Old Squiffy' hands the purse to Robert Ross.

Douglas watched with horror as the war ground on. Nineteen fifteen brought the death of his namesake nephew Bruce, the eldest son of his younger brother Sholto, who was not even eighteen. The grief Douglas felt at Bruce's death must have been heightened when the news came through that Cyril Holland had been killed by a sniper's bullet. Douglas had known him as a boy and had holidayed with him and Wilde several times. In the following year, Pamela Tennant lost her eldest son, Edward, who was only nineteen. Edward's last letter to his mother had described the first day of the battle of the Somme, at which he had been present: 'Death and decomposition strew the ground.' Days later a sniper's bullet ended his life. He died with four photographs of his mother in his pocket.

But 1915 had also brought the culmination of Douglas's own family troubles. In 1914 when Douglas had tried to gain custody of Raymond, the court had consistently refused him. Each time his application had been opposed by his wife and her father. On 30 June 1915, when the case once again came before Mr Justice Eve at the Chancery Court, Olive agreed to stand by her husband and against her father. Even though the boy's parents had come together for the first time to fight for sole custody of their son, the judge decided inexplicably that the arrangements should not change and that the boy's grandfather should have more right to custody than his parents. Had Eve not made this decision, it is just possible that Douglas might once again have tried to live a normal life with his wife and child. But it was not to be. As Douglas had observed the previous year in the same court, he was in 'a position in which one might certainly suppose that an appeal to chivalry and good feeling could not be made in vain to anyone or to any such quarter where such feeling and such chivalry existed'.[45] He was wrong though, and when Eve expressed shock that a photograph of Raymond had appeared in the book *Oscar Wilde and Myself*, Douglas surely realised that, just as his youthful indiscretions had once ruined his chances of marriage, his adult reactions to them were among the causes of the ruin of his family.

Now Douglas grasped that the court's decision meant he was not considered by the law to be a suitable parent for his child. His reaction was understandable if foolish: dismissing once and for all the possibility that any justice could be found in England, he removed his son from Ampleforth and took him to Scotland, beyond the jurisdiction of the English courts, and to Fort Augustus where he could learn at the Benedictine monastery. 'My mother and I decided that the injustice and the iniquity of the whole thing was too much to be borne any longer,' he told William Sorley Brown, 'so I have taken the bull by the horns . . . My position is quite secure, though of course if I went back to England I should be imprisoned for contempt of Court. Words cannot express the contempt I feel for the Court and for the loathsome little worm of a judge, so that really I am thoroughly enjoying the situation.'[46] He took a house, and asked Olive to join them to make up a proper family once more. It was a desperate measure, but the arrangement seemed to work. Douglas reported to his wife, 'Raymond has been having the time of his life and is mad about Scotland and about the fishing. He got 14 trout himself the day before yesterday.' He told her that he was having their wedding ring blessed and a mass said for their reunion. He was hopeful, but worried: 'I do long to see you again, but I always live in fear that you will once more be used as a tool against me by the wickedness of your father and his horrible lawyer. But from all I hear there is nothing that they can do now. Raymond sends his love. He is continually asking when "mummy" is coming.'[47]

As ever Olive was stuck between her attempts to pacify her father and keeping her husband on her side. 'You don't know what people say,' she had written to old Lady Queensberry. 'Everybody I know takes my father's part, and, God help me, I don't know where to turn for advice and comfort.'[48] Eventually she told her husband that she would not meet him again until he agreed to give up his son to the child's grandfather. Douglas's reply is one of the few remaining pieces of evidence that give a good idea of what the Douglases' married life was like.

It is now two years since you deserted me and ever since you have fought against me in every possible way, from the Ransome case onwards, and have put the public insult on me of assisting your father to try to make out that I was unfit to have charge of my own son. Long before that however you treated me with cruelty and brutality. For the last two years we lived together you practically lived with another man. Day after day and night after night I was left alone while you spent your time dining and lunching and supping and going to theatres with Stirling or Clonmel. And as to my having been unfaithful to you I was never so (and as you know all that has been over for 4 years) till you drove me to it by repeatedly telling me in the most insulting language that you were tired of me and that your marriage to me had been one long misery. Indeed before we had been married a year you told me that regularly whenever we had a disagreement about anything. I soon got used to that, but it was during the last two years of our life together in Church Row that you made me see that you really meant it. You *continually* told me that the house and furniture were your property and that I had much better clear out and leave you to yourself. Indeed, although I have known you to have very generous moments you have never really liked to share anything with me as a woman who really loved her husband would be pleased to do . . . It was when I had nothing left except my bare £500 a year, when I was bankrupt and when I was in terrible trouble over the Ransome case and over fighting your battles with your father that you left me. Since then I have gone through unexampled misfortunes and persecutions. I was driven out of the country and had to live in a lodging in Boulogne for 6 months and during all that time you never wrote to me or took the slightest interest in me. And yet now you calmly talk of my having 'cast you off' and 'cut you out of my heart'! I refuse to argue with you about Raymond. Only an abnormal and unnatural woman would ever *desire* her husband to put up with the hideous and humiliating position which you and your father have created for me in that regard. I think you will vainly search history for another example of a woman writing to her husband and offering to come back and live with him *if he will agree to give up his son*. The whole thing is a nightmare.

Yet despite all this, Douglas admitted, 'I am not capable of ceasing to love you. Even if I desired to do so (as I sometimes have) I could not do it altogether . . . But I can keep myself in control and I would far rather never see you again than try to patch up an ignoble reconciliation with you by surrendering my duties and rights as a father.'[49] The result of the situation was more dramatic and disastrous than either of them could have imagined.

One day, Raymond set off fishing as normal. He did not return. Douglas and the monks from Fort Augustus searched every loch and river, fearing that Raymond had drowned. For two days Douglas thought his son was dead. Then he received a telegram from Olive – to tell him that Raymond was with her and Colonel Custance in Norfolk. Custance, through his solicitor George Lewis, had hired a private detective to go to Scotland to the hotel where Raymond and his father were still staying, kidnap the boy and bring him back within the jurisdiction of the English courts.

Once the situation was clear Douglas went to the Lord Advocate in Edinburgh and applied for a warrant to arrest Custance for kidnapping. It was refused – according to Douglas, the Lord Advocate was a great friend of Herbert Asquith. Custance applied for full custody of the boy once more, confident that after Douglas's contempt of court he would get what he wanted. Yet when the matter came up in February 1916 the judge decided that the previous judgment should stand unaltered, with the boy spending two-fifths of the holidays with his father, three-fifths with his grandfather, and that he should return to Ampleforth. But by now Douglas knew the full details of the kidnapping; it had turned out that Custance had been secretly communicating with Raymond all the time the boy had been with his father in Scotland. Custance had planned with him that a car would meet him at a specific point and at a specific time and that he should join the driver. He had bribed Raymond to agree to this with a box of sweets. Once Douglas discovered the truth he announced to the judge that if his own son could plot against him, as he saw it, he would have nothing more to do with him. Typically, when the monks at Ampleforth criticised Douglas's behaviour in renouncing his fourteen-year old son he felt that they 'made terms behind my back with Custance and Lewis'[50] and wrote a bitter sonnet entitled 'English Benedictines'.[51]

> But one child's soul bartered for worldly ease
> While Judas fingers pointed the broad road,
> One heart bereft, one house made desolate –
> Abbot, I tell you, trifles such as these,
> Now light as air, shall be a fearful load
> When with your monks you stand at heaven's locked gate.

Douglas did not see his son for almost a decade. He had been devoted to him for fourteen years, but in Douglas's view love had to reward love and even the renunciation of such love in a fourteen-year-old boy was grounds to disown him. Custance had what he wanted, and Douglas was left with nearly nothing and no one.

7

Cut off from normal family life Douglas moved in with his mother and sister Edith at the beautiful house they had been renting for two years from Lord Monkbretton, Shelley's Folly in Sussex. Since the death of George Wyndham a couple of years earlier, Douglas had only had his mother for support, both emotional and financial. Even T.W.H. Crosland had gone. He had always gravitated towards those who had money and his falling-out with Douglas came about over financial matters.

Crosland brought out the fourth edition of the *Antidote*, and left Douglas to pay for it. It contained another unpleasant attack on Ross. He and Douglas had already fallen out over the Ross trial when Crosland had refused to give evidence for Douglas, claiming that it might damage his prospects in journalistic circles. Douglas, who had sacrificed much to help Crosland, was incredulous, and even more so when Crosland said he would give evidence if Douglas would pay him £50 as an incentive and safeguard against any financial damage to his career. Needless to say Douglas refused.

The two patched things up if only for convenience's sake, when Douglas needed Crosland's help in writing a new book for which he had been given a £200 advance. It was to be entitled *The Wilde Myth*, and Douglas gave Crosland £50 in anticipation of his services. Crosland pocketed it and made off. Consequently Douglas wrote the book on his own over eighteen months. When he delivered it to the publisher, Martin Secker, towards the end of 1916, the book was type-set but the printers suddenly refused to print it and the publisher decided not to carry on with the book. Douglas could not understand why, though he recognised that the work was certainly libellous,[52] but Secker said later that it was simply '*Oscar Wilde and Myself* over again, with a great deal of diatribe about Ross'.[53] He eventually told Douglas to keep the money and try to find a printer himself, which Douglas was unable to do.

The intention of the new book, as explained by Douglas in the MS, was to destroy the cult of Oscar Wilde and Ross, which had also been the intention of *Oscar Wilde and Myself* but which that book had failed in doing. *The Wilde Myth* was repetitive and libellous. Although Ross would not have dared to go for Douglas through the courts again, it was possible that, had it appeared, Asquith would have sued as he was pilloried in it.[54] In its ideas the book contains little that was not already known, and what does not appear in *Oscar Wilde and Myself* is in various pamphlets. The full manuscript of *The Wilde Myth* has survived, though it remains unpublished.[55]

The fall-out with Crosland did no one any favours though it prompted from Douglas one of the few sonnets of this period. Crosland had had his greatest financial successes before he had met Douglas with a series of books, the first of which was called *The Unspeakable Scot*. Douglas called his sonnet 'The Unspeakable Englishman'.

These were some of the saddest days of Douglas's life, and certainly the most futile. He found it hard to create anything of beauty and poetry with his mind twisted by hatred and bitterness to those who had once been close to him. In September 1916 he made an application at Bow Street for a summons to be served against George Moore and his publishers for 'composing, printing, and publishing a blasphemous libel concerning the Holy Scriptures and the Christian religion, contained in a book entitled *The Brook Kerith*'. Douglas's solicitor pointed out that although his client recognised that 'in dealing with religious subjects a person was entitled to attack the fundamentals of religion' he ventured that 'the author of this book had spoken with language of affront, and otherwise than with a feeling of reverence for subjects which the majority of mankind regards as sacred'. But the magistrate said that, in his opinion, the book did not count as legally blasphemous as it was 'based on the assumption – which the author had a perfect right to make – that Christ was merely a man. It had been held over and over again,' he emphasised, 'that to assert in a book that Christ was a man and not divine was not necessarily blasphemy.'[56] Not content with fighting libels concerning himself, Douglas was now trying to defend Christ.

Left with only his mother and his dog, Winston, for company, Douglas regretted the loss of his son. He said later that at this time, 'I gave up all idea of happiness in this life, and clung to Catholicism as my only consolation.'[57] However, relations with Olive perked up when she decided to become a Catholic, which Douglas saw as a signal of her desire to start afresh, but he was largely unoccupied and frustrated. The boy who had shown so much promise had become a man with no future so he picked senseless quarrels. He had grown wary of everyone: if he could not trust his wife, his father-in-law or his son, how could he trust a stranger? A letter to his wife in early 1917 showed the extent of his loneliness. He told her of his dog's death, which had been symbolic: 'It's the last link between us broken. I gave him to you and he was your dog till you got tired of him as you do of everything . . . I have done nothing but cry ever since. He was the last thing I had except my mother.'[58] He consoled himself by writing out quotations from the Bible, including the passage from Romans 8:21, 'The creature itself also shall be delivered from the bondage of corruption into the glorious liberty of the children of God.'

But there was a different side to Douglas in these years, as exemplified by the correspondence he exchanged with Lord Monkbretton. Douglas wrote to him first on 19 November 1917 complaining that in the two years in which he had lived at Shelley's Folly, Monkbretton had not visited or invited the Douglases to his own home even though he lived only a couple of hundred yards away. The letter was full of Douglas's usual tricks: he accused Monkbretton of sympathising with the Ross–Asquith gang and finished by hinting that his lack of cordiality suggested that he was not of the same social class as himself. The reply two days later was a beautiful example of the retort courteous: it merely explained that, for the duration of the war, he had visited no one, and that the tone of the letter he had received did not impel him to take up an acquaintance now. Douglas replied with a guarded apology for his first letter's contents, and added an attack on English Protestants. Monkbretton wrote to accept the apology but suggested that if the family were unhappy with their lodgings he would be willing to release them from their tenancy. In a third letter Douglas told him that he had taken the hint that he and his mother wanted to leave as an attack on her well-being. He concluded the correspondence by telling Monkbretton that no answer to this third letter was required but that if they did meet their relations would be just as they were before the first letter.[59]

Douglas's three letters had brought him back where he had been at the start but with one more person alienated. Surely this was not the same man who had declared in Naples twenty years earlier that his aim was, 'To clutch Life's hair, and thrust one naked phrase/Like a lean knife between the ribs of Time'. His talent seemed to have dried up, he had no ambition, no hope and nothing to live for. He had also engaged himself in a singularly unpleasant act.

8

The First World War had little physical impact on Douglas once he had cocooned himself in Shelley's Folly: he had been busy fighting his own battles. Then, in 1918, the chance came for him to make the public declarations he had wished to make for years, in a libel action which, for once, had not been brought by him. On 26 January 1918 an article appeared in the *Vigilante*, a paper owned by the right-wing maverick MP Noel Pemberton Billing, claiming that, 'There exists in the Cabinet Noir of a certain German Prince a book compiled by the Secret Service from reports of German agents who have infested this country for the past 20 years, agents so vile and spreading such debauchery and such lasciviousness as only German minds can conceive and only German bodies execute.' The article appealed to all the extreme bigotries that such an event as the First World War could throw up. It claimed that the 'Black

Book', as it was called, contained the names of 47,000 'perverts', who would naturally be a threat to British security during this time. One of Billing's informants was Harold Sherwood Spencer who had been invalided out of the army, a man with a grudge and a considerable ability to imagine conspiracies. The extraordinary claims aroused strong public feeling and emotions ran high. But Billing knew what he was doing, and whom he was gunning for, and when the *Sunday Times* carried an advertisement for a private performance, starring Maud Allan, of Wilde's *Salomé* he gave his opinion on the matter. The piece in the *Vigilante* for 16 February read:

The Cult of The Clitoris

To be a member of Maud Allan's private performances in Oscar Wilde's *Salome* one has to apply to a Miss Valdetta, of 9, Duke Street, Adelphi, W.C. If Scotland Yard were to seize the list of these members I have no doubt they would secure the names of several of the first 47,000.

Most of those who read the headline would not have understood its meaning, but to others it was clear, and constituted a gross and defamatory libel on Maud Allan. The article not only appealed to those who saw Wilde's work as depraved but also to those who had been shocked by the career of Maud Allan who, for more than a decade, had entertained the highest echelons of society, even the King himself, with her risqué performances of the dance of the seven veils, which she would execute wearing little more than carefully positioned beads.

Billing's crusade for 'purity in public life' naturally appealed to a great many people, including Alfred Douglas, who supported Billing's attempts to expose the corruption at the heights of society. He, like Billing, saw it epitomised in 'the cult of Oscar Wilde'.

In fact, Douglas had tried to point out the decadence and unhealthy preoccupation with Maud Allan's routines a decade earlier and had come into personal conflict with her. While he edited the *Academy* one of his contributors had written an article claiming that Allan was not a real dancer at all, merely a sensation of the moment whom the public were misguided in applauding. It was not a defamatory article though it made a valid point. 'It would be stupid not to admire the character which has brought about so great a success,' wrote the author of the article, 'but it would be just as stupid to mistake this American "grit" and "bluff" for beautiful art.' Allan threatened to sue so Douglas printed a mild apology to her in the next edition. There the matter might have rested, but Allan and Douglas were both prominent figures who wished their past to remain unknown. Allan, who had grown up in America, had a brother who had committed a particularly unpleasant double murder, which had been widely reported in the American press, resulting in his eventual execution. If this had been widely known in London it would have caused a scandal and highlighted the more gruesome side of Allan's interpretation of *Salomé*.

Shortly after the article appeared in 1908, an incident occurred at a London garden party. Maud Allan arrived and spotted Douglas with two other gentlemen. She strode across the lawn towards them but when they saw her the other men escaped leaving Douglas to bow courteously to the woman who now accosted him. Witnesses saw her lean towards him, hissing some insult at him. Douglas was so used to this treatment that, with no hint of strain and keeping his manners, he simply said, 'But your brother was a murderer!' Allan turned white with rage and hit him across the face with her fan.[60]

The inevitable result of the *Vigilante* article was that Maud Allan and Jack Grein, the play's producer, sued Noel Pemberton Billing for libel – a course Robbie Ross urged them not to take. Ross saw what would happen if they went ahead, and when they did, his worst fears were confirmed. In a trial that became famous as one of the most sensational of the century Billing took charge of his own defence and displayed his ability to bring out people's prejudices over their power of reason. For almost the last time, it was Wilde and his works who stood in the dock at the Old Bailey. There were a number of uncanny echoes of the 1895 trials: Jack Grein, one of the prosecutors, had then represented Alfred Taylor, Wilde's co-defendant; Allan's counsel, Travers Humphreys, was the son of the Humphreys who had agreed to take on Wilde's case in 1895 and who had agreed that he had to prosecute the Marquess of Queensberry. The most significant difference in 1918 was that Queensberry's son, Alfred Douglas, was in court and had been asked to give evidence.

The Billing trial rested on one abhorrent aspect of British life: the intense dislike of foreigners, which was given respectability in wartime. The trial also relied on the common dislike of any sexual preference that stood out from what was seen as the norm. The fact that Billing and others who claimed to be free of sexual vice including one of his key witnesses, a Captain Spencer who was a lunatic, were merely philandering heterosexuals gave the trial an air of the utmost hypocrisy. But it worked for Billing, and when he persuaded the court that people in high society were featured in the 'Black Book' the common man rose up.[61] Public knowledge of Margot Asquith's suspect goings-on as well as her intimacy with Ross, known by both Asquiths to be 'a bugger', genuinely shocked people.[62] Billing was proving his libel, and Douglas could express once and for all in a court of law that he detested every vice with which Ross and Wilde had been associated. Ross was visited by the police – he believed at Douglas's instigation. Christopher Millard had just been convicted and sentenced again for homosexual acts and, as Ross wrote of Douglas, 'the disaster to Millard was for him a very good opportunity'.[63] It was clear from the start who was running the case: Billing had even selected his audience, arranging for maimed soldiers from the front to sit in the gallery, and acted very much as 'the people's advocate'. Mr Justice Darling constantly had to reprimand him and on the second day, at yet another interruption from the judge, Billing snapped. He was trying to get information out of a female witness who claimed to have seen the 'Black Book', and when Darling obstructed this line of questioning he shouted, 'I know nothing about evidence, and I know nothing about law. I come to this court in the public interest to prove what I propose to prove.'

'Very well,' said Darling, 'then you must prove it according to the ordinary rules of evidence.'

'I say this, my lord,' Billing started, but was once more cut short.

'I do not want you to say anything to me. I only ask you to put such questions—'

Darling was not allowed to finish. Billing hit the table, pointed dramatically at the bench and shouted an exchange with the witness:

Billing: 'Is Justice Darling's name in the book?'
Witness: 'It is.'
Darling: 'Just a moment.'
Witness: 'It can be produced.'

Calls for order were ignored and there was pandemonium as the pantomime continued. The witness pointed at Darling and cried, 'If it can be produced in Germany, it can be produced here. Mr Justice Darling, we have got to win this war, and while you sit there, we will never win it. My men are fighting, other people's men are fighting—'

Billing interrupted: 'Is Mrs Asquith's name in the book?'

Witness: 'It is.'

Billing: 'Is Mr Asquith's name in the book?'

Witness: 'It is.'

Billing: 'Is Lord Haldane's name in the book?'

Witness: 'It is.'

The gallery went wild, the press thought it was Christmas, and Darling desperately tried to regain order over a court that had been given the impression that he was doing his best to protect 'high society perverts'.

'It will take more than you to protect these people, my lord,' Billing declared.[64] Accusations flew in all directions, and even Mrs Asquith claimed that it was all 'the dirty work of Lloyd George and Beaverbrook'.[65]

It was into this atmosphere that Douglas emerged to give some of the most poignant and ridiculously over-the-top opinion of the whole case. Billing had been unable to sub-poena Ross, who was ill – he had only weeks to live – so Douglas was able to make all the claims he wanted, which had basically been proven in the courts before. He was also there to take revenge on Darling, who had judged against him in the Ransome case. He went in with guns blazing.

As a collaborator in the translation of *Salomé*, and the only man in court who had been with Wilde throughout the period of its writing, Douglas was a vital witness. Dressed conventionally in a three-piece suit with bow-tie and bowler hat, he started his testimony with a simple historical account of the writing of *Salomé*. Then he got going. Questioned on the nature of the play he said that Wilde intended it to be 'an exhibition of perverted sexual passion excited in a young girl'. He also claimed that it contained a passage that alluded to sodomy, which was the kind of word the excited courtroom wanted to hear. Asked by Billing whether he had been aware that Wilde was a sexual pervert, he said that he had. Then Douglas claimed that Wilde gloried in vice, which was unpardonable, and that he regretted ever having met him. Douglas had only been truthful so far, but now he went further. He said, 'I think he [Wilde] had a diabolical influence on everyone he met. I think he is the greatest force of evil that has appeared in Europe during the last 350 years'[66] (he meant, since the Reformation). 'He was the agent of the devil in every possible way. He was a man whose whole object in life was to attack and to sneer at virtue, and to undermine it in every way by every possible means, sexually and otherwise.' He went on, 'Intellectuals are people who believe in Art for Art's sake, and all that sort of rubbish; but not necessarily wicked people; more or less merely foolish people.' He then identified the 'cult' of Oscar Wilde, the green-carnation wearers, and named members of the cult, including Ross, Millard and Reginald Turner.

Billing manipulated Douglas's answers so that he brought in German names like Krafft-Ebing, author of *Psychopathia Sexualis*. Counsel representing Allan and Grein brought out the letter Wilde had written to Douglas twenty-five years earlier, once again: 'My Own Boy, Your sonnet is quite lovely, and it is a marvel that those red rose-leaf lips of yours should have been made no less for music of song than for madness of kisses.'

Douglas had been goaded too far: 'That is a letter which he wrote to me,' he shouted. 'It has been kept for twenty-five years. It was stolen by that German blackmailer, George Lewis, who is bringing it out for the fiftieth time. I think there are limits to human endurance. Every time I come here this bestial drivel is brought out.' Billing objected to the use of the letter and was told by Darling that should he interrupt again he would be removed from the court. Pressed as to what the letter was Douglas said frankly, 'It is a rotten sodomitically inclined letter written by a diabolical scoundrel to a wretchedly silly youth,' and added, 'You ought to be ashamed to bring it out here.'

Darling ticked him off: 'You are not here to comment on counsel.'

All of the fury Douglas had stored up since the Ransome case, which had been prejudiced by just this sort of interjection, came out: 'I shall answer the questions as I please,' he exploded. 'I came here to give my evidence. You bullied me at the last trial. I shall not be bullied and browbeaten by you again. You deliberately lost me my case in the last trial. I shall answer the questions as I choose, and not as you choose. I shall speak the truth.' Darling threatened to have him removed from the court room. 'Let me be removed from the court,' Douglas said. 'I did not want to come here to be cross-examined to help this gang of scoundrels they have at the back of them.'

So pleased was counsel at the effect that the Wilde letters had on Douglas that he read another. This time Douglas told the court, 'That is the letter that was produced by my father in his effort to smash up Wilde to save me, and that has been the result.' He was actually expressing respect for his father's motives. 'My father comes before the court to save his son, and you lawyers come here twenty-five years afterwards to spit it up again for money, because you have been paid to do it.'

'When did you cease to approve of sodomy?' asked counsel provocatively, but Douglas would not be drawn, knowing it might lead to another trial.

It became clear that Allan's team had a series of Wilde's letters to Douglas – almost certainly given to them by George Lewis, who kept a file of them in his safe and lent them to people who were fighting cases against Douglas. Douglas threatened that if he got hold of the letters he would tear them up so Darling ordered that they be kept out of his reach.

Counsel then held up the letter written by Douglas to Henry Labouchère, part of which had appeared in *Truth*. The letter did more damage to Douglas, but supported the idea Billing was establishing that a substantial number of people at the top of society were sodomites, which was the gist of Douglas's letter, although it had been intended in 1895 to have a somewhat different effect. Douglas attempted to distance himself from it: 'If I were still on Oscar Wilde's side, I should be getting praise from judges and Prime Ministers, and praise from greasy advocates. Like Ross, I should get a testimonial from Asquith and £700 given to me from people in society saying what a fine person I was. Asquith and all these people presented Ross with a testimonial and £700 because he was a sodomite.'

Billing stood up and asked, 'Are you a sodomite today?'

'No, of course I am not.'

Douglas had said in no uncertain terms what he wanted to say. It was left to Billing to point out that Douglas had come to court to testify against perverts when he knew that his own reputation might be harmed. He was held up to the court as a hero.

Douglas's manner during the trial was symptomatic of the way he had behaved for a number of years. Perhaps this was epitomised by a letter he had written four years earlier to the Earl of Clonmel who had questioned his relationship with Olive.

You damned Irish Pig-Doctor,

You have had neither the pluck nor the honesty to answer a straight-forward letter. You make no attempt to deny or explain or apologise for your conduct with regard to my wife. Accordingly, in her ladyship's best interest, I give you fair warning that if I hear of your so much as going within twenty yards of her either in public or in private, I will seek you out and give you the dog-whipping you deserve.

Yours faithfully,

Alfred Douglas.[67]

The verdict of the jury was that Noel Pemberton Billing was not guilty. The gallery rose to its feet as one and the whole court cheered. Darling cried for order in vain, for although people could see his lips move he could not be heard above the noise. Constables tried to clear the mob but it was some time before the jubilant crowd were all out. In the streets those who had waited all day for the verdict were joined by those flooding out. For Billing and his friends it was their finest hour. The crowds greeted Billing loudly on the steps of the Old Bailey and many tried to shake his hand. A few minutes later Douglas came out, and the throng once again went wild, cheering, clapping and backslapping this upholder of British values, this moralist and example. As he stood on the steps of the Old Bailey, which had featured so prominently in his life, waving his bowler hat triumphantly, he received the reception of which he had always dreamed.

9

The Billing case had the result that those involved in it desired. Maud Allan's career was tainted and the works of Oscar Wilde once more appeared as the product of a lascivious pervert. Later many could not understand why the case had been heard. Ross was succinct on the matter: 'The English, intoxicated into failure, enjoyed tearing poor Maud Allan to pieces, simply because she had given them pleasure, and kicking Oscar's corpse to make up for the failure of the 5th Army.'[68] He was understandably upset at the way that Wilde's public image had devalued his work, an anomaly Ross had spent his adulthood trying to correct. In a fit of rage he wrote to the Public Prosecutor telling him what he thought of him, and calling him a 'snob' and a 'bastard'.[69] It was an unusually open attack for Ross, who, though he had certainly been less than honest with Douglas, was not the evil psychopath his former friend believed him to be. But that protracted argument was soon brought to a close, for just before the end of the war he died in his rooms in Half Moon Street. Siegfried Sassoon, a great friend of his, wrote that 'he died of heart failure. It seems reasonable to claim that this was the only occasion on which his heart failed him . . . His death made a difference which could only be estimated in sorrowful conjectures. It deprived us of an ever-ready helpfulness that might have changed many human discords to harmony.'[70] Douglas prayed earnestly for Ross's soul, and continued to do so until the day of his own death.

Douglas himself was not a happy man. He remained in frequent correspondence with his wife, whose conversion had given him hope, but things soured between them every time a full reconciliation looked possible. Letters to her ranged from those addressed to 'My darling little girl'[71] to 'You miserable woman',[72] and they remained apart. The priest who received her into the Catholic Church described relations between husband and wife on the day of her reception as 'very pleasant, though somewhat restrained'. He also recorded her having said that although fond of her husband, 'when [he] got violently angry, she was positively terrified of him'.[73]

Some of Douglas's passion for horse-racing returned when Percy's new wife bought a racehorse. Like Percy, Douglas hoped that it would run in the Queensberry colours, but this was not to be. Percy had remarried, after Minnie's untimely death, partly to try to resolve his financial difficulties. His new wife was Mary Louise Morgan, and he continued to travel the world still trying to make his fortune. He was not successful partly due to his reckless generosity – when he discovered his daughter Violet in his hotel room giving away his cigars and other expensive items to passers-by on the pavement below he was pleased with her for being so thoughtful.[74] If Percy had a fault it was simply bad luck.

He died aged fifty-two on 1 August 1920 in Johannesburg. 'My dear brother's death was a great blow and shock,' Douglas told his cousin Judith Wentworth, daughter of Wilfrid Scawen Blunt, 'though I am happy about him as he died a good Catholic. His body is being brought back to England for burial.'[75] At the funeral of Percy, 9th Marquess of Queensberry, in Westminster Cathedral, there was standing room only. An enormous congregation had turned out to pay their respects to a man who had touched many with his kindness and generosity. The family did not know most of the people there, and many were beggars who remembered Percy for his charity. On one occasion he had gone to one of the poorest areas of the city, the Embankment, with £1,000 in cash and had given some to every beggar he met on the way.[76] He had died nearly penniless, and his son Francis was faced with the daunting prospect of remaking the family fortune. (Alfred Douglas reckoned that between them, his father and brother had lost some £700,000 and all the family property in Scotland.)[77]

Before he died Percy made one more effort to help his younger brother and mistakenly thought he had succeeded. He had persuaded a wealthy friend, one James Conchie, to buy Douglas a paper to edit so that he once again had a viable opportunity to make use of his literary talent. The result was a curse. Douglas called his paper *Plain English*, and Conchie paid £100 for the name of the *Academy*, which was incorporated into *Plain English*. Douglas wanted his new toy to be straightforward in its aims and expressions, and Conchie was in every way the ideal newspaper proprietor for he stood back from its day-to-day running. The first number, of 10 July 1920, opened with an article from the editor, worryingly titled 'Digging up the Hatchet':

Exactly ten years have elapsed since (in June 1910) the editor of this paper, who was at that time editor and proprietor of the *Academy*, sold it (the *Academy*) to two of the richest peers in England, Lords Fitzwilliam and Howard de Walden. The *Academy* was run by the then proprietor and editor at a very heavy financial loss on uncommercial lines in the interests of High Literature, Honest Politics, and Sound Morality. Without financial backing it could scarcely hope to hold its own, and it was only by a series of miracles that it survived as long as it (and the very modest resources of its editor and proprietor) did . . .

Pretty well everything that the old *Academy* under the editorship of Lord Alfred Douglas stood for has been battered into pulp by all kinds of rogues and knaves and fools. The big stick which managed to keep them in a certain amount of order at that time has been lacking, and the forces of evil in consequence, have been having 'the time of their lives'. That time is now over as they are invited to take notice. *Plain English* will carry on the traditions of the old *Academy* in every respect except one – whereas the *Academy* was a venture conducted on lines which not only cultivated an aristocratic disregard for 'business', but actually went to the length of kicking it neck and crop out of the premises whenever it ventured to lift a reproachful face in the office, the present journal, like the Polar bear of our childhood, is 'perwided with claws to prevent it a-slipping on the hice', in the shape of a proper business organisation and a powerful financial backing.

Douglas was setting himself up for another fall. In the wake of the Billing trial moralists like him felt that they held the reins of public opinion, but this soon waned, and as the 1920s progressed paroxysms of rage from the extreme right would seem at their best increasingly futile and, at their worst, comic.

One particular aspect of Douglas's editorship shocks today far more than it did then and that is its anti-Semitism. Douglas was convinced by such stories as the *Protocols of the Learned Elders of Zion*, which confirmed his and the majority of the British public's belief that Jews took positions of power and corrupted the British system for their own benefit.

Plain English aired the prejudices of a good many people, and it was clearly a popular policy. The paper sold only around 350 copies of its first edition, but when Douglas gave up as editor the circulation had increased to 3,000. He found many people to attack and upheld most strongly those Catholic principles threatened by the rising tide of liberalism. He attacked birth-control schemes and other modern phenomena that were anathema to the Pope. If there was an unpopular cause, Douglas supported it – for instance, he expressed strongly pro-Irish Nationalist tendencies after visiting Herbert Moore Pim in Ireland when Pim had shown him the injustices in that country. 'I have no reason to love them and I am not an Englishman,' he told one contributor, 'but to do them justice I think what they suffer from is oversentimentality and inability to get roused over anything.' And Douglas certainly felt strongly when Sinn Fein turned to violence. 'When they begin saying, "we have suffered fearful injustice, therefore are justified in committing murder and suicide and joining secret societies, membership of which implies *ipso facto* excommunication," then I mistrust them and the whole trend of their argument,'[78] he wrote.

Douglas expressed opinions on matters of national and personal significance alike in *Plain English*. He delighted in writing articles on

Mr Justice Eve and Frank Harris. An article in *Plain English* expressed quite clearly what Douglas thought of Harris:

> Frank Harris.
>
> Replying to a correspondent whose letter on the above subject is now printed in our correspondence columns Our reference to Frank Harris as a 'renegade' is based on the notorious fact that all through the War Harris was writing for German-owned and German-edited papers in America (notably in a horrible journal, devoted to a cult of Satanism, called the *International*, and edited by a German named George Silvester [*sic*] Viereck), and that his writings were inspired by sentiments of the utmost hatred of and contempt for this country. Harris backed Germany for all it was worth, and if Germany had won we should, no doubt, have had this foul person editing *The Times* in London, with the assistance of his bosom friends George Bernard Shaw and Alitser [*sic*] Crowley. Our correspondent is right in his conjecture that Harris is 'wanted' by the police. There are at least two criminal charges awaiting him (quite apart from any proceedings which might be instituted by the Treasury for treason) in the exceedingly unlikely event of his ever showing his face in England again. Meanwhile, the *Athenaeum* is praising Harris to the skies, and beslavering him with fulsome compliments, more especially in reference to his book, 'The Confessions of Oscar Wilde', which consists of a mass of crudely and clumsily expressed lies about living persons who, owing to the fact that the book is published in America, are powerless to defend themselves against this scoundrel. Anyone caught selling or dealing with the book in this country would render himself liable to criminal proceedings.[79]

The institutor of those legal proceedings was, of course, Douglas. And when Crosland joined the staff of *Plain English*, the libel cases flooded in.

On 27 January 1920 Douglas was charged with libelling Henry Savage in the course of a letter addressed to the editor of the *Bookman's Journal*. When a copy of Savage's article 'A Bookman's Lost Atlantis' arrived at Douglas's address anonymously, his persecution mania took over. The article linked Douglas's name to that of Wilde. Douglas assumed that Savage had sent it out of spite and told the journal's editor that he should not employ the man. He told a correspondent that he knew Savage to be 'a man of bad character, an associate of the Ross gang', who had once published a paper called the *Gipsy*, which Douglas considered 'filthy' and had slated in the *Antidote*. What Savage wished to sue on, presumably, was the statement in Douglas's letter that Savage was clearly a votary of the cult of Oscar Wilde,[80] who Douglas thought were trying to ruin him. His suspicion that Savage had sent him the article was groundless and nothing was gained from it but another lengthy discussion about the morality or otherwise of *The Picture of Dorian Gray*. The case was dismissed.[81]

10

Of more importance was a case brought by Douglas against the *Evening News*. On 4 February 1921 placards displayed across London announced,

SUDDEN DEATH OF LORD ALFRED DOUGLAS

FOUND DEAD IN A BED BY A MAID

HEART FAILURE AFTER A CHILL

The source of the story is unknown, but when Douglas left the *Plain English* office he bought a copy of the paper and read it. The *Evening News* had elaborated on the story and then, worst of all, had published an obituary that had been turned out at speed by Arthur Machen, who had been a frequent and controversial contributor to the *Academy* under Douglas's editorship. The obituary was headlined,

A GREAT LIFE SPOILT

HOW THE EVIL GENIUS OF THE DOUGLASES DOGGED

LORD ALFRED

The text that followed was not only unfavourable, it was also libellous.

A brilliant and most unhappy career is ended. Lord Alfred Douglas was born, in a sense, under the happiest auspices. He was a Douglas, the son of one of the most ancient families in Britain. He was connected with many of the 'best people' in society, he had brilliant capacities, and showed that he was certain to be numbered among the poets.

He might have done anything and, his poetry excepted, he did nothing and worse than nothing.

The charity which is fitting at all times, but most fitting when we are speaking of the newly-dead, urges that much should be forgiven to this poor, bewildered man, who, with all his gifts, will perhaps only be remembered by the scandals and the quarrels in which he involved himself.

It is a great thing, in a sense, to be born a Douglas, but the family inheritance had gifts from evil fairies as well as from good ones.

It would not be true to say that all ancient races are degenerate, but there are very marked signs of degeneracy in the House of Douglas.

Many of them are violently eccentric, to put the case mildly.[82]

Douglas telephoned a news agency and reported that the *Evening News* article was unfounded. Later editions announced that Lord Douglas was glad to say that he was 'in the best health'. Although the paper carried an apology for the inaccurate report, it said nothing about the defamatory obituary and Douglas sued for libel. The *Evening News* pleaded justification for its contents, and employed George Lewis, knowing that he was the solicitor most willing and able to dish all the dirt on Douglas once more, to represent them. In the ensuing trial, which took place towards the end of the year, Lewis produced the same old letters and brought up the argument with Colonel Custance in an attempt to prove that Douglas would be remembered best for his quarrels and for doing 'less than nothing' with his life.

The trial lasted three days and contained much that was of interest as well as a substantial amount that was simply repetitious. From the outset things looked set to go in Douglas's favour; one of the reasons for this was that Olive sat beside him throughout the trial. Her presence helped to undermine the importance laid on the quarrels with Custance that Lewis tried to make central to the case. But there were damaging revelations. The jury were read a letter (one of only three that have survived)[83] from Douglas to Wilde, undated though probably written in early 1900, in which Douglas had said, 'When are you coming back? I am glad you are enjoying Rome so much. It is certainly a lively place, and life there was really better than Naples. I quite agree with you that the boys are far more beautiful there. In fact, I think they come next to English boys.'[84] In those days, such remarks showed degeneracy in the eyes of twelve men.

The court heard the Labouchère letter and the article in *La Revue Blanche* along with 'In Praise of Shame' and 'Two Loves'. Douglas knew that he could not defend these pieces and admitted that he was ashamed of his letters, though not of the poems since he felt they were merely open to 'misinterpretation'. Questioned about Wilde's letters to him, Douglas said that they were 'idiotic and horrible', though he was more charitable when counsel asked, 'Is it obvious from other letters which have been read that Wilde asked you to return his letters?'

'It is lucky I did not return them,' Douglas replied. 'They would have got into certain hands [presumably Ross's] and we would have had them read today. Whoever stole them took care to take the worst ones. But some of them were very creditable letters, especially those written from Holloway prison.'

At one point Douglas claimed that he had been having an affair with a woman during the last years of Wilde's life, but whether this was true or not (and there is no other evidence to support such a claim) Douglas's aim was simply to rake through as little of the homosexual matter as possible. He admitted much, though. He said that the letters he had written to Wilde showed, 'Moral degeneracy perhaps. Degeneracy means lapse from a higher standard. It does not follow that I may not have risen higher than the average man since. They prove that at that time I was a wicked man, and I certainly was. I have not the slightest desire to conceal it. I was leading a bad life; an immoral, wicked man. I have regretted bitterly, and I have suffered from it all my life.'

Douglas's poem about F.E. Smith, now the Lord Chancellor, and 'Eve and the Serpent' were read too, but the judge, Mr Justice Horridge, seemed rather to enjoy them.

The Custance and Ross cases showed Douglas in a rather good light as far as correcting degeneracy went: 'You still think you will not be remembered for being violently eccentric?' counsel pressed.

'I do not think I shall,' was Douglas's verdict, 'I shall be remembered for quite a lot of other things. The scandals and quarrels will be remembered, but not necessarily against me.' He went on to say, 'I have done many creditable things which have not been mentioned.' Counsel did not enquire what they were.

In his summing-up the judge echoed the words of the Catholic priest who had given evidence for Douglas and who had received him into the Church in 1911: 'I think that a sadder and more horrible life up to 1900 it would be impossible to find. There was this young man, with every promise and every capacity, at Oxford. He, unfortunately, fell under the fascination of this man Oscar Wilde. You may think that Oscar Wilde fell under his fascination; but, at any rate, this connection sprang up between them, which was the most awful thing I should think that ever happened to Lord Alfred Douglas in the course of his life.' He was also emphatic on the point that the question was whether Douglas would 'only' be remembered for his quarrels. It was quite clear that the paper had been irresponsible to publish an account of a death of which they had heard only by telephone from an anonymous tip-off.

The jury decided for Douglas after just fifteen minutes' deliberation and awarded him £1,000 damages. Douglas was pleased that a court had supported him in his claim to recognition rather than infamy. His solicitor, Comyns Carr, told his client that his performance in the witness box had won them the case, though when he looked back on it Douglas had other ideas: 'Owing to the kindness and charity of Sister Mary Vincent, of the Convent of Mercy at Hull, I not only had the prayers of her community but those of two thousand schoolchildren every day for many weeks right up to and during the trial.'[85] He believed fervently that God was helping the reformed sinner, a truly prodigal son.

Douglas's success in the *Evening News* case did not make his life any easier, even though it had secured his finances for a time. Conchie, who had set up *Plain English*, decided to withdraw his support, which upset Douglas. He wrote to him: 'I consider you have treated me very badly and have shown a callous disregard for my feelings and my sufferings which I would not have believed possible in a man who is in other respects so apparently amiable and kind-hearted as I have found you to be. I suppose the fact is that you are one man in "business" and quite another man outside it, and I can only say that I deeply regret that there had ever been any question of business between us.'[86] He also accused him of financial mismanagement and nearly ended up in court. Conchie sold the paper, and Captain Spencer took over the editorship. It had been he who had claimed in the Pemberton Billing trial to have seen the 'Black Book'. Douglas retaliated by setting up a paper of his own, *Plain Speech*, with Herbert Moore Pim as his assistant editor. He took many of the best contributors from *Plain English* with him, but Crosland followed Spencer. For Douglas this confirmed that, regardless of loyalty, he would always follow where the money lay. Even the apologist Sorley

Brown, when writing a biography of Crosland, admitted that on this occasion 'Crosland's course of conduct towards his old friend was thoroughly contemptible.'[87] This was the end of the relationship between Douglas and Crosland and, mercifully, they never met again. *Plain Speech* only survived for a few months. With only the odd donation to support it, it was not financially viable and when Douglas fell ill with influenza it was forced to close.

Though the editing of *Plain English* and *Plain Speech* had not been a great success, it had at least given Douglas the opportunity to do sustained work. The pitfall was that, as with the *Academy*, the papers made him more enemies than friends. Their anti-Semitic content had put many people's opinions firmly against him. Although one of the few specific attacks on Jews came when the famous quatrain

> How odd
> Of God
> To choose
> The Jews.

was published for the first time by Douglas in *Plain English*,[88] the frequent implications that Jewish conspiracies were being worked at high levels in society made many indignant. When the *Morning Post* published a letter from the editor of the *Jewish Guardian* saying that 'It must no longer be a paying proposition for men like Mr Crosland and Lord Alfred Douglas to invent vile insults against the Jews,' Douglas believed he had been libelled and sued. The ensuing case, in mid-1923, showed that Douglas seriously believed that Jews were trying to destroy him to silence his revelations of their activities. Though the case against the *Jewish Guardian* never came to court, that against the *Morning Post* did.

The *Morning Post* case was unfortunate for Douglas. It was clear that he felt he was in the right. When he was questioned as to whether or not he believed that it was the action of a gentleman to make such claims as he had against certain people in government he answered, 'It's the action of a gentleman to tell the truth about people.'[89] Of course Douglas did not always tell the truth about people, although he thought he did, but on this occasion he got himself into more trouble than ever by relying on an uninformed source to make a very serious allegation. In *Plain English* Douglas had claimed that Winston Churchill had been guilty of war-profiteering and that while First Lord of the Admiralty he had, with the help of high-profile Jews, conspired to murder Lord Kitchener. They had allegedly succeeded in 1916 when Kitchener was on board the *Hampshire*. The ship had been sailing for Russia where, according to Douglas, Kitchener would have replaced the 'Bolshevik Jews', who were then setting up the revolution that would come in the following year, with 'loyal men of British birth', thus 'nipping the Russian revolution in the bud'. Apparently it was for this reason that Kitchener and his colleagues ('the finest brains that the country could produce') had had to be killed.[90]

The charge was ludicrous and the evidence flimsy, yet the jury in the *Morning Post* trial decided that Douglas had acted in good faith on the information he had received so was not guilty of invention. The result was that both sides paid their own costs. Douglas thought it a victory, but his satisfaction was short-lived: he had not learnt yet that luck in trials could not last, and that sooner or later he would fall.

At this time, Douglas looked a tired man 'like a hurt boy', according to one friend. His eyes were brilliantly expressive, often merry, but sometimes pained and resentful. The features which in boyhood had been so delicately modelled had grown pronounced, the nose formidable, the corners of the mouth 'turning down petulantly',[91] but underneath lay determination and an urge to self-destruction. Douglas was behaving recklessly, almost daring fate to deal him one more blow. Or perhaps he was simply brave, but he took on the wrong man when, in public and in private, in writing and in speeches, he goaded Winston Churchill into prosecuting him.

Chapter 7

'Wash we our starward gazing eyes with tears'

(1923–1933)

In the *Morning Post* case Douglas had made charges against Churchill and, as far as he could see, had got away with it. In the next trial it became clear that his claims were based on insubstantial evidence, though the fact that Churchill had not attempted to sue him or tried to deny the claims convinced Douglas of his guilt. This method of forcing out the truth had worked with Ross and, to an extent, with Colonel Custance. With Churchill, Douglas should have realised that there were other reasons for his lack of response.

When Douglas first claimed in *Plain English* that Churchill had conspired in the death of Lord Kitchener, Churchill could have sought a legal remedy. As it was, he was a prominent public figure and a court case would do nothing but further publicise the ludicrous libels. Douglas saw *Plain English* as a formidable fighting machine, a weapon that frightened those in high places who wished to exploit their power unnoticed. Churchill saw *Plain English* for what it was: a newspaper with a comparatively small circulation edited by a man who confessed that he was popularly believed to revel in litigation.[1] On occasion Douglas claimed privately that he loathed litigation but from the endless cases he had fought nobody would have guessed this was true. Sir Philip Sassoon wrote to the scholar and patron Eddie Marsh that Churchill bringing a libel action would be ridiculous and 'gratifying to that gentleman [Douglas], who lives for that sort of advertisement and excitement', adding the popularly held opinion that 'I really think it would be paying too high a compliment to this garbage.'[2]

Churchill was wise to avoid prosecuting at first, but Douglas, the passionate believer in conspiracies, would not let the matter drop. In 1923 he was no longer a newspaper editor and had relatively little to fill his days. In 1920 he had been asked to contribute a poem towards a book of homage to Keats in support of the Keats House Memorial Fund. He responded to the request, which had been made to all the important poets in the country, including Housman and Belloc, 'I wish I could do it. But, honestly, my muse has stopped work for a long time now and heaven only knows if and when she will inspire me again.'[3]

He was in his fifties and had no prospect of a new career. He was living in London with his mother and sister, in one of the elegant terraced houses in Draycott Place, just off Sloane Square. Also with them was Douglas's niece, and from her a distinct picture has emerged of life in the household.

When Percy died he had left four children. Of these three were the product of his first marriage to Minnie and all of them were now in their twenties. However, an unknown woman he had made pregnant on his travels had had a girl. Percy took Violet, as she was named, back to Britain, and educated her. She was around ten when her father died, and it is a testament to the close bond between the brothers that Alfred Douglas took her in and brought her up. To her he was not just a benevolent, kindly father figure, he was also a delightful playmate. 'Uncle Alfred' saw her through years that might have been difficult: she accepted that while she was a family member she was also an outsider. The attitude of some of the family towards her was different, as Lady Edith Fox-Pitt, Douglas's sister, made plain. Before her father had died Violet had always been referred to as 'Lady Violet'. Doubtless Percy had found it easier for this to pass as explanations might have been embarrassing. After he died she became 'Miss Violet', which made her ask her aunt why this had come about. 'My dear, don't you know?' replied the formidable-sounding Lady Edith. 'You are an illegitimate!'[4] Uncle Alfred, however, took her around with him, treating her as his own, encouraging and protecting her. The only time she remembers him getting cross with her was when she accidentally cut herself in a restaurant, but it was worry more than anger that sparked him off. On one occasion Douglas wandered into a church with his niece. No sooner had they crossed the threshold than Douglas gave a cry and ran out, dragging Violet with him. 'It's the wrong sort,' he explained.

Despite his affection for Violet, Douglas was still estranged from Raymond, who had by now finished his schooling and was contemplating getting in touch with him. In the meantime, Douglas delighted his niece with stories, rhymes and limericks. He made one up at a meal to encourage her to eat.

The agile gibbon at the zoo
Enjoys his food as much as you.
Put your bib on says the agile gibbon.

The precocious young Rupert Croft-Cooke, already a devoted and loyal fan of Douglas's newspapers and poetry, visited Douglas at Draycott Place. He had been first to Tite Street to find what he thought had been Wilde's house and stood outside it.[5] He told Douglas this and, he wrote, 'For the first time I heard his high-pitched and quite unforgettable laughter, the laughter of a small boy deriding a ridiculous schoolmaster.' Douglas, of course, was still bitter about Wilde. Croft-Cooke explained, 'Moderation was impossible to Douglas. At this time Oscar was a posturing and vicious traitor. Earlier he had been "the Dead Poet" of Bosie's finest sonnet and later he would become the much-wronged man of Bosie's last years. No one who knew Douglas will find these tergiversations strange.' Although Croft-Cooke was deeply interested in Wilde, he tried hard to refrain from mentioning him: 'I did not see him [Douglas] in the way so many have done as interesting chiefly because he had been Wilde's friend. I saw him as a poet, a personality and a hero.'

Perhaps Croft-Cooke's friendship with Douglas was unusually calm because, to start with at least, they were always in agreement. 'I was on his side, whatever the issue. In me he had found someone, a gauche and obscure boy but still someone, who saw these things as he did, for he had the gift, sublime or silly, of convincing himself utterly.' For this reason Douglas spent much time talking to the aspiring poet and *littérateur* during the ensuing months in his little study behind the dining room. From one of the two armchairs beside the fireplace, he would impart his views on poetry to his disciple, always putting the emphasis on reading Shakespeare, 'for if you do that it doesn't matter much what else you read,' and stressing the importance of learning sonnet technique. 'Learn the form, learn to use it. Then when you have something to say it will take shape.'

During these conversations Douglas would sit in his chair 'in his peculiarly fidgety way, twisting his body, leaning suddenly across the chair-arm, moving his hands not in gesticulation but from natural restlessness'. His appearance was apparently most remarkable for its youthfulness. 'His hair was thick and silky, scarcely touched with grey, his face showed lines only as skin which has been clear and feminine in boyhood becomes wrinkled. It remained curiously delicate and his cheeks flushed easily. His hands and wrists were white and slender and his voice had an almost treble pitch when he was excited, delightful when he laughed but shrill when he was angry. He dressed simply, with a liking for heavy boots rather than shoes and a habit of wearing battered hats.' Douglas gave his young friend a characteristic and often repeated piece of practical advice. 'Whenever things seem to really get too much for me,' he said, 'I read the *Lives of the Saints*. It never fails. Try it when you think you're beaten. I learned that a few years ago when I needed miracles to keep me going. You'll see for yourself.'[6] It was only his deeply held faith that kept him going.

Any character sparks a range of responses in different people, but with Douglas the descriptions of his nature and appearance vary wildly. Those who knew him best saw many positive sides to his personality, but if someone was unfortunate enough to meet him when he was in a petulant mood they would view him accordingly. But differences in opinion about his appearance are harder to understand.

In 1921 Douglas had published in *Plain English* an article that constituted an outright attack on the young writer Beverley Nichols, who was much annoyed and wrote to Douglas to tell him so. The response was unexpected, and Nichols recorded that 'In his reply he asked me to lunch, and of course I accepted. How could any inquisitive young man have rejected such an opportunity? It would have been like declining an invitation to cocktails with Alcibiades.' But Nichols clearly found Douglas in defensive mode. 'All I can remember,' he claimed, 'is a blotched and bloated face, glaring across the table, vividly recalling the hideous image on the last page of *The Picture of Dorian Gray*. And a spatter of spiteful recollections, in which he insisted that it was he, Lord Alfred, who had been the inspiration for Wilde's *Salomé* and that it was he who had first coined most of the immortal epigrams in *The Importance of Being Earnest*.'[7] It seems that Nichols confused this encounter with a subsequent even more unfortunate one: it is unlikely that, so soon after the Pemberton Billing trial, Douglas would have claimed any responsibility for *Salome*.

2

Although Douglas had no single occupation at this time he kept busy, and Violet recalls that on some days her uncle would emerge from his study only for meals. He would go through all the newspapers, surveying the political situation and assessing the political persuasions of each. He still hankered after the possibility of editing one himself but suspected that he would never have the opportunity again. His prime concern, during these days, was the business over Churchill, Kitchener, the battle of Jutland and the Jews. In the wake of the 'revelations' he had made at the *Morning Post* trial the 'Lord Kitchener and Jutland Publicity Committee' was formed, consisting of a small group of people who were convinced of the truth of Douglas's allegations. As well as Lady Edith Fox-Pitt, there were a number of others on it associated with Douglas, a general, a colonel and Captain Harry de Windt, a robust man who had been friendly with Douglas and Wilde in the late nineties, and had also been a great friend of Douglas's father.[8] It organised a meeting on 3 August 1923 at the Memorial Hall in Farringdon Street, London, at which Douglas was asked to address a packed hall eager to hear about alleged corruption in high places. The tone of the speech can be judged from its opening sentences:

> Mr Chairman, my lords, ladies and gentlemen – In addressing you this evening I must start by explaining this is the first time that I have ever spoken at a public meeting. My appearances in public hitherto have taken place in the witness-box. (Laughter.) I have got accustomed to it and its accessories, the lawyers, and I confess that I miss them now, especially the lawyer on the other side, for it is my experience that most of one's best points are made under cross-examination. Whether our friend Mr Winston Churchill would agree I rather doubt. (Laughter.) He, as you will remember, went into the witness-box the other day after previously obtaining an assurance from my Counsel that he would not be cross-examined.[9]

Douglas's words were received with enormous excitement by the floor, which gave him a confidence in public-speaking he had never had before. There is no doubt that he believed the sentiments he was expressing and he said that the speech had been written 'entirely out of patriotism and in the public interest and without the slightest malice'.[10] Although he later said that if anyone could have shown him that he was mistaken when he wrote the article in *Plain English* he should not have pursued the matter and would have withdrawn the allegations,[11] at the time he felt he was on the trail of something true and big.

The allegation that Churchill had published a false report of the battle of Jutland so that a group of financiers could bring off a 'large coup' on the New York Stock Exchange was a charge of war-profiteering, which, though serious, did not grip the public imagination. What did excite was the claim that Churchill had been given a large amount of money by Sir Ernest Cassel, a leading Jew, to publish the false report. It later became clear that Churchill had had nothing to do with this report and that the report to which Douglas mistakenly referred had been written by Arthur Balfour when he was First Lord of the Admiralty. However, all of this seemed small fry beside the claim that the *Hampshire*, on which Kitchener had been sailing, was blown up not by a German torpedo but by a time-bomb planted on it. Douglas claimed that he had been told by a German informant that there had been no German vessel, submarine or mine in the area. Douglas believed that Kitchener's mission was to go to Russia to prevent the revolution by replacing the Bolshevised Jews holding key positions by 'loyal men of British birth.' When the revolution had started, the *Morning Post* had approved of it, but Douglas had written to the paper's owners expressing his contempt:[12] 'I thought it simply appalling that the leading Conservative paper should back up the filthy thugs of the Russian Revolution, who shortly afterwards murdered our King's cousin, the Tsar, and his wife and family in a cellar in circumstances of the most horrible cruelty and brutality.'[13]

That Douglas's talk was so well received caused a great deal of concern to many people who were implicated by it. The meeting finished with a call for a government inquiry into the matter and a motion that Lord Alfred Douglas should have a place on any committee of investigation. There was also a plea from one member of the floor to the others to 'do all in your power to bring before the people of this country all that has been told to you by Lord Alfred'.

Douglas's next move was to send a copy of his speech to William Sorley Brown in Galashiels, where he still edited the *Border Standard*. Brown printed it and then, at Douglas's request, published it as a pamphlet. It was Douglas's final attempt to goad Churchill into suing him. Thirty thousand copies were printed and sales were so good that another batch of the same quantity was ordered from the printers. Six thousand copies were sold in a couple of days on the Strand alone and Douglas reckoned that in a couple of weeks more than half a million people would have bought it. He even sent a copy to Churchill with a note saying, 'I challenge you to show your face in the witness box and answer the questions I shall put to you.'[14]

This time Churchill acted. While Douglas and his mother were on the streets selling the pamphlet, the police stepped in, and on 6 November Lord Alfred Douglas was arrested on a charge of criminally libelling Mr Winston Churchill. It was decided by the attorney general that Churchill should not be required to pay for the case himself because it concerned his work for the government. The Chief Magistrate issued the warrant specially to make sure that Douglas was unaware of it until the last moment. When he was taken to Bow Street he announced that he planned to plead justification. He was committed for trial and allowed bail.

The next month the trial of Lord Alfred Douglas came up at the Old Bailey before Mr Justice Avory. Douglas was defended by Cecil Hayes, but from the beginning it was clear what the outcome would be. When Churchill took the stand he volunteered much information about his private finances so that the defence could not make anything of them. He admitted that Cassel had given him £500 as a wedding present in 1908 and that, after the battle of Jutland, Cassel had furnished him with a library. None of this information had come out in the *Morning Post* case and many members of the public were unaware that such gifts were commonplace for politicians. That these facts were brought out by Churchill's own lawyers meant that Hayes could not use then to imply anything sinister in the gifts.

When Douglas took the stand he did not have the opportunity to show off his strong nerve. He was asked whether he had been the author of a letter to the Home Secretary that had appeared in *Plain English*, saying, 'We are not in the least afraid of the Public Prosecutor, because even that official, backed up by the evil forces which control the present Government, has no power to dispense with a Jury. We take the liberty to tell him that if he fondly imagines he will be able to obtain a conviction against us by prosecuting us in the absence of the person whom we have accused (Churchill) he is making even bigger a mistake than the government made when they put up Mr Justice Darling in a vain attempt to secure the conviction of Mr Pemberton Billing.' The prosecuting team now consisted of the Attorney General and the Senior Treasury Counsel: Douglas's aspersions on the legality of the legal profession would harden them against him. However, Douglas was determined to make his point, and complained, 'Every time I tried to present my case to the jury I have been prevented from doing so. I have never been able to tell the jury why I did it or where I got the information, and everything has been stopped. It is the most abominable unfairness I have ever seen in my life.' The judge rebuked him, then said, 'Will you leave the box and not make speeches!' He had to do just that.

Hayes pleaded that Douglas had never done anything in his papers or elsewhere for money, which was true. He also pleaded that Douglas believed everything he had written. This was the problem, but it was not an opinion shared by the judge.

William Sorley Brown gave evidence as the printer of the libel, but he could say little to help Douglas. However, he provided some light relief: when he took the oath he did so at the top of his voice.

'Are you deaf?' enquired the judge.

'No.'

'He comes from Scotland,' said Cecil Hayes, an explanation that the court clearly found adequate.[15]

After Brown had given his evidence it was clear that Douglas's case rested solely on the evidence of Captain Spencer, who had lied his way through the Billing case. Spencer claimed to have had a conversation with Churchill at Lord Haig's luncheon in Dundee in 1919 when, he said, Churchill had confessed to doctoring the report on Jutland to 'get the money out of the Yanks'. Unfortunately for Douglas, Spencer's lies were exposed repeatedly. The Attorney General queried his right to call himself Captain, and dug up two convictions of Spencer's, one for libel and one for insulting behaviour, the first of which had caused him to be sent to prison. He was shown to be a liar and, rather more worryingly, it became clear that an army medical board had, on 17 September 1917, found him unfit for active service and declared him certifiably insane. Although Spencer claimed that the charge of insanity had been a plot engineered to get him out of the army, conspiracy theories did not wash with this court. He alleged that the army had locked him up with a raving lunatic in a cell from which he had escaped disguised in a Red Cross nurse's uniform. As the judge pointed out in his summing-up, it was on the evidence of this man alone that the court were being asked to believe Lord Alfred Douglas's claims.

The judge spoke strongly against Douglas and it took the jury only eight minutes to reach their verdict that Lord Alfred Douglas was guilty of publishing a libel for which he had no justification. Mr Justice Avory was severe but eloquent in his address to the dejected man in the dock:

> Alfred Bruce Douglas, it is to be regretted that your undoubted literary abilities should have been degraded to such purposes as these. If I could have taken the view that you have been honestly deceived into believing the truth of these accusations, I should have taken a different and more lenient course. In view of the fact that in the action tried in the High Court against the *Morning Post* you had full notice that these accusations were untrue, and in view of the fact that the only person upon whom you apparently sought to rely in support of this plea of justification was a person like Harold Spencer, whom you yourself had denounced in your paper as a man unworthy of belief, I must act on the view that you have deliberately persisted in this plea of justification without the slightest excuse, or without the slightest ground for believing that you are now telling the truth in this plea.

Avory then got down to business.

> In view of your previous experience in this Court it is obvious you must be taught a lesson, and like other persons suffer punishment. The sentence of the Court is that you be imprisoned in the second division for six months, and at the expiration of that period find a surety in £100 to keep the peace and be of good behaviour to all His Majesty's subjects, and particularly to Mr Winston Churchill: and in default of your finding a surety that you be imprisoned for a further six months.

Douglas was taken to Wormwood Scrubs in a Black Maria on 13 December. Violet was now without her guardian and Douglas himself would spend Christmas without his family. It was a bleak prospect, but the press revelled in it and a leading article in *The Times* declared the following day that 'To those who have watched the career of the man, it will be regarded as a moderate sentence. For years, in newspapers, and in circulars and in pamphlets, he has conducted a campaign of irresponsible calumny regardless of facts and intrepid in defamatory invective. At last he has been laid by the heels in quite a gentle way, but in a way which we hope – not with great confidence – will teach him a lesson.' *The Times* was uncharitable in its opinion that Douglas would not learn. He did learn and his life was never the same after prison. If the imprisonment of Wilde had been the defining time of his youth, Douglas's imprisonment was the defining time of his old age. At fifty-three, he was in no state to survive six months in the Wormwood Scrubs of the 1920s.

3

There were three divisions of imprisonment in the 1920s. In the first division prisoners could wear their own clothes and have food sent in. There were almost no differences between the second division, into which Douglas went, and the third division (hard labour) except that those in the second division were allowed to write more letters and receive more visits (one of each per month) and that they were allowed a mattress on their plank beds for the first fortnight of the sentence. In every other respect, Douglas had been sentenced to six months' hard labour. When he arrived at Wormwood Scrubs he was put to sewing mail-bags. After ten days of this he was transferred, along with hard-labour convicts, to shovelling coal onto carts then dragging the carts. Throughout December and January, in the icy cold with little to keep him warm, Douglas did the same manual work that Wilde had been forced to do nearly thirty years before. And, of course, the convicts were not allowed to speak to each other.

For the first two weeks he ate and drank little but a crust of bread and half a pint of weak cocoa in the evenings. All other food he was offered he was unable to eat. Even when his diet was changed and he was allowed vegetarian food all he could manage was a tiny piece of cheese and a small pudding, which came three times a week. During the seventh week of his sentence the governor noticed how ill he looked. Next day he was sent to the prison doctor, who weighed him and discovered that he had lost eighteen pounds since his arrival. His efforts to get Douglas more cheese were in vain and finally, 'on the verge of collapse',[16] Douglas was sent to the prison hospital. His health had declined so rapidly that he was not able to walk there himself: a prison officer had to hold him as he shuffled across the yard.[17]

During this time Douglas received a visit from his mother and feared as she left that he would never see her again. She was now approaching eighty, and was frail.[18] He was near the age his father had been when he had died, and Douglas seemed to think that one of them would die before he got out of prison. He must also have remembered that Wilde's mother died while her son was in prison.

In the prison hospital the food was better and Douglas was able to eat. He recovered some of his health, and also had the opportunity to talk to other inmates. He got a sense of the social injustices that existed in the world, and saw at first hand what tragic lives some people lived without being able to write about them. In his accounts of life in prison, it is apparent that he sympathised with the other men, different from him as they were. He recorded with horror that most seemed to be in for bigamy which, as he pointed out, was 'the poor man's substitute for divorce': 'If they had been rich or well-to-do, these prisoners would have got divorces, but being poor they resorted to bigamy.'[19] Douglas heard the most incredible tales: one man told him that he did not mind being in prison, but wept on recalling his wife and children; it turned out that he was in prison with eighteen months' hard labour for having a child by his thirteen-year-old daughter.[20]

Perhaps the only thing that kept Douglas going was his faith. Mass was taken for Catholics by Father Musgrave, who treated him with exceptional kindness, and when the prisoner who played the harmonium at Mass completed his sentence Douglas was asked to take over which, as he said, broke the 'soul-killing monotony'[21] of prison life. There were choir practices, which provided light relief for the organist as the choir was mainly made up of Sinn-Feiners, with whom – although Douglas had changed his views on their politics – he got on personally extremely well, and borstal boys. Douglas remembered one 'choir' member as,

the most extraordinary old chap . . . who had been in prison altogether, on and off, for twenty-nine years. He fancied himself as a solo singer, and sang the solo part in ''Regina Laetare'' at Easter. He also had his own ideas as to how the hymns ought to be sung, which frequently differed from the way they were scored in my hymn-book. I played them as they were written, but he said I was wrong, and Father Musgrave said: ''Never mind, play it his way, it's a tradition of the prison." However, one day Father Musgrave himself remonstrated with him, and said he was wrong; whereupon he replied: "Excuse me, Father, I've been twenty-nine years in prison, and if I don't know how to sing these hymns I don't know who should."[22]

Douglas learnt many things in prison, not least among which were charity and humility. In 1911 he had become an ardent Catholic, but the zeal of the newly converted had brought with it an intolerance of anyone who did not share his dogmatic beliefs. His decade of litigation had partly sprung from an inability to understand other people's faults and their refusal to amend them. After Douglas had been in prison for several weeks, a friend, Alfred Rose, applied to the Home Secretary for him to be given writing materials: he was a distinguished poet who should be allowed to exercise his art. This was just what had happened to Wilde. The officer who listened in on the meeting wrote in his report that Rose had asked Douglas 'if he could write matter like what was written in the Book "De Profundus [*sic*]" '.[23] Douglas agreed to think about it, and writing materials were delivered.

At first Douglas could do nothing, although he invoked the help of his favourite saints, St Antony of Padua and St Thomas Aquinas. Finally he 'conceived the idea of writing a long poem all in sonnets'.[24] He later recorded that he started the poem with difficulty. Then, in a school copybook, he wrote a sonnet, then another, and another, and was amazed to find that they hung together. Altogether he composed seventeen sonnets, and called them 'In Excelsis': unlike Wilde his prison work would not come from the depths but take him to 'the highest'. In this sustained poem he recorded his joy at being in prison, joy in the 'recollection of hard suffering', which, he said, 'will probably be a much greater consolation when one is dying than the remembrance of any amount of pleasure and joy'.[25] It made the intense physical and emotional anguish of the experience rewarding, in that he was atoning for much that had been sinful. In later years Douglas was immensely affected by the attitude of his old school friend 'Sunny' Marlborough, who refused the morphine offered to him on his deathbed to alleviate the pain of his cancer because he wanted to 'bear the pain as an offering in expiation of sins'.[26]

4

Like St John of the Cross in his 'Dark Night of the Soul' Douglas wrote a 'song of the soul at having arrived at the height of perfection'. 'In Excelsis' was the work Douglas had to write to prove to posterity that he was a poet not just of the nineties but one who could endure the twentieth century and produce a poem that would echo as a work of searing faith in the face of adversity and as a testament to spiritual renewal. It has been observed that in this sonnet sequence Douglas also 'purged his heart of hate',[27] in the same way that Wilde had in his prison work: in *De Profundis* Wilde had attacked Douglas but then felt he could forgive him and go back to him. Similarly, in 'In Excelsis' Douglas 'spat out the last of that virulent hatred of Wilde's memory which had succeeded the early reverence for it',[28] and afterwards felt he could return to Wilde, as if facing up to his hatred had rekindled his love.

The first sonnet of 'In Excelsis' was written on 20 February 1924. The next followed three days later, and the sequence was finished on 18 April, Good Friday. When Douglas left prison the authorities refused to allow him to take the manuscript with him, claiming that the notebook was prison property and that even though he had written in it they should keep it. Wilde, of course, had been allowed to take *De Profundis* with him, and Douglas could not understand why he was not allowed to keep his work. Fortunately, he had memorised it and when he was released wrote it all out straight away. Three times during his lifetime, he applied for the manuscript to be returned, but all his attempts failed. The Home Office file on Douglas in which the manuscript was kept was not due for release until 2043.

The manuscript of 'In Excelsis' is of major importance. Shortly before he died Douglas threw away all drafts of his poems and little that reveals his style of working has survived. In 1944 he told George Bernard Shaw about the writing of 'In Excelsis' and explained about the notebook: 'In this book is exactly shown the way I write poetry. On the left is the working out of the sonnet with lines and words and phrases scratched out and rewritten, a regular mess, almost unreadable, written out on the right is the fair, final version'.[29] The manuscript is exactly as Douglas described it, and shows clearly the frantic speed at which some of the ideas for the poem poured out.

The first sonnet in the sequence addresses the idea that lies at the heart of the poem. When Douglas had been in prison in 1914 he had picked up a Bible, which fell open at the passage in which the angel of the Lord appeared to St Peter in prison. In his *Autobiography* he recorded that in 1914 he had prayed hard 'that I might suffer with Christ, be betrayed by all my friends and those whom I loved (except my mother), and taste all the bitterness of His Passion'.[30] In a similar vein of thought the opening sonnet of 'In Excelsis', comparing the roles at the crucifixion of the saint and the repentant sinner crucified with Christ, includes the lines:

> who would stay outside
> When God's in prison? Who would rather choose
> To warm himself with Peter than to bleed
> With Dismas penitent and crucified,
> Facing with Christ the fury of the Jews?

When 'In Excelsis' was first published, it was without this opening sonnet as the editor of the paper believed it anti-Semitic. But this was nothing compared to a later sonnet in the sequence: as well as purging himself of his hatred for Wilde, Douglas also stripped his soul of his 'raucous anti-Semitic fury, his tiresome aristocratic contempt [and all of] the corrosive and acrimonious things which had made him a litigant and blusterer'.[31]

The second sonnet is one of the finest of the set. It is a hymn of glory in humility, prefaced by a quotation from Shakespeare:

II

'For honour peereth in the meanest habit'.
(The Taming of the Shrew)

I follow honour, brokenly content,
Though the sick flesh repine, though darkness creep
Into the soul's unfathomable deep,
Where fear is bred: though from my spirit spent
Like poured-out water, the mind's weak consent
Be hardly wrung, while eyes too tired to weep

Dimly discern, as through a film of sleep,
Squalor that is my honour's ornament.

Without, the fire of earth contemning stars
Burns in deep blueness, like an opal set
In jacinth borders underneath the moon.
The dappled shadow that my window bars
Cast on the wall is like a silver net.
My angel, in my heart, sings 'heaven soon'.

The next sonnets contain much of the most proud sentiments in the poem.

III

I have within me that which still defies
This generation's bloat intelligence,
Which is the advocate of my defence
Against the indictment of the world's assize.
Clutching with bleeding hands my hard-won prize,
Immeasurably bought by fierce expense
Of blood and sweat and spirit-harnessed sense,
I keep the steadfast gaze of tear-washed eyes.

And this discernment, not inherited,
But grimly conned in many cruel schools,
Unravels all illusion to my sight.
In vain, for me with wings, the snare is spread.
Folly imputed by the mouths of fools
Is wisdom's ensign to a child of light.

The following sonnets flow into each other gently and the language becomes ever more complex and spiritual and the meanings manifold. The Shakespearean influence pervades, with echoes of Douglas's most-loved plays. Lines like Hamlet's 'what dreams may come,/When we have shuffled off this mortal coil' (III, ii) are knowingly echoed and lead up to the climax of the sequence, the sestet of sonnet VII (which flowed on to the page with no corrections or amendments), the octave of the same sonnet having been written 'almost verbatim'[32] from Thomas à Kempis' *Imitation of Christ*.

> Could love compel the apertinent retinue
> Of all our essence to some bridge of air,
> Spanning the gulf of that estranging sea
> Which hides the lover from the loved one's view,
> How happy then were we who lothly wear
> This earthy vesture of mortality.

Three of the sonnets turn from the general to the personal as the poet gives full rein to his anger at those forces that work against God and, in sonnet XII, rails at the modern world and its capacity to pervert,

> Have at you, inky scrabblers, base and lewd,
> Whose general pen so greasily enseams
> The venal page with 'birth-controlling schemes,'
> Free love, divorce and devil take the prude.

Douglas included the 'journalistic' terms in the octave of sonnet XII deliberately, his aim being to contrast the poetic language with these everyday harsh realities. He wrote to the first publisher of the sequence, 'I agree that the words mentioned are unpoetical, but the general effect is to get a "punch" just where I want to get it in the interests of Chastity which is really the theme or the heart of the poem.'[33] The next sonnets show Douglas's aristocratic contempt for those, like Wilde, who flaunt immorality.

Sonnet XIII is extraordinary, in that it makes the point about Douglas that so many people have made about him: whatever his faults, he had always 'bayed the pack alone'. The end shows movingly how Douglas saw his state of grace, which he acknowledges was put into disarray when he allowed himself to follow Wilde into homosexual sinning. In the manuscript the last line is highlighted.

> And if, disvouching then my angel's voice,
> I could by natural spirit so outface

The frowning world and its proclaimed offence
Against my friend, shall I not more rejoice
To hate and brave it now, bestead by grace
And my long since recaptured innocence?

XIV

For I was of the world's top, born to bask
In its preferment where the augurs sit,
And where the devil's grace, to counterfeit,
Is all the tribute that the augurs ask
(Whose wedding-garment is a hood and mask).
But God be praised who still denied me wit
To 'play the game' or play the hypocrite
And make a virtue of the devil's task.

I left 'the game' to others, and behold,
This same perversion's priest, this lord of lies
Is now exalted on your altar's height;
His sophist's tinsel is acclaimed pure gold,
And England's course, swayed by his votaries,
Declines upon corruption and black night.

Having completed his rant against his 'friend' Wilde, he turned his anger on the race that he believed had put him where he was – the Jewish plotters who, he thought, had planned to kill Kitchener. Sonnet XV was not published when the sequence was first printed in the papers and was one reasons why Douglas had not been allowed to take the manuscript out of prison. A condition of him having the privilege of writing materials in prison was that he refrained from repeating any of the libels that had put him there. Everything he wrote in prison had to be read, dated and initialled by the prison authorities and they considered that the sonnet XV was a 'thinly veiled' repetition of the libel on Churchill.[34]

Douglas had asserted his attitude towards anti-Semitism in his speech on Churchill, Kitchener and the Jews in which he had said that the *Morning Post* was 'anti-Jewish in the same way that I am anti-Jewish, namely, opposed to Jewish arrogance and evil-doing when they occur, neither I nor the *Morning Post* condemn all Jews indiscriminately'.[35] The sonnet opens:

> The leprous spawn of scattered Israel
> Spreads its contagion in your English blood;

and ends,

> In hidden holds they stew the mandrake mess
> That kills the soul and turns the blood to fire,
> They weave the spell that turns desire to dust
> And postulates the abyss of nothingness.

He completed the penultimate sonnet with a dig at misguided religiosity in the form of the ancient fertility god:

> My star shone clear, my angel smiled, I went
> Down the white way, I could not break my tryst
> With Scotland's honour in an English gaol.
> My soul fares free, my neck was never bent
> To any yoke except the yoke of Christ,
> The Douglas knee will never bow to Baal.

The last sonnet is not up to the standard of some of the others: the language is simpler and it is less densely layered. It ends,

> Follow the star and enter where it rests,
> Be it on palace or on lowly shed.
> What house is this whose hideous bolt and bar
> Groan on the opening? Who are these pale guests,
> These creeping shadows? Whither am I led?
> What iron hold is here? *Follow the star*.

It is clear from the left-hand page workings of this sonnet that Douglas was striving to add something else to it, though he decided against it. In its first version the last line started with a phrase that was then scored through but which contains some of the most revealing words of the poem. Douglas wrote simply: 'Shall I find Christ in gaol?'

The truth is that he did. Finding Christ meant losing his pride, his hatred for those he felt had hated him, and learning forgiveness. That he found Christ in gaol meant that for him gaol had been an ultimately worthwhile experience. It had provided him with the opportunity to write his last lengthy work of poetry, and it had made him again the person who had been loved so much as a young man. In short, as he said in the poem, he had recaptured his innocence.

5

On grounds of good behaviour Lord Alfred Douglas was let out of prison, with his cousin Sholto once more standing surety for him, on 12 May 1924. He went straight to see Alfred Rose and wrote out 'In Excelsis'. He then went to Bruges, where he hoped to recover his health. From Bruges, which he described as 'a real "City of the Soul"',[36] he moved on to Brussels where he was joined by his mother. In his *Autobiography*, Douglas claimed that it took two years to restore his health to its previous state, but he really never recovered properly.

Staying in the same hotel as Douglas and his mother was a young English poet called Norman Roe who was also with his mother. The two were friends of Douglas, who clearly enjoyed having someone with whom he could talk poetry, but it did not last long. On the morning of 10 October, Roe's body was found in a canal. The police thought that he might have committed suicide, but Douglas was sure he had been drunk and fallen in accidentally. In any case, since Roe's mother was away Douglas had to identify the body. The senselessness of his friend's death upset him greatly, and he wrote to Herbert Moore Pim, 'The whole thing filled me with unutterable sadness. I can't see how he *can* have saved his soul, and I certainly get no light on it as I did when my brother Percy died. But he was a Catholic of sorts and had extreme unction.'[37]

After his prison experience Douglas's friends rallied round him. This was partly because he was a changed man for, although he told one correspondent that he had not entirely finished,[38] as far as getting to the bottom of the Jutland business, he was nearly at the end of his career as a litigant. In Brussels he received 'high frequency electric treatment' but it was discovered that his heart was fine. It seems that his illness was simply the result of starvation and the other hardships of prison life.[39] He stayed on the Continent for financial reasons until Christmas, but complained to the ever loyal William Sorley Brown that he was 'horribly tired of being out here. I have no friends here and there is nothing to do, and also I feel it is dull and uncomfortable for my mother.'[40] Luckily money was starting to come in from 'In Excelsis'.

It was published in the *London Mercury* by Sir Jack Squire in the October issue. Douglas had not had a sonnet published by a mainstream paper since 1900 and had certainly never had a poem of this length in somebody else's paper. He was delighted, among other reasons because it forged a new friendship. 'I ought to say,' he wrote to Squire, 'that as I have criticised some of your own work rather roughly I feel that it is truly magnanimous of you.'[41] Squire would not publish the whole work, omitting sonnets I, XII, XV and XVI. However, the faithful Sorley Brown printed the entire sequence in a special literary supplement of the *Border Standard* in November. This included a preface written by Douglas, and a critique from Herbert Moore Pim, entitled 'The World's Greatest Sonnets', that stated Pim's strongly held belief that

> The world is rushing into the horrors which Saint John described; and Douglas has shaken the dust from his feet as a testimony against it. The whole work is so mystical that this seems to express the idea that a symbolic act has been done which had to be done. The best thing that Lord Alfred Douglas ever did for the world was to go to prison and write the finest sonnets in the world.

In the article Pim quoted from a letter he had received from Douglas. 'All I can say about it is that I feel as if someone else had written it, for I can't think how I ever did it.'[42]

'In Excelsis' was printed in book form in December 1924 by Martin Secker. It contained a preface that differed only marginally from that in the *Border Standard* printing. It was dedicated in both its standard and limited, signed editions to Alfred Rose. Sadly, Douglas was soon to discover from Rupert Croft-Cooke that Rose, like so many of his other friends, had let him down badly. Rose had stolen a number of manuscripts from him and sold them through the book dealer Foyle. But

Douglas was making new friends and as he grew older some younger writers became interested in him.

6

Douglas had always railed against modernism and had seen it as the hallmark of an identifiable group of individuals long before they had identified themselves as such. His attacks on what is now known as the Bloomsbury group stood out, and he often felt that he had been made to suffer for them. In the *Academy* he had attacked James Strachey, brother of Lytton, and felt that Strachey's hostile review of 'In Excelsis' was the product of 'an ignoble desire to pay off an old score'.[43] But some young writers regarded him as a 'grand old man of letters'.

Rupert Croft-Cooke was somewhat wary of meeting Douglas after prison, but recorded with amusement that he had bumped into him one evening. Douglas immediately put him at his ease, and the friendship continued. 'I had expected to find him embittered,' wrote Croft-Cooke, 'but prison seemed to have liberated him from tense cords of self-pity and resentment. He now had an irrepressible sense of fun which bubbled up unexpectedly, he laughed without the harsh restraint I remembered, he was gay and young. The outcast licking his wounds was forgotten – here was a man who seemed firmly balanced and contented.'[44] On that occasion Douglas showed his young friend another sonnet he had written in prison, this one called 'To A Certain Judge'. Croft-Cooke read it. 'Do you notice anything odd about it?' Douglas had asked, chuckling. Unable to, Croft-Cooke was finally guided by the poet, who told him to read down the first letter of each line. When he did, the name of the judge, Mr Justice Avory, was revealed. Douglas had thought in prison that he had been unfairly biased during the trial,[45] and had worked out and written the sonnet in the same notebook as 'In Excelsis' but, realising that he would get into trouble for having written it, crossed it out so that the prison officer could not read it and pretended that it was 'clumsy work'. At one point it had been intended as a prologue to the longer poem. To the young man the sonnet seemed a stroke of genius, and he was filled with 'wonderment'.

Shortly after leaving prison Douglas received a fan letter from a

Marlborough schoolboy, who had just discovered the poets of the 1890s. Douglas answered from Belgium and they began 'a long correspondence about how to write sonnets and who was a good poet and who was not'.[46] Douglas was flattered by this respectful disciple and amused by his letters of school life. He nicknamed and addressed him as 'Moth' after Armado's page in *Love's Labours Lost*, because he was 'a well educated infant', and 'possibly because he [thought the lad] might singe [his] wings'.[47] The correspondence brought both parties much enjoyment but was cut short. The boy's name was John Betjeman and he wrote that his parents were 'so shocked at my writing to [Douglas] that they confiscated the letters and I never saw them again'.[48] Then Betjeman had to endure an excruciating father–son talk:

> Bosie in those days went I think fifty times to *The Immortal Hour*, words by Fiona McLeod, music by Rutland Boughton. He thought that was the best thing that had happened in England since Shakespeare. He wrote all about it in letters to me. These letters arrived from Belgium about once a week while I was on holiday in Cornwall. My mother noticed them and must have steamed them open, because one day Nancy Wright, the sister of my friend Ronnie Wright, a fair-haired girl – very pretty but I never thought of sex in those days either with my own or the opposite sex – was invited to stay; and in a rather marked way my mother and Nancy Wright left the room at luncheon and my father took me for a walk up a lane.
>
> You know that he was deaf and could only hear through a speaking tube. And if he didn't want to hear you, he would roll it up and put it in his pocket and he couldn't lip-read very well . . . He said: 'You've been having letters from Lord Alfred Douglas.' I couldn't deny it. 'Do you know what that man is?' I said: 'No.' 'He's a bugger. Do you know what buggers are? Buggers are two men who work themselves up into such a state of mutual admiration that one puts his piss-pipe up the other one's arse. What do you think of that?' And of course I felt absolutely sick, and shattered. And then I thought of this beautiful sonneteer, going to *The Immortal Hour* and writing all those lovely sonnets:

> > I have been profligate of happiness
> > And reckless of the world's hostility,
> > The blessed part had not been given to me
> > Gladly to suffer fools. I do confess

> I have enticed and merited distress,
> By this, that I never bowed the knee
> Before the shrine of wise Hypocrisy,
> Nor worn self-righteous anger like a dress.

My father said: 'You're not to write another letter to that man.' And I didn't. And more and more letters came – 'If I don't hear from you again, I shan't write.' My father did not let me see the further letters that arrived. He put them in his safe.[49]

The attitude of Betjeman's parents was held by many: they feared their son would become a homosexual and wanted him to engage in more masculine activities than *fin-de-siècle* poetry. Yet, amusingly, Douglas's agenda was partly the same. He did not like people who locked themselves away and were precious about poetry, so when he inscribed his *Collected Poems* to Betjeman he included a piece of friendly advice: 'Get out into the open air.'

In 1925 Betjeman went up to Oxford and entered Douglas's old college, Magdalen. When he got there he was in for a shock *vis-à-vis* his opinions of Douglas as a poet. His tutor was C. S. Lewis, who could not agree with his young pupil's belief that Douglas was a better sonneteer than Shakespeare and who did not wholeheartedly approve of the aesthetic, slippered image that Betjeman cultivated, or of the friends he cultivated with equal care, such as John Sparrow and Louis MacNeice. Lewis wrote that at tea in Betjeman's rooms (an invitation to which he considered 'a damned nuisance'[50]) the conversation chiefly revolved around 'lace curtains, arts-and-crafts (which they all dislike), china ornaments, silver versus earthen teapots, architecture, and the strange habits of "Hearties" '.[51] For such an aspiring aesthete to have Lord Alfred Douglas among his acquaintances was a considerable coup, even if Douglas himself had always disapproved of anything he deemed 'unhealthy' or 'unmanly'.

Anthony Powell recalls that Douglas was not much regarded as a poet when he was at Oxford,[52] and among his generation Betjeman was really the only one, until much later on when Evelyn Waugh took an interest, to have anything to do with Douglas as a poet or as a man. Most saw him as merely an interesting historical adjunct to the Wilde affair. Some wanted to latch on to him because of this. Waugh recalled that Raymond Mortimer tried to persuade Reginald Turner to take him to see Douglas by dropping unsubtle hints during a lunch: 'D'you know it sounds absurd but I've never yet met Bosie Douglas.'[53] But there was little point in asking Turner for help: he had been out of favour with Douglas for some twenty years.

The antipathy some 1920s writers felt towards Douglas was largely returned by him. When Betjeman met W. H. Auden at Oxford he was shocked that, like Lewis, the Christ Church undergraduate 'did not think Lord Alfred Douglas was a better sonneteer than Shakespeare'.[54] Auden waited until the 1960s to voice his dislike of Douglas when he reviewed the first edition of Wilde's letters: in the decade after Auden had left Oxford, Douglas had identified him with all the worst aspects of modernist poetry and attacked him constantly.

Of course, the 1920s did not belong to Douglas's generation and, although in so many ways the 1920s echoed the 1890s, those surviving members of the 1890s circle had changed immeasurably. When Douglas had supported Pemberton Billing in 1918 he had thought he was fighting to suppress vice. But the trial had had the opposite effect, as Philip Hoare has written: 'To a generation who had grown up during the war, the Billing trial was a tantalising introduction to Wilde's unnamed crimes, another focus for their generational discontent.'[55] And when Douglas's cousin Pamela Tennant died in 1928 Douglas would have been horrified to witness the goings-on of her son, Stephen Tennant, lover of Siegfried Sassoon, who was described by a friend of the latter as 'a most unworthy man'.[56] It must have been difficult for Douglas to understand how, in just thirty years, 'the love that dare not speak its name' was fashionable. Once again Douglas had backed the wrong horse.

If one thing annoyed him supremely in these post-prison years it was 'modernist' poetry. The poet of the twenties was T. S. Eliot, and the greatest discussion and attention was given to *The Waste Land* in 1922, while Douglas's *Collected Satires*, which appeared in 1926, were largely ignored. Douglas's *Satires* were bound to date considerably more than his other poetry, but to the 1920s reader an acquaintance with the minutiae of his hatreds, legal battles and preoccupations was necessary before they even opened the book. Ironically it was the necessity to be 'in the know' that infuriated Douglas about Eliot's poetry. He despised anything self-consciously clever and believed that it was the cause of most modern artists' problems. He wrote that he wished Swinburne were still alive to deal with T. S. Eliot, Epstein, H. G. Wells, James Joyce, Aldous Huxley 'and a few more who have "fought the good fight" against beauty all their lives with as much energy as (if they had been given to a noble cause) might have earned them the gratitude of their fellows, and the immortality which, in the sphere of art, they will never know,' and declared, 'Ephemeral fame, but lasting oblivion, is the lot of those who wage war on beauty, whether they do it for commercial reasons or simply from a natural hatred of it.'[57] If Douglas had read *The Waste Land* right through, rather than cursorily, he might have seen beauty in it, but not of the kind to which he was accustomed. There was also, for Douglas, the unchangeable fact that Eliot and others did not write in structured forms: to him this meant that they could not, and were sneering at a tradition they should have emulated.

To modern poets, though, the rules to which Douglas and his friends had tried to live up were almost comic in their dictatorial, simplistic origins. Herbert Moore Pim's critique of 'In Excelsis' had finished with a note that ran,

> For those who care to examine 'In Excelsis' or any other poem in a somewhat scientific manner, the writer suggests that the following test, which the average man can easily apply, as proposed by the writer in the *Saturday Review* in 1918, may very properly be used:
> 1 Is the metre right?
> 2 Is the rhythm right?
> 3 Is it intelligible?
> 4 Are the words used properly?
> 5 Is the idea poetical?
> 6 Is it sincere, and on the side of the angels?
> 7 Is it free from exaggerated alliteration?
> 8 Are the rhymes correct?
> 9 Is it free from plagiarism?[58]

It was clear that the changeover from Georgian to modernist would not be smooth, but few railed against the change as strongly as Douglas, who believed that Eliot could not be bothered to learn the art of writing formal poetry and that he was therefore 'not a poet at all'.

7

In 1925 more problems had arisen for Douglas. In March, while he was staying in Nice, he became aware that the old rogue Frank Harris, who lived nearby, was trying to see him. It was obvious to Douglas that Harris wanted to discuss his book *The Life and Confessions of Oscar Wilde*, which had not yet been allowed to appear in England. Douglas was reluctant: Harris had been the butt of many jokes over the years but he had at times been a success. The 1890s had been his heyday, but then he had been able to persuade an audience to listen when he spoke. Wilde had once said, 'I do not know what a football scrimmage is, but I imagine it must be very like a conversation with Frank Harris.'[59]

While admittedly vulgar, short and coarse-looking, there was something about Harris that people did not entirely detest, and indeed his extraordinary tales, most of which were untrue, found him a large number of admirers. He and Douglas had periodic bouts of friendship and Douglas liked the fact that Harris had a great knowledge of Shakespeare as well as being a fine sportsman, and while Wilde had known Harris well before the trials he was arguably never close to him. After his release from prison Harris was generous to Wilde, but also stole ideas from him for his own benefit. *Mr and Mrs Daventry* was based on an idea of Wilde's but it was Harris who wrote the play and claimed the vast majority of the financial and critical credit. He must have contemplated his biography of Wilde from the time of the trials and one cannot help thinking that he saw immortality for himself in befriending the fallen genius.

When Harris's book on Wilde had appeared in 1916 it was quite clear that, although in America nothing could be done about the distortions, if the book been issued in Britain Douglas would have had to sue for libel. Not only did he make Douglas into the villain of the piece, he made things up. Harris's writing style was very readable, a mix of spicy pornography and fiction He masqueraded as a Boswell to Wilde's Johnson but there was little doubt that Wilde had never flattered Harris with the confidences Harris reproduced in page after page of 'verbatim' quotes. As a final insult to Douglas he had also blatantly flouted laws of copyright, reproducing 'Two Loves' and 'In Praise of Shame' along with excerpts of *De Profundis*, as an appendix. Douglas had known of this and had decided never to meet Harris again. However, Harris sent a friend to act as a go-between who told Douglas that Harris had 'discovered quite by chance that his *Life and Confessions of Oscar Wilde* contained a mass of misrepresentations about me, all of which had been dictated to him by Robert Ross or by Wilde himself, and he begged me to meet him so that he might put right the bitter injustice he had done me.'[60]

Douglas, hoping it was possible that someone like Harris could change, agreed to meet him. Harris was delighted and sent a copy of his book *My Life and Loves* to Douglas's hotel in the hope that it might interest him. The pornographic accounts of Harris's sexual adventures appalled Douglas who, after reading only a couple of dozen pages, had it wrapped up and sent back to Harris with a note informing him that he could not bear to have such a book in his possession. Harris tried again, this time with one of his books of *Contemporary Portraits*, which were records of characters he claimed to have known. Unfortunately two of the people 'portrayed' in the book were Wilfrid Scawen Blunt and George Wyndham, both now dead and both cousins of Douglas. Douglas was upset to read of Harris's supposed intimacy with them when, certainly in the case of Blunt, he had only met them once. Harris also claimed to have been a member of the Crabbet Club, which had revolved around Blunt and of which Douglas had been a member, but not Harris. Although these issues did not prevent the meeting taking place, they certainly did not make it easier. Neither did Harris. A witness to the reunion claimed that it started with both men sitting opposite each other, unable to speak and bright red. They finally agreed to write a preface together to correct all the errors.

Harris told Douglas that he was genuinely persuaded that Robert Ross had misled him with information for his biography. He said that when he had written the book it was 350 pages long and that it had increased to its current size of over five hundred after Ross had contributed the information for the attack on Douglas, which Harris had put into his own words.[61] The meeting finished with a a motor ride. Although Nellie, Harris's mistress, said the drive to the top of some nearby cliffs had been intended to show their guest 'what a heavenly place this is', Douglas saw it as part of Harris's plan to intimidate him. Harris knew that Douglas hated heights and, as Nellie recorded in her diary, 'The moment we began to go up my trouble began: Frank sat outside with the driver, Douglas sat inside, he raged, he stormed and swore that Frank and the driver wanted to drive him mad. I said "Oh please don't this was especially arranged as a treat for you." He kept on by the hour "they want to drive me mad" and at length he said I prefer to go to prison for another 6 months, I came to the conclusion that I really was in a closed car with a lunatic and it continued for 6 hours.'[62] Douglas remained convinced, despite Nellie's protestations, that Harris had organised the trip to spite him.[63]

However, the reunion, in some ways, had been a success and Harris and Douglas built up a strong, though temporary, trust in each other. For some reason Douglas believed Harris when he told him that he wanted to do him justice in the new edition of his book and offered many suggestions as to how he might achieve this. He also wrote down for Harris the precise nature of his sexual involvement with Wilde. Douglas's frankness was extraordinary, most obviously because he had always denied in the law courts and elsewhere that he had had any kind of 'immoral relationship' with Wilde. Perhaps, as with Wilde himself, such a denial had been simply a legal necessity, but it is a supreme irony that Douglas should have committed his most frank and incriminating recollections to the man who had revelled in slandering him with lies.

Eventually Douglas returned to England with Harris's assurance that he would write the preface and pass it to Douglas. The result was less than satisfactory, and Douglas informed Harris that it would be impossible for him to allow publication in Britain without Harris taking the libellous passages out of the text. 'I should not like to be forced into a fight with you,' he told Harris in a letter, 'because when all is said, in spite of the frightful injury you have done me (the extent of which you still don't seem to realise), I like you and want to remain friendly with you.'[64] Harris's response to Douglas's gesture of goodwill was to threaten him with the publication of the compromising document he had written a month earlier. This was the last straw, and Douglas told Harris in no uncertain terms what he thought of him.

> I have been re-reading and thinking over your last letter with its blackmailing threat about the letter I gave you concerning my relations with Wilde during the three years before his conviction. I wrote that letter, as you know, as an act of the very highest moral courage to serve as a basis for you as the more or less official biographer of Wilde, so that you privately might know the exact truth (bad enough I admit but a great deal

less bad than you in your black malice and vindictive spite had made it out to be). To write such a letter and give it to a man of your character was, of course, from a worldly point of view, the height of folly on my part. Nevertheless as my actions are not, and never have been, dictated by considerations of worldly wisdom, I don't regret it. I would rather put myself right by telling the truth, even to a heartless enemy, than pose as the possessor of virtue I did not pretend to have all those years ago. The immorality I was guilty of took place more than thirty years ago. I have long since bitterly repented it, you have gone on living like a hog all your life and glorying in it and making money by it . . .

When you have the infernal impudence to write to me as you do and complain about the expense you have been put to in making the corrections of your self-admitted lies from material supplied by me at your own urgent request, you ignore the fact that you have already made thousands of pounds by selling your disgusting book with its filthy lies about me.

Go to, Frank Harris; you are a clumsy fool as well as a rogue. I wash my hands of you. I tried the effect of generosity and kindness on you, but it was simply 'casting pearls to hogs'. I shall take care to let my friends at Nice know the line you have taken up and the way you turned on me with blackmailing menace directly you found you were not going to have things all your own way. Meanwhile you can do what you please about your preface. I have the original with your own autograph corrections and signature and I also have your own letter admitting that practically everything about me in your book is false and humbly apologising. I want nothing more.[65]

'Harris is what he always was,' Douglas told a friend, 'a dirty skunk and as crooked as a corkscrew.'[66] As it was, Douglas himself brought out a new book consisting of Harris's original preface with a letter by himself. It was sold as the *New Preface to 'The Life and Confessions of Oscar Wilde'*, by Frank Harris and Lord Alfred Douglas. Meanwhile Harris raised some more money by getting an American publisher to reprint his original book along with George Bernard Shaw's *Memories of Oscar Wilde* and Douglas's letter on the physical nature of his friendship with Wilde. Harris's book was still banned in Britain, and on two occasions over the next few years when booksellers sold copies of it Douglas received £200 damages. Douglas's *Preface* was scantily reviewed, not, as Douglas thought, because there had been any boycott but because the publishers had sent out so few review copies. It was a constant source of frustration to Douglas that he had to write about Wilde. To Viereck, who was obviously trying to encourage Douglas to do other things, he wrote, 'I can assure you that it is not by my own desire that so much of my time and energy has been spent over this Wilde business.'[67] But Douglas felt he had to write down Harris and others if his reputation was not to languish in posterity from the terrible distortions that had been written. As it was, Harris appeared to have won the day.

8

Nineteen twenty-five also brought about a reconciliation that deeply touched Douglas. When he got back from Nice he found a letter waiting for him from Raymond, who had left Ampleforth and had had a short career in the Scots Guards. He had written to his father imploring him to 'forgive and forget', and adding that although 'I hope we shall be good friends again . . . it must be understood that I retain a strictly neutral attitude with regard to the differences between my grandfather and yourself.'[68] Douglas was delighted to have his son back, forgave everything and gave him all he could of his love and support.[69] 'He is a nice, dear boy,' Douglas wrote at the time, and 'It is a great consolation to me to be friends with him again after all these years.'[70] Douglas became a proud father once more and took Raymond with him to the Continent, staying for a time in Monaco. Soon after the reconciliation of his beloved grandson with the man he loathed Custance died. Whether, as Douglas thought, his death had anything to do with this disappointment it is impossible to say, but the old Colonel's death certainly gave Raymond and his father greater financial stability. Raymond's personal stability, though, was another matter: he had been judged mentally unfit for the army and his behaviour was erratic. However, it took the family some time to realise that Raymond needed to be treated with the same degree of caution as his great-uncle Jim.

Raymond and his father remained on close terms for the rest of their lives but a glitch in their relationship threatened to throw things back a step and, indeed, for a time looked as if it would cause the permanent estrangement of Raymond from both of his parents. Once again Olive and Douglas were on affectionate terms, and although they had realised they could never live together again there were no more quarrels like those of the previous decade. In 1926 an incident brought them even closer together. This was Raymond's announcement out of the blue of his desire to marry a girl of twenty-three called Gladys Lacey. Nothing would have pleased his mother or father more than the idea that Raymond might settle down to a normal family relationship, but he had inherited a tendency of his father to imagine that people were thinking the worst of him. When he announced his engagement, Raymond passed off his fiancée to all the members of his family as a woman of the highest possible birth and social standing.[71] When Douglas and Olive made enquiries they discovered that she was six or seven years older than Raymond, that she had been engaged to and living with another man for three years, that her father was a greengrocer and that her mother ran a pub.

They could not consent to the marriage and not just on snobbish grounds but, as Douglas confided to Pim, because Raymond had lied to and misled them.[72] Neither Douglas nor Olive could condone his having gone out of his way to deceive them and they, along with the Dowager Marchioness of Queensberry and most other family members, told Raymond that on no account could he marry the girl. This caused a temporary split between father and son – worsened by Raymond's violent abuse of Douglas to all their relations – which was repaired the following year, 1927.

The collapse of his marriage plans tipped the balance in Raymond, and in Dinan he had some kind of a brainstorm and became violent. He was taken into a religious establishment kept by the monks of the Order of St John of God. His father was allowed to visit him only once and was shocked by what he saw. For a while he seemed hopeful, and wrote to Pim that the monks had said Raymond would 'almost certainly recover. He knew me when I saw him, he cried and held my hands and begged me not to leave him. It was dreadful. They did not want me to be alone with him, but I insisted. I went in, shut the door and walked straight up to him and made the sign of the cross over him and kissed him. He smiled sweetly at me and for a few minutes he spoke rationally. Then he went off into incoherence.'[73] The monks' hopes were not fulfilled, and Raymond was returned to England. On 26 August 1927 he was sent to St Andrew's Hospital, Northampton, a psychiatric home. There he was certified as a schizo-affective patient and, except for a couple of brief intervals, Raymond stayed there for the rest of his life.

Perhaps it was to fill the gap left by Raymond's removal to St Andrew's that Douglas struck up one of the most enigmatic relationships of these years. Late in 1926 a young man by the name of Ivor Goring turned up on Douglas's doorstep and asked for his help. He said he had no one else and that he was penniless. Ivor Goring was then eighteen. An Old Etonian, he had gone to Oxford, where he had been sent down 'for neglecting his work' though he said that this was 'owing to a disagreement with his tutor', who was apparently 'unsympathetic to the theory of reincarnation, particularly as it involved his pupil in an exclusive study of the poems of Lord Alfred Douglas when he ought to have been reading law'. He said this to Beverley Nichols, whose first book, *Patchwork*, he had admired. In his autobiography, Nichols recalled the young man at some length but did not mention his name. Goring had turned up on his doorstep too. When Nichols opened his front door, he saw

> a tall youth of about twenty, with bright golden hair.
>
> 'Good evening,' he said graciously, 'you are Beverley Nichols?'
>
> I could not deny it.
>
> He nodded and stepped past me, uninvited, into the tiny hall. Over his shoulder, in a casual aside, he said: 'I am the reincarnation of Dorian Gray.'[74]

Nichols said that this happened in the spring of 1925 but it was not until late 1926 that Goring met Douglas. Goring invited Nichols (at Douglas's expense) to luncheon with Douglas and himself at the Café Royal, 'at the same table which was always reserved for Oscar and Bosie'.

It was quite clear that Goring was infatuated, if not with Douglas as an older man, then with the ideal of him as a young one. To all intents and purposes he seemed to want to recreate with Douglas the Wilde–Bosie relationship, with Douglas taking on the role of Wilde. Naturally this was impossible: Douglas was not Wilde, nor had he ever entirely wished to be. If Goring hoped Douglas would hold forth in the Café Royal as Wilde had he was disappointed. Nichols was particularly uncharitable about the meeting: in his eyes Douglas had become a 'podgy, alcoholic blob, with the mean eyes and the double chin and the sinister signature of arterio-sclerosis in the veins at the sides of the forehead! The deterioration in the brain was as marked as the deterioration of the body. Of wit there was none, charity was lacking, malice ruled the board. He talked in jerks, gruffly . . . He cursed the younger generation, the modern girl, and the Labour party.' Nichols's opinion of Wilde was that 'he should have been shaken till his teeth rattled, and told not to be such a damned fool, and plunged into ice-cold baths to discipline himself, and even sent to Enton to get some of the fat off. He should have been forcibly led in front of looking glasses and made to stare at his flabby paunch, and kicked in the buttocks and told to get on with his work and stop talking all that rubbish about his soul being "a stringed lute on which all winds can play".'[75]

At this time there was nothing podgy, alcoholic or mean about Douglas and little remained of the man who had caused such controversies a decade earlier. Douglas, with Ivor Goring for company, became a different man. While he had fought his bitterest legal battles when any of his relationships could be held against him in court he had had to keep away from friendships like the one he now had with Ivor. There was no doubt that the relationship was platonic, but it was then open to misconstruction.

Ivor Goring brought his mother to meet Douglas too. They had been neglected by his father, who was in the diplomatic service, and between them Ivor and his mother had barely a penny. When Ivor had first sought out Douglas, Douglas had helped him in sincere charity. He had told Douglas that 'numerous people (he mentioned several of their names) were ready to do anything for him, but that in every single case he found that they wanted to abuse him'. Douglas let slip the iron façade he had kept in place for twenty years and admitted to Herbert Moore Pim, 'In the end I got very fond of him; he is very good-looking and attractive.'[76]

There is no doubt that Douglas was physically attracted to Ivor, but it was not for this reason that he took him under his wing: 'If I hadn't taken him in,' he told Pim, 'he would have gone absolutely to the devil.'[77] In his next letter to Pim he wrote, 'Of course I want him to be a Catholic, originally that was my main idea, but it is frightfully difficult. So far I have made no progress at all (I can't get him to come to church and have given up trying). But I have put up a terrific fight for his soul . . . I spent the whole of one afternoon, while he was away in London, saying the rosary for him in Church and also had two masses said for him.'[78] In the words of Rupert Croft-Cooke, who knew both men, 'It was pleasant to watch them together – the young man "camping" in a bright and decorous way, Bosie flattered and cheered by this butterfly devotion. This swept the last cobwebs of the Old Bailey from his mind, woke the ghost of the young Bosie.'[79]

As with any relationship involving Douglas, he and Ivor underwent a number of splits, rows and reconciliations, but the end had to come when, in April 1927, Ivor 'got a job on the films with Ivor Novello'.[80] Douglas saw him and his mother off on the *Aquitania* to America, where he went on to have a moderately successful career as an actor. Douglas was saddened by his young friend's departure, and wrote at least two poems about Ivor but only one seems to have survived. This was the last lyric poem Douglas ever wrote and one of only four lyrics he wrote after the 1890s. The fact that he had gone back to a style he had used in that decade was significant for the poem, entitled, preserving the boy's anonymity, *To – With an Ivory Hand Mirror*.

> Look in this crystal pool, and you will see
> (Haloed in gold, enshrined in ivory)
> What Heaven's unopened windows hid from me.
>
> Whence this enchantment, weaving spells that bind
> With sightless cords my visionary mind?
> What angel, dark or shining, lurks behind?
>
> Eyes of the flesh still bind, unfolded scroll
> Hiding its mystery! God knows the whole.
> I guess your face the shadow of your soul.

The poem had come from the man who had been most closely linked to the idea of Dorian Gray and addressed to another who aspired to be the character's incarnation. It is the only poem from Douglas's late period that even hints at the life he had repudiated when he became a Catholic. Douglas knew that he could not pick up the life he had once led. The suppression of a strongly homosexual nature had been fairly easy in the 1910s when his energy had gone into his career in the courts and fighting his enemies. Now, though, that he had entered his last years, a period of calm and reflection, he was unable to deny that, like Wilde, he found youth beautiful, and predominantly male youth.

All those close to Douglas saw that after prison he started to look back more than he ever had before. They hoped he would calm down, and it certainly seemed that he had learned to control his rage when he was slighted. Croft-Cooke wrote that 'now he could laugh even at Harris'.[81] When he sent a copy of his *Collected Satires* to the Prince of Wales it was promptly returned. In days gone by he would have found it impossible not to attack the man who had insulted him in this way. Now he wrote,

> Oh how sorry I am that you should have sent back the book like that. Not on my account but on yours. Common report gives you a splendid character for kindness, generosity and chivalry. Why go out of your way to falsify that report? I have suffered so much all my life (not always unjustly I will admit, for I suppose I deserved some of what I got) that surely *you* might have refrained from 'heaving half a brick' at me. It would not have hurt you to keep the record of my vindication from the worst charges that have been brought against me. It would not have been derogatory to your dignity to acknowledge the receipt of the book I sent you, through your secretary, remembering that though you are the Prince of Wales I am quite as well born as you are and that my ancestors refused a kingdom which yours subsequently usurped. All the same I forgive you and I shall continue to keep good thoughts about you, as becomes a poet in dealing with a prince.[82]

9

In 1927 Douglas and his eighty-two-year-old mother moved to a small and rather dingy house in Hove. There, late in the year, he received a commission to write an autobiography. The request for his memoirs came at a fortunate time and provided him with something to do, but for Douglas the process of writing prose was different from that of writing poetry. As a poet he was disciplined and slaved to produce the effect of perfect ease. As a writer of prose he could not resist the desire to pour words on to the page in the order in which they came into his head. He started writing in the summer of 1927. Financially the work was a godsend, and Douglas told his new friend A. J. A. Symons that his style of entertaining, usually fairly lavish, had been badly hampered by the economic climate.[83]

The Autobiography of Lord Alfred Douglas was finished on 6 November 1927[84] and brought out by Martin Secker in March 1929. It sold so well that it ran into a second edition, appeared in a separate edition in the United States and was translated into German and French. In the preface to the American edition Douglas explained why he had felt the need to write it:

> I wrote it in self-defense and because I was forced to do so, very much against my will, in reply to a campaign of deliberate and frigid lying which has been going on for at least twenty years . . . All history is a fight between truth and lying. Moreover the ultimate truth about anything is not by any means certain to prevail. It is an error of optimism to suppose that truth in the long run is bound to get the better of falsehood, at any rate as far as this world is concerned. It is hard enough for a historian to combat *bona-fide* error, but when, in addition to that, he has to deal with cleverly concocted and deliberate lies, his task may well appear almost hopeless. All he can do is to oppose truth to its enemies and leave it to find its way into the hearts and minds of men of good will. For if truth is not invincible, it is at any rate very powerful.[85]

Of course Douglas's *Autobiography* is as much about Oscar Wilde as it is about himself and, indeed, in foreign editions it was called *My Friendship with Oscar Wilde*. Though the book starts in a conventional enough way with 'I was born on the 22nd of October 1870, in a house called Ham Hill . . .' less than half a dozen pages into the book Douglas makes his first mention of the feuds that had featured in his life. From then on it is downhill all the way. He tried to stick to a chronological time-scale but jumped about maddeningly. He was too desperate to get the facts on to the page and was unable to hold off his attacks on Harris and the other people who had treated him so badly over the years. Though at times the book is a fantastically vivid depiction of an era, the overall effect is of a mass of information, which leaves the reader confused.

The other unfortunate thing about the *Autobiography* is that it contains no evidence of Douglas's sense of humour, that wit 'quite of his own' described by Ada Leverson.[86] Instead he was trying to impress his readers with the good side of his character.

He was deeply honest in it too. He set out, in more forthright language than any other contemporary book, the exact facts of his relationships. The revelations were sometimes scandalous to readers of the day, accounts of his relationships with women in and out of wedlock. But most extraordinary of all was that this was one of the first widely read books in which the author admitted, in no uncertain terms, that he had indeed indulged in homosexual activity. The fact that he was ashamed of it meant that some readers of his time could forgive him. Douglas's idea was that if he told the whole and real truth, as unpleasant and embarrassing as at times it was, he would at least not be accused of whitewashing himself.

Douglas's admissions of homosexual behaviour brought forth a substantial amount of criticism. Late in 1929 he wrote to Symons, 'Have you read [Robert Graves's] *Goodbye To All That*? The author says far more even than I do about "Public School Morals" and enters into details. I wonder whether Squire will say in the *Mercury* as he did about me, that his statements are the "most foolish ever put into writing by a sane man".'[87] On Wilde, Douglas was on safer ground and in an appendix to the *Autobiography* he produced, for the first time, cast-iron proof that he had never abandoned Wilde and proved his financial generosity to him. When he read the book Bernard Shaw told Douglas, with whom he had begun to correspond, that he 'need not worry. Your *Autobiography* and your book anticipating the publication of *De Profundis* in full (*Preface* to Harris) . . . have made your position quite clear; and you need not fear that any biographer will be powerful enough to write you down.'[88] Sadly although there were, as Shaw said, no writers powerful enough to do this a number had the spite to try. One was André Gide, who had featured in a small way in Douglas's life before the turn of the century. He had read *Oscar Wilde and Myself* in Paris in 1918 and had been understandably shocked by it but did not bother to find out why Douglas had repudiated Wilde and the sexual behaviour he had flaunted when Gide had known him, nor whether his attitude had changed in the ten years since. After reading the earlier, repudiated, work, Gide wrote, 'I hope not to die before having unmasked him.'[89] In the French edition of his *Autobiography* Douglas wrote an additional chapter in which he exposed Gide's animosity and vendetta against him. It did little good, though, for whenever he had a chance in writing or in conversation Gide attacked Douglas viciously.

In his *Autobiography* Douglas gives away much of himself without realising it. In one passage he describes how he found the first witness to testify against Ross. He records that he was led to the house, after getting lost and praying to his saint, by a little blond-haired boy, and expresses his belief that the boy was an angel sent to help him.

Of more importance to Douglas at this time, though, was that his *Complete Poems* had been issued in 1928 and that a French poet was translating his sonnets into French.[90] By 1926 eight thousand copies of his volumes of serious poetry had been sold which, as he proudly informed Pim, he had been told was 'a far larger sale than any other living poet, including Kipling'.[91] There were other incidental pleasures during these years. A talk, only his second in public, to the Catholic Poetry Society came in 1931. Douglas actually spoke to the society twice: on the first occasion the light was bad and Douglas had forgotten his glasses so the event was a washout. The second time, he chose to talk about 'The Catholic attitude to certain poets', which was a great success. He spoke about Wilde and berated those in the Catholic Church who had forbidden Abbot David Hunter Blair, who had almost succeeded in converting Wilde to Rome when they had been at Oxford together, from speaking about his old friend in public, fearing it might cause a scandal. Douglas also spoke of Marlowe and Shelley and, in the latter, pinpointed the conundrum that he was 'a very immoral man in some ways, and who was also a blasphemer and a hater of Christianity. He was also of course one of the divinest poets who ever breathed, and Byron said of him "I never knew a man who was not a beast compared to him." '[92] It seemed that Douglas's opinions were becoming more rational. He confessed that he found it impossible to consider Shelley damned, as unrepentant as he was in the eyes of the Church.

This speech to the Catholic Poetry Society marked something of a watershed in Douglas's life. He spoke with fondness of Wilde and was frank about his own attitude to him.

> In the matter of Wilde I am conscious that I have not been consistent. I began in my very early youth by admiring his work inordinately, at a time when it was not generally admired at all. I thought him a man of transcendent genius. This was largely because I knew him personally and was dazzled by his marvellous and unequalled gifts as a talker. One of the tragedies of Oscar Wilde is that he talked so much better than he wrote. I

have never heard anyone come anywhere near his charm and brilliance as a talker. In that line he was supreme. He was the greatest *improvisatore* that ever existed.

Many years later, after he had been dead twelve years and after I had become a Catholic, I reacted violently against him and against all his works. I actually described him in the witness box on one occasion about 14 years ago as 'the greatest force for evil that has appeared in Europe for more than three hundred years.' I was thinking then more of his life than his writings, but even allowing for this, I consider now that what I said was really absurd. Converts are very apt to be censorious and to make a fatal attempt to be more Catholic than Catholics. I have been a Catholic now for more than twenty years and I hope I am now much more charitable and broad-minded than I was just before my conversion or for a good many years after it. After swinging to two extremes in my estimate of Wilde I have now got into what I believe to be the happy mean.[93]

At the end of his speech Douglas concluded that if Catholics were not allowed to hear a lecture on the work of Oscar Wilde then they might as well decide that Shelley, Marlowe and the sonnets of Shakespeare were also not fit to be talked about, which, he finished triumphantly, was absurd. He was pleased with his speech, and the enthusiastic response overwhelmed him. He was touched because, as he told Croft-Cooke, he was 'more used to abuse than praise'.[94]

In 1933 Douglas brought out a book he had considered writing for most of his life. *The True History of Shakespeare's Sonnets* should have been one of the least autobiographical of Douglas's works yet the prime interest in it derives from it being one poet's reaction to another. Dedicated to Olive, the book did not sell well, but it pleased Douglas to have published something on the canon of work that had most inspired him. The reviewer in the *Daily Express* wrote, 'Lord Alfred Douglas, the greatest living master of the English sonnet, has given us in his new book . . . the most sensible and illuminating account of these mysterious works of genius that has yet been published', and the critic expressed a commonly held idea that the most important aspect of Douglas's book was his 'refutation, with a powerful display of evidence, of the theory that there was anything disgraceful in Shakespeare's affection for the boy'.[95] But all this was of a highly personal nature and Douglas clearly felt the need to absolve Shakespeare of the allegations that had plagued the sonnets for centuries. He took up the theory that Mr W.H. was Will Hughes, a boy actor. He could not find cast-iron proof for his theory, though he believed he did later and for this reason it is a shame that more attention has not been paid to Douglas's personal, though thoughtful, writing on the sonnets. He told Bernard Shaw, 'In writing my book I relied far more on my poetical instinct and my knowledge of the text than on the other commentators. Although I read a great many of them, I no doubt missed much that I would have absorbed if I had been more of a scholar.'[96]

10

Perhaps it was because Douglas had given so much thought to Shakespeare and his life that in 1933 and 1934 he produced two of his last sonnets. In the spring of 1932 he accepted an invitation from a young undergraduate to go to Oxford. He had admitted to another correspondent that although he had not been back for more than twenty years, he 'should like to see Magdalen again before I die'.[97] In the opinion of Charles Scott Moncrieff who had been back in 1926, Oxford was 'very much altered and unrecognisable'.[98] To Douglas, however, the joy of being back among youth in the place where he had passed some of his happiest days was enough. John Betjeman had met with Douglas in 1930 and become a good friend, once the business of the unanswered correspondence had been explained. He told Diana Guinness that he had just received a communication from Douglas: 'I am afraid poor old Bosie Douglas must have returned to his old habits,' wrote Betjeman. 'Here is a letter from him to me.'

> I had a glorious weekend at Oxford, the weekend before last. I stayed with Richard Rumbold (a ghastly and pretentious undergraduate J.B.) at Christ Church. I met dozens of undergraduates and they were all perfectly sweet to me. I have almost determined to go back to Oxford and take a degree! I am of course *still an undergraduate* which is a cheering thought. I have written a sonnet (I really think one of my best) about my 'comeback' to Oxford after nearly (forty) years exile. It will be in next week's

Cherwell . . . I too am in love with someone I saw at Oxford: 'who ever loved that loved not at first sight . . .'[99]

It was a curious letter, and uncharacteristic of Douglas's later correspondence. It was not at all like him to be so candid on personal matters. Perhaps the individual he had fallen for was simply proof of his opinion, expressed to Shaw, that there is a great difference 'between the attraction of beauty and the homosexual attraction, and that the one is no evidence of the other',[100] which was the argument he had used for Shakespeare. The sonnet, 'Oxford Revisited', was not one of his best but it had been written, as Douglas said, 'under the influence of genuine feeling'.[101]

Of more note was the sonnet he wrote in 1934, certainly his last great sonnet and possibly his best. It was written as a direct response to Shakespeare's sonnet number 12, which held particular power for Douglas. In the Shakespeare sonnet the author tries to persuade Mr W.H. to live on and have children, not to let his beauty die with him:

> When I do count the clock that tells the time,
> And see the brave day sunk in hideous night;
> When I behold the violet past prime,
> And sable curls all silver'd o'er with white;
> When lofty trees I see barren of leaves,
> Which erst from heat did canopy the herd,
> And summer's green all girded up in sheaves,
> Borne on the bier with white and bristly beard:
> Then of thy beauty do I question make,
> That thou among the wastes of time must go,
> Since sweets and beauties do themselves forsake
> And die as fast as they see others grow;
>   And nothing 'gainst Time's scythe can make defence
>   Save breed, to brave him when he takes thee hence.

In 1934 Douglas finally felt able to write on a topic that had preoccupied him for many years. Whether the poem had anything to do with Wilde or not will never be known, but the links are obvious. Douglas titled it 'The Wastes of Time', in homage to Shakespeare. Shaw had written to Douglas that part of the reason why he thought Douglas's book on the sonnets the best ever written was because 'you yourself have had the experience of Mr W.H.: men fell in love with your personal beauty'.[102] Now Douglas's looks had gone: the face that had once been considered that of Dorian Gray was tired and sagging, the hair, once described as like glistening gold, was thin and grey. Douglas had taken the advice that Shakespeare had given to Mr W.H. but his image would not continue: his son had had no son but was locked up in a psychiatric institution.

> If you came back, perhaps you would not find
> The old enchantment, nor again discern
> The altered face of love. The wheels yet turn
> That clocked the wasted hours, the spirit's wind
> Still fans the embers in the hidden mind.
> But if I cried to you, 'Return! return!'
> How could you come? How could you ever learn
> The old ways you have left so far behind?
>
> How sweetly, forged in sleep, come dreams that make
> Swift wings and ships that sail the estranging sea,
> Less roughly than blown rose leaves in a bowl,
> To harboured bliss. But oh! the pain to wake
> In empty night seeking what may not be
> Till the dead flesh set free the living soul.

Chapter 8

'Till the dead flesh set free the living soul'

(1933–1945)

In the last years of his life Douglas seemed to lose the desire to live. He had no fear of death or any doubt of what would happen when he died, but he found himself ever battered by the worldly troubles and had less energy to fight them. He still mixed in what was called 'society' but was not a regular guest with most people. Lady Violet Powell, wife of Anthony Powell, recalled that in 1933 Douglas had come 'perfectly turned out in white tie and tails' to a party in Hanover Square.[1] He accompanied the actress Hermione Baddeley, wife of David Tennant who was one of Pamela's sons. On this occasion Lady Violet recalls that he 'melted away' from the party 'with the dew of the midsummer morning'.[2] He had little time for formal socialising and had grown suspicious of those people who sought him out only to pump him about Wilde. The only new acquaintances Douglas made were of people who wrote fan mail to him.

During these years he also enjoyed some renewed friendships, and especially with Reginald Turner, who wrote to Douglas shortly before he read the *Autobiography*. He told Douglas that he had nothing but friendly feelings towards him, and Douglas was touched. 'I am delighted to get your letter,' he replied. 'It is sad to think of all the wasted years and the friendship and companionship which we might have had'.[3] Turner had been put in a difficult position by the Ross–Douglas fall-out and was never happy with either side during the feud. However, he strongly sympathised with Douglas and told Ross that he thought any publication of *De Profundis* during Douglas's lifetime would be 'disgraceful'.[4] This made him unpopular with Ross, who proceeded to cause so much trouble for him that the two men split in 1914. Although Douglas and Turner corresponded fondly and frequently from this time, they never met again: Douglas could not coax Turner away from Florence or Turner persuade Douglas to travel further than Paris. He died in 1938.

Another member of the circle Douglas had hoped to see again was Ada Leverson, 'the Sphinx', whose daughter Violet Wyndham sent Douglas her reminiscences of Oscar Wilde. Douglas thanked her, and wrote, 'It brought back so many poignant memories of old days and dear Oscar . . . I *must* talk to the Sphinx when she gets back, and talk to her about all this. What an artist she is! In a few lines she has succeeded in re-creating a perfect impression of Oscar, which no one else has ever succeeded in doing.'[5] He met her once before she died in August 1933.

Douglas watched the whole group of people who had dominated his life slip away one by one. He had been the youngest member of the Wilde circle, only twenty-five at Wilde's downfall, and twenty-six when his first book of poems was published. Ross had been dead since 1918. Harris had died in 1931. George Lewis was dead, and so were Cecil Hayes, Edward Clarke, Edward Carson, Judges Avory and Eve, and F. E. Smith. Christopher Millard, who had lived after Ross's death on a small legacy Ross had left him, had died at the end of an unhappy life punctuated by prison sentences. Adey was still alive, but was in a lunatic asylum. Siegfried Sassoon told the story:

After the War he retired to a fine old manor house in the west of England – a property which he had inherited as a young man. His oddity then became actively apparent, and for a while he was happy. Having got it into his head that the house contained hidden treasure, he employed a number of workmen to pull the place to pieces. Free cider flowed like water while More Adey gleefully superintended his party of demolitionists, walking about in a long black cloak, with a tame rook perched on his shoulder. No treasure was found, and the poor old lord of the manor was finally removed from the scene to live on for a few years as a certified case of mental derangement.[6]

John Gray, whom Douglas had replaced as Wilde's lover, and who had converted to Rome and become a priest, died in 1934. Robert Sherard, though, was still alive. He had spent his life trying to whitewash Wilde from any claim that he was a sexual sinner and had written a large number of books to this effect. Douglas encouraged him to see the picture more fully, but Sherard would not budge except to recognise that much of what Ross had told him was false. He, like Harris and Ransome, had relied on the source who had provided the anti-Douglas information.

Olive – 'You are the only girl I have ever loved or even *looked* at seriously'.

Raymond aged nine.

The father . . .

. . . and
respectable
newspaper
editor.

Olive – 'I loved you as a tired child loves sleep, / I lived and laughed and loved, and knew not why'.

Haunted by the family furies – Raymond.

Douglas in his sixties. 'Those whom the gods love grow young'. (Oscar Wilde)

Above A weekend with the Queensberrys and Coopers – 'something to look forward to in my rather dismal existence'. From left to right, Douglas, Duff Cooper, Lady Queensberry, Edward Stanley, Lady Diana Cooper, Lady Mappin and Francis Queensberry.

Right George Bernard Shaw at the time of his correspondence with Douglas, during which a socialist became a Saint.

Above With Marie Stopes – 'There is nothing more for me to do but die'.

Right The last photograph 1944, 'If you came back perhaps you would not find / The old enchantment, nor again discern / The altered face of love'.

If there was one person who could not be persuaded by what other people thought and who continued even in his seventies to pursue his ruggedly individual path it was Bernard Shaw. He had never been one of Wilde's intimate circle, and he had met Douglas only once. From 1931 until Douglas's death the two men continued a lengthy correspondence. Douglas had first written to Shaw about Harris, a mutual contact, and it was with Harris that they had their one and only meeting, in 1895 at the Café Royal. On that occasion Wilde had asked Harris, who had been lunching with Shaw, to go into the witness box and testify that *The Picture of Dorian Gray* was not an immoral book. At this point Douglas had entered the room. The tone changed as Harris begged Wilde not to proceed with his action against the Marquess of Queensberry but to take his wife and children with him and escape to France. Such a cowardly course of action, in Douglas's view, was unthinkable and he had stood up, made a comment on the kind of friend who advised this course of action, and stormed out of the restaurant, Wilde following him.

None of those who had taken part in it forgot the incident at the Café Royal. Harris saw it as proof that Douglas dictated to Wilde, and Shaw saw in this impetuous youth the same style that he saw in the older man when he wrote to him forty years later. Douglas had explained the incident at the Café Royal to Harris in a letter: 'All I know is that if I had gone into the box I would have won the case for Wilde . . . At the very worst, even if he had lost the case, there would have been no subsequent criminal prosecution of Wilde. All the sympathy and all the feeling would have been on our side instead of on Queensberry's . . . When therefore you and Shaw gave your advice, based on a one-sided knowledge of the facts, I resented it, and I was terribly afraid that Oscar would weaken and throw up the sponge.'[7] Of course, Douglas had been determined that he and Wilde would nail his father. As it was, Shaw and Harris came to see that their advice would have been good in the short term for Wilde though perhaps not for his reputation in the eyes of future generations.

It seems that Shaw and Douglas had preferred to forget about their earlier, rancorous exchange in the *Academy* about Shaw's play *Getting Married*. Shaw's correspondence gave Douglas much pleasure and the opportunity to argue, debate, flare up and sympathise. The exchange of letters, published in 1982, gives a fascinating insight into how two men with opposite points of view in almost everything could yet become friends. The two duelled constantly. But from the first letter, in which Shaw had berated Douglas, 'Why should you who have been so unjust to many good men, expect justice for yourself? Are you not wise enough yet to pray God to defend you from it? Does your conscience never reproach you for the reckless way in which you exploited Crosland's phobia for calumny in the *Academy*?'[8] he became the man who supported Douglas in every way, a father figure and supporter to someone who desperately needed both. And Douglas needed no reminding of the injustice he had done to many men. He was acutely conscious that there were many people with whom he should have been reconciled. With some he managed to make his peace, for instance with the writer Douglas Goldring. In 1933 Douglas wrote:

> Dear Mr Goldring,
>
>   You will be much surprised to hear from me after such a long time. But the fact is that for *years* I have been meaning to write to you. When I was editing *Plain English*, in the very first number, there was a review of a book (or rather two books) of yours. The article was most unfair and ill-natured. I need hardly say that I did not write it myself and did not see it till it was in type in the paper. But I vaguely intended to say something about it to you at a later date to put it right. But I put it off and it went out of my mind. Recently I have been suffering remorse about it, and I write this very belated expression of regret. I remember your poem about the daffodils in the *Academy*. I greatly admired it, and so did Pamela (then) Tennant. So please forgive me, if indeed you have not long forgotten all about the incident of the review, which is quite likely.
>
>   Yours sincerely,
>   Alfred Douglas.[9]

He admitted to Jack Squire that 'for years of my life I was goaded and insulted and attacked and baited, and not being a Saint (by a very long chalk) I did sometimes hit out indiscriminately, but my nature is not like that. My chief desire is to spend the rest of my life at peace, and in "charity with all men" '.[10]

2

During these last years family life for Douglas settled down. Olive lived near him in Hove and the two would lunch often at each other's houses, keeping in almost daily contact. His niece, Violet, recalled that Olive and he would have found it impossible to live together during these years: both had the sense to realise how far to take their friendship. They knew if they had to stay together for any protracted period of time they would get on each other's nerves.[11] Their relationship was loving and affectionate. When Olive heard of the help given to her husband by Shaw she told him, 'I have always admired [Shaw] as a great man of genius . . . but now I simply love him for his kindness to you.'[12] In letters Douglas would address her as his 'Darling Mouse-girl' and sign himself 'your devoted Boy'.

Douglas's nephew, the Marquess of Queensberry, rented a flat for him in St Anne's Court, Hove, and Lady Edith Fox-Pitt and the Dowager Marchioness moved into an apartment in the same building. Betjeman reported to his wife that he had lunched 'with Bosie yesterday in his new flat, which is in the basement of a back street in Brighton. He thinks it absolutely lovely.'[13] Indeed Douglas did and told William Sorley Brown that he was 'very comfortable' in his new flat 'with a lot of very nice furniture'.[14] He was, nevertheless, unable to stop worrying: with his mother in the same building he could see her deterioration. The Dowager Marchioness of Queensberry was now ninety-one, and her family had had to accept that she would not live much longer. She entered a nursing home for a while then returned to her flat to die. She had cancer and the illness was long and painful, though she and her son took much solace from the fact that she had become a Catholic. She died within the faith that had sustained her for so many years on 30 October 1935. Douglas's mother had helped him, pampered him, flattered him and perhaps damaged him too, but she had done everything she could to support him. 'The pain of losing my darling mother has been simply unbearable,'[15] Douglas told Croft-Cooke after the burial had taken place in the cemetery of the Franciscan friary in Crawley. The priest who conducted the service told Douglas afterwards, 'We have just buried a saint,' which helped greatly to console him. He told a friend that the blank left in his life by his mother's passing could never be filled.[16] To

Croft-Cooke, he poured out his grief more fully. 'She gave me, all her life, the most wonderful and perfect love that ever mother gave to son. I feel at present as if I don't know how I shall go on living without her.'[17]

3

Although 1935 brought this greatest tragedy to Douglas, it also brought one of his greatest joys, for the publishers Rich and Cowan decided that they wanted to bring out his poems in two volumes, *Lyrics* and *Sonnets*, both with a new preface by the poet. The project caused him much contemplation. There were two problems. First he was on terms of the greatest affection with his wife and the bitter sonnets written after her desertion and published in previous collections upset him and he knew they would upset Olive. The solution to this was simple and he took them out of the new edition. A greater problem, though, was the early work. The publishers assured him that the inclusion of poems from the 1890s, which he had previously suppressed, would help sales but this alone did not sway Douglas.

The preface to *Sonnets* was an eloquent and brief discussion of the sonnet form and contains only one swipe – at 'Mr T.S. Eliot and company' for their 'deadly and dismal heresies' of anti-formalism.[18] The preface to *Lyrics* is somewhat different in style, and includes Douglas's explanation for having allowed, after nearly forty years, the suppressed poems to appear. In the preface to the 1919 *Collected Poems* he had written:

> I am well aware that having written these poems I cannot escape responsibility for them, and I have no kind of doubt that after my death they will eventually be reprinted. My reason for omitting them from this edition is that, although there is no actual harm in them, they lend themselves to evil interpretations, and the fact that they have been so interpreted by those whose interest has been to attack and defame me, and that they have actually been used against me in the law courts by the very persons who most applauded them at the time they were written, has given me a distaste for them which such poetical merits as they may possess are insufficient to dispel.

He quoted this in the 1935 *Lyrics* and went on to explain, 'All the poems referred to in the above paragraph are now reprinted in this volume and in the companion volume of my sonnets published by Messrs. Rich and Cowan. I have taken this step after considerable hesitation on the unanimous advice of all the friends and critics, including a Catholic priest, whom I consulted.'[19]

Douglas's emphasis in these prefaces was on what made a poet. He reiterated his belief that poets were not simply born, they had to work at their art and that, just as a man who learns to paint is not an artist and a man who learns how to churn out poetry is not a poet, so also it is as impossible to become a poet simply by having poetical thoughts as it is to try to be a painter if you do not know how to hold a brush. It was a simple argument that expressed an opinion held by many people.

The two books of poems appeared in a de luxe edition, which Douglas said was 'quite the most beautiful book I ever saw',[20] as well as an ordinary edition. They sold well, though they were not as prominently reviewed in the press as Douglas would have liked. He attributed the boycott in certain areas to the fact that he had dared to speak out against Eliot when most people, in his opinion, were going along with an emperor's-new-clothes trick. Harold Nicolson was particularly kind about the books in the *Daily Telegraph*. Out of gratitude for his review Douglas must, characteristically, have written to Nicolson and requested a meeting, for they lunched together early in 1936 and Nicolson recorded the event in his diary.

There is little trace of his good looks left. His nose has assumed a curious beaklike shape, his mouth has twisted into shapes of nervous irritability, and his eyes, although still blue, are yellow and bloodshot. He makes nervous and twitching movements with freckled and claw-like hands. He stoops slightly and drags a leg. Yet behind this appearance of a little, cross, old gentleman flits the shape of a young man of the nineties, with little pathetic sunshine-flashes of the 1893 boyishness and gaiety. I had fully expected the self-pity, suspicion and implied irritability, but I had not foreseen that there would be any remnant of merriment and boyishness. Obviously the great tragedy of his life has scarred him deeply.[21]

Shaw was another who recognised the tragedy of Douglas's life but he also saw, as few have, that Douglas's finest achievement and rebuttal to his critics was his poetry. In a published preface Shaw wrote, 'Not until 1935, 40 years after his father struck him down, did Douglas play his ace of trumps by publishing his poems in two volumes which his worst enemies cannot open without exclaiming almost at every page "For this be all thy sins forgiven thee".'[22]

Douglas gave Shaw copies of his two books when they were published and wrote to him, 'I would really like you to have them as you have really been very kind to me lately, and the whirligig of Time now surprisingly exhibits you in the light of a friend . . . You will never convert me to your views, or to Socialism, but at any rate now you have succeeded in turning me into one of your admirers!'[23] Shaw replied, 'You certainly have a first-rate talent for the most difficult forms of verse: sonnet sequences come from you as easily as limericks; but where's your epic? If I could sing like that in words I should by this time have left more verses than Shelley did . . . Are you lazy?'[24]

Douglas was hypercritical rather than lazy. The early poems he had written had been highly praised by critics who knew what they were talking about and for whom Douglas had much respect. The trouble was that great praise early on had destroyed in him the ability to achieve his potential. Having written a number of sonnets in his twenties, which were considered by some of the best judges of the day to be among the greatest works of poetry in the language, the thought of following them with anything less good horrified him. Therefore after 'The Wastes of Time' most of Douglas's attempts to write poetry had been impossible and anything which was contemplated never got beyond the stage of working-out. He had reached the stage he had described in a sonnet thirty years earlier. In 'Silence' he had written, 'This is deep hell, to be expressionless/To leave emotion inarticulate.'

But he was finally being universally recognised as an eminent poet. Humbert Wolfe, writing in the *Observer*, wrote in a review of *Sonnets*, 'Everywhere are scattered lines so invulnerable that it is fair to claim for Lord Alfred the position of one among the first of English sonneteers.'[25] A number of events proved that this was so.

4

In 1928 Douglas had received a book of poems from a woman calling herself Francis d'Avilla, though her real name was Fabienne Hillyard. The gift prompted the inevitable thank-you letter from Douglas and a correspondence began, which continued until Douglas's death. The relationship was important to Douglas, and was strengthened by a number of mutual friends. D'Avilla expressed her admiration for Douglas in her letters, which delighted him. He wrote playfully, 'You will spoil me and make me conceited if you don't take care.'[26] Her opinion that Douglas was one of the great poets was expressed in her translations of his poems into French, the first of which she sent him in 1930. She translated the 'To Olive' sonnets, 'The Dead Poet', 'To Autumn', 'Behold, Your House Is Left Unto You Desolate', 'The Unspeakable Englishman', 'Oxford Revisited' and many more over the years. He told her in one letter that her translations 'are all admirable. I do not intend to criticise them or to pick holes because you must do the translations in your own way. You are a conscientious artist and nothing that I could say would make you do them better. If you are satisfied so am I. A translation of poetry must be unhampered. You must translate them just as you would do if I were dead.'[27]

Lord Alfred Douglas's *Poèmes*, translated by Francis d'Avilla, was published in Paris in 1937. It was an important event not only in Douglas's career as a poet but for English poetry. Harold Nicolson observed that the publication marked the first time that an English poet had had a translation of his poems published in French in his own lifetime since Lord Byron. Douglas saw it for what it was: 'a great honour'.[28]

In 1935 Douglas received a letter from Sir Arthur Quiller-Couch (known as 'Q'), professor of English literature at Cambridge. As Anthony Powell writes in *Faces In My Time*, 'For forty years Q pretty well laid down what verse ought to be given a chance to survive.'[29] Quiller-Couch wrote to Douglas to say that he wanted to include some of his sonnets in his forthcoming *Anthology of Sonnets (1500–1935)*. Douglas was one of only three living poets to be honoured by inclusion in this volume but, as Quiller-Couch had written to him, 'You know very well that I rate you among the very first' of English poets.[30] It was an opinion that was no longer held by only a few. The newspaper owner Lord

Beaverbrook wrote to Douglas telling him that for years he had expressed the opinion, both in public and in private, that Douglas's sonnets are 'the best work of our time',[31] and when the 1935 *Sonnets* and *Lyrics* appeared he claimed that Douglas's reputation was now 'unassailable and unique',[32] while John Buchan postulated that one of the '*To Olive*' sonnets was 'the finest written in our day'.[33] Yet when W. B. Yeats compiled his *Oxford Book of English Verse* in 1936 he did not include any poems by Douglas, thus incurring the wrath not only of Douglas but of a good many of his supporters. 'Although I am not a great admirer of Yeats,' Douglas admitted, 'if I had been editing a modern anthology, I would have considered it the height of bad manners and bad taste to leave him out.'[34] Because Douglas had attacked Yeats in the preface to his 1919 *Collected Poems* it seemed clear that Yeats had got his own back in this snub. Douglas sent him a telegram, whose content revealed the kind of aristocratic pride that had provoked some of Douglas's famous telegrams in the 1890s.

> Your omission of my work from the absurdly named *Oxford Book of Modern Verse* is exactly typical of the attitude of the minor to the major poet. For example Thomas Moore the Yeats of the nineteenth century would undoubtedly have excluded Keats and Shelley from any anthology he had compiled. And why drag in Oxford? Would not Shoneen Irish be a more correct description?[35]

This riposte made Douglas an even stronger enemy than he already had in the Irish poet who, it was rumoured, told publishers and printers not to bring out any work by Douglas. However, it also brought the support and encouragement of the compiler of the original *Oxford Book of English Verse*: Sir Arthur Quiller-Couch wrote to him saying, 'It must be the "Oxford" that stirs your gall. You should take it as a high compliment that you are not included in Mr Yeats' gallery . . . *What* an anthology, and *what* a preface.'[36] Quiller-Couch went on to include a number of Douglas's poems, including 'Impression de Nuit', in the new edition of the *Oxford Book of English Sonnets*, not, as his biographer has claimed, out of loyalty[37] but out of a genuine respect and belief that Douglas ranked as a sonneteer with Shakespeare.

In 1937 the composer Havergal Brian was looking for a text to use in a new work he was preparing. He turned to Douglas's poems and was immediately struck by one he had written in 1897, which closed with the lines,

> No joy is here but only neutral peace
> And loveless languor and indifference,
> And faint remembrance of lost ecstasy.

Brian wrote to Douglas and requested permission to use 'Wine of Summer' as the text in his Fifth Symphony, to which Douglas gladly agreed. When Brian played it to Douglas on the piano, Douglas was so moved that he immediately told Brian that he would allow him to set any of his other poetry to music.

Seeing his work made into another form of art gave Douglas great pleasure; seeing his life made into one did not. In 1935 Douglas learnt that a play called *Le Procès d'Oscar Wilde* was on in Paris. The author was a man called Maurice Rostand. As soon as he heard of it Douglas realised that the play, with Wilde, Douglas, Queensberry and Harris as the principal characters, would be an appalling travesty[38] of facts that had now been proved beyond dispute in Douglas's favour, yet he felt disinclined to do anything about it. He admitted that he was tired of the whole Wilde business.[39] When, however, Norman Marshall proposed to put on an English version of the play at the Gate Theatre, Douglas intervened. The play was basically a dramatisation of ideas in Harris's book and would have done him irreparable damage if it had been produced as it was. He told Marshall that he would allow the play to go ahead if he took out libellous passages from the script. He would also write a preface to the published version of the play. He explained why he had taken this course of action: it was 'not because I considered then, any more than I do now, that a play dealing with more or less contemporary facts and passions may not lightly be presented on the stage, but simply because Monsieur Rostand's play was a travesty of the truth and a deliberate mis-representation of well known facts. It is sufficient to point out that the whole idea of Rostand's play was based on the false assumption that I had never seen or spoken to Oscar Wilde again after he came out of prison.' Douglas ended, 'Devoted as I still am and always shall be to the memory of this brilliant and wonderful man and conscious as I am and always shall be of my own failings . . . Wilde was the author of what I consider to be, apart from Shakespeare, the finest comedy in the

English language.' He also made clear where he apportioned the blame for the whole tragedy: 'Let England bear the responsibility for what she did to him, ''From the beginning when was aught but stones/For English Prophets?'' '[40]

The corrections were made, and the play went ahead, but Douglas explained that it would be too painful for him to see it.

He saw one other play about Wilde and himself, though, by Leslie and Sewell Stokes. It was put on in 1938 at the Arts Club where Douglas had no right to alter anything as it was a private club. The two writers asked him for his opinion of it which he was only too pleased to give. The reaction of the young man playing Lord Alfred Douglas to the appearance of the man himself, with his wife, backstage, an old and weary vision of what he had once been, can only be imagined.

Although the constant revival of Douglas's relationship with Wilde often annoyed him, he was sometimes happy to speak to people about it. He always appreciated young admirers who showed him some act of kindness, either practical or in the form of praise for his poetry, and treated them well, usually with an invitation to tea. Harford Montgomery Hyde, who had lived in Wilde's old rooms at Magdalen which Encombe had inhabited while Douglas was there, received a letter from Douglas asking to see the rooms again before he died. Sadly he was unable to fulfil this plan while Hyde was there.[41] However, Hyde, who already had an interest in Wilde and who subsequently wrote a biography of him and 'Bosie', became friendly with Douglas and, as well as corresponding with him regularly, visited him in Hove. In conversation with Douglas, Hyde came to understand the quarrels that had peppered his life, and he remembered particularly Douglas's attitude to André Gide. Gide's memoir *Si le Grain ne Meurt* (*If I Die*) with its tales of Douglas and Wilde in Northern Africa profoundly shocked Douglas, and when he read it, in 1929, he wrote to Gide to tell him what he thought.

Dear Gide,

I have been trying to read your book *Si le Grain ne Meurt*, but frankly I find it ugly, squalid and boring. I read first the malicious and perfidious passage about myself and marvelled that a man who, I supposed, desired to be regarded as a gentleman should 'give himself away' to such a degree. Supposing that what you say about my immoral conduct thirty-five years ago is true, still what a frightful cad you must be to reveal to the world secrets which were confided to you by a man who was your friend and who never injured you by thought word or deed! No gentleman could possibly do such a thing.

Then I read the other part of the book and I began to understand your psychology. I feel sorry for you now. It must be frightful to have such a life to look back upon, beginning with your 'mauvaises habitudes' at the age of about four. Poor wretched creature, I will put you in my prayers. I will apply to you the charity which you denied to me. It would be easy for me to set the law in motion against you. I could have your libellous and malignant book destroyed and suppressed, and I could have you up before the Police Correctionnelle. But I prefer to leave you to the judgment of decent people when they have read my *Autobiography* which is now being translated into French. You will take then, definitely, the place you have chosen for yourself with Frank Harris and Robert Ross. That is of course unless you have the grace to be sorry for what you have done and to ask forgiveness (not of me because I have now forgiven you) but of whatever God you believe in. I am a Catholic and it is not so difficult for me to forgive injuries. But God alone can forgive sins (especially spiritual sins which are worse than sins of the flesh). When you have read my *Autobiography* you will see how grossly and cruelly you have wronged me about my attitude to Wilde, for whom I sacrificed my whole life after his downfall, and for whom I did what you have never done for any friend of your own.

Yours sincerely,

Alfred Douglas.[42]

He might have forgiven Gide but Douglas found it difficult to hide what he thought of him. When Hyde asked him what he thought of Gide some of the old fire returned: 'Gide is a shit! Like a person who has an abscess on his bottom and continuously displays it to the world.'[43]

5

There were others who asked for, and received, Douglas's opinions on his contemporaries. James Agate had lunch with him for the first time in February 1937 and came away from the occasion, at which he felt

Douglas was 'obviously best side out', with pleasant memories of 'lively' talk, which had inevitably settled on the Wilde circle. He recorded, 'My impression of A.D. was that he has mellowed. I think I should like a little of him very much.'[44]

One afternoon in the late 1930s Hugh Kingsmill, who had written a biography of Frank Harris, travelled to Hove to visit Douglas, and later recounted the event to Hesketh Pearson, later a biographer of Wilde. Douglas appeared to him surprisingly 'simple and unsophisticated'.[45] After lunch, during which conversation was restricted by the presence of Lady Edith Fox-Pitt, the two men talked over the inevitable subjects: Harris, Gide, Sherard, Wilde and others. Clearly Kingsmill found Douglas heavy going and was not in sympathy with him, but nevertheless several things stood out from the visit.

> The thing that appealed most to my imagination during the afternoon was our walk along the front. A bitter east wind; Douglas wizened and bowed; his nose jutting out from beneath his soft hat. If anyone had been told by God (he would not have accepted it from lesser authority) that one of these two men had been the handsomest man in England in his youth, he must have picked me out. We struggled along, left the promenade and made for a bun shop to get some cakes for tea. I thought of the world-wide hurricane that had raged over Douglas . . .
>
> Best touch of all, which much endeared me to him, was as we neared the bun shop. I said something about Harris having made out that Wilde was heartless. 'He was the kindest chap,' said Douglas, 'the kindest chap.'[46]

A subsequent occasion saw Malcolm Muggeridge driving Kingsmill and Pearson to tea with Douglas. To Pearson, Douglas's constant shifting movements, symptomatic of his pent-up energy, gave the impression of a discontented man:

> . . . it was more like a meal for lads of fourteen or fifteen than for men, two of whom were nearer fifty than forty. We sat up to the table, just as we had done in our teens, and faced a spread of buttered toast, scones, cream cakes, jam puffs, tarts, and all that class of confectionery which we had viewed with satisfaction as schoolboys; so we could only guess that the usual gatherings at Douglas' flat were juvenile, especially as we three

were grouped round one end of a long table with the house-master sitting at the other. The conversation, between mouthfuls, was agreeable but uninspiring, and we were relieved when, no longer in front of the pastry, we sat by the fire and discussed poetry.

Douglas was amiable and urbane, though he showed irritation when a theory he had put forward about Shakespeare's Sonnets provoked Kingsmill's disagreement. He talked chiefly about himself and his poetry, as indeed we wished him to do, though he made a few friendly references to Shaw and Wilde and some less friendly ones to Robert Ross and Frank Harris. I did not think it opportune to remind him that he had once written me a violent and menacing letter because I had described Ross in print as a pleasant little man. All his life he had suffered from sudden rushes of blood to the head, when he would emulate his father and bombard perfectly inoffensive people with the most virulent abuse merely because they had said something of which he disapproved. This letter-writing frenzy is a well-known form of dementia, frequently indulged in by people who feel that they are not getting enough attention. Douglas was subject to the complaint throughout his life, and so preposterous were many of his communications that sensible recipients either tore them up or laughingly displayed them as curiosities. Probably no one would have been more surprised than Douglas if he had been shown his letters a year or two after they were written. He was too much absorbed in himself to be conscious of the existence of others except in reference to his own immediate feelings. His self-absorption was curiously illustrated after the tea-party I have described. He accompanied us to the street, shook hands, waved a farewell and as he turned away to re-enter the block of flats both Kingsmill and myself experienced the odd feeling that, for him, we had completely ceased to exist. So strong was the impression that each of us took several seconds to recover the consciousness of his own identity.[47]

For a man who had been led, not unwillingly, into conversation about himself and those who had formed his circle as a youth it is not surprising that Douglas had appeared self-absorbed. Perhaps without realising it, Muggeridge, Kingsmill and Pearson had, for an afternoon, seen into the world of Alfred Douglas as it was in old age. Douglas acknowledged the childishness of his attitude and tastes: he admitted to one correspondent in 1931 not only that he had an 'infantile complex', but also that he had more sympathy with schoolchildren than with any other group of people.[48] This is not such an ominous statement as it might at first appear: to Shaw, who accused him of having an 'infantile complex', Douglas, agreeing with the diagnosis, wrote: 'You will find the same phenomenon in most of the great poets, not excluding Shakespeare (in the sonnets). All real poets have an infantile complex. Also, there is the best authority for believing that the possession of an infantile complex is the only way to get into the Kingdom of Heaven.'[49] Which settled it. For a man who had led a far from ideal childhood it was only natural that Douglas as an old man should want to replay that period of his life which, due to its relative simplicity, he most hankered after, but this time without the malicious and abusive father.

The visit of Muggeridge, Pearson and Kingsmill put them on good terms with Douglas, and Douglas gave constant support and encouragement to Pearson during the writing of his *Life of Oscar Wilde*, although Pearson was not particularly graceful in acknowledging him in later editions of the work. While Douglas lay on his deathbed he gave time to Pearson, carefully and conscientiously correcting and advising on the proofs. In an Appendix to the book Pearson made a studied, though rounded, attack on Douglas which does Pearson few favours. He made much of the single occasion on which he pushed Douglas's patience too far, but failed to credit the numerous occasions when Douglas treated him with magnanimity. Fortunately Douglas was not alive to see his kindness thrown back at him – but he did not miss Malcolm Muggeridge's attack, which he found impossible to understand.

6

In 1936 Rich and Cowan, pleased with the success of the *Sonnets* and *Lyrics*, asked Douglas for a new book of memoirs. It is obvious from the text that the writing of this book gave Douglas much pleasure. As A. J. A. Symons wrote to him, 'It is a great deal more happy in tone than I had expected, and catches just the cadence of your voice when you are holding forth and at your best. Behind all the sentences there is the note of your enjoyment; I surmise that you must have had more pleasure in the writing of it than any of your other books.'[50] Douglas regarded

Without Apology as a kind of foot-note to the *Autobiography*.[51] The title was one of his most apt and is taken from *Romeo and Juliet*: 'What, shall this speech be spoke for our excuse?/Or shall we on without apology?' (Act I, Scene 4)

He opened the book with this quotation, then wrote:

I have just looked up the word 'Apology' in the dictionary, and I find that its first meaning is given as: 'something spoken to ward off an attack,' and that its second meaning is: 'a defence or justification.' It is only in its third sense that it means what it is generally taken to express in modern usage – namely, 'a frank acknowledgment of offence'.

It was in the first two senses that Newman used it when he wrote his *Apologia*; and if I reject it, even in those senses, as a description of this book of desultory memoirs, this does not imply that I have not done a lot of things which I regret and which I would avoid doing again if I had the chance to re-live my life. It simply means that in this book I am not 'climbing down' on the main issues. I have often behaved badly and I have often behaved foolishly; but, as it happens, I find that, on the whole, the things that I have been most blamed for are exactly the things I would do again to-morrow if I had the chance. The things I regret are, generally speaking, the occasional compromises and the (infrequent) runnings away from high attitudes which I failed to carry right through to their ends. In short, what I regret in my life is just that part of it which worldly wisdom applauds. Spiritually speaking, of course (and inevitably), one is bound to realise and to admit that one has failed to do what one ought to have done. Unless one is a saint – which happens only in the case of one man or woman in a million – one cannot possibly avoid realising that one has often failed miserably. But that is a matter for oneself and one's conscience, and does not concern the 'gentle reader' of memoirs, however gentle he or she may be.

All one is constrained to do in relation to the aforesaid gentle reader is to say: 'This is what I did, and this is why I did it.' Life lands one in a certain position (whether by one's own faults, or merely by fatality or the fault of others, really matters very little); and finding oneself in that position, one acts according to one's temperament, one's convictions and one's courage or lack of it. On the whole, I think that it is a mistake to allow the opinion of the world to influence one. A thing does not become right because the world says it is right, any more than it becomes wrong because the world says it is wrong. One can act only according to one's lights, and if one is in good faith, one may hope that in the long run justification will result, even if not in this world or in one's own lifetime.[52]

Unfortunately after Rich and Cowan had passed the book for publication and the printers had type-set it, they were advised by libel lawyers not to publish it. Douglas was greatly upset and annoyed that they followed this advice. 'I carefully refrained from making it dangerous,'[53] Douglas informed Shaw, and Symons told his friend, 'Heaven help those who can see libels in this breezy, amiable recital of things past. Why it is the most benevolent, the least pugnacious, the least controversial of all you have done.'[54] It was probably the attacks on Yeats, H. G. Wells and other living authors that persuaded Rich and Cowan not to take the book on, but Douglas did well out of their decision: he was allowed to keep the advance and his book was published by Martin Secker in April 1938.

The writing of *Without Apology* had clearly been speedy. Douglas told Francis d'Avilla in a letter written a year before the book finally appeared that in a month he had written 40,000 words – more than half of it.[55] The speed of composition shows in the book: as in the *Autobiography*, Douglas's mind worked too fast for his pen and the ideas are not sustained. Although in *Without Apology* the jumping around can be justified, since the book is not intended as a chronological work, the confusion that flawed the earlier work is still in evidence. *Without Apology* is, however, the most enjoyable and revealing of Douglas's prose works. Shaw told him, 'The book is extremely readable: I enjoyed reading it very much.'[56] The factual events had been covered in the *Autobiography* and here Douglas had more room for anecdotes. James Agate wrote that it was 'intensely readable and human', as well as being 'a record of some pretty good quarrelling'.[57] What Agate most admired was that the author could laugh at himself, which Douglas had not revealed in his writings before.

Douglas went out of his way to be as fair as he could in his new book. Most obvious was his desire to correct the impression given in his *Autobiography* that he had disliked his time at Winchester, so here he told the world about his schoolboy love affairs, including the one with Maurice Turner. He did not know that Turner had been dead for almost thirty years, killed in 1910 in a hunting accident.[58]

He also attempted to reconcile himself in memory at least with his father. Having reviled him during the earlier part of his life then unconsciously emulated him in the middle period, he was now able to forgive him. His uncle, the Reverend Archibald Douglas, had told him in 1911 that Queensberry's deathbed conversion meant that 'When you meet there will be no cloud, there is none now, for even if his purgatory is not by, there is no cloud where there is peace.'[59] So, as he did when he was a child, Douglas expressed a kind of love for his father, despite everything, in affectionate stories about him.

On Wilde, Douglas put down several important anecdotes as well as opinions. Perhaps the most interesting comments come in a passage during which he discusses the imbecility of modern 'artists' and 'critics'. He attacks Yeats, Eliot, Auden, Epstein and H. G. Wells for creating works that are 'ugly' and 'incompetent'. He emphasises that nobody but himself seems to dare to criticise them while the fashion of the moment is to slate Wilde as a dramatist and to sneer at *The Ballad of Reading Gaol* as not sufficiently 'highbrow'. This sparks off an account of the time when he questioned Wilde over the meaning of the refrain in the *Ballad*, 'all men kill the thing they love'. At first Wilde would not answer the question, saying that any phrase in poetry could mean any number of things.

> On another occasion, and with a view to confirming my own opinion, I asked Wilde what he meant by his phrase about killing the thing one loves, and this time he said, '*You* ought to know.' This instantly gave me the clue I wanted. I do not want to 'rub it in,' but of course what he meant was that if one loves anyone very much one is very apt to destroy him or her, or, more exactly, to destroy the image of the person created in one's own mind which is in truth what one loves and worships. You create an image of the beloved, and then gradually and inevitably you kill it.[60]

Douglas fends off the attacks on Wilde and himself, and reclaims Wilde as a great moralist who realised on his deathbed that 'good is good and evil is evil' and that rejection of this simply leads to hell. He put a large number of ghosts to rest and he looked forward to peace now it was written. But a problem surfaced immediately.

In *Time and Tide* of 30 April 1938, Malcolm Muggeridge reviewed a number of recently published books. He made some general comments, then wrote of the cyclical nature of learning and the effect of time on literary endeavours. 'Browning seems no longer fabulous, Tennyson a man and a brother; but Wilde! – how inconceivable is Wilde. Who would suppose it possible that anyone should talk about "doing beautiful work in art" and get away with it?' After quoting from *Lady Chatterley's Lover* he moved on to Eliot, Auden and Isherwood, writing that the process of the ageing of works of literature 'goes on inexorably. *The Waste Land* is better left unread, *The Ascent of F6* has already an ominously morning-after-the-night-before flavour. Each generation, each year, sheds its leaves, and they lie heaped up along our way, to be rustled through, as children rustle through fallen leaves on autumn walks. One thing only is certain about tomorrow – that today's urgency, fashions, apprehension, certainties, projects and despair, will seem as empty then as yesterday's do today.' The article was one that Douglas might have enjoyed had it not been that both he and Wilde were classed as 'fading, falling leaves'. Of Douglas's book Muggeridge wrote:

I had this sensation of rustling through the fallen leaves of a remote yesterday in reading Lord Alfred Douglas' entertaining volume of reminiscences, *Without Apology*. He evokes a world in which words like 'genius,' 'artist,' and 'beauty' had as rich a content as, now, words like 'proletariat,' 'class-war,' 'Communism,' and 'Fascism.' The controversies he so spiritedly continues are almost forgotten. Other controversies have replaced them, also to be forgotten in their turn. Who now cares that Frank Harris' picture of Wilde in his *Life and Confessions of Oscar Wilde* is distorted? Who will be comforted by learning that Chapters 16 and 17 in Lord Alfred Douglas' (now, he explains, repudiated) book *Oscar Wilde and Myself*, which contain 'a very skilful, I might say brilliant "cutting-up" of Wilde's poetry, his prose, and his plays . . . were written by T.W.R. Crosland [*sic*], and not a word of them is by my hand?' Who will not sigh over Lord Alfred Douglas' remark, in a letter written to his mother in 1897, that he regarded Wilde as 'a martyr to progress'?

How strange they seemed to me, the figures Lord Alfred Douglas writes about so vivaciously, how strange the world to which they belonged:

Apropos of Oscar's ultimate reception into the Church, I recall that just before he started his fatal libel action against my father at the

Old Bailey, he said to me one day: 'If I win this case, as of course I shall, I think we must both be received into the dear Catholic Church.'

There seemed a great chasm between them and us. 'My *dear* Windermere, manners before morals' – it was a twilight to be followed soon by oppressive darkness, and in this twilight forms were shadowy, voices thin and silvery; it was a pause portending disaster.

A great wave of materialism had been gathering force, and stood poised, ready to crash, groaning and frothing. Wealth had been accumulated, how much wealth? The earth was scarred and torn where it had bled wealth, the hands which had gathered up this wealth were blackened and grazed, people clustered thickly round each scar like flies round a sore. This wealth seemed real. It was golden sovereigns. Jingling golden sovereigns – 'My *dear* Windermere, manners before morals'; jingling golden sovereigns, seek admission to 'the dear Catholic Church'; jingling golden sovereigns, do 'beautiful work in art'; jingling golden sovereigns, be a martyr to progress.

Then, jingling golden sovereigns, go to war, and lo! suddenly the golden sovereigns are pieces of paper, soon tattered, blown by the wind and sodden by the rain, fragile and combustible. The wave of materialism crashed, and its fury is not yet nearly spent; the whole edifice of wealth, progress and knowledge collapsed, and that little jingling of golden sovereigns was quite submerged in the resultant noise and confusion.[61]

Douglas did not need this harsh reminder that he was a survivor. He was aware that his time had passed, and Muggeridge's words brought him down, with an unpleasant bump, to earth. To make matters worse his review was followed by one of George Orwell's new *Homage to Catalonia* under the headline 'A Really Important Book'. With some of his old fighting spirit Douglas wrote to the editor of *Time and Tide*:

Sir, – My autobiographical books seem to have a peculiar effect on your reviewers, male and female. Ten years ago you published a very spiteful and offensive notice of my *Autobiography* by 'Sylvia Lynd' (I hope I have got the name right), and now my new book *Without Apology* appears to have had a disastrous effect on the proletarian mind of Comrade Muggeridge. My withers remain completely un-wrung, but I cannot help wondering what is at the back of this strange exhibition of utterly unprovoked malice and stupidity. My book is just a book of memoirs and literary criticism, and no one reading Mr Muggeridge's outpourings in your columns would get the slightest idea of what it is about or what it is like. Also may I ask why Mr Muggeridge should drag in an obscene passage from another author in connection with my book which is impregnated with moral purpose and sound Catholic philosophy? Unless Mr Muggeridge was drunk when he wrote the review, it is difficult to account for his clumsy and heavy-footed offensiveness. Will he or you please explain?

   I am, etc.,

     Alfred Douglas.

It was a lame showing for Douglas, to which Muggeridge replied, simply, 'I was not drunk.'[62] 'I am told by a friend of his that he had no intention of being rude or offensive to me,' Douglas wrote to Shaw, 'but I can hardly swallow this.'[63]

7

The publication of *Without Apology* brought Shaw and Douglas even closer together, and the financial worries that had troubled Douglas after the book's initial rejection by Rich and Cowan had been solved when Shaw offered, without prompting, to guarantee a £100 overdraft for Douglas. Sorley Brown was soon informed of the state of relations between these two grand old men of literature. 'He now calls me "Childe Alfred,"' Douglas told him, 'and is rewriting his preface to Harris in the light of *Without Apology*.'[64] Shaw's nickname for Douglas came from an old ballad used in *King Lear*, 'Child Rowland to the dark tower came', a heroic and noble figure, and Douglas approved it. 'I think it rather appropriate,' he told Shaw, '(partly because I often come to dark towers, though I generally get out of them all right and escape by magic casements) and partly because it has a pleasant sound and nimbly and sweetly recommends itself.'[65] He also found a nickname for Shaw, and wrote to him,

'It's amazing and satisfactory beyond words that you should turn out, after all, to be a sort of saint. I never could really love anyone unless he or she were good, however brilliant and gifted and clever. Nearly all the men I have been devoted to have been really, I fear, rather bad, though I have always tried to 'kid' myself into thinking that they were really good at the back of it all.

In church last Sunday when the priest read the Gospel, which was that beautiful passage 'I am the Good Shepherd, I know my sheep and mine know me' (I quote from memory), when he came to 'other sheep I have which are not of this fold' I immediately thought, 'That's dear Bernard Shaw'. It explained everything about you in a flash and showed that I had always misjudged you, though (honestly) I always did like you without knowing why.[66]

In view of this Douglas told Shaw that the most appropriate name for his new-found saint was St Christopher. The correspondence between the atheist-Communist St Christopher and the sixty-seven-year-old Childe Alfred provided both men with fun and frustration, with Shaw sending Douglas the latest free-thinking pamphlets and Douglas telling Shaw that 'I continue to say rosaries for you and to put you on pedestals.'[67]

If the friendship that had developed between Douglas and Shaw seemed improbable, it was nothing compared to the relationship that started up late in 1938 between Douglas and a woman signing herself Marie Carmichael. She had written to Douglas to express her admiration for his poetry and enclosed some of her own verse. A correspondence soon developed with Mrs Carmichael sending her poems to Douglas for him to comment on them. He encouraged her, telling her that, of course, she could never expect financial reward for her writing, adding that he had made only about £500 in royalties from his poetry during his whole career.[68] But, he added, 'If you are a real poet nothing on earth will stop you writing poetry,'[69] although poetry-writing was 'a desperate blood and sweat business'.[70] The two got on well, since Douglas appreciated any admiration shown for his work and enjoyed giving lessons in poetic technique to this eager student.

Early in 1939 he told his correspondent that he felt her poetry, which was all about 'love', did not have the 'proper subject matter for the highest poetry'. 'All your poetry is about physical passion,' he noted, and, 'The best poetry is not about that. When Shakespeare wrote about love he sublimated and spiritualised it, and the same applies to all the best poets.' He had held this view for years, and it explained the lack of poetry production in his later life:

> I have impossible ideals about poetry, I know only too well. That's why I never write it now. I can't do better than I've done already and I refuse to do worse.
>
> 'In Excelsis' I believe to be my highest point, and I admit that it's frightfully difficult and metaphysical and has not the lyrical grace of my earlier work. But why should I want you to write in the same way or on the same lines as I do? That would be absurd![71]

Late in 1938 Douglas had been hit by a bad case of bronchitis. His new correspondent sent him a gift, possibly of money, which, though it embarrassed Douglas, pleased him enormously. Having been near to death, he confided to her on Christmas Eve,

> I have been incapable of thinking or doing anything. My illness is now in its fourth week and I really came to the conclusion that my 'number was up'. My wife, who is much better off than I am, is ill in London, and we are separated for Xmas for the first time in many years. Neither of us can move out of the house . . .
>
> As it happens I am just now desperately hard up. My nephew Queensberry told me the other day that he could not go on paying the rent of my flat. Although I have been ill, I have not had a doctor as I can't afford it, and I know if he came he would simply tell me to get a nurse and remain in bed all the time, or go to the South of France, all of which is wildly impossible. I really think however that I have staved off pneumonia and that I will now gradually get back to health . . . So your kindness has cheered me in my loneliness.[72]

So distressed was his new friend by Douglas's plight that she offered to help him financially to make life more bearable for him. Douglas decided now that they should meet. For him this was simple, for her less so: it meant she had to tell him what she had been keeping from him all this time. In February 1939 she revealed her true identity, signing herself Marie Stopes. Douglas was astonished, as she had always been 'a bête noire of mine', he admitted to Shaw.

Shaw wrote to Douglas about Marie Stopes, whom he had known for some time: 'As a staunch R.C. you will have to keep off the subject of birth control with its prophetess. She is about fifty, a tremendous scientific swell, as litigious as you used to be, about as soothing as a bombardment and liable to drop into reckless poetry and drama at any moment.'[73]

Douglas wrote to her,

Dear Mrs Carmichael, I was astounded to see the signature on your letter received this morning. I had not the remotest idea that you were Marie Stopes. It is really very extraordinary because (as you perhaps know) I have in the past criticised you rather strongly. Naturally as a Catholic I disagree with your views about birth control. But now that you have written one so many kind letters and shown so much interest in me and my poetry and my health and my worldly condition, I feel remorseful to think that I have ever had unkind thoughts about you.[74]

This settled it and Marie Stopes, author of *Married Love*, came to tea with Douglas. Shaw wrote to Stopes, 'There are only three Immortals now living – myself, Bosie and you'.

The meeting was clearly a great success, and resulted in Stopes inviting Douglas to her home, Norbury Park, for a weekend. Poetry, of course, was their common ground, but both were strongly opinionated. As long as they kept off birth control and the other topics that had made Stopes famous but which would upset Douglas, they got on perfectly. She understood Douglas's fits of rage if someone pushed him too far on delicate topics, and she reluctantly admired his strong-willed behaviour. Her biographer explained that 'Although she had no love for homosexuals, she had a keen understanding of the reasons for homosexuality.'[75] She saw only the good in Douglas's personality, adored his sonnets, and was always annoyed that the world had not wholly recognised him as the great artist he was. Having Shaw as a mutual friend helped the relationship and Stopes learned quickly how to deal with Douglas. She kept an account of his stay in her diary:

On Saturday, 18th March, 1939, Lord Alfred Douglas, Mrs Monro and Mr Webster Evans came for the week-end. I had been rather afraid of having Lord Alfred Douglas, knowing that he is reported to be very quarrelsome and uninterested in anything except poetry. I took an early opportunity of telling him laughingly that my husband was very illiterate and laughed at poetry, and that my son despised it. He responded charmingly and developed an amusing geniality and wide interest, talking about hunting and shooting, a number of well-known people he had stayed with or who were related to him, and was full of humorous anecdotes and very much the man of the world, appreciating good food and wine and making altogether very entertaining company. Talk naturally tended to a monologue as everyone was only too interested to listen to him. He told me he often stayed with hunting people and was accustomed to an environment which despised poetry.

At dinner we had Knox and Mrs Knox, son-in-law of Ernest Shepard and Editor of *Punch*, and Ernest Shepard. Lord Alfred Douglas told us that the acting copy of *The Importance of Being Earnest* made Earnest ten years older than Wilde had intended him to be, because Alexander was so pleased with himself in the part that he made the dialogue suit himself. Lord Alfred Douglas talked to Gielgud at his recent reproduction, in which Gielgud played the part for the age of twenty-nine, the age Wilde had really intended.

In the evening I managed to get the circle close round Lord Alfred and led him gently to talk about poetry, Oscar Wilde, etc. The same applied at tea time however, when Mrs Monro and he had a talk about Eliot and his poetry. Mrs Monro losing her temper, Lord Alfred nearly losing his temper, Lord Alfred maintaining that Eliot was not a real poet and Mrs Monro violent that he was. I tried after a bit to steer the conversation away from Eliot and got it on to Wilde again, when Lord Alfred became extremely interesting and reminiscent. He told us that he was personally with Wilde, staying with him and in and out of his study all the time he was writing *The Importance of Being Earnest*; that they talked and laughed about it and a number of the jokes were the repartee Lord Alfred had made himself to Wilde and which were worked up and incorporated in the play.

He told us that they were staying in rooms with a balcony at Worthing. The house was then called, I think, 'The Haven', and Lord Alfred had recently been down and found it, though the name of the street and the house have both been changed, but he found an old fisherman who remembered it under its old name. The beautiful large room he and Wilde had had, had been spoiled by partitioning, but otherwise the house was unchanged.

He told many anecdotes of Wilde's vivid wit in conversation and said none of his writing was so witty and brilliant as his quite spontaneous talk. It was often said that Wilde thought out his repartee and witticisms beforehand, but Lord Alfred said this was not so and they were quite spontaneous and quite as brilliant when he was alone with Lord Alfred and when there was a big company. We played chess and he played the way I do enjoy it, very rapid moves, and we were very level in sets of three, I winning two out of three in one set, and in another set he winning two out of three.

The last morning, Monday morning, when the others had gone, he had an hour's talk with me by the fire, read one of my published poems ('The Brother'), which he said was very good indeed, and he liked it very much. He also read the published Ballad 'King Canute' and he asked me to give him the volume and when I did he asked me to write in it. He told me he appreciated very little modern poetry so I felt the compliment greatly.

We talked of deeper things, religion and his feeling. I urged him to write some more poetry, particularly one or two more sonnets. He turned his head into the back of the arm-chair, almost crying, and said, 'I cannot. I wish I were dead. There is nothing more for me to do but die. I should like to die. My life is done.' I told him that with his wisdom he must not feel that, and I felt in lots of ways that older people were selfish to younger people by not giving them the ripe mellow results of their experience of life. He then started talking of Tennyson and said, 'Look what rubbish Tennyson wrote in his last years. You would not have me do the same? And then Tennyson did that one lovely thing, "Crossing the Bar", but he did that on his death bed, and I could not do anything less than I felt to be my best' . . .

Before the time came to go he appeared to cheer up, looked out at the beautiful view from the window, admiring it and said, 'I love your house.' He was very appreciative of the week-end and asked me to come and see him again in Hove.[76]

When Stopes's biographer, Keith Briant, who had met Douglas with her, read this account in the drawing room of Norbury Park after Stopes's own death, it brought the whole event painfully back to life for him. 'I found myself,' he wrote, 'hearing the high-pitched, time-weary voice of Alfred Douglas evoking the ghost of Oscar Wilde and the days of the nineteenth century when he was a beautiful youth with the world at his feet, instead of a broken-down, impoverished old man.'[77]

Douglas's financial situation was indeed difficult. Olive gave him £400 a year from which he had now to pay for his flat. He had become increasingly worried at his financial situation and feared that he might have to move. In desperation he wrote to Shaw:

> Do you think there would be any chance of my getting a civil list pension for services to literature? Even if it was only a hundred and fifty pounds a year that would just pay the rent of my flat and enable me to go on living here instead of having to eke out a miserable existence in lodgings . . . I don't know how these things are worked, but I suppose strings can be pulled. I am in the good books of the Prime Minister [Neville Chamberlain], from whom I received a very friendly letter a fortnight ago in reply to one I wrote him about the political situation. I don't think he would have answered my letter (as I don't know him personally) unless he had agreed with what I said. I believe he is an admirer of my poetry.[78]

Shaw told him of the normal procedure for such a request: 'The usual course is to send a letter to the P.M. with a string of well-known signatures, at least six, ten if possible, setting forth the literary achievements of So-and-so, and stating that he or she is "in straitened circumstances" (this is indispensable) and is disabled by age or infirmity from earning a living, therefore is in need of and eligible for a civil list pension.' To which he could not resist adding, 'As your literary achievements include a criminal libel on a cabinet minister and six months' expiation thereof, I have some doubt as to the success of this course.'[79]

8

Douglas expressed his anxieties to Marie Stopes too, and at once she set about getting up a petition to Neville Chamberlain. Douglas wrote to John Betjeman and, mentioning that the petition was being got up by Marie Stopes, asked him who he thought should be included. He suggested T. S. Eliot, Beverley Nichols, Evelyn Waugh, Graham Greene, Hugh Walpole, Edmund Blunden and Elizabeth Bowen.[80] Douglas sent the list on to Stopes, though scrawled out the names of Eliot and Nichols – neither would feel particularly favourably towards him.

The response to Stopes's letter was good and the result was a truly impressive list of names. Shaw thought his own signature would harm Douglas's chances so it was omitted, but the final fourteen names were James Agate, Edmund Blunden, Lord Clonmore, Sir Arthur Quiller-Couch, St John Irvine, John Gielgud, Christopher Hassall, Harold Nicolson, Sir John Squire, Sir Hugh Walpole, Evelyn Waugh, Humbert Wolfe, Virginia Woolf and Marie Stopes. Douglas had requested wisely that there should be no purely social figures in the list. Quiller-Couch further affirmed his high opinion of Douglas's work by including three of his sonnets in the updated version he published in 1939 of *The Oxford Book of English Verse*. Humbert Wolfe, who died the following year, wrote to Douglas to tell him that 'It is a great privilege to be able to have affixed my signature among many more distinguished to this trifling attempt to recognise one of the greatest sonneteers in the language.'[81]

Evelyn Waugh had never had any personal contact with Douglas. It was Douglas's great friend Lord Tredegar who asked him to sign the petition, and though Waugh felt that Stopes was 'a preposterous person,'[82] he agreed to sign. 'I am very sorry indeed to hear of Lord Alfred Douglas' distressed condition and am glad to do anything I can to advance his claim to public recognition,'[83] Waugh wrote to Stopes. Douglas was amazed when he saw Virginia Woolf's name on the petition. He admitted to Stopes that he greatly admired her novels and it seems curious that this single modernist should have so appealed to Douglas when none of the others did. One of the reasons he was so surprised to see her signature was because her husband, Leonard, had damned Douglas's *Autobiography* in the *New Statesman* in 1929. Douglas, who saw these writers far too quickly as groups who stuck to each other's opinions, wrote Virginia Woolf a letter, the only known direct exchange between the two.

Dear Mrs Woolf,

I am quite overwhelmed to find that your name is among the 14 of those who have signed the 'petition' on my behalf to the PM which Dr Marie Stopes has got up. I had an idea that I was not at all *persona grata* with Mr Leonard Woolf, and this makes it all the more pleasing and gratifying to receive this mark of your generous kindness to a poor poet. I have indeed been greatly touched by the kindness of so many eminent people many of whom are personally unknown to me. I have been going through a rather bad time lately, and the whole thing has been a great consolation which will persist even if the petition fails to materialise. Please be assured of my gratitude.

> Yours most sincerely,
> Alfred Douglas.[84]

Although he was never going to understand Eliot, in these years Douglas recanted his earlier opinions on some writers but reinforced his distaste for others. In 1919, in the Preface to the *Collected Poems*, he had made some slighting remarks about Rupert Brooke's poetry, which as one of the first newspaper editors to print Brooke he felt he was justified in doing. In 1939, when he was going to be quoted on this opinion he retracted it: 'At that time I felt rather disgusted at the way he was over-rated and boosted by people who had no qualifications to judge poetry,' adding, 'But really so many much worse ''poets'' have been acclaimed as masters since that time that Brooke shines by comparison. I think he was quite a decent minor poet and if he had lived longer he *might* have written something first-rate.'[85]

By comparison, though, Eliot was not just considered 'not a poet' but actually 'the supreme enemy of poetry now living', who, Douglas thought, had 'disastrously corrupted the taste of the rising generation'.[86] The Sitwells remained among those for whom Douglas had little patience. In *Without Apology* Douglas had pointed out how misguided Edith Sitwell's adoration of Pope was, compared him with Shakespeare, and concluded that although Pope knew how to write poetry 'the poetry was not there to write. He had no vision and no romance.'[87] In a private letter he fulminated, 'Fancy that Sitwell creature praising Dylan Thomas! It just shows what her supposed knowledge and judgement of poetry is worth. All the Sitwells make me sick! but she is the worst of the 3.'[88] But, of course, the Sitwells and Douglas never had anything to do with each other. Douglas and Hugh Walpole did however. They had exchanged several letters before Marie Stopes brought them together for a weekend at her house. Walpole wrote in his diary, 'He is so obviously a gentleman, full of little courtesies, delicacies, that, as gentlemen are now as rare as dodos, he seems remarkable. He loves to talk of his ancestors fighting in border raids, of Oscar whom he now always defends. When someone he hates like Wells is mentioned, he gets so angry that all his crooked features light up . . . He is a real poet – witness 'the ribs of

Time', one of the finest lines in all English poetry – but he has a streak of craziness running through his charm and talent.'[89]

After their weekend Douglas wrote to thank Stopes and mentioned that he thought Walpole 'a pleasant fellow', although 'I cannot see many signs of him being really interested in the great issues of either life or literature.'[90] Walpole appeared well disposed to Douglas and said he would put in a good word for him with the Prime Minister. However, when Downing Street sent their reply to the application for a state pension the letter informed Stopes that although Chamberlain had 'great sympathy with [Lord Alfred Douglas] in his difficulties, he regrets that he has not felt able to submit his name to the King for the award of a pension'.[91] The rejection was a serious blow to Douglas. Like Wilde, when he had no money, he became suspicious and began to believe, incorrectly, that Walpole had double-crossed him and deliberately 'queered' his application for a pension. Eventually the truth emerged from a new young friend of Douglas's: Richard Rumbold was the son of a captain of the Royal Yacht Squadron and the nephew of the ambassador Sir Horace Rumbold. Douglas repeated what he had heard about the pension saga to Stopes: 'He says that there was a lunch party at No. 10 and that Chamberlain was entirely in favour of it and said, "He is a fine poet and ought to have it." Then someone (Richard either didn't know or would not tell me who it was) raised objections (based on the Wilde scandal!) and Chamberlain reluctantly gave in.'[92] At seventy he had to suffer poverty because of the follies of his youth. He explained to Stopes that, although the loss of the money was bad enough, what hurt him most was 'the wounded feeling that I have so many enemies'. He continued, 'I have been badly treated all my life (though I don't deny that it is partly my own fault) but I began to think that the hostility and unfairness had died down. Now I find that it is still there.'[93]

9

One way of earning money was still open to Douglas, and that was his writing. Several short projects brought him a small amount and gave him obvious pleasure to write. One such project was the preface to a book by John Piper, which appeared in the summer of 1939. *Brighton Aquatints* owed much to John Betjeman, a friend of Piper who had introduced him to aquatinting, a technique Piper went on to study in London. It was also Betjeman, who travelled down to Brighton or Hove frequently to lunch with Douglas and his wife at one or the other's flat, who suggested that Douglas write the preface. Piper and Douglas arranged to meet and, after an enjoyable lunch together Douglas wrote his short, nostalgic work. The book therefore consisted of twelve aquatints of the town and Douglas's preface, which began, 'Looking with admiration, not un-mingled with emotion, at these charming aquatints of Mr Piper's, it is surprisingly borne in on me that there is still a good deal left of the old Brighton which I knew in my youth.' He goes on to recall his time in the city as a boy between the ages of twelve and sixteen when he would stay in the city to visit his father in lodgings in Oriental Place, days spent with his sister on the pier, watching the performing fleas, a man with a performing dog, Spot (whose only 'performance' so far as Douglas could remember was to 'die on the spot for the Queen'), or staring into the aquarium. He remembered them making their own amusement long before the days of 'picture theatres, or wireless, or gramophones'. It is one of Douglas's most charming shorter works. He finished,

> I had almost forgotten all this till I saw Mr Piper's aquatints and discovered that the Brighton of my youth is still in existence, and that nearly all the old landmarks remain exactly as they were. If only I were fourteen instead of seventy, no doubt I could easily recapture that first fine careless rapture of the middle eighties and the early nineties. It is probably still there if one could only come by it. In any case, I notice that in the long run nearly everyone ends by coming to live (and die) in Brighton. When I say 'everyone' I mean, of course, just what the papers mean when they announce that 'everyone now agrees' that so-and-so is the case. I mean that I could give at least a hundred cases of people I know, among what the Paris newspapers used to call *les High-lifers*, turning up late in life and announcing that they now live in Brighton. Refreshing myself with another glance through Mr Piper's aquatints, and looking back with my mind's eye to Oriental Place, I arrive at the conclusion that they might easily do worse.

Brighton Aquatints was published by Duckworth who, early in 1939, asked Douglas to write a life of Oscar Wilde for their 'Great Lives' series. At first Douglas was unhappy with the idea, but he needed the money. Yet there were things he did not want to write about again: the life of Wilde brought back too many memories, both of happier and more bitter times. The book was to be no more than thirty thousand words in length, but there was much Douglas knew he had to tackle. In July he confided to Stopes,

> I am beginning to think I cannot possibly do it as I find that when I begin to remember all the details of the old tragedy, and the frightful experiences I went through, it upsets my mind and causes me a tremendous amount of mental disturbance and distress, on my own, as well as Wilde's account . . .
>
> It seems to me that if I do the book at all I shall have to go into the whole question of homosexuality. I am very reluctant to do this. I *hate* the whole thing myself, and wish to God I had never even known or heard anything about it. But there it is, and fairness to Wilde would compel me to say that he was cruelly and unjustly treated, because people who have that attraction for their own sex ought not really to be blamed for it.
>
> What they can be blamed for is giving way to instincts which they cannot help but which they ought to control. But how many people in this world do control their instincts completely? And if they fail to do so, as Wilde did, how can it be right to treat them as criminals and send them to prison? Now if I say all of this in a book, it will be quite difficult to defend homosexuality (I mean the acts not the instinct which no one can help if he or she happens to be 'built that way').[94]

Although he had difficulty with it, Douglas wrote a lengthy and eloquent defence of Wilde in his new book, although it was only 'the assurance that Wilde died a Catholic that has enabled me to undertake the task of writing this book'.[95] But more important was that Douglas, with astonishing bravery in view of the then prevailing attitude, wrote a brilliant defence of homosexuality, telling his readers that, although as a Catholic he regarded it a sin, just as many other forms of sex were sinful, it should not be crime. The opinions are those he held as a young man writing in the *Mercure de France* and *La Revue Blanche* in 1896, but now with the perspective of a Catholic.

> The violent prejudice which existed against homosexuality in those days – half of it, as I believe, simulated and hypocritical – made it almost literally

impossible for anyone to say a good word for any person who was known to be addicted to it. Mr Robert Sherard, for example, was all his life a fanatical hater of the vice. He not only hated it but he utterly failed to understand anything about it, and, as I have already pointed out, looked upon it as an appalling form of madness. Yet just because he tried to defend Wilde's character and to speak up for his genius, he was attacked and vilified by people who thought, or pretended to think, that no one could say a good word for a homosexualist unless he were inclined to be 'that way' himself. In those days the vice was considered far worse than murder. Even at this day, when a tremendous change of opinion has taken place on the subject, I have no doubt at all that there are a number of people who believe that it is a form of 'devilish insanity'. It is, of course, simply a sin of the flesh, and is no worse than adultery or fornication. Sooner or later the criminal law will have to be revised on the basis of admitting this fact, which involves the principle that the law is not concerned with sin but merely with crime. Sometimes a sin is also a crime (for example, a murder or theft) but this is not the case with homosexuality any more than with adultery.[96]

Several times Douglas announced to friends that he had decided to give up and return the £30 advance, but as Shaw told him, 'A job's a job. Have you anything better to do?'[97] Of course he hadn't so he forged ahead.

Shaw's original advice to Douglas about the writing of his new book was, 'Whatever you do don't start the old solemn recriminations; and get as much detergent fun into the case as you can.'[98] Douglas took the first piece of advice and tried hard to keep the personal grievances out of the book; as a result it is his fairest and most balanced book. Without going into personal vilification of Ross, Douglas attempts to prove once and for all that Ross was the villain of the Wilde affair.[99] Now that he had understood that Wilde had not attempted to keep *De Profundis* from him, he had forgiven him, and was free to speculate. He expressed his wish that he had been allowed into the witness box in 1895, and said that if he had had the courage he and Wilde should have stood up together in the box, openly witnessing to what they believed in: homosexual passion. 'Between the two of us, neither of us being without brains and courage, we might have made a certain amount of history. I don't believe he would have got off even so, but we would have at least "put up a terrific show'', and the result could not possibly have been worse than it was'.[100]

Douglas called his new book *Oscar Wilde: A Summing Up*. It was his last word on Wilde. 'I am glad I've written it,' he told a friend. 'It will set things right for ever.'[101] In the book he recaptured Wilde the man, the companion, the raconteur, and the atmosphere of gaiety the two men had enjoyed half a century earlier. On one of the last occasions on which he met Rupert Croft-Cooke, Douglas told him, 'The worst of *De Profundis* is that it makes our friendship seem a solemn sort of thing, crossed with terrible quarrels. But we were laughing most of the time – often at one another. There were whole days we laughed our way through. I remember once at Torquay going into a hotel for breakfast – I forget why now – and being told by the waiter that there was some nice fish. 'If you knew the breeding habits of fish you would scarcely call them *nice*,' said Oscar. Not a remark to treasure perhaps, but it led us into endless absurdities . . . That's what people, simple unintellectual people, loved about Oscar – he could make them laugh. Even the wretched young men who gave evidence against him. Far more than cigarette-cases and meals at Kettner's. He made the dullest of them gay and amusing. He brought out oddity and humour in them which they never knew they possessed.'[102]

However, he could not go along with Shaw's suggestion that he should get as much 'detergent fun' as possible into the life: there is no 'comedy or farce in the frightful tragedy of Oscar Wilde's terrible pilgrimage,' he wrote.

But without knowing it he also proved an assertion of Shaw's about his own life. It was a passage from Shaw's preface to Harris, which Douglas quoted in *A Summing Up*.

Please let us hear no more of the tragedy of Oscar Wilde. Oscar was no tragedian. He was the superb comedian of his century, one to whom misfortune, disgrace, imprisonment were external and traumatic. His gaiety of soul was invulnerable: it shines through the blackest pages of his *De Profundis* as clearly as in his funniest epigrams. Even on his deathbed he found in himself no pity for himself, playing for the laugh with his last breath, and getting it with as sure a stroke as in his palmiest prime. Not so the young disciple whose fortunes were poisoned and ruined through their attachment. The tragedy is his tragedy, not Oscar's.[103]

He closed his book with a sonnet he had written about Wilde around 1903, after his marriage, when Wilde was still on his mind but when his life was fast moving on: 'Forgetfulness'.

> Alas! that Time should war against Distress,
> And numb the sweet ache of remembered loss,
> And give for sorrow's gold the indifferent dross
> Of calm regret or stark forgetfulness.
> I should have worn eternal mourning dress
> And nailed my soul to some perennial cross,
> And made my thoughts like restless waves that toss
> On the wild sea's intemperate wilderness.
>
> But lo! came Life, and with its painted toys
> Lured me to play again like any child.
> Oh pardon me this weak inconstancy.
> May my soul die if in all present joys,
> Lapped in forgetfulness or sense-beguiled,
> Yea, in my mirth, if I prefer not thee.

10

The publication of *Oscar Wilde: A Summing Up* was set back some months by an event Douglas believed would not happen. As late as 27 August 1939 Douglas was informing Marie Stopes 'I don't think there will be a war.'[104] He had been proved right a year earlier when he had made the same conjecture and many others believed that war was imminent. Now he made rash predictions, which were ill-founded. A letter from Douglas was published in the *Daily Telegraph* on 1 September, saying he did not think there would be a war. On 7 September he wrote to Stopes, 'I think we shall wipe the floor with Hitler, and very speedily too. I was banking on my belief that he was clever and not a lunatic. But evidently he is raving.'[105]

The most dramatic effect of the war on Douglas was on his income, which diminished from all quarters. Just how poor he was is hard to guess, but William Plomer, who visited him, said that he 'was not ostentatious about his poverty'.[106] When he had money it appears that he spent it on other people, entertaining them or giving them presents: an eleven-year-old girl, Norma Reeves, lived with her parents next door to him in St Anne's Court, befriended him and in return he wrote nonsense verse for her and gave her a bicycle which, her parents told him, became 'the pride and joy of her life'.[107] Douglas had been flattered when the little girl had asked for his autograph and from then on he acted as a godfather figure to her, helping her with a severely limited-edition magazine she was producing, the circulation of which he proudly informed Shaw, is 'going up by leaps and bounds and there will be four typed copies of the next number'.[108] Her sudden departure to Birmingham, when her father had to change jobs due to financial insecurity, saddened Douglas, who loved to have young people around him to treat and amuse.[109] But when Sir Arthur Quiller-Couch wanted to invite Douglas to stay for the weekend, his wife apparently objected: 'My dear Arthur, we can't have that man here with small children in the house.'[110]

Raymond was due to inherit from Olive the majority of her estate as it was feared that anything left to Douglas would be swallowed up by the Official Receiver since he was still a bankrupt. From St Andrew's Hospital Raymond wrote to his mother of the war, 'I dread to think what the aftermath will be, the world was none too pleasant to live in, in many ways, before.'[111] By 1940 he was writing, 'Today is the 13th year I have been here, dreadful!'[112] He was occasionally allowed out and even at times to travel alone to luncheon meetings with his parents and other family members. His father's great-nephew, the present Marquess of Queensberry, remembers Raymond coming to lunch and recalls him seeming fairly normal. But he was not, and every time it looked as though he might be released there was some setback. He had some of the odd mannerisms of his father, described by Anthony Powell, who met Douglas at a wedding. 'He had curious movements', wrote Powell, 'entering a room almost as if about to turn a cartwheel.'[113] Douglas and his own father had betrayed signs of paranoid schizophrenia, but this was more evident in Raymond. However, while Queensberry and Douglas had been ordered to take rest cures in spa towns, Raymond was treated with electroconvulsive therapy and narcosis.

Marie Stopes made a second application to secure a state pension for Douglas in 1941, but Chamberlain had left office and Churchill had to make the decision. Many of those who had originally signed the petition thought it hopeless although some stalwarts, like Virginia Woolf, did not give up.[114] Bernard Shaw wrote to one supporter about the second pension attempt and informed her that Douglas's allowance from his nephew, who was experiencing hard times, was going to drop. Even so he saw that, 'The treasury will not class Alfred as one of the deserving poor if he has £250 a year, which it considers munificent for a poet; but he might have a chance as one of the undeserving rich.'[115] However the Ministry of Information informed Stopes that a second application would not be advisable. They wrote that '[Douglas] once attacked Churchill in a very bitter manner'. This might mean that 'the Prime Minister's native generosity would rather prejudice him in his favour, on account of this attack, than against him', but 'On the other hand I gather that there would be much criticism in the House and I fear that Alfred Douglas might be wounded by what was said.'[116] Douglas was resigned to his fate: 'I am a b . . . fool,' he told Stopes, 'and it was stupid and rather contemptible of me to suppose that my enemies would ever allow me to get a pension. The people who get pensions are people who keep quiet and give no trouble and never disagree with anyone on one side or the other.'[117] The worry over the money eclipsed all possibilities of enjoying life. 'The number of times I wish I were dead is very considerable,' he told Stopes. Incidental friendships and acquaintances, lunches with, among others, Ivor Novello brought little comfort. Money governed everything. He spent a weekend at the Duchess of Westminster's home in Surrey, met Duff and Lady Diana Cooper and was charmed, but he could not accept an invitation to stay at the Dorchester as Lady Diana's guest because he had spent all his spare money on a taxi to Surrey.[118] In his *Autobiography* Douglas had written, 'I believe the most constant cross I have had to bear is precisely that of being born, and having had to go on all my life being, a lord without money.'[119] Now, in his old age, he really felt it.

Lady Diana Cooper proved a godsend to Douglas, who wrote to her after they met and sent a copy of his Shakespeare sonnets book with a description of what would appear in a new edition: in the archives of Canterbury he had discovered reference to a Will Hews, an apprentice to Marlowe's father. The conjecture was that the boy had been taken up by Marlowe then Shakespeare, which fits perfectly with the hypothesis put forward in Douglas's book, which might answer the question of who Mr

W.H. was. Lady Diana was fascinated and asked Douglas to come and see her some time. In his reply he expressed his desire to do so and added that it would be 'something to look forward to in my rather dismal existence'.[120]

Offers were made to Douglas of ways out of his situation but none was suitable. He had made a new friend, Adrian Earle, who had come to his attention because he had wanted to buy some Douglas manuscripts. The two men grew close and by mid-1943 Douglas had decided to make him his literary executor. It is clear that Earle, who showered books on Douglas, had set out to achieve this objective, but he was also a great help to him. In 1942 he had offered to take Douglas away to a place in the country to live, but Douglas rejected the notion outright: neither he nor Olive could bear to be separated completely, and he visited her at least two or three times a week.[121]

As the war carried on, Olive's money diminished as did her husband's allowance. Douglas only moaned about his money troubles to those who he knew could help him out and to Marie Stopes more than most. A letter he wrote on his birthday in 1942 is particularly pitiful:

> I know that I *ought* to rely on Providence and 'consider the lilies' and the sparrows and so forth, but you must remember that I am old and worn out (72 today) and that I have been through fearful trials (have you ever read my *Autobiography*?) and that I cannot control my health. Up till a few years ago I was full of courage and almost demoniacal energy and ready to face anything, but nowadays I find that things get me down (chiefly because worry stops me from sleeping). I never got over that imprisonment in Wormwood Scrubs. It simply destroyed my health. I have never been the same since. Then now, consider my position, I have not really enough to live on comfortably (even when the rent is paid for me) and I am in a constant state of worry and anxiety about ways and means.[122]

As more and more plans fell through, Douglas wrote to Earle from his sickbed: 'There seems to be a curse on me. If only I could die and get out of all this misery. I am distracted and can't write sense.'[123]

There *was* a way out, however, and it was suggested by the indomitable Marie Stopes. She decided that the way to keep Douglas out of poverty and worry was to grant him an allowance herself and to encourage others to do the same. She made sure that Douglas occasionally met Lady Diana Cooper: 'I thought he was delightful,' she reported after first meeting him.[124] She, along with Stopes, worked tirelessly for Douglas and eventually secured money for him from Lord Tredegar and two MPs, Henry (Chips) Channon and Alan Lennox-Boyd, who were married to Guinness sisters. Channon and Lennox-Boyd liked him. 'He was very pathetic . . . alone, poor, almost friendless,' wrote Channon in his diary. 'Alan and I melted towards him, especially when he told us that he can no longer afford to keep his flat, for which Francis Queensberry pays the rent. I do not know what will become of him. I think I shall give him a small allowance, and then perhaps someone will be kind to me in my advanced age.'[125] In the same year Channon and Harold Nicolson supported Douglas's application to the Home Secretary for the return of the manuscript of 'In Excelsis', which the prison officials at Wormwood Scrubs had confiscated at the time of his release. Citing De Profundis as a precedent, Douglas and the others argued that the manuscript was the property of the poet, not the prison services. Channon wrote to Osbert Peake, the Under-Secretary of State for the Home Office, telling him 'Alfred Douglas is a very old man living in the most distressing circumstances. All he has left are the memories of his literary career, and it is not unnatural that he should wish to collect his MSS and put them in order before he dies.'[126] Of course, Douglas wanted the only working manuscript that remained so that he could sell it, and the Home Office knew this when they turned down the application, informing Douglas and his supporters that the rule that prisoners must not benefit financially from their imprisonment had to be maintained. Really, though, they wanted to avoid the publicity which the sale of such an item would create, especially because it would almost certainly take place in the USA.

Douglas was also experiencing political difficulties. As always he could not refrain from entering into any argument about which he felt strongly. Letters to the papers were fired off with alarming regularity, about the Bolsheviks, the Fascists, Ireland and much else. A pamphlet he had written, Ireland and the War Against Hitler, was circulated round both Houses of Parliament and made a small impression. With many others, Douglas was strongly of the belief that southern Irish ports should be seized by the British authorities. 'Politically you have the brains of a grasshopper,' Bernard Shaw told him, 'and you have far too much courage.'[127]

Two months ago I wrote a letter to *The Times* which, characteristically, that paper would not print, saying that unless we took over the Irish ports, with or without the consent of Mr de Valera, we deserved to lose the war against Germany. Since I wrote that letter many of our ships have been torpedoed in waters contiguous to the Irish ports and the situation has steadily deteriorated. Foolishly, idiotically one might say, we tried, twenty years ago, to propitiate our implacable Irish enemy by kindness and generosity. The experiment has been a complete failure both from the Irish and the English point of view. We abandoned our friends in Ireland in the vain hope of propitiating our enemies; and the result has been what it always has been and always will be in similar conditions. Now is the time to act. If we wait till Germany has actually landed an army in Ireland (which is liable to happen any day), it may be, it probably will be, too late. It is for the armed forces of the Crown to act because the present crisis is not a political but a strategic one. Fortunately we now have a Prime Minister whose courage is unassailable and indomitable. This was not the case when Lloyd George surrendered to Sinn Fein.[128]

Douglas indeed respected the policies and actions taken by the Prime Minister. The old argument that had made Churchill his enemy had long faded into insignificance. Now, in mid-1941, Douglas was persuaded by his nephew Francis Queensberry, who was a friend of Churchill, to write a poem about the Prime Minister. 'I told Francis that it was quite impossible, but directly I got down to it it came fairly easily,'[129] Douglas told Francis d'Avilla. Queensberry, who professed to a great admiration for his uncle's poetry and knew much of it by heart, read the new sonnet to a house party at Leeds Castle where Osbert Sitwell was among the guests who proclaimed it a masterpiece. Douglas could not agree with them on this, but admitted that it was 'not too bad'.[130]

Queensberry sent a copy of Douglas's sonnet, 'Winston Churchill', to the man himself. Churchill wrote to thank Queensberry, and passed on a message for Douglas: 'Thank you very much for the sonnet you sent me which I shall keep and value. Tell him from me that "Time Ends All Things".'[131] It was a noble and fitting end to the squabble. The sonnet appeared in the *Daily Mail* on 4 July 1941:

> Not that of old I loved you over-much,
> Or followed your quick changes with great glee,

While through rough paths of harsh hostility
You fought your way, using a sword and crutch
To serve occasion. Yours it was to clutch
And lose again. Lacking the charity
Which looks behind the mask, I did not see
The immanent shadow of the 'Winston touch'.

Axe for embedded evil's cancerous roots.
When all the world was one vast funeral pyre,
Like genie smoke you rose, a giant form
Clothed with Addisonian attributes
Of God-directed angel. Like your sire
You rode the whirlwind and outstormed the storm.[132]

The Churchill sonnet led Douglas into writing three more, all, as he freely admitted, *'vers d'occasion* written for propaganda purposes'.[133] Nevertheless they went down well and earned him some extra money.

During these last years Douglas's writing also included a small amount of prose. He wrote a preface to a book of poems by Marie Stopes. He did not want to do this but felt that he should as a form of thanks for her loyalty and perseverance on his behalf. Rather more difficult was a preface he wrote to a book by Frances Winwar entitled *Oscar Wilde and the Yellow Nineties*. The book was a rehash of Harris and libellous of Douglas. He agreed to allow its sale if his notes were added. Nevertheless the preface gave him no joy to write. He was fed up with having once again to write about a matter he thought he had settled many years before. Winwar's book was slack and badly researched but it was another piece of work that would strengthen the myth that Douglas's role in Wilde's life was that of nemesis. An opportunity also arose to do something he had never done before: when he met the ballet agent Poppoea Vanda she asked him to write a scenario for her company. Douglas suggested *Vanity Fair* and wrote it. Vanda was delighted and proclaimed it the finest scenario for a ballet she had ever seen. Sadly the restrictions of the war meant that it was never produced.[134]

Of more importance was a talk that Douglas was invited to give to the Royal Society of Literature on 2 September 1943. It was his only lengthy public speech on poetry and it was an opportunity he had wanted for years. The platform was perfect and Douglas decided to make an all-out attack on modern poets, calling his talk 'The Principles of Poetry'. 'I have gone bald-headed for T. S. Eliot and other heretical ''poets'' in my lecture,'[135] he told Francis d'Avilla, and indeed he had. Articles appeared in the papers about the event before it had even happened. One columnist wrote at the end of a lengthy and positive article in which he expressed hope that the lecturer would speak in the 'best Lord Alfred tradition', 'I congratulate the Royal Society of Literature on the honour they have done in his old age to one of the greatest English poets.'[136] The writing of the lecture was a great burden to Douglas and he had required help from a friend, with much borrowed from the earlier prefaces to his poems,[137] but it did what he wanted. The talk centred on the horror Douglas felt for poetry that was not primarily concerned with beauty and the fact that naturally this sort of poetry was mainly anti-formal. Douglas displayed his contempt for Eliot by quoting a passage from his 'Aunt Helen' and comparing it with a piece of news from the paper he had turned into 'verse' by splitting up the lines. Quiller-Couch told him, 'I purred over your address to the R.S.L. and again over your news that the hearers took it with joy. Indeed there are signs – even in poor old Cambridge – that sensible people are sickening of the T.S. Eliot game (has he ever written 3 consecutive lines of poetry in his life?) of perpetually ''debunking'' beauty and sneering at it. 'Tis a fearsome thing, this spread of ''culture'' in the U.S.A. Middle West! And this fellow Pound, with his Mussolini!'[138] Quiller-Couch, who died the following year, added that he had hope for the future of poetry as long as Douglas was alive.

The talk was indeed a success and came out as a pamphlet later in the year. Among those who expressed their admiration for it was Augustus John, who told Douglas, 'I find your observations tremendously stimulating because profoundly true and their general sense could be applied with equal justice to much that passes for painting nowadays. What must be your satisfaction to realise, as you of course do, that in your own practice of the Art of Poetry you have illustrated with supreme distinction the principles exemplified in the masters.'[139]

A reprint of *Sonnets* in 1943 helped to keep up Douglas's reputation, as did two radio broadcasts. The second was a five-minute programme in which Douglas read four sonnets, the prologue to *Romeo and Juliet*, Milton 'On His Deceased Wife', Wordsworth's 'Toussaint l'Ouverture' and his own 'Beauty and the Hunter'. Although the BBC has never been able to track down the reels that contain this short programme, there is a recording of him reading 'Beauty and the Hunter'. The poem, written shortly before he became a Catholic, betrays strongly Catholic mystical influence.[140]

> Where lurks the shining quarry, swift and shy,
> Immune, elusive, unsubstantial?
> In what dim forests of the soul, where call
> No birds, and no beasts creep? (The hunter's cry
> Wounds the deep darkness, and the low winds sigh
> Through avenues of trees whose faint leaves fall
> Down to the velvet ground, and like a pall
> The violet shadows cover all the sky.)
>
> With what gold nets, what silver-pointed spears
> May we surprise her, what slim flutes inspire
> With breath of what serene enchanted air? –
> Wash we our starward gazing eyes with tears,
> Till on their pool (drawn by our white desire)
> She bend and look, and leave her image there.

11

Depression set in almost permanently during the war years. Weariness had long since taken over the youthful jollity. Before the outbreak of war Douglas had made his last trip to Oxford and told Shaw, 'I am full of melancholy here in Oxford. Yesterday I walked round the cloisters of Magdalen and the whole place was peopled with the ghosts of my boyhood friends, most of whom are dead.'[141] It was very much the same impression that one surviving friend also had. In 1941 George Montagu, now Earl of Sandwich, received a letter from Edmund Phipps, Douglas's collaborator on the *Pentagram* and contributor to the *Spirit Lamp*. 'Magdalen is looking lovelier than ever! Full of ghosts, for me – Tiler Reid, Jane [Encombe] and Bosie.'[142] The past that Douglas had known and loved had all gone. Even Clouds, where he had loved staying, was empty, the Wyndhams dead. It had been demolished in part to make it a more convenient size. As a symbol of the way the world had changed there could be nothing more stark for Douglas: the privileged lifestyle had disappeared and what was left of Clouds was now sold and became a treatment centre for alcoholics and drug addicts.[143]

As the fighting raged on abroad, Douglas lost more of those who had formed his circle. A. J. A. Symons, who had been writing the book that he and Douglas believed would vindicate once and for all Douglas's role in the Wilde scandal, exposing the lies of Ross and Harris, died before he could finish his work in 1941, the same year that Virginia Woolf, fearing another attack of mental illness, loaded her pockets with stones, waded into the river Ouse and drowned. Douglas had even outlived the younger generation.

William Sorley Brown, Douglas's defender, correspondent, friend and admirer for some thirty years, died in 1942. In 1943 the only other important survivor of the Wilde circle died and Douglas assured Robert Sherard's widow that he would pray for him always.[144] He was in bed with bronchitis and could not attend the funeral. A promising young poet called Raoul Pugh who had befriended Douglas was killed on active service at the age of twenty-two. Then Hove was bombed. Douglas described it to Adrian Earle: 'A stream of German planes came shimmering just over the tops of the trees in St Ann's Wells Gardens. They were not more than 100 yards off as I watched them from my window and looked as if they were coming right at this building.'[145] Four people living in the same road as Douglas were killed in the raid and two houses were completely destroyed.

Douglas's health was failing rapidly now, and he was vulnerable to chills, fevers and colds; he found it impossible to sleep and took to writing his letters in the early morning to keep off the worry he felt lying awake in bed. In one letter to Earle he said, 'I write this at 10.45 and I am looking forward with misery to a sleepless night. Or rather I know I shall go to sleep and then wake up at about 4 in the morning and lie awake worrying till I get up for breakfast. St Jude and all my saints seem to have deserted me. When I was younger and stronger I could face these situations, but now I am helpless before them.'[146]

Olive was also very ill, and having delusions too. Her health declined rapidly throughout 1943 and early 1944. On 11 February 1944 Douglas spent several hours with his wife, holding her hand as she lay semi-conscious in bed. The next morning Olive's maid telephoned to tell him that his wife had died in the early hours. She had refused to go back to the Catholic faith, from which she had lapsed shortly after her conversion, so Douglas's fears for her soul were great.[147]

The main beneficiary of Olive's will was Raymond, who was allowed to attend his mother's funeral. Everything she had left Douglas was seized by the Official Receiver for his bankruptcy. 'I think this a cruel piece of injustice and cruelty, but it is on a par with the way I have been treated all my life,' he later told his nephew Queensberry. 'I am now almost penniless. My health is still awful though it looks as if I may not die yet which is a pity.'[148]

For a time after Olive's death Douglas was allowed to occupy the flat where she had lived. His loyal friend Lord Tredegar would come with his wife and stay in one of the Brighton hotels, entertaining him to tea. The Tredegars would see others at the same time and introduce their friends to Douglas. On one occasion the writer Hector Bolitho was present. He left an account of the occasion.

> I remember a big sitting-room, with grey shadows outside, and the miserable winter tide beyond the sea wall; Alfred Douglas walking in, slowly, with a sad face but quick, lively eyes. Then some naval cadets from H.M.S. King Alfred joined us and our hostess, Olga Tredegar, tried to manage a rather confused conversation; the boys on one side talking of war; on the other, Alfred Douglas talking of poetry. There was a tough little midshipman who had never heard of Alfred Douglas. He no doubt felt that his place was with the erudite, so he piped up: 'Oh, I know a poem right through. I learned it at school. Milton!'
>
> Instead of frowning at the interruption, Lord Alfred Douglas said: 'I love Milton. Which poem was it?'
>
> The boy began, but his memory failed. Alfred Douglas prompted him, line by line, so that the midshipman navigated his way to the end of the sonnet. After this, Lord Alfred Douglas turned the conversation to the Navy, so the boy would feel that he was in home waters. It was a charming gesture from an old, distinguished poet to an eager boy.[149]

At last Raymond was judged fit to leave St Andrew's Hospital and live in his mother's flat. Olive's maid, Eileen, was to look after him. She was described by one visitor as 'a vast gorgon of a woman', with 'wide hips, pendulous breasts at her waistline, sloping shoulders and a large head with a fringe of mangy black hair, but nearly bald on top'.[150] Douglas was delighted and looked forward to establishing a normal father–son relationship once again. After about a week he decided to take two new friends, Edward and Sheila Colman, whom he had met through Richard Rumbold, to meet his son. Things did not go according to plan. A short time before the Colmans were due to arrive at the flat Raymond had a brainstorm: he began throwing things out of the window into the street until Eileen managed to stop him.[151] St Andrew's was phoned and the staff came to collect him straight away. It was a sad let-down for Douglas, the proud father who had wanted his new friends to meet his son.

After Raymond had gone back to St Andrew's, Eileen helped Douglas for a time but she was not a welcoming sight and nearly scared off one young visitor. This was Donald Sinden, who was acting in repertory in Brighton, and had been interested when, at a meeting of the Sussex Poetry Society, someone had mentioned that Lord Alfred Douglas lived nearby. Shortly before this occasion he had been lent ('with malice aforethought', he now thinks) a biography of Oscar Wilde. He had not known until now that '*the* Lord Alfred Douglas' was still alive, so he decided to visit him.

After a short interrogation from Eileen someone spoke from behind her in the hall, the voice of a stooping man, 'with grey hair, bleary eyes and pouches under them and a bulbous nose'. Douglas invited his young visitor in and was obviously impressed by Sinden's talk about his poetry. He invited the young man to come to tea the following week and a pleasant friendship began. During Sinden's ensuing visits Douglas finally got round to talking about Wilde and other people he had known who might interest the aspiring actor. Some way into the friendship Douglas revealed to Sinden a side of his character that had once dominated it. Sinden had found a copy of *Oscar Wilde and Myself* in a local bookshop and had been confused by the sentiment in it. He produced it one day while visiting Douglas:

Bosie leaped to his feet, his whole body twitching, his face became deathly white and his eyes glared, he spluttered and mucus ran from his nose and mouth. He seemed to be choking and his eyes grew larger and sightless . . . At last he managed an intake of breath and screamed, 'WHERE DID YOU

GET IT? WHERE DID YOU GET IT?' I was deeply shocked and tried to explain.
He snatched the book with jumping hands – for a moment I thought he
was going to throw what had cost me two shillings and sixpence on the
fire.' Instead, Douglas sat down with a pen and wrote on the fly-leaf:
'This book (nearly all of which was written by T.W.H. Crosland) has
long since been repudiated by me. It does not represent my real views
about Wilde as I have explained in numerous places. I much regret that it
was ever published. Alfred Douglas Sep. 1944.'

Sinden wrote that he felt guilty in recounting this story since on every
other occasion they met, and in every way, Douglas was to him 'a very
kind old man'.[152] But Douglas could not bear the thought that his final
word on the subject of Wilde was not *the* final word on Wilde.

Sinden took Douglas out to lunch twice in Brighton, 'praying that he
would not stray from the three shillings and sixpence table d'hôte'. On
being offered a drink Douglas replied, 'No, thank you. The wages of gin
is breath, as Oscar would have said.' They continued to meet at intervals
for the rest of Douglas's life and Sinden was one of the last visitors
Douglas received.[153]

In the autumn of 1944 Douglas suffered a serious heart-attack, which
left him nearly paralysed. He had earlier tried to make some money by
selling most of his possessions, including his pictures and furniture.
Because of the flying-bomb scares the auction at Sotheby's was sparsely
attended and raised only £298. 'Bloody sickening' was how he described
it.[154] At the same time he threw away all those papers he thought it
unnecessary to keep. All he retained were his manuscripts and some
letters, including those from Shaw. The heart-attack had been brought on
by the shock he received when a letter from the Custance family solicitor
told him that the annuity left him by Olive, on which he had relied, had
been reduced by taxation from £500 to £163. The capital sum was then
taken by the Official Receiver.

Douglas spent a month in a nursing home in Hove. From there he
wrote to Marie Stopes, 'I never expected to be so old. I expect I shall
hang on for a few months but don't see how I can expect to recover.'[155]
Two days later his condition was so serious that he was given Extreme
Unction by a priest, which cured him with miraculous efficiency. His
childishly simple belief in miracles had been justified. The feeling of
suffocation, which had been with him for days, had gone and he was well

enough to walk. Edward and Sheila Colman, who ran a farm in Lancing, not far from Hove, offered to put him up and nurse him back to health. With fresh farm produce and such generous company Douglas was able to live his last months in comfort, security and relative happiness. He was well enough to rewrite his will and cut out Adrian Earle. Earle had let him down badly: among other things it became obvious that he had stolen ideas from Douglas and claimed them as his own. Douglas therefore decided that he would leave his books, manuscripts and copyright to Edward Colman as his literary executor.

Though Douglas recovered noticeably with the Colmans it was obvious that his improvement would not last. A doctor had diagnosed that the heart trouble dated from a rheumatic fever he had suffered at twenty-five. A cardiograph of Douglas looked, in his own words, 'like a map of the Himalayas'.[156] 'My miraculous recovery from Extreme Unction was, I fear, only a dying flicker, as I'm worse than ever now,' he told Shaw. In December 1944 the correspondence with Shaw drew to a close. Douglas's last letter to him ended, 'I'm afraid I am too far gone for care now, and I don't expect to recover. I'm not afraid of death and have many consolations, but the long process of dying is painful and miserable. I wish it were over. Your devoted, Childe.'[157]

Shaw wrote the final letter, continuing the theme of the correspondence that had been the result of continual clashes between atheist and Catholic. The friendship, during which they had only met once, was brought to a fitting close with a reconciliation of their beliefs.

Dear Childe Alfred,

In jumping to a conclusion be careful not to jump too far. The Unction cured you. Only for a day; but it did cure you for that day, proving that you are not incurable. The problem is to cure you for many days and not too many years, but enough.

I have nothing to contribute but my strong wish that the problem will be solved, which is my form of prayer, and as good, I hope, as anybody's . . .

From your letters I should say you have a lot of life left in you yet.

There are many degrees of belief. The child of eight believes; so does the vieillard of eighty-eight, but not in the same light. Though I discard the Aztec touch, I have more faith in the consecrated wafer than I do in digitalis, and agree with Mephistopheles that blood is *ganz besonderes saft* [quite a special juice].

    Good night.

      G.B.S.[158]

Douglas was happy to die because he had been able to resolve his quarrels. He had written to Marie Stopes as long ago as 1939 about Ross, who had been, in his opinion, his worst enemy. He had masses said for Ross because 'I felt that as he was my greatest enemy and spent 10 years of his life trying to ruin me and my reputation I ought to try to help him, as of course I've forgiven him.'[159] He made a kind of reconciliation with Vyvyan Holland, the only surviving son of Oscar Wilde. They met for the first time for half a century at a ball in the late thirties. 'We chatted on general subjects for about five minutes and then parted,' wrote Holland.[160] When they had last met Vyvyan Holland had been a boy of nine and Douglas twenty-five. It was always a source of sadness to Douglas that relations between himself and Vyvyan could not have been better.

But this was a time for making peace with the world and nobody was more aware of this than Douglas. The days of quarrelling were long gone and he was touched when, during his illness, a flood of letters and phone calls came from well-wishers. 'I didn't know I had so many friends,'[161] Douglas told Marie Stopes. She received her last letter from Douglas on 3 February 1945. He now signed himself, 'with love, yours affectionately, Bosie'. The most improbable of friendships had turned into one of the most affectionate.

Robert Hichens, who had written *The Green Carnation* after meeting Douglas in Cairo in the early 1890s, was now being pressured by his publishers to reissue the book he had voluntarily suppressed at the time of the Wilde trials. Douglas was asked if he would object to a new edition and he assured Hichens that he would not. He had tried to set things right and if he had not it was too late now.

To Churchill, Douglas had made one last communication, in December 1944:

Dear Mr Churchill,

    I write this letter from what is probably my death-bed. I was given extreme unction 3 days ago. I am writing to you as a dying man to implore you after your magnificent speech about Greece the other day, not to fall into the pit of dishonour which would be the result of the betrayal of Poland to people whom you yourself described, not so long ago, as 'bloody baboons'. I am too ill to write more, but I beg you to consider that if you let down the Poles your own reputation, which is now at the highest peak, will be irretrievably damaged in the eyes of posterity.

> Yours sincerely,
> Alfred Douglas[162]

Churchill replied immediately, thanking him for his letter, promising that he would not let down the Poles and finishing, in his own hand, 'I trust your health may be restored.'[163]

Among those who visited Douglas at Old Monk's Farm, the Colmans' home, were his nephew Queensberry, Donald Sinden, Hesketh Pearson and, with Lord Tredegar, Terence Rattigan. The Colmans had selflessly helped him at a time when he had little to give them in return. Occasionally a small amount of money would come to Douglas, from a betting win or a royalty cheque, in which case he took them to lunch.

Having had to sell his piano two years earlier Douglas now found much comfort in being able to sit for hours at theirs. He would play all sorts of things. He had a particular love of *The Beggar's Opera*, a work that had been composed due to the patronage of his ancestors. Chopin's *Ballades* remained favourites, and his copy reveals that he tackled all of the hardest, and scribbled in the fingering and pedalling. Considering he had not had lessons since he was at school, his facility at the piano was impressive. As well as Bach he would still play from the copy of Mozart sonatas he had bought at Magdalen in 1890, and added a couple of newer songs to the collection. He sang to Graham Peel's setting of Housman's 'In Summertime on Bredon' and also liked 'My Little Grey Home in the West':

> There are hands that will welcome me in
> There are lips I am burning to kiss
> There are two eyes that shine just because they are mine,
> And a thousand things other men miss.

Yet although there was the occasional day on which he felt lively, his health was declining and breathing became hard. He had already had

Extreme Unction twice. Visitors found him tired and weak, which made conversation difficult. In March he was in bed and clearly on his way out. It was what he had wanted for years. At times his faith had been the only thing that had kept him going and it was all he had to help him through death. A priest, Father Corley, visited him at least once a day and administered the sacraments. On St Patrick's Day, three days before he died, Douglas was well enough to talk to Sheila Colman about the serious attitude to saints in Ireland, but his energy did not last long.

Douglas's last act was a characteristic one and for someone who had lived such a contradictory life it was an appropriate finish. On the morning of Saturday 17 March 1945 he scribbled a faint note in pencil for Sheila Colman: 'Mixed bark doubles – Nicholson's mounts.' As far as last literary efforts go it takes some beating. It was a bet he wanted her to place for him at the bookmaker's that afternoon. The horse lost.[164] Half a century earlier in Paris, Oscar Wilde had remarked of Douglas's gambling that '[Bosie] has a faculty of spotting the loser, which, considering that he knows nothing at all about horses, is perfectly astounding.'[165]

In the early hours of the morning of Tuesday 20 March, Douglas's night nurse called the Colmans to his room. His breathing had become increasingly laboured and she sensed that death was not far off. Edward and Sheila Colman took it in turns to hold his hand, but he was probably not conscious that anyone was present.

He had made his peace with the world and with his God, and so, at about four in the morning, Lord Alfred Douglas breathed for the last time.

*   *   *   *

Douglas had mentioned several years earlier that he wished to be buried with his mother, in the cemetery of the Franciscan Friary in Crawley. A requiem mass was celebrated before the burial and a small number of people turned out for it. Raymond was not allowed out of St Andrew's Hospital for the funeral, but other members of the family were present; including Lady Edith Fox-Pitt, his sister, who lived on until 1963. Douglas's nephew, Francis Queensberry, attended, as did his brother, Lord Cecil Douglas. The Colmans were both there and held a reception afterwards. Others among the small crowd of no more than thirty mourners included Harford Montgomery Hyde, who was home on leave, Francis d'Avilla, Donald Sinden,

Adrian Earle, Lord Tredegar and Father Corley, who had helped Douglas so much at the end.

After his death, as many people had suspected, books poured out abuse about Douglas. Vyvyan Holland was able to publish the full version of *De Profundis* for the first time, the obstacle of a libel case now being out of the way. A biography of Douglas written in 1948 by William Freeman was not granted permission to include Douglas's copyright material. The following year for some reason the Marquess of Queensberry collaborated with Percy Colson on an extremely offensive book: the authors of *Oscar Wilde and the Black Douglas* were also not allowed to quote from copyright work. This book deeply upset other members of the Queensberry family because, as Lady Edith Fox-Pitt wrote to Marie Stopes, 'Alfred can no longer defend himself.'[166] Marie Stopes herself brought out a book on Douglas in 1949; it contained the text of a lecture she had given. Quirky and eccentric, it is a loving view of Douglas by his friend.

'St Christopher' died at Ayot St Lawrence, his home of forty-four years, on 2 November 1950 after a fall in his orchard. He was ninety-four. His death was mourned across the British Empire, indeed, across the globe. In India the government adjourned a cabinet meeting when the news came through, and the lights were dimmed on Broadway. The last line he ever wrote would have appealed to his 'Childe Alfred'. The play, *Why Should She Not*, concluded 'The world will fall to pieces about your ears.'

In her will, Olive had asked for her ashes to be scattered at sea. It was not until 1950 that her wishes were fulfilled, and the remains of the woman Lord Alfred Douglas had loved were scattered over the sea front near her home in Brighton.

Also in 1950, the ashes of Robert Ross were interred in the tomb of Oscar Wilde, Père Lachaise cemetery, Paris.

Raymond Douglas died on 10 October 1964, at the age of sixty-one, in the hospital where he had spent the majority of his life. Francis, the 11th Marquess of Queensberry, died in 1954. He was succeeded by his son David, the present Marquess, whose greatest moment in the House of Lords was perhaps his speech in favour of reform of the Criminal Law Amendment Act, which decriminalised homosexual love. Among his children is a daughter, Lady Alice Douglas, who several years ago began to work with prisoners at Wormwood Scrubs. She married an inmate.

Lord Alfred had written many times that he looked forward to death.

He looked forward to meeting his father and Wilde again, both of whom, being converts, were of course in heaven. He looked forward to meeting again the mother who had doted on him and the brothers he had loved, Percy, whose conversion to the Church made his position certain and, of course, Drumlanrig, whom Douglas rarely mentioned, but whom, in the Kinmount days, he had loved so much. And he looked forward to being a boy once more. From Thomas à Kempis, Douglas had got the idea that in heaven you could be whatever age you wanted to be, and Douglas wanted to be free of the troubles that had haunted him incessantly throughout maturity.

Perhaps the best view of Douglas was written by him in one of his beautiful sonnets 'To Olive'. He had no doubt that his vision would be fulfilled.

> I see you all bedecked in bows of rain,
> New showers of rain against new-risen suns,
> New tears against new light of shining joy.
> My youth, equipped to go, turns back again,
> Throws down its heavy pack of years and runs
> Back to the golden house a golden boy.

Notes

I have used abbreviations in the notes to refer to the following locations where manuscripts are held.

Berg   The Berg Collection, New York Public Library, New York
BL   The British Library, London
Bodleian The Bodleian Library, Oxford
Hyde   The Hyde Collection, in the possession of the Viscountess Eccles (Mary Hyde), Somerville, New Jersey
Maggs   Catalogue of the sale of Douglas family letters, Maggs Bros., London
NLS   The National Library of Scotland, Edinburgh
Princeton Manuscripts Division, Department of Rare and Special Collections, Princeton University Library
PRO   Public Record Office, Kew, London
Texas   The Humanities Research Centre, University of Texas, Austin
Clark   The William Andrews Clark Memorial Library, University of California, Los Angeles

Introduction

1 John Betjeman to Rupert Croft-Cooke, 8 June 1962. In Candida Lycett-Green (ed.), *Letters*, vol II, 1996, p. 233.
2 Lord Alfred Douglas, *Without Apology*, 1938, p. 308.

Chapter 1

1 The Marquess of Queensberry and Percy Colson, *Oscar Wilde and the Black Douglas*, 1949, p. 11.

2 The Black Douglas features in several novels and stories of Sir Walter Scott such as *The Tales of a Grandfather*.

3 See contemporary letter from the Duchess of Marlborough to Viscountess de Longueville, n.d. BL. MS 63650, f. 70.

4 Henry Blyth, *Old Q, the Rake of Piccadilly. A Biography of the Fourth Duke of Queensberry*, 1967, p. 42.

5 *Ibid.*, p. 216.

6 Queensberry was reported to have offered a large reward to anyone able to find the body of his brother. *Dumfries Standard*, 16 August 1865.

7 In Lady Florence Dixie, *The Story of Ijain: or, The Evolution of a Mind*, 1903.

8 The poem by Queensberry entitled 'The Spirit of the Matterhorn' was published in the *Spirit Lamp* when Lord Alfred Douglas edited it.

9 See Gladstone to Queensberry, 18 April 1881. Maggs, p. 9.

10 *The Autobiography* of Lord Alfred Douglas, 1929, p. 1.

11 Fanny Montgomery to Benjamin Disraeli, 31 August 1868. Bodleian.

12 *Autobiography*, p. 2.

13 *Ibid.*, p. 7.

14 *Ibid.*, p. 9.

15 'Here and There', *Harrovian*, vol. VII, no. 8.

16 *Autobiography*, p. 14.

17 *Ibid.*, p. 14–15.

18 *Ibid.*, p. 15.

19 *Ibid.*, pp. 16–17.

20 *Ibid.*, p. 17.

21 *Ibid.*, pp. 8–9.

22 *Ibid.*, p. 26.

23 See Hugh Trevor-Roper, *Hermit of Peking*, 1979, p. 299.

24 Sir Edmund Trelawny Backhouse, *The Dead Past*, 1943, p. 26. Bodleian. MS ENg. misc. d1225, MS Res.d.332.

25 John Stokes, 'Wilde at Bay: the Diaries of George Ives', in *English Literature in Transition 1880–1920*, vol. XXVI, no. 3, 1983, pp. 178–179.

26 *Autobiography*, pp. 25–6.

27 Described by W. G. Ward who was quoted by his son, Wilfred Ward. *Autobiography* of Lord Alfred Douglas, pp. 18, 26, 28.

28 *Ibid.*, p. 28.

29 *Ibid.*, p. 17.

30 Patrick Braybrooke, *Lord Alfred Douglas, His Life and Work*, 1931. He was told by Douglas in a letter that there was nothing that he could offer that he had not written in his *Autobiography*. The result was simply a rehash and exaggeration of Douglas's book.

31 *Without Apology*, p. 159.

32 *Ibid.*, pp. 229–30.

33 Maurice Ashley, *Churchill as Historian*. Quoted in Hugo Vickers, *Gladys, Duchess of Marlborough*, 1979, p. 66.

34 *Autobiography*, pp. 9–10.

35 *Without Apology*, pp. 244–5.

36 Introduction to John Piper's *Brighton Aquatints*, 1939, p. iii.

37 *Without Apology*, p. 240.

38 *Autobiography*, p. 2.

39 *Without Apology*, pp. 160–64.

40 *Ibid.*, p. 241.

41 *Ibid.*, p. 173.

42 *Ibid.*, pp. 168–73.

43 'In Excelsis', sonnet XI, *Sonnets*, 1935, p. 69.

44 Sandwich became a notable art collector and his will, dated 3 December 1962, pp. 1–4, shows that on his death he left works by, among others, Van Gogh, Degas, Constable, Bonnard, Cézanne, Matisse, Augustus John, Modigliani, Gauguin and Renoir, many of which he bequeathed to the nation.

45 *Autobiography*, p. 93.

46 *Ibid.*

47 *Without Apology*. p. 165.

48 The identification of the editors of the *Pentagram* is possible thanks to the donation of the marked copies of Sir Edmund Bamfylde Phipps to the Rare Book and Manuscript Library, University of Columbia, New York.

49 *Pentagram*, no. 6, p. 25.

50 *Ibid.*, p. 23.

51 *Ibid.*, no. 3, p. 13.

52 *Autobiography*, p. 51.

53 *Pentagram*, no. 2, p. 6.

54 *Ibid.*, no. 10, p. 44.

55 *Autobiography*, p. 57.

56 *Pentagram*, no. 10, p. 41.

57 *Autobiography*, pp. 48–9.

58 *Ibid.*, p. 49.

59 John Stokes, 'Wilde at Bay: the Diaries of George Ives', in *English Literature in Transition 1880–1920* vol XXVI, no 3, 1983, pp. 178–179.

Chapter 2

1 *Without Apology*, p. 174.

2 *Autobiography*, p. 50.

3 *Ibid.*

4 *Autobiography*, p. 52.

5 Lord Alfred Douglas, *Oscar Wilde and Myself*, 1914, pp. 36–7.

6 President's notebook, Magdalen College archives, PR1/1/10.

7 Lord Alfred Douglas to Francis d'Avilla, 18 May 1930. Berg.

8 *Autobiography*, p. 52.

9 Preface to *Sonnets*, 1935, p. 10.

10 *Ibid.*, p. 11.

11 *Without Apology*, p. 243–4.

12 *Agnostic Review*, 11 November 1905.

13 *Autobiography*, p. 64. There was no way that Harris could have known the details of the meeting since only three men were there and Harris was not privy to their confidences at the time. He invented what he thought to be a likely scenario for the benefit of his readers.

14 Lady Colin Campbell, quoted in H. Montgomery Hyde, *The Trials of Oscar Wilde*, 1973, p. 50.

15 Douglas to Harris, 20 March 1925; Douglas MSS, Texas.

16 *Autobiography*, p. 215.

17 Douglas to Harris, 20 March 1925; Douglas MSS, Texas.

18 Jerusha Hull McCormack, *John Gray, Poet, Dandy and Priest*, 1991, p. 49.

19 André Gide, *Si le grain ne meurt*, (tr. D. Bussy), New York, 1935, pp. 300–1.

20 Harris claims in his *Life of Wilde* that Ross told him this, and Douglas heard the story from Harris as recounted in his letter to Robert Harborough Sherard, 26 September 1932. Hyde.

21 See Lord Alfred Douglas to William Andrews Clark, 7 February 1930; Clark.

22 Preface to *The City of the Soul*, 1911, pp. ix–xi.

23 *Academy*, vol. XXVI, no. 643, 30 August 1884, p. 134.

24 Tim d'Arch Smith, *Love in Earnest*, 1970, p. 30.

25 Shaw to Douglas, 4 July 1931. Mary Hyde (ed.), *Bernard Shaw and Alfred Douglas, A Correspondence*, 1982, p. 11.

26 *Lyrics*, 1935, p. 111.

27 Rupert Hart-Davis (ed.) *Selected Letters of Oscar Wilde*, 1979, p. 107.

28 Edmund Phipps contributed to the *Spirit Lamp*, vol. III, no. 1.

29 Campbell Dodgson to Lionel Johnson, 8 February 1893. In Hart-Davis, *Selected Letters*, p. 109, n. 2.

30 *Ibid.*

31 *Ibid.*, p. 110.

32 Wilde to Dodgson, postmark 23 February 1893. In Hart-Davis, *Selected Letters*, p. 109.

33 G.P. Jacomb-Hood, *With Brush and Pencil*, 1924, p. 116.

34 Wilde to Douglas, March 1893. In Hart-Davis, *Selected Letters*, p. 111.

35 See Richard Ellmann, *Oscar Wilde*, 1987, pp. 374–7.

36 *Morning Post*, 7 March 1912: Stuart Mason, *Bibliography of Oscar Wilde*, 1912, p. 209.

37 John Addington Symonds to Lord Alfred Douglas, 29 January 1893. Hyde.

38 *Autobiography*, p. 78.

39 *Ephemeral*, no. 1, 18 May 1893, p. 2.

40 Ibid., no. 3, 20 May 1893, p. 23.

41 *Artist*, April 1893, p. 113.

42 D'Arch Smith, *op. cit.*, p. 53.

43 Note to the German translation of *De Profundis*, Hart-Davis, *op. cit.*, p. 242, n. 3.

44 Wilfrid Scawen Blunt to Judith Lady Wentworth, 11 August 1894. BL, 54115.

45 *Without Apology*, pp. 37–8.

46 Elizabeth Longford, *A Pilgrimage of Passion, The Life of Wilfrid Scawen Blunt*, p. 292, n.

47 Ibid., p. 293.

48 Wilfrid Scawen Blunt to Lady Anne Isabella Noel Blunt, 15 August 1894. BL, 54103.

49 Douglas to Mr Underhill, 14 June 1893. Magdalen College archives, MS 1009.

50 Queensberry to Lord Alfred Douglas, 1 April 1894. In H. Montgomery Hyde, *The Trials*, p. 71.

51 Douglas, *Oscar Wilde and Myself*, 1914, p. 34.

52 *Without Apology*, p. 181.

53 *Autobiography*, p. 59.

54 Douglas, *Oscar Wilde: A Summing-up*, 1940, p. 96.

55 *De Profundis*. In Hart-Davis, *op. cit.*, p. 160.

56 Gekoski, catalogue 18, summer 1994, p. 29.

57 *Ibid.*, p. ii.

58 H. Montgomery Hyde, *Lord Alfred Douglas*, 1984, p. 55.

59 William Rothenstein to Margaret Woods, 28 October 1893. Quoted in: Mary M. Lago and Karl Beckson (eds), *Max Beerbohm and William Rothenstein – Their Friendship and Letters 1893–1945*, 1975, p. 24, n. 1.

60 Hart-Davis, *Selected Letters*, pp. 113–14.

61 See Ellmann, *op.cit.*, pp. 382–3.

62 Stanley Wintraub, *Reggie: A Portrait of Reginald Turner*, 1965, p. 49.

63 Robert Hichens, *Yesterday*, 1947, pp. 60 ff.

64 Max Beerbohm to Reginald Turner, 12 March 1894. In Rupert Hart-Davis (ed.), *Letters to Reggie Turner*, 1964, pp. 91–2.

65 *Autobiography*, p. 74.

66 Lord Alfred Douglas to Lady Queensberry, 2 February 1894. Hyde.

67 *Ibid.*

68 *Sonnets*, 1935, p. 23, n.

69 Foreword to the second edition, Frances Winwar, *Oscar Wilde and the Yellow Nineties*, 1941, p. xvi.

70 *Ibid.*

71 *Autobiography*, p. 88.

72 H. Montgomery Hyde, *The Trials*, p. 71.

73 *De Profundis*. In Hart-Davis, p. 167.

74 H. Montgomery Hyde, *The Trials*, pp. 73–4.

75 Ibid., p. 71.

76 William Freeman, *The Life of Lord Alfred Douglas, Spoilt Child of Genius*, 1948, p. 103.

77 *Without Apology*, p. 235.

78 H. Montgomery Hyde, *The Trials*, p. 1.

79 Maggs, p. 4.

80 *Ibid.*, p. 5.

81 W.E. Henley considered one of the ballads for inclusion in the *New Review*. See letter from George Street to Douglas, 10 December 1894. Hyde.

82 *Lyrics*, 1935, p. 29.

83 *St James's Gazette*, 18 January 1895. In Rupert Hart-Davis (ed.), *More Letters of Oscar Wilde*, p. 103.

84 Longford *op. cit.*, p. 292.

85 *Without Apology*, p. 39.

86 *Ibid.*

87 30 June–1 July 1894. Fitzwilliam Museum, Cambridge.

88 Lucas D'Oyly Carte to Lord Alfred Douglas, 22 March 1892. Hyde.

89 Douglas to Queensberry, June 1894: Rupert Hart-Davis (ed.), *The Letters of Oscar Wilde*, 1962, p. 446.

90 *Oscar Wilde and Myself*, p. 204–5.

91 *De Profundis*. In Hart-Davis, *Selected Letters*, pp. 167–8.

92 Queensberry to Lord Percy Douglas. Maggs, p. 4.

93 Lady Florence Dixie to Lord Percy Douglas, 19 December 1899. Maggs, p. 7.

94 Lady Paget Walburga, *In My Tower*, vol. I, p. 5.

95 H. Montgomery Hyde, *The Trials*, p. 74.

96 *Ibid.*

97 The papers relating to the divorce were released in 1994.

98 *The Times*, 25 October 1894.

99 *Ibid.*

100 *Ibid.*

101 *Ibid.*

102 *De Profundis*. In Hart-Davis, *Selected Letters*, 1979, p. 169.

103 *Ibid.*, p. 168.

104 *Ibid.*

105 Mackail and Wyndham, *The Life and Letters of George Wyndham*, vol I, p. 280.

106 Related by Mrs Violet Conagham in conversation with the author, 9 August 1997 and 30 September 1997.

107 Wilde to George Ives, postmark 22 October 1894. In Hart-Davis, *Letters*, p. 375.

108 Queensberry to Montgomery, 1 November 1894. Quoted in Ellmann, *op. cit.*, p. 402.

Chapter 3

1 Letters from Queensberry to Percy Douglas, Minnie and solicitor, 18 February to 23 May 1895. Maggs, p. 3.

2 *Ibid.* Quoted in The Marquess of Queensberry and Percy Colson, *Oscar Wilde and the Black Douglas*, p. 58.

3 *Ibid.*

4 Wilde to Ross, 13 May 1897. Quoted in Hart-Davis, *Selected Letters*, p. 255.

5 See H. Montgomery Hyde, *The Trials of Oscar Wilde.*

6 See Douglas to Frank Harris, quoted in foreword to *A New Preface to 'The Life and Confessions of Oscar Wilde' by Frank Harris*, 1925.

7 See Sir Edward Clarke to Robert Harborough Sherard, 16 September 1929. This letter is reproduced in full with a comprehensive discussion of this whole matter in Appendix B, H. Montgomery Hyde, *The Trials*, pp. 328–33.

8 See Douglas G. Browne, *Sir Travers Humphreys, A Biography*, 1960, pp. 36–7.

9 Oscar Wilde to the editor of the *Evening News*, 5 April 1895.

10 Max Beerbohm to Ada Leverson, 3 March 1895. Quoted in Katherine Lyon Mix, *Max and the Americans*, 1974, pp. 10–11.

11 *De Profundis.* In *Selected Letters of Oscar Wilde*, p. 170.

12 Julie Speedie, *Wonderful Sphinx, The biography of Ada Leverson*, 1993, p. 72.

13 *Ibid.*, p. 72.

14 H. Montgomery Hyde, *The Trials*, pp. 133–4.

15 Douglas Murray, 'The Comedy of Suffering', unpublished MS, 1996, p. 3. in Eton College archives.

16 *Reynolds*, 7 April 1895.

17 *Ibid.*

18 Charles Russell to the Hon. Hamilton Cuffe, Director of Prosecutions, 5 April 1895. Quoted in H. Montgomery Hyde, *The Trials*, p. 151.

19 Maggs, p. 10. This cutting belonged to the Marquess of Queensberry and the most vituperative phrases are underlined in ink.

20 George Wyndham MP to his father, the Hon. Percy Scawen Wyndham, 7 April 1895. Quoted in *Without Apology*, pp. 310–12.

21 *Autobiography*, p. 108.

22 See *Autobiography*, pp. 121–2.

23 Oscar Wilde to Ada and Ernest Leverson, 9 April 1895. In Hart-Davis, *Selected Letters*, p. 133.

24 Oscar Wilde to Robert Harborough Sherard, 16 April 1895. In Hart-Davis, *Selected Letters*, p. 135.

25 Oscar Wilde to Ada Leverson, 23 April 1895. In Hart-Davis, *Selected Letters* p. 135.

26 Alfred Douglas to More Adey, September 1896. Quoted in Rupert Croft-Cooke, *Bosie*, 1963, pp. 150–51.

27 H. Montgomery Hyde, *The Trials*, pp. 264–6.

28 *Autobiography*, p. 111.

29 Alfred Douglas to Percy Douglas, 1 May 1895.

30 Lord Alfred Douglas, 'An Introduction to my Poems with some reflections on the Oscar Wilde case', *La Revue Blanche*, 1 June 1896.

31 *Ibid.*

32 *Autobiography*, p. 35. See also Wilde to Douglas, 20 May (?) 1895; in Hart-Davis, *Selected Letters*, pp. 137–8.

33 *Autobiography*, p. 112.

34 Queensberry to Stoneham. See Queensberry and Colson, *op. cit.*, pp. 61–2.

35 Maggs, p. 3.

36 *Ibid.*

37 Queensberry and Colson, *op. cit.*, pp. 67–8.

38 *Ibid.*

39 Alfred Douglas, *Star*, 25 May 1895.

40 Alfred Douglas, *La Revue Blanche*, 1 June 1896.

41 H. Montgomery Hyde, *The Trials*, p. 272.

42 See Hesketh Pearson, *The Life of Oscar Wilde*, 1946, pp. 205–6.

43 Queensberry to Lady Percy Douglas, 11 March 1895. Quoted in Queensberry and Colson, p. 59.

44 Alfred Douglas to Sir Edward Clarke, 26 May 1895. Quoted in H. Montgomery Hyde, *The Trials*, pp. 328–9.

45 Alfred Douglas to W. T. Stead, 15 November 1895. Sold at Sotheby's, London on 19 July 1994. Lot 150.

46 Lionel Johnson to More Adey, 13 July 1895. Princeton.

47 Alfred Douglas to Percy Douglas, 20 June 1895. Maggs, p. 13.

48 Edmund Phipps to Lord Alfred Douglas, 24 December 1895. Hyde.

49 *Illustrated Police News*, 1 June 1895.

50 *News of the World*, 26 May 1895.

51 *Daily Telegraph*, 27 May 1895.

52 See the programme for the first production of Stoppard's *The Invention of Love* at the Cottesloe Theatre, autumn 1997.

53 H. Montgomery Hyde, *Lord Alfred Douglas*, p. 226.

54 Croft-Cooke, *Bosie*, p. 133.

55 Douglas petition to Queen Victoria, 25 June 1895. In H. Montgomery Hyde, *Oscar Wilde: The Aftermath*, 1963, pp. 203–4.

56 PRO HO 45/24514.

57 Alfred Douglas to Percy Douglas, 5 August 1895. Maggs, p. 16.

58 Alfred Douglas to the editor of *Journal du Havre*, 1 August 1895. See *Lord Alfred Douglas*, p. 93.

59 Douglas wrote the article in English. It was then translated into French by Henry D. Davray of the *Mercure de France*. The original French translation is in the Rare Books Department of Princeton University Library: Lord Alfred Douglas, 'Oscar Wilde', bound MSS, O'Connell, CO213. AM 16891. p. 38, translation in Box 1, File 35.

60 *Autobiography*, pp. 114, 126–9.

61 *Without Apology*, pp. 268–9.

62 The sonnet contains echoes of Keats's sonnet about Leigh Hunt.

63 Alfred Douglas to Percy Douglas, 1 April 1896. Maggs, p. 15.

64 The four journalists picked out for attack were Henry Fouquier, Georges Vanor, Francisque Sarcey and Henry Bauer.

65 *De Profundis*. In Hart-Davis, *Selected Letters*, p. 188.

66 Copy of *Poems*, 1896, inscribed by Lord Alfred Douglas to Walter Spindler. In the collection of Mrs Sheila Colman, curatrix of the literary estate of Lord Alfred Douglas.

67 Stephane Mallarmé to Alfred Douglas, 24 March 1897. In Rosemary Lloyd (ed. and tr.) *Selected Letters of Stephane Mallarmé*. University of Chicago, 1988, pp. 220–21.

68 *Without Apology*, p. 270.

69 *Lyrics*, 1935, p. 31.

70 Wilde to Douglas, *c.* 20 May 1895. In Hart-Davis *Selected Letters*, pp. 137–8.

71 More Adey to Alfred Douglas, 1897. Hyde.

72 Lord Alfred Douglas to Ada Leverson, 13 September, 1895. Clark.

73 The initiative for this came from the governor of Reading Prison, Major J. O. Nelson.

74 As with Douglas's poem of the same name, the title is taken from the opening lines of Psalm 130.

75 Lady Wilde died on 3 February 1896 in London after being refused permission to see her younger son one last time.

76 More Adey to Alfred Douglas, 1899. Clark.

77 Wilde makes his interpretation of the intentions of Percy and Lady Queensberry clear in his letter to Ernest Leverson, March 1895. In Hart-Davis, *The Letters of Oscar Wilde*, p. 385.

78 Oscar Wilde to Robert Ross, 1 April 1897. In Hart-Davis, *Selected Letters*, pp. 240–45.

79 In a statement in 'The Library of William Andrews Clark, Jr.' (San Francisco, 1922), II, p. 70, Robert Ross claimed that he had sent a typescript to Douglas on 9 August 1897, and that Douglas had acknowledged receipt of it. In his *Autobiography*, p. 135, Douglas details what he did with the Ross letter which contained 'quotes' from Wilde (whether they 'had been written or merely repeated by word of mouth' Douglas did not know). The date of receipt of this is proved by a letter from Douglas to More Adey, written from Nogent-sur-Marne, 30 June 1897, now in the Clark library, University of California, Los Angeles. In this letter Douglas says that he has just received an 'enormous envelope' from Ross which has turned out to be 'a typewritten statement' which Ross had said that he would send. This would date the arrival of the letter to which Douglas refers as being several weeks prior to the date on which Ross claimed he sent *De Profundis*.

80 Alfred Douglas reviewed Ross's expurgated version of *De Profundis* in *Motorist and Traveller*, 1 March 1895. Reprinted in full in *The Aftermath*, pp. 208–10.

81 *Autobiography*, p. 135.

82 Alfred Douglas to Percy Douglas (undated), from Villa Casa, Capri. Maggs, p. 15.

83 Alfred Douglas to Percy Douglas, 21 August 1897. Maggs, p. 16.

84 'The Travelling Companion', *Lyrics* 1935. p. 50.

85 Oscar Wilde to Alfred Douglas, 4 June 1897. In Hart-Davis, *Selected Letters*, p. 290.

86 *Autobiography*, pp. 151–2.

87 The cigarette case was auctioned by Bonhams of London on 30 September 1997 and fetched £14,500. See *The Times*, 22 August 1997.

88 Douglas, *Oscar Wilde, A Summing-Up*, Note to illustration on p. 134.

89 Oscar Wilde to Alfred Douglas, 31 August (?) 1897. In Hart-Davis, *Selected Letters*, pp. 305–6.

90 Oscar Wilde to Robert Ross, 21 September 1897. In Hart-Davis, *Selected Letters*, p. 308.

91 Alfred Douglas to Lady Queensberry, December 1897. Quoted in *Without Apology*, pp. 297–9.

92 Alfred Douglas to More Adey, 15 October 1897. Maggs, p. 20.

93 Oscar Wilde to Robert Ross, 1 October (?) 1897. In Hart-Davis, *Selected Letters*, pp. 309–10.

94 *Autobiography*, pp. 157–8.

95 Lord Alfred Douglas to Sir Rupert Hart-Davis, 26 October 1937. In the collection of Mr Merlin Holland.

96 *Sonnets*, 1935, note to p. 32.

97 See Douglas, *The True History of Shakespeare's Sonnets*, 1933, p. vi.

98 See Hart-Davis, *Letters*, pp. 649, 647, and; note p. 664.

99 Croft-Cooke, *Bosie*, pp. 163–4.

100 Lady Queensberry to More Adey, 13 November 1897. See Croft-Cooke, *Bosie*, pp. 164–5.

101 Alfred Douglas to Lady Queensberry, 7 December 1897. Quoted in *Without Apology*, pp. 302–5.

102 *Ibid*.

103 *Autobiography*, p. 159. See also Alfred Douglas to More Adey, 20 November 1897. Clark.

104 Oscar Wilde to Robert Ross, 2 March 1898 (?). In Hart-Davis, *Selected Letters*, pp. 329–30.

105 Alfred Douglas to Lady Queensberry, 7 December 1897. Quoted in *Without Apology*, pp. 302–5.

106 Oscar Wilde to Robert Ross, 18 February 1898 (?). In Hart-Davis, *Selected Letters*, p. 327.

107 Oscar Wilde to Reginald Turner, 11 May 1898. In Hart-Davis, *Letters*, p. 738.

108 Alfred Douglas to Oscar Wilde, 20 September 1898. In H. Montgomery Hyde, *Lord Alfred Douglas*, pp. 121–2. This is incomplete and the last of the three surviving letters from Douglas to Wilde.

109 Oscar Wilde to Robert Ross, 25 November 1898 (?). In Hart-Davis, *Selected Letters*, p. 345.

110 Preface to the first edition of *The Pongo Papers*, (1907). Reprinted in *The Complete Poems of Lord Alfred Douglas*, 1928, pp. 135–8.

111 Lord Alfred Douglas, *Tails With A Twist: Animal Nonsense Verse* (also including four poems from *The Placid Pug and Other Papers*), Batsford 1979.

112 See the 1911 edition of *The City of the Soul*: 'Some Press opinions', p. 136.

113 In the Headmaster's Collection, Winchester College.

114 *Autobiography*, pp. 51–2.

115 *See catalogue, Leonard Smithers and the 1890's part II*: The Booth collection of books published by Leonard Smithers. Phillips in London, 13 June 1996. p. 27, lot 364.

116 Captain Anthony Ludovici to Rupert Croft-Cooke. In Croft-Cooke, *Bosie*, pp. 175–6.

117 Bodleian. Walpole MS 35 (e 180).

118 Croft-Cooke, *Bosie*, p. 301. Croft-Cooke recalls Douglas saying this in conversation with him in 1922.

119 Lord Alfred Douglas to Robert Ross, 11 February 1895. Hyde.

120 Captain Anthony Ludovici to Rupert Croft-Cooke. In Croft-Cooke, *Bosie*, pp. 175–6.

121 Introduction by Douglas to the 1907 reprint of *The Pongo Papers and The Duke of Bewick*.

122 Arthur Symons, *Aubrey Beardsley*, 1966, p. 12.

123 *Autobiography*, p. 124.

124 Croft-Cooke, *Bosie*, p. 178.

125 *Autobiography*, pp. 122–5.

126 Lord Archibald Douglas to Lord Alfred Douglas, 2 July 1911. Hyde.

127 Wilde to George Ives, postmark 22 February 1900. In Hart-Davis, *Letters*, p. 816.

128 Alfred Douglas to Percy Douglas, 7 March 1900. Maggs, p. 15.

129 *Wykehamist*, no. 374, p. 223.

130 *Autobiography*, pp. 182–3.

131 Alfred Douglas to Percy Douglas, 19 December 1900.

132 *Without Apology*, pp. 252–3.

Chapter 4

1 *Autobiography*, p. 181.

2 *Ibid.*, pp. 163–7.

3 *Ibid.*, p. 211.

4 Lord Alfred Douglas to Olive Custance, 20 June 1901. Berg.

5 Lord Alfred Douglas to Olive Custance, 24 June 1901. Berg.

6 *Autobiography*, p. 212.

7 *Ibid.*

8 George Wickes, *The Amazon of Letters: The Life and Loves of Nathalie Barney*, 1977, pp. 58 ff.

9 Nathalie Barney poem to Olive Custance, no date. Berg.

10 *Autobiography*, p. 205.

11 Lord Alfred Douglas to Olive Custance, 20 August 1901. Berg.

12 Olive Custance to Lord Alfred Douglas, no date. Berg.

13 Lord Alfred Douglas to Olive Custance, September 1901. Berg.

14 Lord Alfred Douglas to Olive Custance, 2 October 1901. Berg.

15 Lord Alfred Douglas to Olive Custance, 23 October 1901. Berg.

16 Lord Alfred Douglas to Frank Harris, 19 October 1901. Texas.

17 Lord Alfred Douglas to Olive Custance, 1 November 1901. Berg.

18 Lord Alfred Douglas to Olive Custance, 13 November 1901. Berg.

19 *New York Herald*, 23 December 1901, p. 3.

20 Lord Alfred Douglas to the editor, *New York Herald*, Tuesday 24 December 1901, p. 4.

21 *Autobiography*, p. 190.

22 Lord Alfred Douglas to the editor, *New York Herald*, Tuesday 24 December 1901, p. 4.

23 *New York Herald*, Tuesday 24 December 1901, p. 4.

24 *Autobiography*, p. 191.

25 Lord Alfred Douglas to Olive Custance, 20 December 1901. Berg.

26 *Ibid.*

27 *Autobiography*, p. 188.

28 The MS shows only slight variations to the published version.

29 Lord Alfred Douglas to George Sylvester Viereck, 3 January 1902. Hyde.

30 *Autobiography*, p. 192.

31 Lord Alfred Douglas to George Sylvester Viereck, January 1902. Hyde.

32 Lord Alfred Douglas to Olive Custance, 27 January 1902. Berg. The comment echoes Wilde's famous quip on Max Beerbohm.

33 *Autobiography*, p. 196.

34 *Ibid.*, p. 194.

35 *Without Apology*, p. 56.

36 *Autobiography*, p. 195.

37 For instance the poem appeared among the select number in the *Augustan Books of Poetry* edition of Douglas's poems in 1926.

38 *Autobiography*, pp. 195–6.

39 Lord Alfred Douglas to Olive Custance, 11 February 1902. Berg.

40 Lady Queensberry to Lord Alfred Douglas, 4 March 1902. Hyde.

41 Herbert Warren to George Montagu, 18 May 1902. The archives of the Earl and Countess of Sandwich, Dorset.

42 Croft-Cooke, *Bosie*, p. 203.

43 Elizabeth Longford, *A Pilgrimage of Passion. The Life of Wilfrid Scawen Blunt*, p. 373.

44 John Betjeman to Ian Fletcher, 18 January 1974. In Candida Lycett-Green (ed.), *Letters*, vol. II, p. 469.

45 Croft-Cooke, *Bosie*, p. 204.

46 Mary Hyde (ed.), *Bernard Shaw and Alfred Douglas, a Correspondence*, p. 217.

47 Lord Alfred Douglas to Lady Alfred Douglas, 28 August 1902. Berg.

48 Lord Alfred Douglas to George Sylvester Viereck, 6 June 1903. Hyde.

49 Lord Alfred Douglas to Walter Ledger, 3 June 1902. 'The Letters of Robert Ross to Walter Ledger, 1902–1918', Bodleian, MSS Ross 4.

50 For instance, Holbrook Jackson, *The Eighteen Nineties*, 1927.

51 *Motorist and Traveller*, 1 March 1905.

52 Compton Mackenzie, *My Life and Times III*, 1964, p. 225.

53 Croft-Cooke, *Bosie*, p. 209.

54 Lord Alfred Douglas to Lady Alfred Douglas, 23 July 1905. Berg.

55 *Sonnets*, 1935, p. 39. n.

56 Essay by Max Meyerfield, written in 1914, copied in the hand of Robert Ross. Hyde.

57 Douglas, *The True History of Shakespeare's Sonnets*, p. 102.

58 *Sonnets*, 1935, p. 40. n.

59 Lord Alfred Douglas to Lady Alfred Douglas, 13 September 1905. Berg.

60 Reprinted in Brocard Sewell, *Olive Custance, Her Life and Work*, 1975, p. 35.

61 Copy of *The Placid Pug* in the library of Princeton University. Meeting with Turner related in Lord Alfred Douglas to Lady Alfred Douglas, 24 July 1905. Berg.

62 Lord Alfred Douglas to Lady Alfred Douglas, 5 September and 22 October 1906. Berg.

63 Alice M. Head, *It Could Never Have Happened*, 1947, p. 43.

64 *Ibid.*

65 Lord Alfred Douglas to George Sylvester Viereck, 24 December 1904. Hyde.

66 Lord Alfred Douglas to George Sylvester Viereck, 6 June 1903. Hyde.

67 The poem appeared as 'Before the Dawn' in the 1909 *Sonnets*, and as 'Premonition' in collections thereafter.

68 Lord Alfred Douglas to Lady Alfred Douglas, 22 January 1906. Berg.

69 Olive Custance to Lord Alfred Douglas, no date. Quoted in *Autobiography*, p. 204.

70 W. Sorley Brown, *The Genius of Lord Alfred Douglas*, 1913, pp. 29–31.

71 *Autobiography*, p. 201.

Chapter 5

1 Although the light verse appeared in several papers, Douglas's sonnets, with the exception of 'Sois Sage O Ma Douleur', did not get into the press until 1924 when 'In Excelsis' was published in the London *Mercury*.

2 *Autobiography*, p. 220.

3 Lord Alfred Douglas to Lady Alfred Douglas, 2 May 1907. Berg.

4 Alice M. Head, *It Could Never Have Happened*, p. 44.

5 *Ibid.*, p. 42.

6 *Autobiography*, p. 220.

7 See Lord Alfred Douglas to Michael Field, n.d., from the *Academy* Office. British Museum. 45851, f.218.

8 William Sorley Brown, *The Life and Genius of T.W.H. Crosland*, 1928, p. 209.

9 Maureen Borland, *Wilde's Devoted Friend – A Life of Robert Ross*, 1990, p. 126.

10 Head, *op. cit.*, p. 43.

11 *Without Apology*, p. 54.

12 Mary Hyde (ed.), *Bernard Shaw and Alfred Douglas – A Correspondence*, p. 207. The letter exchange appeared in *Academy* on 30 May and 6 June 1908.

13 George Bernard Shaw to Lord Alfred Douglas, 25 May 1908.

14 Lord Alfred Douglas to George Bernard Shaw, 25 May 1908.

15 George Bernard Shaw to Lord Alfred Douglas, 27 May 1908.

16 Lord Alfred Douglas to George Bernard Shaw, 29 May 1908.

17 George Bernard Shaw to Lord Alfred Douglas, 31 May 1908.

18 Lord Alfred Douglas to Ada Leverson, n.d., 1908. National Library of Scotland.

19 Lord Alfred Douglas to Lady Alfred Douglas, 29 October 1908. Berg.

20 *Sonnets*, 1935, p. 54 n.

21 *La Revue Blanche*, 1 June 1896.

22 Preface to *Sonnets*, 1935, pp. 9–11.

23 *Autobiography*, pp. 222–3.

24 *Ibid.*, p. 223.

25 Letters exchanged between Blunt and Douglas, 15–17 August 1909. Fitzwilliam Museum, Cambridge.

26 William Freeman, *The Life of Lord Alfred Douglas, Spoilt Child of Genius*, p. 207.

27 *Autobiography*, pp. 232–3.

28 Freeman, *op. cit.*, pp. 208–9.

29 *Ibid.*, pp. 209–10.

30 Lord Alfred Douglas to Lady Alfred Douglas, 21 July 1909. Berg.

31 Freeman, *op. cit.*, pp. 211–14.

32 *The Life and Genius of T.W.H. Crosland*, pp. 240–41.

33 Hilary Spurling, *Ivy – The Life of Ivy Compton-Burnett*, p. 242.

34 *Sonnets*, 1935, p. 53. n.

35 See Lord Alfred Douglas to John Lane, 13 September 1911. Bodleian, MS Walpole d.4.

36 The MS was sold at Sotheby's, London, on 17 July 1997, Lot 220, with the letters from Douglas to W.A. Gordon. It is now in the Hyde collection.

37 Lord Alfred Douglas to Lady Alfred Douglas, 27 November 1911. Berg.

38 Lord Alfred Douglas to More Adey, 21 December 1900. Clark.

39 Lord Alfred Douglas to John Lane, 13 September 1911. Bodleian, MS Walpole d.4.

40 Freeman, *op. cit.*, p. 218.

41 *Daily News*, 16 March 1909.

42 The letters discussing the negotiations for the deal are among the twenty-three from Wyndham to Douglas in the Hyde Collection.

43 Lord Alfred Douglas to Lady Alfred Douglas, 14 October 1911. Berg.

44 Wilfrid Scawen Blunt in his diary, 7 June 1911. Fitzwilliam Museum, Cambridge.

45 Lord Alfred Douglas to Wilfrid Scawen Blunt, 7 June 1911. Fitzwilliam Museum, Cambridge.

46 Wilfrid Scawen Blunt in his diary, 10 June 1911. Fitzwilliam Museum, Cambridge.

47 *Ibid.*, 11 June 1911.

48 Head, *op. cit.*, p. 45.

49 Vyvyan Holland, *Son of Oscar Wilde*, reissued 1988, p. 195.

50 Lady Alfred Douglas to Robert Ross, 24 February 1909. Ross TS. Clark.

51 Robert Ross to Lady Alfred Douglas, 26 February 1909. Ross TS. Clark.

52 Lord Alfred Douglas to Robert Ross, 1 March 1909. Ross TS. Clark.

53 Sir Frederick Kenyon to Robert Ross, 29 October 1909. British Library, Add. MSS 50141.

54 Sir Frederick Kenyon to F.S. Salaman, 19 June 1913. British Library, Add. MSS 50141.

55 Robert Ross to Sir Frederick Kenyon, 5 November 1909. British Library, Add. MSS 50141.

56 H. Montgomery Hyde, *Lord Alfred Douglas*, p. 175.

57 Lord Alfred Douglas to Lady Alfred Douglas, 3 June 1911. Berg.

58 Freeman, *op. cit.*, pp. 227–8.

59 See Robert Ross to Carlos Blacker, 7 May 1912. In Maureen Borland, *Wilde's Devoted Friend – A Life of Robert Ross*, p. 164.

60 Arthur Ransome, *Oscar Wilde: A Critical Study*, 1912, p. 157.

61 Lord Alfred Douglas to Robert Ross, 6 March 1912. Ross Deposition. Clark.

62 George Lewis to Lord Alfred Douglas, 7 March 1912. Ross Deposition. Clark.

63 *Autobiography*, p. 135. In this account Douglas claims that he threw the letter in the river; in the letter to Ross in 1912 he claims he threw it into a fire.

64 Lord Alfred Douglas to Robert Ross, 9 March 1912. Ross Deposition. Clark.

65 Lord Alfred Douglas to Robert Ross, 4 November 1912. Ross Deposition. Clark.

66 *Autobiography*, p. 159.

67 *De Profundis*, in '*Selected Letters of Oscar Wilde*', p. 174.

68 Lord Alfred Douglas to Robert Ross, 1 November 1912. Ross Deposition. Clark.

69 *Ibid.*

70 Ross Deposition. Clark.

71 See *Autobiography*, p. 43.

72 Marie Belloc Lowndes, *A Passing World*, 1948, pp. 178–9.

73 Robert Ross to Lord Glenconner, 30 November 1912. Ross Deposition. Clark.

74 Robert Ross to Mrs Asquith, 30 November 1912, copy Hyde.

75 Lord Alfred Douglas to Robert Ross, 30 November 1912, copy Hyde.

76 *The Genius of Lord Alfred Douglas*, p. x.

77 *Ibid.*, p. xi.

78 *Ibid.*, p. 19.

79 T.W.H. Crosland, 'The First Stone', 1912, p. 7.

80 *Ibid.*, p.30.

81 *Autobiography*, p. 136.

82 Lord Alfred Douglas to Rev. Henry E. G. Rope, 15 January 1920. Clark.

83 Lord Alfred Douglas to a newspaper editor, 24 July 1911 (copy). Hyde.

84 Lord Alfred Douglas to the Duke of Richmond, 5 October 1912. Hyde.

85 *Autobiography*, p. 54.

86 Douglas, *Oscar Wilde and Myself*, p. 288.

87 The Marquess of Queensberry and Percy Colson, *Oscar Wilde and the Black Douglas*, p. 145.

88 In Tim d'Arch Smith, *Love In Earnest*, p. 53.

89 Lord Alfred Douglas to Christopher Millard, 11 November 1913. Hyde.

90 *Star*, 2 April 1913.

91 *Star*, 3 April 1913.

92 Lord Alfred Douglas to the Home Secretary, 2 April 1913. PRO HO 144/21591.

93 Lord Alfred Douglas to the Home Secretary, 4 April 1913 and official's comments in PRO HO 144/21591.

94 Lord Alfred Douglas to the editor, *The Times*, 9 April 1913. PRO HO 144/21591.

95 Lord Alfred Douglas to the Home Secretary, 10 April 1913. PRO HO 144/21591.

96 Arthur Ransome, *Oscar Wilde: A Critical Study*, 1912. p. 157.

97 *Ibid.*, p. 182.

98 *Ibid.*, p. 196.

99 Details of the trial were published in *The Times*, 18–19 and 22–23 April 1913.

100 *De Profundis*. In Hart-Davis, *Selected Letters*, pp. 305–6.

101 Oscar Wilde to Lord Alfred Douglas, 31 August (?) 1897. In Hart-Davis, *Selected Letters* pp. 305–6.

102 *De Profundis*. In Hart-Davis, *Selected Letters* pp. 239–40.

103 Lord Alfred Douglas to Robert Ross, 1 March 1909. Ross TS. Clark.

104 Lord Alfred Douglas to More Adey, 23 April 1913. MSS Clark.

105 *Autobiography*, p. 257.

106 *The Complete Poems of Lord Alfred Douglas*, p. 100.

107 Alice Head in conversation with Hilary Spurling, in Spurling, *op. cit.*, p. 328 n.

108 *Autobiography*, pp. 30–31.

109 Wilde, *The Importance of Being Earnest*, Act I.

Chapter 6

1 *Autobiography*, p. 137.

2 *Ibid.*, p. 210.

3 W. Sorley Brown, *The Life and Genius of T.W.H. Crosland*, 1928. p. 311.

4 Douglas, *Oscar Wilde and Myself*, p. 18.

5 *Ibid.*, pp. 39–40.

6 The identity of the woman named D.E. in the *Autobiography* can be deduced from the letters of Lord Alfred Douglas to Nathalie Barney in the Doucet Library, Paris. Doris Edwards subsequently became Doris Carlyle.

7 *Autobiography*, pp. 259–60.

8 Lord Alfred Douglas to Lady Alfred Douglas, 3 June 1913. Berg.

9 Lord Alfred Douglas to Lady Alfred Douglas, 12 August 1913. Berg.

10 Lord Alfred Douglas to Lady Alfred Douglas, 19 September 1913. Berg.

11 Lord Alfred Douglas to Lady Alfred Douglas, 15 September 1913. Berg.

12 Lady Alfred Douglas to A.J.A. Symons, 2 December 1925. Bodleian. MS Walpole d.4, f.15–16.

13 See *Lord Alfred Douglas*, p. 197.

14 Lord Alfred Douglas to Frank Harris, 2 November 1913. Texas.

15 As early as 1906 Millard had edited *Impressions of America by Oscar Wilde*, also under the name Stuart Mason.

16 Rupert Croft-Cooke, *Bosie*, p. 255.

17 Lord Alfred Douglas to Christopher Millard, 11 November 1913. Hyde.

18 Lord Alfred Douglas to Colonel Custance, 29 March 1914 (pamphlet).

19 *Autobiography*, p. 266.

20 W. Sorley Brown, *Crosland*, pp. 309–10.

21 *Ibid.*

22 Croft-Cooke, *Bosie*, p. 258. n.

23 William Freeman, *The Life of Lord Alfred Douglas, Spoilt Child of Genius*, pp. 230–9.

24 Margery Ross (ed.), *Robert Ross: Friend of Friends*, 1952, pp. 260–1.

25 Vyvyan Holland, *Time Remembered After Père Lachaise*, 1966, p.65.

26 Robert Ross to Edmund Gosse, 17 October 1913. Brotherton Library, Leeds University.

27 *Oscar Wilde and Myself*, p.296.

28 *Ibid.*, p.23.

29 *Ibid.*, pp. 10–11.

30 *Ibid.*, pp. 22–3.

31 *Ibid.*, p. 67.

32 *Without Apology*, pp. 60–1.

33 André Gide, *Journals 1889–1949*, 1967 edn, p. 307.

34 Lord Alfred Douglas to George Sylvester Viereck, 9 September 1913. Hyde.

35 Charles Lander to the Home Office, stamped 20 July 1914. PRO HO 144/21591.

36 Essay by Max Meyerfield, written in 1914, copied in the hand of Robert Ross. Hyde.

37 *Autobiography*, p. 281.

38 *Ibid.*, pp. 282–3.

39 *Ibid.*, p. 286.

40 *Ibid.*, p. 43.

41 Lord Alfred Douglas to Lady Alfred Douglas, 30 November 1914. Berg.

42 Lord Alfred Douglas to S.M. Ellis, 1 December 1914. Berg.

43 Lord Alfred Douglas to Lady Alfred Douglas, 10 December 1914. Berg.

44 Lord Alfred Douglas to Jack Squire, 6 February 1934. Berg.

45 Lord Alfred Douglas's plea before the Court of Chancery in the action against Colonel Custance over the custody of Raymond Douglas, p.15. Hyde.

46 Lord Alfred Douglas to William Sorley Brown, 22 August 1915. NLS.

47 Lord Alfred Douglas to Lady Alfred Douglas, 4 September 1915. Berg.

48 Lady Alfred Douglas to Sibyl, Dowager Marchioness of Queensberry, 14 January 1913. In Brocard Sewell, *Olive Custance, Her Life and Work*, 1975, p. 25.

49 Lord Alfred Douglas to Lady Alfred Douglas, 14 August 1915. Berg.

50 *Autobiography*, pp. 262–4.

51 The sonnet was later renamed 'The Erastians' and it appeared as such in the 1928 *Complete Poems*.

52 Lord Alfred Douglas to Mr Drake, 8 June 1929. Hyde.

53 *Bosie*, pp. 278–9.

54 Lord Alfred Douglas to Mr Drake, 8 June 1929. Hyde.

55 Merlin Holland, 'Biography and the art of lying', in Peter Raby (ed.), *The Cambridge Companion to Oscar Wilde*, 1997, p. 10.

56 *Daily Express*, 7 September 1916.

57 *Autobiography*, p. 264.

58 Lord Alfred Douglas to Lady Alfred Douglas, 3 January 1917. Berg.

59 Correspondence between Lord Alfred Douglas and Lord Monkbretton. Bodleian.

60 Felix Cherniavsky, *The Salome Dancer*, 1991, p. 20.

61 See Philip Hoare, *Wilde's Last Stand*, 1997, passim.

62 Douglas had written to Asquith on 22 January 1915 demanding to know why Asquith was still befriending Ross. He also wrote to Winston Churchill on 21 May 1915 emphasising what he had said to the Prime Minister. Both letters are in the Bodleian Library Oxford, MS Asquith 26.

63 Robert Ross to Walter Ledger, 4 April 1918. Bodleian. MS Ross 4.

64 Court accounts from the *Daily Mail* and *Morning Post*, 31 May 1918. Also Michael Kettle's 'Verbatim Report' of the trial brought out by the Vigilante Society, pp. 92–3.

65 Stephen Koss, *Asquith*, 1976, p. 234.

66 Michael Kettle's 'Verbatim Report' of the trial brought out by the Vigilante Society, pp. 172–80ff.

67 Lord Alfred Douglas to the Earl of Clonmel, 30 January 1914. Hyde.

68 Robert Ross to Charles Ricketts. In Margery Ross, *op. cit.*, pp. 333–4.

69 Maureen Borland, *Wilde's Devoted Friend, a life of Robert Ross*, p. 283.

70 Siegfried Sassoon, *Siegfried's Journey*, 1945, p. 84.

71 Lord Alfred Douglas to Lady Alfred Douglas, 21 November 1918. Berg.

72 Lord Alfred Douglas to Lady Alfred Douglas, 8 August 1917. Berg.

73 'Lord Alfred Douglas and his Wife', an article by the Rt. Rev. W.F. Brown, Bishop of Pella, in an unidentified paper, written shortly after Douglas's death. Hyde.

74 Conversation with Violet Conagham, 9 August 1997.

75 Lord Alfred Douglas to Lady Judith Wentworth, 17 August 1920. BL. ADD MS 54155.

76 *Autobiography*, pp. 186–7.

77 *Ibid.*, p. 3.

78 Lord Alfred Douglas to Reverend Henry E. G. Rope, 1 September 1920. Clark.

79 *Plain English*, vol. I, p. 361.

80 Lord Alfred Douglas to Reverend Henry E. G. Rope, 15 January 1920. Clark.

81 William Freeman, *Lord Alfred Douglas, Spoilt Child of Genius*, pp. 252–4.

82 *Evening News*, 4 February 1921.

83 The three surviving letters from Lord Alfred Douglas to Oscar Wilde are all in the William Andrews Clark Memorial Library, UCLA.

84 *Daily Telegraph*, 25, 26 and 29 November, 1921.

85 *Autobiography*, p. 309.

86 Lord Alfred Douglas to James Conchie, 14 October 1921. Hyde.

87 Sorley-Brown, *Crosland*, pp. 391–2.

88 Douglas, *Collected Satires*, 1926, p. 55.

89 H. Montgomery Hyde, *Sir Patrick Hastings: His Life and Cases*, 1960, pp. 110–17.

90 Douglas had met Kitchener in 1893 when he was in Cairo. In their highly unreliable book *Oscar Wilde and the Black Douglas*, Douglas's nephew Francis and Percy Colson claim that there had been some kind of a sexual encounter between the two men. In the unlikely event that there had been, it was something Douglas wished to forget.

91 Rupert Croft-Cooke, *The Glittering Pastures*, 1962, p. 127.

Chapter 7

1 Lord Alfred Douglas to Lady Judith Wentworth, 17 March 1920. BL, ADD MS 54155.

2 Sir Philip Sassoon to Sir Edward Marsh, 3 February, no year (almost certainly 1923). Berg.

3 Lord Alfred Douglas to Dr George C. Williamson, 20 August 1920. John Keats Memorial Volume, Princeton General MS [Bd.].

4 Conversations with Violet Conagham, 9 August and 30 September 1997.

5 The house numbers in Tite Street had changed by this time and so, as Croft-Cooke realised afterwards, he had probably stood staring at the wrong house.

6 Rupert Croft-Cooke, *The Glittering Pastures*, 1962, pp. 126–31.

7 Beverley Nichols, *The Unforgiving Minute*, 1978, p. 51.

8 *Autobiography*, pp. 153–4.

9 'The Murder of Lord Kitchener and the truth about the Battle of Jutland and the Jews', *Border Standard*, 1923, p. 1.

10 *Without Apology*, p. 183.

11 *Ibid*.

12 Douglas published a bitter pamphlet in 1918 entitled 'Fashionable Intelligence about the "Morning Post"'.

13 *Without Apology*, pp. 143–4.

14 Martin Gilbert, *Sir Winston Churchill*, 1976, vol. V, pp. 21–3.

15 William Freeman, *Lord Alfred Douglas, Spoilt Child of Genius*, p. 271.

16 Preface to 'In Excelsis', 1924, p. 9.

17 *Autobiography*, pp. 310–12.

18 *Without Apology*, pp. 185–6.

19 *Ibid.*, p. 187.

20 *Ibid.*, p. 187.

21 *Ibid.*, p. 193.

22 *Autobiography*, p. 314.

23 PRO HO 144/21591.

24 *Autobiography*, p. 314.

25 *Without Apology*, p. 194.

26 *Ibid.*, p. 36.

27 Rupert Croft-Cooke, *The Numbers Game*, 1963, p. 79.

28 *Ibid.*, p. 80.

29 Lord Alfred Douglas to George Bernard Shaw, 9 February 1944. In Mary Hyde (ed.), *Bernard Shaw and Alfred Douglas, a Correspondence*, p. 169.

30 *Autobiography*, pp. 277–8.

31 *The Numbers Game*, p. 79.

32 *Sonnets*, 1935, p. 65 n.

33 Lord Alfred Douglas to Sir Jack Squire, 10 July 1924. Berg.

34 PRO HO 144/21591.

35 'The Murder of Lord Kitchener and the truth about the Battle of Jutland and the Jews', *Border Standard*, 1923, p. 2.

36 Lord Alfred Douglas to Sir Jack Squire, 27 July 1924. Berg.

37 Lord Alfred Douglas to Herbert Moore Pim, 17 October 1924. Queen's University, Belfast.

38 Lord Alfred Douglas to R. N. Green Armytage, 22 November 1924. Berg.

39 Lord Alfred Douglas letter addressed to 'My Lord Bishop', 22 October 1924, Berg.

40 Lord Alfred Douglas to William Sorley Brown, 17 October 1924. NLS.

41 Lord Alfred Douglas to Sir Jack Squire, 20 June 1924. Berg.

42 *Border Standard*, 1 November 1924.

43 Lord Alfred Douglas to the editor, *Spectator*, 25 January 1925. Hyde.

44 *The Numbers Game*. p. 77.

45 *Ibid.*, p. 78.

46 John Betjeman to Rupert Croft-Cooke, 8 June 1962. In Candida Lycett-Green (ed.), *Letters*, vol. II, p. 232.

47 Foreword by John Betjeman to the 1890s catalogue compiled by Dr G. Krishnamurti, 1974, p. 10. Betjeman thought he was christened Moth after the character in *A Midsummer Night's Dream*.

48 John Betjeman to Rupert Croft-Cooke, 8 June 1962. In Lycett-Green, *op. cit.*, vol. II. p. 232.

49 Bevis Hillier, *Young Betjeman*, 1988, pp. 116–17.

50 Walter Hooper (ed.), *All My Road Before Me. C. S. Lewis*, 1991, p. 436.

51 *Ibid.*, p. 437.

52 Violet Powell to the author, 1 February 1998.

53 Evelyn Waugh, *Diaries*, 1995, p. 297.

54 'W.H. Auden at Oxford', in *Coming Home: John Betjeman*, selected and introduced by Candida Lycett-Green, 1997, p. 483.

55 Philip Hoare, *Wilde's Last Stand*, 1997, p. 228.

56 Lady Ruth Head to Janet Ashbee, 9 November 1933. In the private collection of Mr Angus Graham-Campbell.

57 *Without Apology*, pp. 56–7.

58 Herbert Moore Pim, in *Border Standard*, 1 November 1924.

59 Rupert Croft-Cooke, *Bosie*, p. 322.

60 Lord Alfred Douglas to William Sorley Brown, 18 May 1925. NLS.

61 Lord Alfred Douglas to Herman Finck, 29 August 1925. Berg.

62 Philippa Fullar, *Frank Harris*, 1975, p. 367.

63 Lord Alfred Douglas in conversation with Rupert Croft-Cooke. See Croft-Cooke, *Bosie*, p. 326.

64 Lord Alfred Douglas to Frank Harris, 4 September 1925. Texas.

65 Lord Alfred Douglas to Frank Harris, 16 September 1925. Texas.

66 Lord Alfred Douglas to George Sylvester Viereck, 25 February 1926. Hyde.

67 Lord Alfred Douglas to George Sylvester Viereck, 23 September 1925. Hyde.

68 *Bernard Shaw and Alfred Douglas, a correspondence*, p. 218.

69 Lord Alfred Douglas to Herbert Moore Pim, 20 May 1926. Hyde.

70 Lord Alfred Douglas to Frank Harris, August 1925. Texas.

71 Lord Alfred Douglas to Herbert Moore Pim, 20 May 1926. Hyde.

72 Lord Alfred Douglas to Herbert Moore Pim, 18 May 1926. Hyde.

73 Lord Alfred Douglas to Herbert Moore Pim, 22 April 1927. Hyde.

74 Beverley Nichols, *Sweet and Twenties*, 1958, pp. 228–9.

75 *Ibid.*, pp. 230–31.

76 Lord Alfred Douglas to Herbert Moore Pim, n.d., *c.* August to December 1926. Hyde.

77 Lord Alfred Douglas to Herbert Moore Pim, n.d., *c.* August to December, 1926. Hyde.

78 Lord Alfred Douglas to Herbert Moore Pim, 31 December 1926. Hyde.

79 Croft-Cooke, *Bosie*, p. 331.

80 Lord Alfred Douglas to Herbert Moore Pim, 22 April 1927. Hyde.

81 Croft-Cooke, *Bosie*, p. 329.

82 Lord Alfred Douglas to the Prince of Wales, 1 July 1926, copy Hyde.

83 Lord Alfred Douglas to A. J. A. Symons, 9 June 1927. Bodleian. MS Walpole.

84 See the MS of the *Autobiography*, Bodleian: In the Walpole papers, vol. III, p. 587.

85 Preface to the American edition of the *Autobiography*, 1932, p. 7.

86 Julie Speedie, *Wonderful Sphinx, the biography of Ada Leverson*, 1993, p. 38.

87 Lord Alfred Douglas to A. J. A. Symons, 17 December 1927. Berg.

88 George Bernard Shaw to Lord Alfred Douglas, 16 April 1931. In Mary Hyde, *op. cit.*, p. 3.

89 André Gide, *Journals*, 1889–1949, 1967 edn, p. 307.

90 The poet was Francis d'Avilla, also known as Fabienne L. E. C. Hillyard.

91 Lord Alfred Douglas to Herbert Moore Pim, 20 May 1926. Hyde.

92 MS of Douglas's talk to the Catholic Poetry Society, pp. 9–10. Hyde.

93 MS of Douglas's talk to the Catholic Poetry Society, pp. 20–22. Hyde.

94 Croft-Cooke, *Bosie*, p. 335.

95 *Daily Express*, 23 March 1933.

96 Lord Alfred Douglas to George Bernard Shaw, 1 July 1933. In Mary Hyde, *op. cit.*, p. 19.

97 Lord Alfred Douglas to H. Montgomery Hyde, 28 April 1930. In H. Montgomery Hyde, *Lord Alfred Douglas*, p. 285.

98 Charles Scott Moncrieff to Douglas Goldring, 3 June 1926. Princeton, General MSS (misc.) CO140 GL GOO.

99 John Betjeman to Diana Guinness, 29 May 1932. In Candida Lycett-Green, *Letters*, vol. I, pp. 106–7.

100 Lord Alfred Douglas to George Bernard Shaw, 1 July 1933. In Mary Hyde, *op. cit.*, p. 19.

101 Lord Alfred Douglas to John Gawsworth, 24 August 1932. Berg.

102 George Bernard Shaw to Lord Alfred Douglas, June 1933. In Mary Hyde, *op. cit.*, p. 15.

Chapter 8

1 Lady Violet Powell to the author, 10 February 1998.

2 Lady Violet Powell, *Within the Family Circle*, 1976, p. 177.

3 Lord Alfred Douglas to Reggie Turner, 6 May 1929. Hyde.

4 Reggie Turner to Frank Harris, 24 March, n.y., Texas.

5 Lord Alfred Douglas to Violet Wyndham, 21 November 1932. Berg.

6 Siegfried Sassoon, *Siegfried's Journey*, 1945, pp. 35–6.

7 *Autobiography*, p. 97.

8 George Bernard Shaw to Lord Alfred Douglas, 16 April 1931. In Mary Hyde (ed.), *Bernard Shaw and Alfred Douglas, a Correspondence*, p. 4.

9 Lord Alfred Douglas to Douglas Goldring, 15 January 1933, Princeton General MS [Misc.].

10 Lord Alfred Douglas to Sir Jack Squire, 8 February 1934. Berg.

11 Conversations between Violet Conagham and the author, 9 August and 30 September 1997.

12 Lord Alfred Douglas to George Bernard Shaw, 6 May 1938. In Mary Hyde, *op. cit.*, p. 46.

13 John Betjeman to Penelope Betjeman, 18 September 1935. Candida Lycett-Green (ed.), *Letters*, vol. I, p. 155.

14 Lord Alfred Douglas to William Sorley Brown, 9 April 1935. NLS.

15 Lord Alfred Douglas to Rupert Croft-Cooke. In Croft-Cooke, *Bosie*, p. 338.

16 Lord Alfred Douglas to Francis d'Avilla, 18 November 1935. Berg.

17 Lord Alfred Douglas to Rupert Croft-Cooke. Quoted in Croft-Cooke, *Bosie*, p. 338.

18 Preface to *Sonnets*, 1935, p. 9.

19 Preface to *Lyrics*, 1935, p. 7.

20 Lord Alfred Douglas to Francis d'Avilla, 13 December 1935. Berg.

21 Nigel Nicolson (ed.), *Diaries and Letters of Harold Nicolson, 1930–1939*, 1966, p. 261.

22 George Bernard Shaw's Preface to Frank Harris, *Life and Confessions of Oscar Wilde*, 1938. p. l.

23 Lord Alfred Douglas to George Bernard Shaw, 3 January 1936. In Mary Hyde, *op. cit.*, pp. 20–21.

24 George Bernard Shaw to Lord Alfred Douglas, 8 October 1937. In Mary Hyde, *op. cit.*, pp. 21–2.

25 Humbert Wolfe, in *Observer*, 12 January 1936.

26 Lord Alfred Douglas to Francis d'Avilla, 18 January 1930. Berg.

27 Lord Alfred Douglas to Francis d'Avilla, 26 April 1930. Berg.

28 Lord Alfred Douglas to Francis d'Avilla, 11 April 1930. Berg.

29 Anthony Powell, *Faces In My Time*, 1980, p. 115.

30 Sir Arthur Quiller-Couch to Lord Alfred Douglas, 28 August 1935. Hyde.

31 Lord Beaverbrook to Lord Alfred Douglas, 16 March 1933. Hyde. Beaverbrook had expressed this opinion in the *Evening Standard* and the *Daily Express*.

32 Lord Alfred Douglas to Francis d'Avilla, 13 December 1935. Berg.

33 Croft-Cooke, *Bosie*, p. 336.

34 *Without Apology*, p. 22.

35 Bodleian. MS Walpole. d.4. 33.

36 *Daily Express*, 2 December 1936.

37 A.L. Rowse, *Quiller-Couch – A Portrait of Q*, 1988, p. 218.

38 Lord Alfred Douglas to Robert Sherard, 1 March 1935. Hyde.

39 *Ibid*.

40 Preface to Norman Marshall's English version of Maurice Rostand's play about Oscar Wilde.

41 H. Montgomery Hyde, in Gabriel Austin (ed.), *Four Oaks Library*, 1967, p. 86.

42 Lord Alfred Douglas to André Gide, 7 May 1929. Copy in the collection of Mrs Sheila Colman.

43 H. Montgomery Hyde, *Lord Alfred Douglas*, p. 289.

44 James Agate, *EGO 3*, 1938, pp. 82–3.

45 Malcolm Muggeridge and Hesketh Pearson, *About Kingsmill*, 1951, pp. 138–9.

46 *Ibid*.

47 Hesketh Pearson, *The Life of Oscar Wilde*, 1960, pp. 375–6.

48 Lord Alfred Douglas to Cornelia Mary Streator, 29 June 1931. Clark.

49 Lord Alfred Douglas to George Bernard Shaw, 6 July 1931. In Mary Hyde, *op. cit.*, p. 28.

50 A. J. A. Symons to Lord Alfred Douglas, 10 April 1938. Hyde.

51 Lord Alfred Douglas to W.A. Gordon, 16 July 1942. Hyde.

52 *Without Apology*, pp. 9–11.

53 Lord Alfred Douglas to George Bernard Shaw, 29 January 1938. In Mary Hyde, *op. cit.*, p. 28.

54 A. J. A. Symons to Lord Alfred Douglas, 10 April 1938. Hyde.

55 Lord Alfred Douglas to Francis d'Avilla, 20 April 1937. Berg.

56 George Bernard Shaw to Lord Alfred Douglas, 18 April 1938. In Mary Hyde, *op. cit.*, p. 30.

57 James Agate, *Daily Express*, 19 May 1938.

58 He died on 17 February 1910.

59 Lord Archibald Douglas to Lord Alfred Douglas, 2 July 1911. Hyde.

60 *Without Apology*, pp. 46–8.

61 Malcolm Muggeridge in *Time and Tide*, 30 April 1938, pp. 598–9.

62 Lord Alfred Douglas's reply in *Time and Tide*, 7 May 1938.

63 Lord Alfred Douglas to George Bernard Shaw, 23 May 1938. In Mary Hyde, *op. cit.*, pp. 54–5.

64 Lord Alfred Douglas to William Sorley Brown, 10 May 1938. NLS.

65 Lord Alfred Douglas to George Bernard Shaw, 10 May 1938. In Mary Hyde, *op. cit.*, p. 49.

66 Lord Alfred Douglas to George Bernard Shaw, 6 May 1938. In Mary Hyde, *op. cit.*, p. 48.

67 Lord Alfred Douglas to George Bernard Shaw, 10 May 1938. In Mary Hyde, *op. cit.*, p. 49.

68 Lord Alfred Douglas to Marie Stopes, 1 October 1938. BL. MS 58494.

69 Lord Alfred Douglas to Marie Stopes, 3 October 1938. BL. MS 58494.

70 Lord Alfred Douglas to Marie Stopes, 5 November 1938. BL. MS 58494.

71 Lord Alfred Douglas to Marie Stopes, 7 January 1939. BL. MS 58494.

72 Lord Alfred Douglas to Marie Stopes, 24 December 1938. BL. MS 58494.

73 Lord Alfred Douglas to George Bernard Shaw, 20 February 1939. In Mary Hyde, *op. cit.*, pp. 105–6.

74 Lord Alfred Douglas to Marie Stopes, 14 February 1939. BL. MS 58494.

75 Keith Briant, *Marie Stopes, a Biography*, 1962, p. 194.

76 *Ibid.*, pp. 203–5.

77 *Ibid.*, p. 203.

78 Lord Alfred Douglas to George Bernard Shaw, 14 April 1939. In Mary Hyde, *op. cit.*, pp. 106–7.

79 George Bernard Shaw to Lord Alfred Douglas, 17 April 1939. In Mary Hyde, *op. cit.*, p. 107.

80 John Betjeman to Lord Alfred Douglas, 21 May 1939. BL. Stopes Papers, MS 58494.

81 Humbert Wolfe to Lord Alfred Douglas, 3 July 1939. Hyde.

82 Evelyn Waugh, *Diaries*, 1995 edition, p. 649.

83 Evelyn Waugh to Marie Stopes, 25 May 1939. Stopes Papers, BL. MS 58494.

84 Lord Alfred Douglas to Virginia Woolf, 30 June 1939. Berg.

85 Lord Alfred Douglas to Mr R. B. Marriott, 3 November 1939. Clark.

86 *Ibid*.

87 *Without Apology*, pp. 54–5.

88 Lord Alfred Douglas to Adrian Earle, 3 July 1943. Clark.

89 Rupert Hart-Davis, *Hugh Walpole, a Biography*, 1952, p. 413.

90 Lord Alfred Douglas to Marie Stopes, 2 October 1939. Stopes Papers, BL. MS 58494.

91 Anthony Bevin to Marie Stopes, 12 March 1940. BL. MS 58494.

92 Lord Alfred Douglas to Marie Stopes, 22 April 1940., BL. MS 58494.

93 Keith Briant, *Marie Stopes, a Biography*, 1962, p. 219

94 Lord Alfred Douglas to Marie Stopes, 12 July 1939., BL. MS 58494.

95 Douglas, *Oscar Wilde: A Summing Up*, p. 14.

96 *Ibid.*, pp. 15–16.

97 George Bernard Shaw to Lord Alfred Douglas, 20 June 1939. In Mary Hyde, *op. cit.*, p. 115.

98 George Bernard Shaw to Lord Alfred Douglas, 29 June 1939. In Mary Hyde, *op. cit.*, p. 115.

99 Lord Alfred Douglas to Franklin P. Rolfe, 30 December 1940. Clark.

100 Douglas, *Oscar Wilde: A Summing Up*, pp. 25–7.

101 Croft-Cooke, *Bosie*, p. 352.

102 *Ibid.*, pp. 364–5.

103 *Oscar Wilde: A Summing Up*, p. 7.

104 Lord Alfred Douglas to Marie Stopes, 27 August 1939., BL. MS 58494.

105 Lord Alfred Douglas to Marie Stopes, 7 September 1939., BL. MS 58494.

106 William Plomer to Rupert Croft-Cooke, In Croft-Cooke, *Bosie*, p. 347.

107 Lord Alfred Douglas to George Bernard Shaw, 30 May 1939. In Mary Hyde, *op. cit.*, p. 113.

108 Lord Alfred Douglas to George Bernard Shaw, 3 September 1938. In Mary Hyde, *op. cit.*, p. 93.

109 See William Freeman, *The Life of Lord Alfred Douglas*, pp. 300–1.

110 A.L. Rowse, *Quiller-Couch – A Portrait of Q*, 1988, p. 5.

111 Raymond Douglas to Lady Alfred Douglas, 8 September 1939. Berg.

112 Raymond Douglas to Lady Alfred Douglas, 27 August 1940. Berg.

113 *Faces In My Time*, p. 115.

114 See Virginia Woolf to Marie Stopes, 24 February 1941. Stopes Papers, BL. MS 58495.

115 George Bernard Shaw to Lady Diana Cooper, 9 April 1941. Cooper Papers in the College Library, Eton.

116 Letter from the Ministry of Information to Marie Stopes, 24 February 1941. BL. Stopes Papers, MS 58494.

117 Lord Alfred Douglas to Marie Stopes, 5 March 1941. BL. MS 58495.

118 Lord Alfred Douglas to Marie Stopes, 21 January 1941. BL. MS 58495.

119 *Autobiography*, p. 4.

120 Lord Alfred Douglas to Lady Diana Cooper, 14 February 1941. Cooper Papers, College Library, Eton.

121 Lord Alfred Douglas to Adrian Earle, 12 December 1942. Clark.

122 Lord Alfred Douglas to Marie Stopes, 22 October, 1942. BL. MS 58495.

123 Lord Alfred Douglas to Adrian Earle, 1 March 1943. Clark.

124 Lady Diana Cooper to Marie Stopes, 13 February 1941. BL. Stopes Papers, MS 58495.

125 R. Rhodes James (ed.), *Chips, The Diaries of Sir Henry Channon*, 1967, p. 338.

126 Sir Henry Channon to Osbert Peake, 13 November 1942. PRO HO 144/21591.

127 George Bernard Shaw to Lord Alfred Douglas, 14 November 1940. In Mary Hyde, *op. cit.*, p. 135.

128 *Ireland and the War against Hitler*, 1940 pp. 36–7.

129 Lord Alfred Douglas to Francis d'Avilla, 7 July 1941. Berg.

130 *Ibid.*

131 The Marquess of Queensberry and Percy Colson, *Oscar Wilde and the Black Douglas*, p. 143.

132 In several sources, including H. Montgomery Hyde's biography of Douglas, the second word of the last line of the octave has read 'imminent'. The word is 'immanent'. See Lord Alfred Douglas to Marie Stopes, 31 May 1941. BL. MS 58495.

133 Lord Alfred Douglas to Francis d'Avilla, 3 May 1944. Berg.

134 For information on the ballet, see Lord Alfred Douglas to Adrian Earle, 8 and 22 August 1942. Clark.

135 Lord Alfred Douglas to Francis d'Avilla, 27 August 1943. Berg.

136 *Evening Standard*, 3 July 1943.

137 See *Bernard Shaw and Alfred Douglas, a correspondence*, p. 155, n. 2.

138 Sir Arthur Quiller-Couch to Lord Alfred Douglas, 5 December 1943. Hyde.

139 Augustus John to Lord Alfred Douglas, 5 February 1944. Hyde.

140 See John Stratford, *The Poetry of Lord Alfred Douglas*, in *Book and Magazine Collector*, no. 133, April 1995, p. 70.

141 Lord Alfred Douglas to George Bernard Shaw, 18 October 1938. In Mary Hyde, *op. cit.*, p. 96

142 Edmund Phipps to the Earl of Sandwich, 24 July 1941. The archives of the Earl and Countess of Sandwich, Dorset.

143 Caroline Dakers, *Clouds, The Biography of a Country House*, 1993, pp. 236, 259–60.

144 Lord Alfred Douglas to Mrs Robert Sherard, 1 February 1943. Reading University Library. MS 1047 1/3.

145 Lord Alfred Douglas to Adrian Earle, 12 March 1943. Clark.

146 Lord Alfred Douglas to Adrian Earle, 3 March 1943. Clark.

147 Briant, *op. cit.*, 1962, p. 229.

148 Lord Alfred Douglas to Francis Queensberry, 12 January 1945. Maggs, p. 21.

149 Quoted in William Freeman, *The Life of Lord Alfred Douglas*, p. 308.

150 Donald Sinden, *A Touch of the Memoirs*, 1982, p. 47.

151 Communicated to the author by Mrs Sheila Colman.

152 Sinden, *op. cit.*, pp. 47–9.

153 Sinden, *op. cit.*, pp. 49–50.

154 H. Montgomery Hyde, *Lord Alfred Douglas*, p. 329.

155 Lord Alfred Douglas to Marie Stopes, 24 November 1944. BL. MS 58495.

156 See Mary Hyde, *op. cit.*, p. 187 including n. 2.

157 Lord Alfred Douglas to George Bernard Shaw, 9 December 1944. In Mary Hyde, *op. cit.*, p. 195.

158 George Bernard Shaw to Lord Alfred Douglas, 12 December, 1944. In Mary Hyde, *op. cit.*, p. 195.

159 Lord Alfred Douglas to Marie Stopes, 13 February 1940. BL. MS 58494.

160 See Vyvyan Holland, *Son of Oscar Wilde*. pp. 192–3.

161 Lord Alfred Douglas to Marie Stopes, 27 November 1944. BL. MS 58495.

162 Lord Alfred Douglas to Winston Churchill, 16 December 1944, copy Hyde.

163 Winston Churchill to Lord Alfred Douglas, 29 December 1944. Hyde.

164 This note is now in the Hyde collection.

165 Hart-Davis, *Letters*, 1962, p. 732.

166 Lady Edith Fox-Pitt to Marie Stopes, 1 February, 1950. BL. Stopes Papers, MS 58494.

Select Bibliography

The following works of Douglas are the principal ones cited in the text:

Poèmes, Paris, *Mercure de France*, 1896

Sonnets, London, The Academy Publishing Company, 1909

The City of the Soul, (3rd edition) London, John Lane, 1911

Oscar Wilde and Myself, London, John Long, 1914

Collected Satires, London, The Fortune Press, 1926

Complete Poems, London, Martin Secker, 1928

Autobiography, London, Martin Secker, 1929

Lyrics, London, Rich and Cowan, 1935

Sonnets, London, Rich and Cowan, 1935

Without Apology, London, Martin Secker, 1938

Oscar Wilde, A Summing-Up, London, Duckworth, 1940

The Principles of Poetry: An Address Delivered by Lord Alfred Douglas before the Royal Society of Literature on September 2nd, 1943, London, The Richards Press, 1943.

Borland, Maureen, *Wilde's Devoted Friend: a life of Robert Ross*, Oxford, Lennard Publishing, 1990

Briant, Keith, *Marie Stopes: A Biography*, London, The Hogarth Press, 1962

Sorley Brown, William, *The Genius of Lord Alfred Douglas*, Galashiels, The Author, 1913
 The Life and Genius of T.W.H. Crosland, London, Cecil Palmer, 1928

Croft-Cooke, Rupert, *The Glittering Pastures*, London, Putnam 1962.
 The Numbers Game, London, Putnam 1963
 Bosie. The Story of Lord Alfred Douglas, His Friends and Enemies, London, W.H. Allen, 1963
 Feasting with Panthers, London, W.H. Allen, 1967

Crosland, T.W.H., *Collected Poems*, London, Martin Secker, 1917

Custance, Olive (ed. Brocard Sewell), *Selected Poems*, London, Cecil Woolf, 1995

d'Arch Smith, Timothy, *Love in Earnest*, London, Routledge and Kegan Paul, 1970

Ellmann, Richard, *Oscar Wilde*, London, Hamish Hamilton, 1987

Freeman, William, *Lord Alfred Douglas, Spoilt Child of Genius*, London, Herbert Joseph Limited, 1948

Harris, Frank, *Oscar Wilde: His Life and Confessions*, New York, The Author, 1916
   Oscar Wilde, London, Constable and Company, 1938
   Frank Harris, His Life and Adventures, London, Richards Press, 1947

Hart-Davis, Rupert (ed.), *The Letters of Oscar Wilde*, London, Hart-Davis, 1962
   Selected Letters of Oscar Wilde, Oxford, OUP, 1979
   More Letters of Oscar Wilde, London, John Murray, 1985

Head, Alice M., *It Could Never Have Happened*, London, Richards Press, 1947

Hichens, Robert, *The Green Carnation*, London, The Unicorn Press, 1949

Holland, Merlin, *The Wilde Album*, London, Fourth Estate, 1997

Holland, Vyvyan, *Son of Oscar Wilde*, London, Rupert Hart-Davis, 1954, (new edition Oxford University Press, 1988)
   Time Remembered after Père Lachaise, London, Victor Gollancz, 1966

Hoare, Philip, *Wilde's Last Stand*, London, Duckworth, 1997

Hyde, Mary (ed.), *Bernard Shaw and Alfred Douglas, a Correspondence*, London, John Murray, 1982

Longford, Elizabeth, *A Pilgrimage of Passion: The Life of Wilfrid Scawen Blunt*, London, Weidenfeld and Nicolson, 1979

Lycett-Green, Candida (ed.), *The Letters of John Betjeman,* 2 vols., London, Minerva, 1995, 1996

Montgomery Hyde, H. (ed.), *The Trials of Oscar Wilde*, London, William Hodge, 1948 (new edition Dover Publications, 1973)
   Oscar Wilde: The Aftermath, London, Methuen, 1963
   Oscar Wilde: A Biography, New York, Farrar, Straus and Giroux, 1975
   Lord Alfred Douglas, London, Methuen, 1984

Pearson, Hesketh, *The Life of Oscar Wilde*, London, Methuen, 1946

Pullar, Phillipa, *Frank Harris*, London, Hamish Hamilton, 1975

Queensberry, The Marquess of, and Colson, Percy, *Oscar Wilde and the Black Douglas*, London, Hutchinson, 1949

Roberts, Brian, *The Mad Bad Line: The Family of Lord Alfred Douglas*, London, Hamish Hamilton, 1981

Sewell, Brocard, *Olive Custance, Her Life and Work*, London, The Eighteen Nineties Society, 1975

Sinden, Donald, *A Touch of the Memoirs*, London, Hodder and Stoughton, 1982

Speedie, Julie, *Wonderful Sphinx, the Biography of Ada Leverson*, Virago Press, 1983

Stopes, Marie, *Lord Alfred Douglas: His Poetry and Personality*, London, The Richards Press, 1949

Stratford, John, 'The Poetry of Lord Alfred Douglas', *Book and Magazine Collector*, No. 133, April 1995

Wilde, Oscar, *The Collected Works of Oscar Wilde*, Glasgow, HarperCollins, 1994

Wintermans, Caspar, *Halcyon Days: Contributions to* The Spirit Lamp, New Hampshire, Typographeum, 1995
   '*Lord Alfred Douglas*' Netherlands, *Maatstaf* no. 8, August 1995

from Oscar

To the gilt-mailed
Boy.

POEMS.

at Oxford,

in the heart
of June.

Wilde's inscription in the copy of his poems which he presented to Lord Alfred Douglas.

Illustration Credits

The Autobiography of Lord Alfred Douglas 1929; I/1, 8; II/5 bottom, 11 bottom; III/5 top. Columbia University, Alfred Douglas Papers, Rare book and Manuscript Library; I/6 top. Artemis Cooper III/11 top. *The Cycling World Illustrated* 1896; II/6. Lord Alfred Douglas *Collected Poems* 1919; III/4 bottom. Lord Alfred Douglas *Poems* Paris 1896; II/7. Copyright © Estate of Sir William Rothenstein, by permission: I/11. Executors of the Estate of Lord Alfred Douglas; I/2; III/1, 2, 14 below. Merlin Holland; II/6, 9 bottom, 10 top. Hulton Getty Picture Collection; II/1, 2 top; III/7 top, 8 bottom, 12 bottom. *The Life and Genius of T W H Crosland* by W Sorley Brown 1928: III/6 top left. *The Life of Lord Alfred Douglas, Spoilt Child of Genius* by William Freeman 1948; II/5 top; III/3 top. Magdalen College Library and Archives Oxford, photos John Gibbons Studio; I/9, 10. Princeton University Library, Robert H Taylor Collection, Department of Rare Books and Special Collections: text page 361. Private Collections; I/4 bottom, 5 top left; III/6 top right and bottom, 10 bottom. Courtesy of the present Earl and Countess of Sandwich: I/5 top left. *Scottish Field*: I/3 top. *The Spirit Lamp* 1893; II/3 bottom. *Marie Stopes A Biography* by Keith Briant 1962; III/13 top. University of California Los Angeles, the William Andrews Clark Memorial Library; II/4, 8 top. University of South Florida Library, Special Collections: III/9 top. The Warden and Scholars of Winchester College, photos Derek Dine; I/5 top right and bottom, 7 bottom.

Index